FAITH IN THE COUNTRYSIDE

A Report presented to
The Archbishops of Canterbury
and York

CHURCHMAN PUBLISHING
1990

Cover photograph:
Mike Williams, by courtesy of the Countryside Commission

Faith in the Countryside
was first published in 1990 by
Churchman Publishing Limited
117 Broomfield Avenue
Worthing, West Sussex BN14 7SF

Publisher: Peter Smith

Represented in
Dublin; Sydney; Wellington;
Kingston; Ontario and Wilton, Connecticut

Distributed to the book trade by
Bailey Book Distribution Limited
(a division of the Bailey and Swinfen Holdings Group)
Warner House, Wear Bay Road
Folkestone, Kent CT19 6PH

ISBN 1 85093 274 3

Typeset and printed by
Bourne Press Limited, Bournemouth

Terms of Reference

1. To examine the effects of economic, environmental and social change on the rural community.
2. To describe the changing nature of the Church in the countryside.
3. To examine the theological factors which bear upon the mission and ministry of the Church in rural areas.
4. In the light of the above, to make recommendations for consideration and action.

Members of the Commission

The Right Honourable Lord Prior PC (Chairman)
Former Cabinet Minister; Chairman of The General Electric Company plc
The Right Reverend Peter Nott (Vice-Chairman)
Bishop of Norwich
Mrs Patricia Batty Shaw CBE JP DL
Former Rural Development Commissioner
The Reverend Canon Andrew Bowden
Rector of Coates, Rodmarton and Sapperton with Frampton Mansell
Chaplain to the Royal Agricultural College, Cirencester
The Reverend John Clarke
Director, Arthur Rank Centre
Member of the Methodist Church
Mr John Dunning JP DL
Cumbrian farmer and businessman
Mr Henry Engleheart DL
Suffolk farmer and landowner
Representative of the Roman Catholic Church
Mr Robin Grove-White
Senior Research Fellow, Lancaster University
Former Director of the Council for the Protection of Rural England
The Reverend Dr Brian Horne
Theologian and lecturer, King's College, University of London
Mrs Pat Kelly
Representative of the National Federation of Women's Institutes
Mrs Clare Laflin
Member of the United Reformed Church
Mr David Lambert
President of the National Union of Hosiery and Knitwear Workers
Representative of the Trades Union Congress
The Reverend Martin Leigh
Vicar of Baslow, Derbyshire
Member of the Board of Governors, Church Commissioners

Faith in the Countryside

The Venerable Richard Lewis
   Archdeacon of Ludlow
Mr Brian McLaughlin
   Representative of the National Farmers Union
   Author of the Department of the Environment study on Rural Deprivation
Mr Humphrey Norrington
   Executive Director, Barclays Bank plc
Dr Alan Rogers
   Senior Lecturer in Rural Planning, Wye College, University of London
The Right Reverend Anthony Russell, D Phil
   Bishop of Dorchester
Mr Edward Smith (died May 1989)
   Deputy Secretary, Ministry of Agriculture, Fisheries and Food
Sir John Starkey Bt DL
   Nottinghamshire farmer and landowner
   Church Commissioner
Mrs Elaine Storkey
   Lecturer in sociology and theology, Open University

Joint Secretaries

Mr Ewan Harper
The Reverend Jeremy Martineau

Preface

Your Graces,

As far as rural England was concerned, I think we all presumed at the start that it was more a matter of bringing together available knowledge than of exploring fresh ground. The report shows that this is far from being the case and that there is a constantly changing picture. The absence of an agreed definition of what constitutes a rural area means that statistical information is limited and the ability to assess needs is consequently difficult. But we met and heard from a large number of people and were able to build up from that an impression of a wave of deeply significant changes taking place and the effect they were having on rural life.

In recent years there has been a remarkable change in the make-up of the rural population. This has brought to villages a growing number of incomers with higher proportions of the elderly and the more affluent among them. The overall picture leaves no doubt about the tensions between those who traditionally regarded the countryside as their own and their work place, and the new arrivals. Interest in the countryside is by no means the preserve of those who live and work there; urban dwellers too have claims on and aspirations for the countryside they wish to enjoy. The integration of new villagers is a challenge for voluntary organisations and particularly for the Church, among whose tasks is the reconciling of differences in the local community.

We have devoted much time to a study of the theological factors and implications of the changing attitudes and patterns of life in rural communities and the views of the urban population about them. We felt that the mysteries of creation and the spirit of community were subjects which went to the heart of the Church in our rural areas, and that there were differences between rural and urban churches which needed discussion. Although our theological discussion has been a continuing aspect of our work and has emerged from our rural context, we have placed our reflections towards the beginning of our report

v

because we feel that it points the way towards our conclusions. The difficulty has been to find simple and meaningful ways of expressing the spiritual response many people make to the peace and beauty of the countryside, sensing in these the ever present but unseen hand of God.

In order to present our material in the clearest possible way, we have divided the report into three main sections, comprising an introduction (which includes theology), the rural context, and the rural church. It would be misleading to suggest that these are separate from each other and we emphasise that the Church has no being and no future if it is not grounded in contemporary life, as an integral part of the world it seeks to serve. A continuing theme throughout our work has been the need for the Church to reflect this integrity in all aspects of its life.

The method of the Commission has been to break itself down into working parties pursuing specific areas of study and to seek written and oral evidence from a wide range of interested and authoritative organisations and individuals. Government departments and agencies have been forthcoming, with four Ministers giving personal evidence. A similar presentation was made by the Opposition's front bench environmental team.

Despite the weight of evidence being submitted to the Commission in London, or perhaps because of it, it was felt essential for members of the Commission to travel widely to test what had been submitted. Our travels also enabled us to gather local evidence and to meet those members of the general public who wished to speak to us. Four regional visits, one led by the Bishop of Norwich and three by me, were made to the North East, North West, West Midlands, and South West, ensuring that those areas less well represented on the Commission received a fair hearing. Visits have been made by small teams to 41 dioceses to hear the views of local rural churches and diocesan bodies. Throughout these visits we have been warmly welcomed and are most grateful to local authorities, rural community councils, dioceses and many private individuals for the frankness they showed us and for their very considerable generosity and hospitality. Commissioners have frequently been given meals and a bed by private individuals as their contribution to our work, and their warmth and friendship have been deeply appreciated.

The work of the Commission would not have been possible without generous financial support from a number of benefactors. Foremost amongst these have been:-

Brunswick Public Relations Ltd
The Englefield Charitable Trust
The Ernest Cook Trust
Esso Petroleum plc
The General Synod of the Church of England
The Jerusalem Trust
The Methodist Church
The Tudor Trust
United Biscuits (Holdings) plc
The United Reformed Church
His Grace the Duke of Westminster
The Garfield Weston Foundation

We have received constant support from the Church Commissioners in the form of a valuable grant, equipment and a full-time secondee, initially Sian Mosford, and latterly Lucy Thirtle. The Corporation of The Church House generously made offices available to us without charge and the Bank of England supported us by seconding Derek Chetwin on a full-time basis. Touche Ross produced and presented to the Commission a valuable report on parish shares.

My thanks go also to the members of the Commission who have given so freely of their time and expertise. We have developed a friendship and loyalty unusual in such affairs, and this is due largely to the unstinting efforts of our Joint Secretaries, Ewan Harper and Jeremy Martineau, supported initially by Diana Gallimore and then by Sarah Johnson. I am also grateful to those who have helped us considerably as consultants, Dr Grace Davie, the Revd Dr Leslie Francis, Professor Philip M'Pherson, Professor Howard Newby, the Revd Canon Claude Rutter and Lady Warner.

We welcome your appointment of Jeremy Martineau as Archbishops' Rural Officer to follow up the findings of this report within the Church of England, with other Churches and with secular bodies.

Throughout, we have been conscious of our position following *Faith in the City*. We have greatly valued the work of that Commission, particularly in what it said about the community and the importance of context. Our report should be read in conjunction with it, as we have tried not to repeat it. Above all, we have been aware that both Commissions were ultimately concerned about the people of one nation and one Christian Church. A report like ours can look fragmented, but it is addressed to the nation and Church as a whole, seeking to unite and reconcile, and to create a deeper understanding of the context and needs of one part of society.

Our report is unanimous.

The Rt Hon Lord Prior PC

Contents

Faith in the Countryside

Page

Chapter 1
Introduction:
The Countryside as
an Arena

The pastoral image

1.1. Were a latter-day Cobbett to explore England's rural areas in 1990, his initial impression would surely be one of purposeful prosperity. He would pass through thriving small towns, quiet villages, and well-maintained hamlets, surrounded by the symbols of successful farming.

1.2. Most of us share such images of the English countryside - balanced communities and well-tended landscapes, predominantly pasture in the west and arable in the east, with an infinity of subtly varied local characteristics at every turn. The countryside still seems reassuringly stable, a refuge from the thrust of technology and the tough realities of work and competition in the cities.

1.3. This view of the rural idyll has the power of myth. But too often it leads us to feed fantasies and avoid facing up to what is really happening. For the countryside is no more impervious to change than our towns and cities. It is just that such change tends to occur less obviously, in ways barely noticeable to people living in the midst of it. Indeed, most of us have not appreciated these patterns. It is vital we should do so, if we are to think creatively about the future, and plan the role the Church must play in rural areas in the decades ahead.

Change and tension

1.4. The truth is that social and economic forces, often with a national or international impetus, are transforming rural England. In the 1980s, such processes accelerated - varied and uneven in their occurrence, but far-reaching in their impacts. Wherever the Commission has looked, it has been struck by a sense of flux and change behind the deceptively familiar facade.

1.5. Almost every aspect of rural life has altered significantly since the Second World War. There have been substantial shifts in the structure of the rural population, traumatic changes to the patterns of agricultural production, new problems associated with the emergence of a changed working base for the rural economy, and social transformations arising from the movement of growing numbers of professional people out of the cities into the rural areas. Not surprisingly, the consequence of such change has been increasing tensions in rural life.

1.6. These tensions are reflected in new questions that are now asked of the countryside. Should the rural areas be developed only in ways consistent with traditional patterns of employment - or in ways less inhibited by the past? What sorts of rural communities should be encouraged in the late 20th century, and with what mixes of population? Who 'owns' the countryside, and what rights and obligations should such 'ownership' entail? What priority should be given to nature as opposed to people? Whose interests should come first - those of established rural dwellers, or those escaping from conurbations to new forms of living?

1.7. Such questions bear on the interests of far more people than simply those living in rural areas. They engage the needs, aspirations and interests of the urban majority too. What goes on in rural England has to be seen in relation to the needs of a predominantly urban society. Only superficially is it true that rural affairs are a minority concern. They affect 80% of the land mass of our island, yet much of the population is effectively disenfranchised from influencing the decisions which affect them. What happens in our countryside is and ought to be the concern of all of us.

1.8. Increasingly the environmental issue provides a framework within which all others are being seen. The 1980s witnessed escalating public concern about mankind's relationship with the natural world, at the global as well as the most local levels. Indeed, the stability of the very climate of the earth itself now appears to be at risk from the accumulated activities of our industrial societies.

1.9. This awakened public concern bears acutely on England's rural areas, both directly and indirectly. Land use decisions are more keenly contested; retention of wild habitats of flora and fauna on farmland have become matters of continuing controversy; disputes about new housing and industrial development, and about pollution of rivers and aquifers, are increasingly intense; public expectations of access to the countryside are growing. So too is national support for environmental bodies. Indeed, the Royal Society for the Protection of Birds, National Trust, and Woodland Trust have themselves become some of the country's largest landowners, reflecting widespread concern at the state of much of the country's natural heritage. Environmental factors will have a growing importance in future decisions about rural land, not least because the countryside is the most immediate and familiar focus through which such concerns can be expressed.

1.10. Such themes are far from exhaustive. There are many more changes in the pipeline. The processes of European integration represented by '1992' will have further impacts on living and working patterns in much of England. Much of this will be controversial, as it touches us culturally and socially. Drives like those behind the Channel Tunnel, the biotechnology and information technology industries, and the newly privatised water and electricity industries will maintain the domestic pressure for change too, with the rural areas affected at least as much as the urban. The 21st century is likely to be no quieter than the 20th.

1.11. How then should such factors, and the prospect of more such turbulence, affect our conception of the countryside as a whole? The proper starting-point is that no single over-arching conception now suffices. In a complex society like ours, there is now an immense variety of distinct understandings and expectations of our rural areas. Some of these complement one another. Frequently they are in conflict.

1.12. For example, many farmers continue to see the countryside as predominantly their workplace (as in an important sense it is), in which their activities should be granted the precedence they have had historically. But many new rural dwellers have a quite different view, arguing that farming has become an industry and that, where its activities impinge on others in the community, it should be restrained like other industries. Similarly, developers, frequently co-ordinated nationally, may see rural land largely as an undeveloped resource, replete with opportunities for new commercial activity and the creation of wealth. Others urge greater modesty and restraint in the way land is used. Again, growing numbers of people find in the countryside a focus for peaceful enjoyment, and for re-establishing their connections with historical and spiritual continuities. But to energetic and socially constrained younger people this same quiet may be a focus of frustration and resentment at what Sydney Smith called "a healthy grave". There are tensions, too, between the outlooks of landowners, new as well as long-established, with a rooted stake in the rural status quo, and those of socially more marginal groups, be they homeless urban families, potential smallholders, small developers, ramblers or even 'alternative' communities. There are real and continuing tensions between all of these outlooks and many others besides. That they are rehearsed and reported repeatedly and instantaneously on the national news media simply makes them all the starker.

The arena

1.13. In the 1990s, therefore, England's rural areas may be best understood as an arena - an arena in which different concerns and aspirations, stimulated by social and economic change, meet and must somehow be reconciled.

1.14. But they are an arena in deeper senses too. For the differences they harbour are not only between interests; they also concern the way the countryside itself is understood. Indeed, some distinct assumption about the meaning of the countryside is implied in each one of the social and economic outlooks the Commission has encountered. This reality is much more than a merely theoretical or academic matter. It is reflected at every level of experience - in the multifarious reports on rural issues that appear each year, in the activities of pressure groups, in the policy priorities of governments and local authorities, and in the everyday lives of people.

The stance of the Commission

1.15. The Commission's report is thus written at a crucial historical moment for the English countryside. Not only are economic, industrial and technological processes stimulating unprecedented change, but moreover these are emerging in the context of quite new attitudes and priorities towards nature and the environment, the impacts of which are intensified by the ubiquity of our modern communications media.

1.16. The questions facing the Commission in the first part of its programme have arisen largely from these tensions. They took shape through evidence from many people and organisations involved in farming, planning, policy-making, tourism, conservation, recreation, housing, public utilities, rural services, community programmes and education.

1.17. The approach of the Commission's members to all of these questions has been shaped naturally by their own Christian understanding. However, articulating the framework of that understanding, in the context of the new circumstances we have encountered, has been far from straightforward. Like most forms of knowledge, fresh theological insight does not generally emerge, pristine and complete, independently of social circumstances. Almost always, gains are made when social and historical forces present an imperative for us to seek fresh and enlarged understanding. Theological insight is rooted in mankind's experience - and it tends to develop most dynamically when the pressure of events forces it to do so.

1.18. That has been the Commission's experience in the present case. The changes - and other concentrations of forces precipitating further change - in England's rural areas, and in our understanding of them, are now so substantial that they confront theology itself with fresh questions. We consider some implications of this in the chapter that now follows.

Chapter 2
Theological
Reflections

Creation

2.1. On any sunny weekend millions of people leave the cities and towns of England and go out into the countryside. What drives so many from such a variety of backgrounds to spend as much time as possible in rural surroundings? What are they seeking? And what do they find? Most will give simple answers: they feel 'at rest' or 'refreshed' in the countryside. They may even speak of being 'renewed' by contact with what they call nature. There is a sense of release from an urban environment of mechanical noise, commercial pressure, speed and high technology which is experienced as destructive. In his evidence to the Commission, Sir Laurens van der Post expressed his belief that the desperate loneliness and sense of 'not being known', which are common features of modern human lives, are caused not merely by the estrangement of human beings from one another in large urban communities, but also by the estrangement of human lives from the non-human world of nature. That feeling of 'wholeness' and 'healing' bestowed by contact with nature in the countryside is for many close to religious experience and is frequently expressed in religious language.

2.2. Yet there are contrary experiences too: of the fragility of nature and the vulnerability of the countryside in the discovery of polluted streams and rivers or diseased and dying wild life. The destruction of natural habitats and the presence of toxic waste are not only harsh reminders of an environmental crisis which puts in jeopardy the enjoyment of weekend leisure, but are also pointers to a far larger crisis which threatens every aspect of life on the planet. And it is because of the religious dimension of the experience of the countryside that its pollution and destruction are perceived, not merely as ugly or

7

dangerous in themselves, but as desecration. The righteous anger of many supporters of 'green' policies is, in a real sense, a religious emotion: the warning of the modern German theologian, Jurgen Moltmann, written 5 years ago does not seem exaggerated:

> "Faced as we are with the progressive industrial exploitation of nature and its irreparable destruction, what does it mean to say that we believe in God the Creator, and in this world as his creation? What we call the environmental crisis is not merely a crisis in the natural environment of human beings themselves. It is a crisis of life on this planet, a crisis so comprehensive and so irreversible that it cannot unjustly be described as apocalyptic."

The need for a world view

2.3. When the Commission set about its task two years ago of producing a report on rural areas for the Church of England, it quickly became evident that we would be addressing some of the most serious questions about life on the planet as a whole, and not merely questions about life in the English countryside. Before practical questions concerning the Church and society in rural areas could be considered, these deeper issues had to be faced: the relationship between the human and non-human worlds, the meaning of the quasi-religious experience of nature, and the truth about human personhood. We were aware of the urgent need of the Church to say something morally and spiritually meaningful in the context of the human race's increasing anxiety about the future in its problematic relationship with nature. The urgency of that need has grown in the years of our deliberations. We recognised immediately the complexity of this crisis which involves, on the one hand, the need to provide food, housing, health, education and prosperity for a world population which is growing, and, on the other, the necessity of preserving diminishing resources and the protection of the human and natural environment. Hard decisions have to be made in situations in which claims - whether for housing or food, conservation or growth - frequently seem not only competitive but mutually incompatible. On what grounds can decisions be taken? Has the Christian Church something distinctive and positive to offer to the debate on the crisis of the environment? Our most pressing requirement, as an Archbishops' Commission, was to discover "a context of reference concerning what human beings and nature are, and what they may both become in the light of the overall purposes of God" (A R Peacocke, *Creation and the World of Science*, Oxford 1979).

Our work needed to be rooted in theology; for if a theology that has no practical application is irrelevant, so conversely, a practical programme which is not founded upon a comprehensive vision of the destiny of creation and the human race is vulnerable to the pressure of unscrupulous manipulations and fashionable ideologies.

The task of theology

2.4. It is as mistaken to suppose that Christian theology is a kind of abstract philosophy produced by religious experts remote from the turbulence of everyday existence as it is to suppose that a Christian life can be lived in isolation from the fears and anxieties, the needs and perplexities of the ordinary world. Unfortunately even churchpeople often have a view of theology as a kind of impenetrable science which seems to have very little to say about their everyday concerns; or if they do see some usefulness in it, they see it as something touching only their private, interior lives, unrelated to the public, historical events of the world outside. But it is, in reality, not so. The revelation of God's truth in the events of history and, uniquely, in the person of Jesus Christ, is a revelation to and in the world. It is, moreover, a revelation whose meaning is discovered in and shaped by the particular historical circumstances in which Christians of different ages and different societies have found themselves. The revelation, though given, (for it is the truth of the unchanging God that we are discussing) is always in need of interpretation: that interpretation is called theology; a living, changing, growing process, and it is fundamental to our enterprise. The long and continuous process of interpreting the Christian message and articulating Christian truth is achieved in a kind of dialogue: a dialogue that is conducted not only between those who belong to the community of believers, but also with those who seem to be indifferent or hostile to the Gospel which the Church proclaims.

2.5. The dominant theme of the Old and New Testaments is the drama of salvation: the account of human pride, folly and rebellion redeemed by the loving action of the Creator. But in the face of contemporary realities like the ecological crisis and environmental destruction it has become unreal to speak about salvation as though it were a doctrine solely about human redemption and unrelated to the integrity of the whole of the natural order. We are compelled to recognise that there is needed a reconsideration and possibly a re-interpretation of a Christian theology both of creation and human personhood. We are beginning to see the deeper and wider implications of St Paul's words in the eighth chapter of his letter to the Romans:

> "For the creation waits with eager longing for the revealing of the Sons of God ... because the creation itself will be set free from its bondage to decay and obtain the glorious liberty of the children of God. We know that the whole creation has been groaning in travail until now ..." (Romans 8, vv 19-22)

2.6. That which the Church has always implicitly known has now to be made explicit in the clearest possible way: that human beings are related to the non-human universe as well as to each other and are not individual souls to be plucked out of their material bodies on the day of salvation. We are, as St Paul indicates, part of a universe which waits for the consummation that has been promised by God in Christ's death and resurrection. A doctrine of God as creator and lover of the material world implies the necessity of living in that world and being responsible for it in such a way that the attitudes of society as a whole to this relationship with nature will be transformed. Central, then, to a Christian world view at this stage of our history is a Christian doctrine of creation.

The biblical perspective

2.7. Two creation stories appear in the opening chapters of the book of Genesis. They were composed in the light of long reflections on the history of the people of Israel, whose developing awareness of God's purposes for them led them to ascribe the origin of the world and its continued existence to the same divine source. It is therefore not only to the opening chapters of Genesis, but to the whole range of biblical literature that we must turn to discover the biblical perspective on creation.

2.8. What emerges is the concept of a God who is the only source of the universe: the origin of all things. The opening words of the first chapter of Genesis are only a concise formulation of the utterance in the prophecy of Isaiah:

> "I am the Lord; that is my name.
> I will not give my glory to another,
> nor my praise to idols."

There is no independent area of 'nature' which does not reflect God, or refer back to its maker. The theme which re-appears throughout scripture is "I am the Lord, and there is no other. Apart from me, there is no God."

2.9. Just as God is the only origin, the alpha and omega of creation, so creation lives constantly before the face of God. The psalmist sings out: "The heavens are telling the glory of God, the earth shows forth his handiwork." We are told that the God who dresses the poppy in its startling coat also sees into the depths of our hearts and knows even the number of hairs on our heads. The intimacy and detail of God's knowledge of creation is echoed powerfully in the realisation that there is nowhere we can go where God is not present. Again the psalmist muses:

"Lord you have searched me and you know me.
You know when I sit and when I rise;
You perceive my thoughts from afar.
You discern my going out and my lying down;
If I go to the heavens you are there;
If I make my bed in the depths, you are there." (Psalm 139)

2.10. Those who experience the breathtaking view from the mountain top, or thrill at the minute details of a butterfly's wings, are already discovering something about the God whom the Bible discloses and the Church proclaims. It is in fact this very sense of wonder, joy and well-being which points us to *shalom* - that Hebrew concept of wholeness and release which comes from being at peace with God and recognising our place in the universe. So even though those who rush to the countryside for fresh air after the dirt of the cities may not articulate this theologically, they are nonetheless experiencing something of the God who created the universe and whose glory is to be perceived in and through it.

2.11. John Baker, Bishop of Salisbury, has noted that the Old Testament is "permeated with what we can only call an affectionate and admiring approach to nature ... the faithful obedience of non-human creatures to the divine will is contrasted with the faithlessness and perversity of men:

'Even the stork in the heavens knows her times;
and the turtle dove, swallow and crane
keep the time of their coming;
but my people know not the ordinance of the Lord.'

"This admiration of nature finds its climax in the Book of Job, where the wonders of the natural order are used for a didactic purpose unique in the Bible and perhaps in all ancient literature: namely, to make the point that man's whole attitude to what goes on in the created order is wrong, because it is totally egoistic, totally anthropocentric. If he were

11

to stop for even a moment to consider the universe as it actually is, he would see that by far the greater part of it has no relevance to him at all."

2.12. It is from the folly of this "totally egoistic, totally anthropocentric" attitude that the exploitation of natural resources and the consequent destruction of the environment derives. Yet it must be recognised that within the biblical perspective itself a clear indication is given that in the created order the human creature occupies a place of central significance.

Humankind as the image of God

2.13. "Then God said, Let us make man in our own image after our likeness; and let them have dominion over the fish of the sea and over the birds of the air and over the cattle and over all the earth and over every creeping thing that creeps on the earth." (Genesis 1, v 8)

2.14. Max Nicholson, a former director of the Nature Conservancy Council, expressed a popularly held view of that text when he wrote:

> "It is a tragedy that of all the great religions of the world it should have been one of the very few that preaches man's unqualified right of dominance over nature which has become the most powerful influence through the agencies of ancient Judaism and modern Christianity."

A similar view is held by Jonathon Porritt : "We shall continue to see a worsening ecological crisis until we reject that central Christian axiom that nature has no reason but to serve man."

2.15. There is no doubt that this account of creation places man at the apex of the natural order and in doing so acknowledges the power that is at his disposal. There is also no denying the fact that, for the most part, Jewish and Christian teaching has interpreted the concept of dominion in terms of control and domination. The environment has been viewed as existing for the sake of the human species; a setting for the splendours of that species which conquers and subdues it. At the same time, Jewish and Christian teaching has been uneasily aware of the paradox in the story , for this same account of creation declares that every element in the created order is precious to the God who "saw that it was good". Throughout the Old Testament (most conspicuously in the Book of Job) there are regular reminders that the infinite variety and complexity of creation might exist for purposes which defy human comprehension.

2.16. Meanings other than subjugation and domination lie within this notion of dominion. These meanings come to light when the idea of dominion is placed, as it should be, in the context of the image of God. At the very least, this implies that the human being is the kind of creature who was able, like the Creator in whose image it is made, to see that the creation was good and who was capable of exercising the kind of creative care which would enable the whole natural order to achieve its proper end.

> "From the perspective of theology, man is clearly made the focal point in the interrelations between God and the universe. He is given a special place within creation with a ruling and priestly function to perform towards the rest of created reality." (Thomas Torrance, *Divine and Contingent Order,* Oxford 1981)

2.17. We may also see the human being as the microcosm of creation: a creature in whom the rest of nature is gathered. This may at first seem an arrogant concept; in fact, it is just the opposite for it compels the human race to recognise its responsibility towards the non-human world. It even reverses the normal 'western' perception that the world exists for the sake of the human race; indeed - and, paradoxically, because the human species is the most powerful - humanity is seen as existing for the sake of nature.

2.18. 'Dominion' can be seen as the working out of the meaning of 'image'; an expression not of the exploitative powers of the human species, but of the loving power of God for the integrity of creation.

2.19. Moreover, the image is not to be confused with the origin. The human species, though the most powerful in the world, does not own the world or have absolute right of the world. The dominion that is exercised is part of the representative function the human being has as the representative of God. It is a gift of grace bestowed by the sovereign Creator on his free creatures for particular purposes. It is the abuse of this freedom, the foolishness of believing in human autonomy, together with the assumption of the absolute right to ownership and leadership that lies at the root of the wanton destruction of the environment and the callousness towards animal and plant life.

2.20. In arguing for the restoration of the doctrine of creation to a central place in Christianity, we are not arguing for a return to a pre-mechanical age, or for the Church to become wholly identified with certain environmental pressure groups in this country. Christianity cannot be either Luddite or Utopian. It is not possible or desirable to 'un-make' what has already been made in the course of the scientific achievement of the last four centuries, and in a world where moral choices are often choices between conflicting goods or conflicting evils, the environment can never remain intact. The use of any kind of technology will always involve some destruction and loss in the natural order. What can be prevented is wanton destruction: destruction which is caused not because it has been chosen as the lesser of two evils, but because motives of power and greed have over-ridden the respect due to, and the care of, that which God has created and loved.

2.21. In arguing for this restoration, Christians are firstly addressing themselves and are doing so with a sense of penitence. Others, not necessarily Christian, have pointed the way forward and have not always received the committed support of the Church. It is in this spirit that we seek a new understanding.

Our relationship to creation

2.22. The growing awareness in Christian circles about the importance of the natural world can be seen in the consultations that have been held at St George's House, Windsor, under the general title 'The Christian Attitude to Nature'. At the end of 1988 the Church of Scotland published *While the Earth Endures,* on the specific question of the proper relationship of the human being to the non-human world. Three analogies are suggested: the steward, the custodian, the companion:

> "1. We are Stewards of God's Creation. Stewardship implies the manner in which we treat the world around us. A Steward does not ruthlessly exploit or exhaust the resources entrusted to him. He does not shelve or try to shift his responsibility for any situation, nor let it grow worse through neglect. He thinks not solely in terms of the present, but has a responsibility for the future.
>
> 2. We are Custodians or Trustees of God's Creation. A Trustee holds his trust because he is responsible. It means leaving the inheritance in at least as good a condition as he received it and, if possible, in an enhanced state for the future. No person worthy of trust will abuse that confidence by allowing his trust to be degraded, neglected, or reduced to ugliness.
>
> 3. We are Companions. Companionship expresses the interdependence of each constituent part. We co-exist and

share our world together. The role of companion excludes the possibility of adversarial tactics with nature - that attitude of confrontation and control which was thought until recently to be an essential part of the scientific method."

2.23. More significant, perhaps, than any of these descriptions is that of human beings as the priests of the created order. The priest has an intermediary role: of representing God to the world and the world to God. "The true vocation of the human person is to be the priest of creation - to stand before the creator on behalf of all creation (intercession), and in turn to interpret the good intention of the creator to and for all." (*Towards an Affirmation on Justice, Peace and the Integrity of Creation*, Working Paper for the World Convocation on Justice, Peace and the Integrity of Creation 1989) This is not a new or narrowly ecclesiastical notion; it has a long history in the theology and spirituality of Eastern Orthodox Christianity, and has been a persistent, though not powerful, theme in Anglican thought since the seventeenth century:

"Man is the world's High Priest: he doth present

The sacrifice for all: while they below

Unto the service mutter an assent,

Such are springs use that fall, and winds that blow."

(George Herbert, *Providence*)

2.24. The time has come for this description of humankind's relationship with nature to be explored further, and more vigorously accepted. The idea of the human being as creation's 'representative', which is at the heart of the meaning of priesthood, is a vital element in the understanding of what it is to be human. The non-human world of animals, plants and inorganic matter cannot represent its own interests; this world needs a voice and champion, now as never before. It is the human race which threatens it, and unless the human being recognises and acts out his role as representative, the free and willing agent of God's purposes, human attitudes will remain at the level of the manipulative or sentimental, and human influence will be demonic.

2.25. It is specifically as Christians that we attach such importance to this concept, because central to this understanding is the person of Jesus Christ himself. He is the mediator; through him and in him God is known. He is the priest, the one who represents God to the world and the world to God. Human beings have a real priesthood, but it is derived from Christ's own priesthood. Christians, above all, should recognise this: because we are members of his Body, we share in his mediatorial work of healing and restoration.

> "This priestly role of man must take on a redemptive form - that is how we should view man's relationship to nature. It is his task to save the natural order through remedial and integrative activity, bringing back order where there is disorder and restoring peace where there is disharmony." (Thomas Torrance, *Divine and Contingent Order*, Oxford 1981)

Sin and idolatry

2.26. The creation stories of Genesis 1 and 2 describe the harmony between God, humankind and nature, that integrity of the created universe which is God's purpose. There is order, peace and wholeness, a beginning full of promise and hope. But as history unfolds there is soon revealed, in W H Auden's words, "the promising child who could not keep his word for long".

2.27. The third chapter of Genesis contains the account of the fall of Adam from a state of harmony. It is told as a simple story, but it touches mysterious depths, which it does not attempt to explain in detail, except that the origin of evil is traced to the freedom conferred on man, which he abuses. The consequence of Adam's disobedience does not affect humanity alone, but the natural world as well: "cursed is the ground because of you".

2.28. For the first hearers of these stories, as for us, the lessons are not about the remote past, but parables of present reality. What theologians call 'original sin' is to be found, not merely in the beginning, but in every generation. The desire to be independent of God, to be the controller of one's own destiny, to live as if there were no other purpose greater than the gratification of human desires: these are observable characteristics in all ages. The sign of that corruption is not only to be discerned in the way humans behave towards one another but towards the rest of creation.

2.29. It is of great importance to recognise the reality of this corruption, which can infect humanity's relationship to the created universe in subtle as well as obvious ways. It is not difficult to understand that human sin lies behind the destructive exploitation of the environment, or callous treatment of animal and plant life. It is not so easy to see danger in reverence for nature. But it is here that the corruption can take its most insidious forms disguised as apparent good.

2.30. Respect and reverence for nature can pass with subtle ease to idolatry, that is, ascribing to the natural world an ultimacy which belongs only to God. It is good when we perceive the natural world as beautiful, refreshing, life-enriching, and of intrinsic value because it is created and lovingly sustained by God. But there has always been a tendency, which is reasserting itself strongly in our environmentally-conscious age, for the created world to become the focus of religious adoration as the source of meaning, wisdom, virtue - of life itself. This attitude is as unbalanced, false, and potentially dangerous as selfish exploitation, though it is far more subtle. But subtlety is a characteristic of temptation, as the biblical account makes eloquently clear.

2.31. The doctrine of the Fall underlines, albeit in a negative way, the essential integrity of the human and non-human which is one of the principles, as we have seen, of the biblical doctrine of creation. Its realism also provides a warning against the kind of utopian attitudes which are sometimes found amongst well-meaning ecologists, as well as a neo-Victorian faith in the inevitability of progress and human perfectibility.

Redemption and hope

2.32. The Christian world view whilst recognising the reality of corruption nevertheless is one imbued with hope. This hope is not merely that human beings will be restored to a right relationship with God and with each other, but that the "groaning in travail of the whole of creation" will be heard by the God who loves it and will find restoration and peace. The vision of the new creation is not a nostalgic attempt to recover the primitive idyll of the lost Garden of Eden. Its orientation is towards a future proclaimed by Jesus Christ as Kingdom of God. This Kingdom has already been inaugurated by Christ himself, the Son of God and Son of Man. It is on the basis of his appearance in history that Christians hope for the future. In the light of Christ's mission, the words of Genesis 1:28 are interpreted in a new way: not as a licence to subdue the earth, but to serve it and offer it to its creator. When St Paul writes to the Christians at Colossae that Jesus Christ is "the image of the invisible God, the firstborn of all creation", he is writing about the Christian hope. He is articulating the mysterious connection between the act of creation and the act of redemption. Their essential unity is to be seen in the person of Christ, the Incarnate Lord. For in his flesh God, the author and origin of creation, became part of creation. Jesus Christ is now identified as the one "by whom and through whom all things were created" (Colossians 1:16). He is the one in whom all things hold together, and because he is the pivotal point of the entire cosmos he can offer the hope of a new world.

Personhood

2.33. An unfolding of the biblical themes of creation, sin, redemption and hope has thus provided a starting point for our theological reflections on the natural world and our relationship to it; but the work of the Commission has also been involved in another area of theological dialogue, that which concerns human communities and human relationships. In the months before compiling this report, the Commission has spent many weeks visiting rural communities and listening to evidence from people living or working in them. We have been struck by the varieties of rural community. In some parts of the country, the pattern is still of traditional farming areas, but there are increasingly commuter villages, retirement communities, tourist-based areas, and communities where many different patterns of livelihood co-exist. There has emerged a need therefore for some underlying definition: what do we mean by community? How are we to develop a concept of community from a Christian position?

2.34. This innocuous little question in fact plunges us into a problematic issue because in raising it we are challenging deep assumptions of our day. For the overriding emphasis is placed not on community, but on the individual. What is more, 'community', like 'society', has often been derided as a vague, almost meaningless term. The Prime Minister has been quoted as saying that there is no such thing as 'society', there are only individuals and their families. Statements such as this both summarise and reinforce the contemporary preoccupation with the individual. But they also assume that the concept of 'individual' is somehow less problematic that that of 'society' or 'community'. It is clear, then, that any theology of community will first have to address the notion of the individual. It will also need to explore a theology of personhood.

2.35. One of the problems is that 'person' and 'individual' have become virtually synonymous. A 'person' is largely identified by his or her individuality, separateness, difference from others. Being a person is still predominantly associated with being rational, having choices, possessing a memory and being able to recall. In fact it was Boethius

(AD 487-524) who provided Western European culture with what was to prove a most lasting definition of 'person', namely: an individual substance of rational nature. Such influential philosophers as Aquinas in the thirteenth century, Descartes, Leibniz and Kant of the Enlightenment and the modern existentialists have never challenged, but developed this concept of the person as referring to that unique, distinctive, isolated, egocentric, self-conscious individual. The eighteenth century Moralists took the concept into debates on ethics. Thomas Payne used it in political theory and Adam Smith carried it into economics with his focus on individual enlightened self-interest. So this understanding of human personhood has undergirded our thinking in so many areas of life: political theory, economics, morality, art, religion, psychology and science. It has had profound repercussions for even such issues today as the provision of health care, the maintenance of rural services, the level of taxation and the educational curriculum.

Human autonomy
2.36. The early Christian writers saw nothing incompatible between a view of personhood focused on individual differentiation and one in which the individual derived ultimate meaning in relationship with God. But by the end of the eighteenth century Enlightenment, that link had been strongly severed. For human rationality had no need of God. All that was possible could be known by the light of reason unaided by revelation. And what defined human personhood was not some equation of rationality plus creatureliness, but autonomy: the state of being self-determinant, subject to no higher authority. This notion of the individual's ultimate independence from God is the one which dominates most of our thinking about the person today. The rights, sovereignty, freedom and autonomy of the individual are upheld as basic tenets of faith in much contemporary decision-making.
2.37. There are many examples of the way in which the autonomy and self-determination of the individual has undergirded the mind-set of our culture. It lies, for example, at the basis of consumption economics. The consumer is defined as an autonomous individual purchasing commodities. We talk of consumer sovereignty and autonomy as though the consumer were a self-defining unit whose decisions remained independent of others. And yet the consumer is not autonomous, but through patterns of trade, credit, waste, and use of resources, affects everyone else.

2.38. A still deeper view of the autonomy of the isolated individual is evidenced in the modern art, drama and literature which has been influenced by existentialism. Because the human person has no roots other than those of his own making, he is ultimately alienated from the rest of the universe. There is no God to refer to, no community to identify with, no relationship where we are ultimately knowable. Even love is illusory, for love depends on intimacy, on the possibility of knowing and being known. So the true human condition is one of estrangement and aloneness. It is a state of constantly "knocking on the door of the universe and finding nobody home". As one theologian has put it: "This is the end of the line: this notion of person, the seed of which was planted in the fifth century, can produce no more flowers."

The biblical perspective

2.39. It will not come as a surprise, therefore, to discover that the Commission has gone in a different direction for its theology of the person. In fact, it begins with a rejection of the post-Enlightenment view of human autonomy and reasserts a biblical position of humankind created in the image of God. So again it is as creaturely rather than autonomous that we understand the meaning of human personhood at its deepest level. Human identity is vested in being God's image, of reflecting God in the rest of creation.

"So God created man in his own image,
in the image of God he created him,
male and female he created them." (Genesis 1, v 27)

2.40. But this immediately brings in a second element which profoundly undermines the emphasis we have pinpointed earlier. There is no attempt to define personhood in terms of the irreducible ego, but instead the definition incorporates relationship and community. To be a person is to be in relationship: ultimately in relationship with the God who has made us, and knows us, and in whom we find our identity, but also in relationship with other persons and with the rest of the creation.

"Then the Lord God said, 'It is not good that man should be alone, I will make him a helper fit for him'." (Genesis 2, v 18)

This account of the creation of human community is of a man and woman: the image of God as male and female, inextricably bound to make up the fullness of human personhood. The understanding that the meaning of personhood is relational is implied throughout much of scripture as God establishes rules for relationships, communal norms, mutual responsibilities. The Ten Commandments are not a charter of individual human rights, but a code of relational duties and respect which we must offer one another. Just as the very being of God is that of a community (the notion of the Trinity is implicit even in the account of the creation of Adam and Eve), so in reflecting God's image human persons are linked with each other as common creatures, and joint image-bearers.

2.41. It is clear from much of the Old Testament that the concept of community is the one into which so many other important concepts feed. Norms of justice, mercy, compassion, not lying or stealing, the cancellation of debts, paying a fair wage, are all aimed at healthy communal living and at ensuring there will be no poverty in the land. Some of the instructions are distinctly biased towards the disadvantaged and against accumulation.

> "Do not take advantage of a hired man who is poor and needy, whether he is a brother Israelite or an alien living in one of your towns. Pay him his wages each day before sunset, because he is poor and is counting on it. Otherwise he may cry to the Lord against you and you will be guilty of sin."

> "Do not take the cloak of the widow as a pledge."

> "When you harvest the grapes in your vineyards, do not go over the vines again. Leave what remains for the alien, the fatherless and the widow." (Deuteronomy 24, vv 14, 17, 21.)

Nor does the New Testament depart from this motif. The person again is the person-in-community, and care and love are the hallmarks of living in relationship with others. "Give to the one who asks you and do not turn away from the one who would borrow from you." (Matthew 5, v 42) The supreme expression of community is the picture of the body of Christ, which St Paul outlines to the young church at Corinth:

> "The body is a unit, though it is made up of many parts ... if the foot should say because I am a hand, I do not belong to the body, it would not for that reason cease to be part of the body ... But in fact God has arranged the parts of the body, just as he wanted

> them to be ... The eye cannot say to the head I don't need you! And the head cannot say to the feet I don't need you! On the contrary, those parts of the body that seem to be weaker are indispensable." (1 Corinthians 12, vv 12-22)

There is no concept here of any isolated, self-determining individual. Instead, a person is only fully personal when in proper relationship with Christ and with others. We are not most personal when we are most distinctive. Instead, we are most personal when we are dependent on the community to grow and relate and love.

Community

2.42. We can begin to see here how a theology of personhood and a theology of community begin to reflect each other. At its heart a theology of personhood stresses the ultimate dependence of the person: first on God the creator for all of life and meaning, and second upon the communal and created context into which God has placed us. Nevertheless, the uniqueness of the person does not in any sense disintegrate by stressing that the person is ultimately relational. Nor does this uniqueness become meshed into a world soul, or universal spirit: the alternative to individual autonomy is not pantheism or Eastern mysticism. Rather it is that our uniqueness lies in the relationship each of us has with God: the God who can search each one of us and know our hearts. We therefore retain personal responsibility, both for our responsiveness to God and for our rejection of God. We are personally accountable for the sins we commit and for the relationships we violate. The injustice we perpetrate and the lack of compassion we show will be laid at our feet.

2.43. At the same time we are communal. Our identity is defined relationally, and there is also corporate responsibility for justice, fairness, peace and right relationships within which we contribute our voice. So from this theological standpoint there can be no purely individual redemption. Salvation in Christ involves working for freedom and justice for others. It involves carrying the message of reconciliation into areas of community which are torn apart and opening up the possibility of repentance and forgiveness. It means moving from the knowledge of personal peace and restoration - *shalom* - in relation to God, to pleading the cause of the disadvantaged, the victim of unfairness, greed, or exploitation. It is part of our response to God to help to create conditions where others in community can experience care and well-being. For the Church to be truly committed to enabling persons to grow will involve the task of ensuring that society is organized in such a way that human beings can enter freely into these relationships of spiritual and material exchange that we call loving relationships.

Implications of this theology

2.44. We have seen in this chapter a number of features which make up the theological basis of some of the Commission's work. We have noticed here that person and community are inextricably linked. But we still need to see how these insights could direct us in our own analysis of the evidence we have received. One way into this might be to turn to an underlying question.

2.45. What is community? In seeing the changes in our rural areas, are we witnessing the breakdown of community? Is community to be identified with traditional work patterns and 'organic' relationships based in this case around the land, or can community be understood in any wider sense?

2.46. Fundamental to the notion of 'community' is the idea of persons-in-relationship, and of shared norms. So a community is one where people draw together to express their relatedness by focusing on things they have in common. Traditionally, this used to be centred around the land, and around farming as an activity, a work pattern and a way of life. Yet any group which shares concerns, norms, patterns of mutual support, is a community. So it is possible to build communities which look very different from those of the past and yet which give people space to grow and be enriched.

2.47. However, that is frequently not the case. For the growth of individualism is affecting and destroying community life in many rural areas. Some of the views of the person which we have outlined in this chapter, those of self-determination, privacy and isolation, have been carried into the rural areas and have made the village a very lonely place. What is more, those principles so crucial for communal life – justice, corporate responsibility, protection of the disadvantaged – are seemingly being eroded by public policy in many areas of our country, and this again affects rural communities very deeply. It is from this standpoint that our report will be documenting some of these issues as they occur in various forms in rural life.

2.48. For just as we are called to be stewards of the earth and its resources, we are also called to be guardians of each other. Our calling is to neighbourliness, to love, to compassion and mutual care. Our hope then is that our theology of creation, of person and of community will be persuasive, and will encourage a departure from those other views of the environment and of the individual, which are currently producing so many problems for our earth and our societies.

Chapter 3
A Restructured Countryside

3.1. One of the powerful images which we have of the English countryside is that it is an idyllic 'world apart', a place which is isolated and insulated from the rest of the hectic, urban-centred world. In consequence, a common focus of complaint which newcomers to rural areas have concerns the intrusion of elements of the modern world into their chosen rural haven. But this image of an entirely isolated countryside was always false, and never more so as we near the end of the twentieth century. The new national and international economic structures, new technologies, changing political views and the relocation of many thousands of urban people to rural areas are major influences which must not be ignored in our understanding of the countryside.

3.2. The changes with which we are concerned are much more significant than a simple continuation of past trends; still less do they constitute a temporary aberration. They imply a radical alteration or restructuring of the way in which economies are made up, with equivalent changes in the societies which operate them.

3.3. Four key and inter-related elements seem to us to be especially crucial to aid our understanding of the English countryside as we approach the end of the century:-

1. The changing national and international economic order.
2. The implications of new technologies.
3. The demographic turn-round and social change.
4. Changing political and economic approaches.

The changing national and international economic order

3.4. The most striking feature of the rural economy has been the decline of the significance of farming as an employer of labour.

Although agricultural activities still occupy by far the major part of the land area of England and Wales, even in rural areas only one in seven of the workforce was, according to a recent official estimate, engaged in agriculture. The decline in coal mining jobs has also hit many rural communities. Nationally, employment in manufacturing has also declined (even though, as a result of heightened productivity, output has risen), but the decline in rural areas has been much less, so the share of rural areas in manufacturing jobs has generally gone up. This seems to reflect mainly the greater ease of capital-intensive expansion in the countryside, land being less scarce than in urban areas.

3.5. The expansion of manufacturing in rural areas springs mainly from the growth of existing rural factories; new branch plants plus complete relocations account for only a quarter to a third of the urban-rural difference in growth. High hopes are placed on the increasingly important small business sector: there is indeed increasingly a climate of opinion that the benefits of operating in small units outweigh the economies of scale of larger units except for the most major industries. Branches of large firms are of course at the mercy of pressures experienced and decisions made at a distance, whether elsewhere in the UK or abroad. We experienced the significance of these matters on our diocesan visits. In South Derbyshire, there seemed hope that the creation of a major Toyota installation would provide jobs for rural workers; conversely, in the Forest of Dean recent lay-offs of 300 workers by Rank Xerox had depressed the local people.

3.6. The growing impact of the European Community is a further important factor, with European companies enjoying a greater fiscal freedom to move anywhere, subject to planning permission, and with companies outside the Community seeking the best locations within the Community to establish their bridgeheads. It should be noted that this greater freedom implies greater competition, with not only overseas companies freer to invest in the UK, but UK companies freer to set up manufacturing plants elsewhere in Europe, or to import components manufactured by European companies. With this freedom to locate new plant wherever market forces indicate, the UK stands to gain its fair share of investment.

3.7. In this dynamic situation, a new importance attaches to planning decisions. Considerations of environmental fitness are at the top of the agenda right across the Community, so that these should not affect decisions differently in the UK from elsewhere. But over-insistence on unobtrusive industry in rural areas - the gentrification of rural industry to match that of rural dwellings - could drive new plants elsewhere in Britain or even overseas.

3.8. Note, however, that manufacturing investment will not lead to a corresponding increase in manufacturing employment. We are, perhaps, now in a post-industrial phase in terms of employment, with more new employment to be found in service industries. To some extent, as manufacturing industry moves out of cities, the cities are reverting to their old function of being centres of service, trade, administration and culture; but increasingly new technology is facilitating a growth of service industries in the rural areas.

The implications of new technologies

3.9. There are three major sets of new technologies which seem to have a special importance for rural areas. These are new manufacturing technologies, new communication technologies and new biotechnologies.

3.10. The first of these results from micro-electronic innovation, leading to the application of computerised production methods in existing industries and the growth of brand-new industries. First the protection of, and then adjustment to the decline in, traditional methods and traditional industries have absorbed much of Britain's economic potential, and reduced Britain's competitiveness, in the post-war and indeed in the inter-war periods. The rise of new businesses has often favoured the growth of smaller firms, some of them in the rural areas, although it is important to remember that not all rural industry is 'hi-tech'. Some of the implications of these trends for rural areas are touched on later.

3.11. The most recent developments in communications technology are those which permit the transmission of information, and of the manipulation of data, from a distance. One result of this can be the establishment in a remote area of branches of large firms to handle, for example, data processing. These are beneficial, but of course are subject to the 'eggs-in-one-basket' dangers, which any large employer in such an area can bring. Another outcome is the growth in 'tele-commuting', including handling information from home. This has been made possible by the development of workstations, which at a reasonable cost can give access to a central computer and enable the information obtained to be used to formulate conclusions and reports, and then transmit it. A tele-commuter can be an employee of a company, or an independent networker, contracting to supply his or her services. A networker may sometimes be an employee who has left his parent company and who makes a contract with that company. This can in itself generate employment, the typical Rank Xerox networker employing three to five people. The parent company saves vast overheads: the social benefits of networking are the ability of workers to combine family responsibilities with a career, the absence of disruptive relocations, less risk of redundancy because of not being tied to one employer, the ability to combine a career with writing a book, study, charitable work, etc, and the ability to reduce the working week as retirement approaches.

3.12. To conclude on this point, the trend is now firmly established which was identified some years ago by the American geographer, Brian Berry, when he wrote:-

> "Traditionally we have moved the body to the experience; increasingly we will move the experience to the body, and the body can therefore be located where it finds the non-electronic experience most satisfactory."

Put another way, we can now move work easily to people rather than the other way round. That work can be done anywhere and can therefore be located where people choose: and many, in exercising that choice, will choose the English countryside.

3.13. A third set of technological developments will also be important, and perhaps in ways which we now find difficult to imagine. These are the biotechnologies - the application of advanced science-based technology to biological materials. English rural areas will, we are sure, again be on the receiving end of these critical developments.

3.14. At the simplest level, these new industries, particularly in agriculture, horticulture and the bio-medical sciences, are already making their impact. Biotechnology-based industries often need clean atmospheres for their delicate products, and employ small but highly-skilled staff who do not wish to work in dirty, congested towns and cities, so the countryside is often a popular place for these new firms.

3.15. But the countryside implications of biotechnology are much more far-reaching than that. Agricultural over-production in Europe is already giving concern and raising questions of surplus rural land and what to do with it. Yet much of the massive increase in agricultural production has been accomplished with an agricultural science based upon relatively old technologies (fertilisers, machinery, herbicides, etc).

The potential, especially through genetic manipulation of future productivity increases, could be enormous, and the impact upon the farmland of rural England could be equally far-reaching. The knock-on effects upon the economy and society of the countryside could be very radical. At the same time, not only are there major moral and social issues raised by these technologies, but also we need to be aware how vulnerable our increased productivity would be if we became unduly dependent on a reduced number of strains of plants and breeds of animals, and these fewer strains and breeds became subject to newly-developing diseases and pests.

The demographic turn-round and social change

3.16. A third set of major changes concerns a development that is already recognised and commented on - the change in the number and structure of the rural population. The significance of these trends for rural England is already becoming apparent. In a paper especially produced for the Commission, Champion and Townsend stated unequivocally: "The key feature common to all broad areas of rural England is population growth." Their work, and that of others, has shown how the historical model of rural problems being seen as based in rural depopulation has in recent decades been reversed. Whilst London and the other major urban centres have tended to lose people, London and the principal cities losing ten per cent of their people between 1971 and 1981, the remoter, largely rural districts of England and Wales increased their population over the same period by a similar amount.

3.17. We now know that this process of 'counter-urbanisation' is not a simple one. It waxes and wanes in its relative importance to such an extent that some authorities have doubted its permanence as a demographic characteristic over significant periods of time. Moreover, it is clear that population loss has in no way totally disappeared from the scene. Thus between 1971 and 1981 more than half of all the parishes in Northumberland actually lost people and the equivalent figure for Suffolk was more than one in three. However, the broad pattern remains clear and we are convinced that it will continue. All rural regions will record some area of loss, and northern and western counties may well have more of these. Overall, however, the picture will be of increasing rural populations.

3.18. Those broad generalities, however, hide some critical demographic and social changes which will be important for rural

England. Rural populations will not be insulated from national trends. Thus we can expect smaller families and households, with more people living alone and more households with children and a single parent. Again, our society is an ageing one, with more people surviving to old age and even great old age. Indeed, if anything these trends will be especially strong in rural areas. Thus the migration of older people to the countryside, coupled with the location of younger people at early stages in their careers in urban and suburban zones, will tend to increase the geriatric feel of many rural areas.

3.19. Behind these demographic and social changes there is a sociological revolution at work. The people who choose consciously to move to the countryside are frequently different from those whom they join in the villages. They tend to be wealthier, to be overwhelmingly middle class, to have attitudes and mores which are different from the indigenous population. Above all, they have lifestyles which are noticeably different from their long-standing rural neighbours. Several years ago now, the sociologist Howard Newby commented on this change by arguing that the old 'occupational' rural community, strongly based upon agricultural employment, had been replaced by an 'encapsulated' one where the rump of the old farming-based village society found itself both outnumbered and surrounded by a new, different urban-orientated society in the village. More recently the geographer Nigel Thrift has argued that, over much of the South of England, rural society has all but vanished, to be replaced by a 'service class' of ex-urban and transformed local residents whose involvement with strictly rural industry and attitudes is minimal.

3.20. These analyses may be viewed as extreme, but the fact remains that there has been, and is continuing, a major social recomposition of rural society, fuelled not least by the attractions of rural living and the possibility of significant capital accumulation through the rural housing market. The end results of these demographic gains, and the associated social changes, provide a constant thread throughout all of our Report. Competition for rural housing; the loss of village-based services; the problems and tensions associated with observable differences of wealth in rural society; the rise of articulate pressure groups concerned to express their particular views; the ageing of rural congregations; the pressures upon vicars to minister to lonely single person households. These are but some of the tensions which we have observed both in our evidence and our visits and all have as their root the complex demographic and social trends we have just outlined.

Changing political and economic approaches

3.21. A fourth and final set of major changes, which we believe are helping to restructure our rural areas, concerns the changes which seem to be happening on the political front. These matters are rather more uncertain than the broad population changes which we have just described, but they are potentially just as important. They are operating both within national boundaries and within a broader European framework.

3.22. Put simply, there are a number of (often conflicting) developments which point to quite radical changes in the relationships between the state and society in general, and rural society in particular. Most obviously, the 1980s have seen a concerted effort by government to increase the role of the private sector in both the ownership of capital resources (such as housing) and in the operation of services which previously were largely delivered by the state itself. This process is, of course, still in train and as with every political phenomenon, it is subject to change and even reversal in the future. Nonetheless, we believe that there has been sufficient change in this area for it already to have had a major and long-lasting effect upon rural life in England. As such it deserves comment. Perhaps the most obvious effect of these radical shifts in the political paradigm can be seen in the privatisation of resources and services. Thus more rural houses are now owner-occupied and there are fewer council houses available to rent. Equally, the provision of essential services, such as telecommunications, are now subject to market forces and pressures of demand rather than need.

3.23. There are less obvious, but equally far-reaching, developments elsewhere. There is little doubt that the agricultural lobby is now far less powerful than once it was, and no longer can it be assumed that a Conservative Member of Parliament for a rural seat will be impressed by the farmers' and landowners' lobbies.

3.24. A political scenario which some might consider strikes a more optimistic note could be one whereby local rural democracy is given a fresh impetus. Admittedly the outlook may not look bright here. Local government at both county and district level has seen its powers restrained and its activities emasculated in recent years. Moreover, there is, especially by comparison with other European countries, a relatively poor tradition of vibrant parish government in England. However, the increase in rural population and in particular the change to an increasingly articulate, locally-concerned rural population might be seen as presaging a burgeoning of local democracy where, albeit within a wide national and even European structure, local village communities are encouraged to decide more for themselves.

3.25. Even more uncertain are the changes which may come about with our increasing integration with the other countries of the European Community, especially after 1992. Overseas interest in both housing and businesses is already clear in the southern counties of England. Where will this leave the English countryside? It may be that the attraction of rural areas which have been noted above and elsewhere in this Report will apply to the broader European Community, with consequent pressures of counter-urbanisation and re-industrialisation. Or it may be that some of the prosperity which has come to the English countryside in recent years will itself be attracted further south in Europe. Either way, the differential benefits which occur will be less evident in the rural areas of the north and the west of England and will thus widen the regional divide which is more and more apparent.

3.26. A European perspective was very rarely referred to at our open meetings and outside the strict farming community. But evidence given to us from Brussels suggests that, with the various pressures for the reform of the Common Agricultural Policy (CAP), there is a strong possibility of a rural rather than simply agricultural emphasis developing within Community policy. Since the admission of Greece, Spain and Portugal a new political presence has been apparent, representing the interests of the poorer southern and essentially Mediterranean parts of the EC. With 25% of the Greek population, 21% of the Portuguese and 14% of the Spanish, together with 15% of that of the Republic of Ireland, working in agriculture, and by British standards relying on very small holdings, it was to be expected that agricultural support would assume a more social emphasis, seeking to support the infrastructure of rural society rather than just food production. This could well link with those lobbying in the more prosperous north for farming policies which would take more account of green issues, concentrating on more sustainable farming methods and the quality rather than quantity of food. Care for animal rights and welfare could also form part of this.

3.27. Although Article 39 of the Treaty of Rome imposed an obligation to try to ensure a fair standard of living for the agricultural community, it did not insist that this was achieved solely through the application of the CAP. It was represented to us that even if agriculture had seen the major part of EC funding into rural areas in the past, it was not expected to receive such a high level of direct funding in the future. By using the structure funds more extensively, a policy initiated in 1987 had already led to a doubling of the structure fund during the period 1987-93. Of the 58 areas receiving help under this only one, Devon and Cornwall, was in England, although three others were in the UK: Highland and Islands, Galloway and Mid Wales. A more broad-based rural policy seeking to strengthen the base of the rural economy was advocated in the EC policy discussion document *The Future of Rural Society*, published in September 1988.

3.28. Within the policy debate in February 1990, the Agricultural Commissioner has advocated a new fund to help with structural reform in rural areas. Part of this would be aimed at encouraging farmers to enter environmental and management contracts with local government or other relevant bodies. The Commission is arguing for more co-ordinated growth in rural areas, less dominated by agriculture and therefore directed at promoting rural industries and tourism in those areas where it is appropriate.

3.29. The nub of this is that there is a layer of supra-national government in Europe which has the potential seriously to affect our rural areas. It is likely to be directed financially towards the poorer regions, and could be influenced significantly by closer relations with the countries of Eastern Europe, where agriculture is lagging and a rural dimension to policy is weak. In either event it must be probable that Britain and the more advanced agricultural countries will see their position weakened as recipients of subsidies, whether for strictly agricultural purposes or for the broader policy areas designed to strengthen rural areas.

3.30. With this debate well engaged in Europe it is important that British interests are strongly represented on a broader front than just agriculture. When we raised this with different ministries we were left with a clear view that they felt that the EC would not move either quickly or decisively in this direction. No one British ministry was responsible for a rural policy or even overseeing a rural dimension to policy in general, with the effect that those EC countries with a more co-ordinated and politically powerful rural lobby could well seize the initiative and manoeuvre policy in their interests. From our EC evidence, we were left with a firm impression that Europe would move ahead with the development of distinct rural policies, and was likely to shift funds from one part of the budget to another in order to achieve them, whether or not the UK was an active contributor to the debate.

It seemed to us to be a policy dimension about which British people should be more aware, and we were encouraged that the House of Lords Select Committee on the European Communities, Sub-Committee D: Agriculture, was examining the subject in greater detail.

3.31. These final suggestions on changing political structures are, of course, in some respects speculative and seem less certain than the elements of demographic, economic, social and technological change which we mentioned earlier. Nonetheless, they fit within the general picture which we have outlined in this chapter - that of an English countryside which is no longer cut off from major national and international trends, and which is in the swim of change and not just carried along, affected by the 'backwash' of urban-centred development. It is in this broad context that we need to move now to consider in more detail the questions of employment and industry, democracy and society with which any vision of the countryside must engage.

Chapter 4
The Environment and
Rural Development

4.1. We have said it before - the countryside is now an arena in which many priorities, some of them conflicting, are struggling for recognition. Nowhere is this more true than on environmental questions. Much of the striking growth in concern for the environment in Britain over the past decade has had the countryside as its immediate focus. There have been continuous disputes, local, national and international. How are these to be understood? What importance do they have?

4.2. The term 'environmental' is an elusive one. Most obviously, it points to a range of concerns about human health and well-being - concerning local amenity, the use and misuse of natural resources, and the pollution of the atmosphere, soil and water, and the disposal of wastes - on which the welfare of all of us depends. It is bound up inescapably with questions of justice and equity. One person's livelihood may be another's pollution. There is little disagreement that these concerns have been neglected seriously, and their importance underestimated, until very recently.

4.3. However, 'environment' has also acquired a more far-reaching significance. For growing numbers of people, environmental concern has become a medium through which they have been able to articulate anxieties about accelerating trends in contemporary existence. It has been through environmental disputes that unease about the pace of change, and about our apparent powerlessness in the face of evermore enveloping technological development, has been expressed, initially outside the framework of conventional politics, but now, increasingly, within it. Underlying this has been a spontaneous, indeed religious, recognition of humanity's deep relatedness to the rest of nature.

4.4. The Commission has received evidence, and had much discussion, on all of these matters. This is not surprising, since a great deal of recent environmental concern in Britain has focused on the countryside. The explanation for such a focus is in part social and cultural; much of our literature and painting celebrates rural (or imagined rural) values, and the protection of these values has been the concern of many of the best-organised environmental groups. But it also reflects the fact that it is in the countryside above all that nature abounds, and that it is there that we can celebrate it or abuse it.

Local planning

4.5. Thirty years ago, there was significantly less conspicuous controversy than today about the ways in which environmental conflicts were handled in Britain, whether in the country or the towns. Problems were treated as being of one of two kinds - those relating to land use and those relating to pollution. The former were handled through the system of county and district development plans, and planning permissions, under the Town and Country Planning Acts, or through private acts of Parliament. The latter were treated quite separately by a variety of pollution inspectorates and agencies, such as the Alkali Inspectorate and river authorities, and through the civil courts.

4.6. But the growth of environmental controversy in the 1970s and 1980s has brought to light - indeed, has reflected - serious gaps in these arrangements. Modern pollution problems demand much more integrated handling than can be provided by the former ad hoc agencies working pragmatically with particular industries. Moreover, the increasingly international complexities of many of the problems - and the economic and social implications of adequate controls - mean they must now frequently be addressed through internationally negotiated actions. Hence British practice is having to adapt, frequently uncomfortably, under European pressure, and out of a recognition of the need for a global approach to such daunting crises as atmospheric ozone depletion and, above all, the greenhouse effect.

4.7. In the same way, our town and country planning system has had little purchase on some of the most controversial recent land use conflicts in the countryside. For example, many farming activities have lain outside the scope of direct public influence - even though, in the 1970s and 1980s, the impacts on nature of modern agricultural technologies became a matter of widespread debate and concern.

4.8. The changed demographic patterns referred to in earlier chapters, and the steady adaptation of much of industry, and most of our rural communities, to patterns of living dependent on the private car, have also created escalating new pressures on our planning machinery. Recent rows about proposed 'new villages' in rural Hampshire and Oxfordshire, for example, have reflected tensions between new market forces and some established residents. These tensions themselves have flowed from the increasing location of hi-tech industries outside the old manufacturing centres. Where new industries - and new jobs - go, the housing pressures have tended naturally to follow. In the face of such problems, the long established balance between local planning control and national priorities as seen from Whitehall is now experiencing acute strain.

Growing strains

4.9. Over and above these issues, the Commission has become aware that still more troubling tensions lie behind the way environmental issues arise in our rural areas. The countryside is important for the range of specific uses to which it can be put. But, increasingly, it is also valued by many people for its own sake. This is a self-reinforcing phenomenon; as more people, increasingly the better-off, move into rural or semi-rural areas in pursuit of patterns of living not available in the conurbations, their preferences have become more significant at a local political level, when new developments are under discussion. Their views frequently link with those of the growing national memberships of conservation bodies such as the Royal Society for the Protection of Birds, the Council for the Protection of Rural England, Friends of the Earth and the National Trust, in favour of rural areas dedicated to 'natural' and recreational values.

4.10. In the background, now making themselves felt on the fringes of local controversy, are growing anxieties about new global environmental questions, such as the greenhouse effect. What sense is there in planning new and faster local roads, or out-of-town shopping centres based on ever greater private car ownership, if by doing so we intensify such global problems, however marginally? Concerns of this kind, unheard of in planning controversies two decades ago, are likely to be a growing feature of environmental debate in the countryside in the 1990s.

4.11. It is not hard to foresee the potential conflicts these trends in public attitudes will trigger when they interact with powerful economic and social forces now in the pipeline, both technically and at the European Community policy level. A recent task force report of the European Commission has warned of the likely severe environmental impacts of '1992'. The current pressures in food production are toward an increasingly efficient agriculture requiring less and less land. In Britain's rural areas such trends would open up increasingly large tracts of rural land for other uses. Obvious candidates for alternative uses will be footloose hi-tech manufacturing firms and the tourist industry in all its many guises. Similarly, the privatised water and electricity supply industries may well bring substantial blocks of hitherto undeveloped countryside, much of it in areas cherished environmentally, onto the market in the 1990s. It is not difficult to picture the conflicts with environmental values that lie ahead, with unsatisfactory consequences all round, if such possibilities are not anticipated adequately. The evidence the Commission has received suggests that our institutions have not yet fully absorbed the likely implications.

Contending interests

4.12. Given the tensions that now exist, what may have been adequate arrangements for establishing policies in the past may no longer be appropriate for the future. There is a striking 'apartheid' of policies affecting environmental planning in rural areas. The Ministry of Agriculture continues to be responsible for farming and the food-producing industries, in Whitehall and Brussels, whilst, despite the controversies of the past decade, the interests of the environment and of the rural poor are handled quite separately, by the Department of the Environment and the Departments of Health and Social Security respectively. Such political arrangements are mirrored in the pressure groups and trade associations most involved in rural policy. The Farming Unions, the Country Landowners' Association (CLA) and the Timber Growers' Association reflect the dominant concerns of their members; the environmental groups are seen as doing likewise for theirs. And industrial associations, like the House Builders' Federation and the Confederation of British Industry, press their own, quite distinct, imperatives.

4.13. However, a number of interests are conspicuously under-represented in this constellation of pressure groups. The rural poor, and the underpaid, have repeatedly been the victims of the changes that have overtaken rural areas in recent years. What is more, the interests of the urban population are also under-represented. The reality is that 80% of Britain's land area is owned by a small number of people. In the Commission's view, too often the under-represented interests are treated as marginal when public policies for the countryside are debated, whether in relation to the desirability of encouraging more small-holdings or unconventional work-places away from the conurbations, or improved public rights of access to rural areas for recreational purposes.

4.14. Thus the obvious strengths of established arrangements - for example, that many of the key issues for our rural areas are represented vocally by important sectoral groups - should not be allowed to conceal their limitations for the future. At a national level, the present balance of rural policies has emerged largely through a series of battles, the outcomes reflecting the economic and political strengths of sectoral interests, rather than from any more consensual process. Environmental interests, whether locally in amenity societies, or through the established national associations, have sought to organise themselves to operate as effectively as possible within this 'pluralist' framework, with the result that they too risk losing sight of the full range of economic and social priorities that policies for our rural areas should embrace.

4.15. To summarise the argument up to this point: the evidence we have received suggests that public concern for the environment in our rural areas, quite as much as nationally and internationally, is straining the established frameworks of planning and pollution control. Moreover, new economic and commercial developments now in motion are likely to increase the tensions still further in the 1990s. With this in mind, we see a need not only for new policies, but also for new machinery to help ensure that balances are struck.

Wider issues

4.16. The changes to local environments discussed above need to be seen in a wider context. The truth is that the intensity with which much environmental argument is conducted reflects the importance of what is at stake for our very existence as full persons. The countryside is not simply of instrumental value. It is also the focus of much deeper hopes and expectations. The lives many of us lead in advanced industrial society are becoming more and more complex and vertiginous, and increasingly bound by technological and organisational systems over which we feel less and less control. In these circumstances, it is as if nature, with its ingenuity, apparent autonomy and vulnerability, is becoming steadily more important, in reminding us of deeper continuities of existence of which we are all a part.

4.17. Moreover, as we have argued in Chapter 2, all of us need access to nature and the non-human, and nature itself needs our commitment and consideration. However parochial or self-interested particular land use disputes may appear, these deep needs are seldom far from the surface. People's identification with place and community, and their urge to safeguard and engage with familiar local countryside, are thus impulses of profound - indeed divine - importance. They need to be given real weight in public decisions. Indeed, the opportunity to experience and express such needs ought to be much more widely spread.

4.18. There are several levels at which advances can be made. First, our existing machinery of planning control remains an asset for the community as a whole. It provides a robust framework through which public choices about local development can be made. But it could be used more creatively. We welcome the Secretary of State's proposals for encouraging more affordable housing for local needs. But there is also scope for use of covenants, or Section 52 agreements, to acquire conservation benefits from developers or landowners when substantial housing developments of an orthodox kind are proposed in rural communities. Local communities should be enabled to benefit directly, as part of the process of agreeing to such schemes: new 'common land', or major schemes for new, free access to adjacent countryside dedicated to public use, should be made a quid pro quo of new development schemes. Alternatively, a proportion of the profit should be rolled over directly to the local community, for its own, named, conservation purposes. The Commission is aware of the lurking moral ambiguities in this area. The dangers of corruption are not insignificant. Nevertheless, the potential benefits for communities are such that the possibilities should be investigated seriously.

4.19. An important corollary is that the needs of urban dwellers for greater opportunity to enjoy and use the countryside should be given high priority. This has at least two dimensions. First, despite the good work of the Countryside Commission, National Trust and others, many people in the cities have little opportunity to become familiar with nature and open spaces. Greater public prominence should be given to their needs. Second, there is evidence of an unsatisfied yearning for readier access to rural land on the part of unorganised, even marginalised, social groups. When questions of public access and use of rural land are considered, the needs of these groups too need to be given greater emphasis than in the recent past.

4.20. For example, Government and local authorities should apply themselves to the question of how more rural land, in the form of small-holdings, could be made available for the use of people seeking access to farming on a part-time, or low-input, basis. We suspect the existence of a substantial latent demand for such opportunities. Greater attention should also be given to providing more opportunities for public recreational use of the countryside, not least by ensuring that public rights of way are well-maintained and publicised, in all parts of the country. An immediate step of great potential benefit would be for Government to enact promptly the recommendations of the 1986 Common Land Forum, thus securing proper management of, and public access to, hundreds of thousands of acres of common land, much of it in beautiful areas. (In 1986, the Forum, a round-table of all the principal environmental and land-management organisations concerned with common land, agreed proposals for legislation on these matters.)

4.21. It has been suggested to us that access to conservation 'services' from rural land should be put on a more explicitly commercial footing. That is, that rural landholders should be entitled to charge the community financially for the 'services' it gains from them, in terms of rights of way, public access, nature conservation, landscape enjoyment, and the like.

4.22. We see merit in the notion that landholders should be recompensed for particular positive initiatives to further environmental ends in the community's interest. However, we are troubled by the notion of a full cash economy for such intangibles. Nature and its enjoyment - not to mention public rights of way established across rural land from time immemorial - are not 'owned' by landholders; care should be taken to avoid any such implication. Positive payments will be needed from central Government to farmers, on the lines of the premiums in Environmentally Sensitive Areas, designated under the Agriculture & Food Act 1986.

4.23. Plainly, the development of such public priorities will need more than the good will of district planning authorities to bring it about. As the Town & Country Planning Association have stressed in the recent report *The Future Planning of the Countryside*, underlying economic and social trends affecting the countryside are at odds with many of the community's present expectations of it. The need for a regional, or at the very least an enhanced county, level of planning seems to us compelling in this context. Desirable as it may be that local decisions should prevail where possible, more synoptic views of land availability and of commercial and economic pressures are vitally necessary, if such forces are to be shaped and channelled in the community's wider interest. With the increasing integration of the European Community, local planning authorities in Britain will have to be aware of the new freedom of movement of manufacturing industry, and the pressures this may place on their long-established local land use policies. Counties, preferably co-ordinating their activities through regional bodies like the South East Regional Planning Conference (SERPLAN), will need to build conservation priorities ever more firmly into their thinking about future strategies for land use planning, in ways which do not frighten off new investment. In this context, we welcome the growing number of County Council initiatives, for example, in Shropshire, Lancashire and Cumbria, to undertake comprehensive county-wide 'green audits' for the first time, involving a wide spread of interests and expertise. Other local authorities should follow these precedents with the determination to see them through.

The national level

4.24. However, in a political culture with as continuous a history of strong central government as Britain's, the role of national government will continue to be crucial. Better balances between development and nature conservation, between the priorities of enhanced food production and reduced pollution impacts, and the like, must be led by government.

4.25. In the agricultural sphere, there is a strong case for an increasing shift of emphasis in policy towards encouraging more environmentally-benign husbandry. This suggests the need for greater financial incentives to support moves towards lower input farming systems, particularly if, as seems likely, ever-increasing yields mean that less and less land is likely to be required for mainstream food production. In such circumstances, the arguments for farming in many parts of the country to be encouraged to develop on lines, and on a unit scale, appropriate to secure conservation and recreational values are very strong indeed.

and on other forms of fossil-fuelled energy consumption in industry and the home. Such changes will be without precedent. They will present massive challenges to our political and social institutions.

4.31. However, the Commission has noted that many of the steps needed to begin addressing the worst trends contributing to the greenhouse effect also make sound sense for other social and environmental reasons, and could bring immediate benefits in a number of the fields mentioned in this chapter. Less private and more public transport could benefit the less well-off in rural communities, and others besides. So too could policies designed to ensure that social services - for schools, shops and health - can be provided more locally, to reduce the need to travel. In employment terms, it is arguable that lower-input agriculture could bring greater human benefits than present practices. And so on. There appear to be strong arguments for moving in these directions anyway, quite apart from any new political requirement which may arise from governments moving to initiate more determined action to mitigate trends in global climate.

4.32. Similarly, the arguments for greater public review and control over the development of pervasive new technologies should be seen as strengthened by the experience of the greenhouse effect. The Commission is convinced of the need for far greater scrutiny of claimed technical advances before they are developed or disseminated socially. Scientific ingenuity is an immense asset to society, provided it is made properly responsive and sensitive to the deepest interests of us all. This suggests the need for Parliamentary and public enquiry processes on such matters to be greatly strengthened.

4.33. England's rural areas have been exposed to many of the most important technological trends in modern industrial society. Public environmental concern has been one important signal of this. These trends and their implications need to be kept under much more systematic review by Parliament, for the benefit of society as a whole.

Recommendations

1. In order to reduce the tensions relating to access to the countryside, local communities should be enabled to benefit directly when new housing developments are approved from, for example, the creation of new common land or increased free access to public areas of countryside, or from receiving a proportion of the planning gain to be used for their own named conservation purposes. (4.18)

2. Greater priority should be given to the need of urban dwellers to enjoy and use the countryside, while not losing sight of the necessity to provide the maximum amount of green open space in the urban areas themselves. (4.19)

3. When considering questions of public access and the use of rural land, the needs of unorganised and marginalised social groups need to be given greater emphasis. (4.19)

4. Legislation should be put in hand to implement the recommendations of the 1986 Common Land Forum. (4.20)

5. Payment should be made to farmers and other land owners, for example, on the lines of premiums in Environmentally Sensitive Areas, for facilitating the community's enjoyment of rural land, including the creation and maintenance of new rights of way. (4.22)

6. The balance between economic needs, and those of environment and access, should be struck at the level of regional planning, rather than being decided piecemeal. This balance then needs to be worked out locally through county and district authorities, with parishes being consulted. (4.23)

7. The urban fringe should be defined in statutory plans with a strategy for these areas.

8. Financial incentives are needed for lower-input farming systems. (4.25)

9. Machinery is needed for more systematic public scrutiny and evaluation of proposals for developments in the field of bio-technology. (4.27)

10. The Government should commission a thoroughgoing review of transport facilities in the rural areas, in the context not only of social and economic needs but of environmental pressures and the greenhouse effect. This should include consideration of the adequacy of public transport, and of the accessibility of services. (4.31)

11. The growing impacts of modern technology on the environment emphasise the need for more adequate debate and research, linked to Parliamentary processes, into how these can be evaluated. (4.33)

12. Research should be undertaken into the scale and speed of development which small communities and the environment can assimilate without detriment.

Chapter 5
The Economy in Rural Areas

5.1. The economy of rural England in 1990 is complex and fast-changing. Not only are there substantial variations between different regions of the country in the balance of economic activities which are emerging, but perceptions of activities appropriate to rural areas also vary.

5.2. Nonetheless, certain patterns are clear. Agriculture is still overwhelmingly the dominant land use, but it is becoming increasingly less important as a rural employer. Moreover, as agriculture has become less labour-intensive, new patterns of economic activity in the towns and villages of rural England have grown, in turn reflecting and reinforcing changes in the structure of the rural population. As we note however, incomers to the countryside - whether commuting to the conurbations, working locally or simply enjoying retirement - tend to be wealthier than were their predecessors in the converted cottages and farmhouses many of them now inhabit.

5.3. Our investigations have tended naturally to focus on the problem areas of rural economic life. Much of England's rural economy is healthy and vigorous. At the most conspicuous level, in agriculture, the hi-tech manufacturing sector, and service industries such as tourism, there is abundance of innovation and competitiveness. Moreover, at the local level the Commission has gained an impression of considerably more inventiveness and adaptation in the less 'formal' areas of the rural economy than tend to be reflected in the available official statistics. For example, we have been impressed by the evolution in some parts of the country of new small-scale manufacturing and service enterprises serving local or specialist markets, in a fashion masked by official small business statistics.

5.4. Such developments are a reflection of the undoubted prosperity for better-off sections of the population, who have been moving increasingly into the rural areas. However, such positive trends by no means benefit everyone. What follows below therefore examines the problems arising in the rural economy as reflected in the evidence and statistics we have received.

5.5. The variations in these patterns county by county are considerable. The Town and Country Planning Association has suggested in a recent report (*The Future Planning of the Countryside*, July 1989) at least four different categories of rural area in England, each with its own sharply distinctive balance of economic activities. The rural areas overall have been more successful in attracting new jobs than the major cities over the past three decades, but, as the Commission has discovered, the details of the picture are fast changing and hard to pin down.

5.6. Thus the evidence received by the Commission suggests a complex picture of parallel economies developing in different parts of England. Whilst agriculture continues to dominate in much of both upland and lowland England, its significance for local communities as a whole is diminishing and its interests no longer command automatic priority. Small manufacturing industries, including mobile hi-tech plant, and the service industries now play an increasingly important parallel role in the rural economy as a whole.

5.7. In the paragraphs that follow we examine some of those trends in more detail and some problems to which they give rise. We also look to ways in which, in the remoter regions of the country at least, the interests of the economy might be reconciled better with those of the environment.

Employment trends

5.8. This section will attempt to examine the trends in the rural employment base not as a statistical exercise per se, but more for their implications for those primary areas of concern to the Commission - the population and the environment of rural areas. In order to examine these latter issues, however, it is necessary to paint some picture of how the rural employment profile appears to the Commission from the evidence that has been presented to us.

5.9. Early records show that even in 1800 less than 40% of British people worked on the land. By 1981 that had dwindled to just 2%, a lower percentage than in any other member of the EC where other heavily industrialised countries like West Germany and France registered over 5% and 7% respectively. During 180 years, then, there was in Britain an extremely sharp fall in agricultural employment.

5.10. However, national statistics by definition obscure important local variations in the relative importance of any employment sector and, in spite of this sharp decline, agriculture is still the direct source of one in seven jobs in rural areas: the Ministry of Agriculture, Fisheries and Food (MAFF) has calculated that in 1986 those working in agriculture accounted for around 15% of the UK rural workforce. Furthermore, many jobs in manufacturing, construction, and transport in rural areas are dependent upon agriculture, so its employment significance extends beyond that which is measurable within a narrow sectoral definition. Although the data tend to be patchy, there is clear evidence that in some rural counties in England and Wales agriculture can still account for up to 30% of the rural workforce.

5.11. Recognising the significance of agriculture to rural employment it is important to consider recent and prospective trends within that industry. Between June 1978 and June 1988 the numbers engaged nationally fell from 758,000 to 665,000, a ten-year fall of 93,000 or 12%. Some forecasts are that there could be a loss of a further 90,000 jobs nationally in the following ten years, to 1998, and indeed in the twelve months ending June 1989 there was a fall of 15,000. The spread and nature of the forecast fall will vary considerably, but it is expected to include both full-time farmers and part-time workers, even where these are members of the family. An analysis by the National Farmers Union (NFU) suggests that the greatest loss will continue to come from medium-sized farms as agriculture polarises between large agri-businesses and small part-time and hobby holdings. Evidence is that women have been particularly affected by the drop in part-time seasonal work. As full-time working on farms has reduced, so more rural people have been forced to become self-employed. This leaves them vulnerable, facing the risks on their own of finding work to fill in the gaps between seasonal jobs. On a larger scale there has been a growth in contracting services, in part due to the high cost of equipment, and in part a response to the problems of holding on to labour at times of low activity. It is recognised that these activities are not recorded in some agricultural employment statistics, and it is likely therefore that the significance of agriculture as an employment sector is somewhat understated. At the same time, some of those leaving direct employment in the industry become contractors, and to that extent the numerical declines experienced and forecast are overstated.

5.12. In general, though, what happens to people leaving agriculture is not clear. Evidence given to us shows that farming is an industry with an elderly workforce, and that therefore a growing number of people go into retirement if they can afford it. EC evidence was that they identified this trend across Europe. Even so, we met farmers, particularly tenants, who felt that they could not afford to retire, partly because they would have had to surrender their house and could not afford their own - a position which had not applied to the previous generation. As most agricultural holdings across Europe are owner-occupied this is not a problem on a European scale, but it still needs to be considered.

5.13. For hired farm workers the position was represented as being particularly hard. Even though their redundancy was often attributable to the effects of public and EC policy through the reduction of support prices, there were no retraining or special compensation schemes for agricultural workers as there had been for steelworkers and coal-miners. Even where restructuring was occurring through policies like 'Set-Aside', the support went to the farmer whose cropping pattern was changed rather than to the worker who lost his job. (Under the Set-Aside Scheme farmers receive annual payments to take at least 20% of their arable land out of agricultural production.) Because the full-time hired worker is rarely found on European farms the position in the UK has not been easily understood in Brussels as it does not form a significant part of European experience. It is likely therefore that any support will have to come from a national rather than a European scheme. Because of the scattered nature of farm employment and the spasmodic incidence of redundancy, it is clearly much harder for public policy to focus on training or special help, unlike the possibilities offered in concentrated areas like a mining village, or Corby when the steel mills closed there. Nonetheless no attempt has been made to increase the cash compensation to help the redundant farm-worker to reach a training centre to prepare for other employment. Because they have been scattered, they have been unable to group together to bring political pressure to bear: but they have a case which we feel needs closer examination and an imaginative response.

5.14. With an average of 85% of rural people employed outside the agricultural sector, it is other sectors which are increasingly more important to the rural economy in terms of employment. Despite the contraction of manufacturing jobs nationally, over the period 1960-87, the number employed in manufacturing in rural areas grew. The argument that there has been a significant redistribution of manufacturing jobs between urban and rural areas is based on percentage changes. Growth over this period in rural manufacturing jobs sounds significant at 20% - especially when contrasted against falls of 62% in similar employment figures in London, and 56% in the major conurbations. The extent of the alleged 'shift' can be seen more sharply when the numbers are examined. The 20% covered only 104,000 jobs, but there was a massive decline over all other areas of 3.12 million. Although rural manufacturing jobs have grown usefully in rural terms, in national terms they are much less significant. But within this perspective, manufacturing is an important component of the rural economy, with nearly a quarter of total rural jobs reflecting 15% of those in national manufacturing.

5.15. Otherwise, national trends in employment shifts by sector have been reflected within rural areas, and there was indeed a downturn in rural manufacturing jobs from the mid-1970s to the mid-1980s. The only sectors to have increased their employment nationally between 1971 and 1987 were public and private services, and this growth pattern is paralleled in rural areas. Over that period, service jobs in rural areas grew by 672,000, in stark contrast with all other sectors which taken together lost 144,000 jobs, leaving a net gain for rural areas of 528,000.

5.16. The position has not been consistent across the country. Not all regions enjoyed the same level of growth in employment in their rural areas. The three southern regions of South West, South East, and East Anglia together with the North West and Yorkshire and Humberside recorded the most rapid growth, varying from 20% to 35% between 1971 and 1987. Across the period the rural areas in every region recorded growth, with the North being the lowest at 11%. The North West, which recorded the lowest growth in the period 1971-81, recorded the highest during 1981-87. Although our regional visits emphasised that significant variations can exist not just intra-regionally, but within regions themselves, the overall picture was confirmed as one of reasonably full employment - even in many of the Rural Development Areas (RDAs) which had been selected in 1984 by the predecessor of the Rural Development Commission (RDC) for special support because of high unemployment.

Small businesses

5.17. Just as rural branch plants of large firms played an important part in the growth of rural jobs in the 1960s and 1970s, so small businesses have been equally significant in the 1980s. The small business sector is of growing importance in this country. Around 96% of UK firms registered for Value Added Tax (VAT) are small, and these account for 25% of the total workforce, 36% of private sector employment and 20% of Gross National Product (GNP). 11% of all employed adults in this country are self-employed, and 22% of the self-employed have between one and five employees. Small firms employing fewer than 20 people were responsible for the major part of net job generation in the period 1985-7; it is noteworthy, however, that numbers employed by firms with 20 to 49 employees fell, possibly indicating the difficulties involved in expansion.

5.18. Many small businesses in the more attractive parts of the country are linked to tourism. Indeed, in its forecasts for the future of the rural economy at a time of agricultural decline, the EC (COM (88) 501) singles out tourism as the most significant business for rural areas right across Europe. In the most popular areas like the Lake District, many farms offer accommodation, while some have extended their enterprise to the conversion of farm buildings and the provision of specialist holidays. While it is not every area which can easily capitalise on its natural beauty for tourism, opportunities are presenting themselves more widely, even in areas less used to tourists. With more leisure time available and with the more popular areas often becoming intolerably crowded, people are looking elsewhere for interesting places to visit and stay, seeking theme and activity holidays which are often less dependent on the beauty of the landscape.

5.19. We were told by the Tourist Boards, the RDC and others, that in promoting such areas it was important to develop advertising illustrating a range of interesting local activities. Their experience was that it was difficult for isolated attractions to succeed on their own, and therefore it was important for them to seek each other out and to group together. As tourism is increasingly offering rural employment, albeit often on a seasonal and relatively low paid basis, and has helped to provide part-time work for women in particular, it is an activity which needs every encouragement. It can be an important second income for rural households.

On our visit to Carlisle diocese we saw a number of small farms close to Hadrian's Wall where the wife's holiday business was the key income, with farming becoming effectively a supplement which nonetheless contributed to the experience of a rural holiday, especially when children met animals.

One tenant farming couple near Bolton Abbey in the North Yorkshire area of the Bradford diocese had just converted a former cow-shed into a tea-shop, with the old hay-loft sporting a fascinating model train layout which nearly caused the Commission member concerned to be late for his next appointment!

We saw others whose craft businesses were aimed at a tourist clientele, with a range of activities varying widely from knitted products to specialist foods. Many of these were personal in character with some making use of homeworkers as suppliers. Most of the businesses we saw were not highly capitalised but had nonetheless involved indebtedness to start them off.

5.20. The rural church has many things to offer the tourist and too often underestimates not only its own potential to attract visitors, but also the obligation on it to do so in order to help the local economy. Church buildings and their contents are a goldmine of social history and works of art from early medieval times.

In church buildings, sculpture, wood carving, memorials, and brasses all create interest for tourists - especially if they are well presented and explained. Pilgrimages linking churches to each other form just one of the imaginative schemes emerging from the work of Lincoln diocese's tourist officer. We turn to the evangelistic opportunities emerging from tourism in Chapter 11.
At Lanercost Priory in Cumbria stalls sell locally produced products varying from pottery to chutneys as

> **well as the usual books and postcards. A group of people find their ministry helping others obtain a market through the priory.**

5.21. The 1980s have also seen an indigenous development. Many of the new people in rural areas are affluent, with high disposable incomes, and they have sought out higher value goods and services. This has led to demand for crafted as opposed to standardised goods, and has provided a niche for rural industries. It is not surprising, therefore, that the continued very fast growth in employment in the 1980s in some rural areas (see 5.16.) has embraced craft jobs involving glass, pottery, and furniture, as well as financial and business services (in southern areas in particular), and village industries dealing with software, computerised injection moulding and micro chips.

5.22. New technology is stimulating a further area of small businesses, and, from the evidence we have received, will continue to do so for the foreseeable future. People involved in software writing, computer-aided design work, graphics and a range of financial services told us that they had settled in an area because they liked it, could afford a house there, and had good enough communications to enable them to travel as needed. For some this even meant access to airports because their business had an international clientele. As information becomes increasingly available through databases, this trend is likely to accelerate, with more home-working and less daily commuting. For example, a teacher's wife in a Dorset village works for the Atomic Research Council, relaying her results by telecomputer to Harwell. Again, Rank Xerox has licensed former employees as contractors, who typically employ several people. Finding such employees, however, can be a problem for these licensees, which raises again the issue of rural job training and the sort of skills needed for an area of business most likely to expand rapidly.

5.23. Even if the 100 or so tele-cottage experiments throughout Europe, providing key telecommunications on a village service basis, are slow to develop in the UK, the signs are that both private and corporate investment will continue to swing this way. Such developments, as well as bringing new highly paid jobs to a locality, create a new multiplier in the economy among those who service them. Nevertheless these self-employed contractors are vulnerable and their incomes often lack security. The expansion of this work can depend on the upgrading of British Telecom installations, and this process is likely to be slower in remote areas where distance and expected returns make investment less attractive.

5.24. Whatever the nature of its business, the small business sector has been encouraged by public policy with a plethora of support projects, often concentrating on assistance with capital, premises and advice. The responsibility lies between local authorities, the Department of Trade and Industry (DTI), the Department of Employment and MAFF, with each offering its own range of advice, incentives and assistance. Despite the good intentions, this apparent overlap easily leads to confusion, as we learnt from a number of people, wishing either to set up or expand their businesses. One key difficulty in rural areas is that of knowing or easily finding out what help is available. In some areas we have seen and welcomed the move towards 'one-stop shops' co-ordinating these activities, and helping clients to sift through the alternatives available to them. There is often a narrow dividing line between this type of advice and training and they frequently overlap.

5.25. Evidence from small rural towns suggested that much of the encouragement of small rural businesses rests on the shoulders of local banks and other professional firms. However, special training and counselling is offered by the countrywide chain of Local Enterprise Agencies. There are 255 of these in total in England, with 78 being in rural areas. They have been created through a partnership involving the public and private sectors, making available to clients the knowledge of experienced counsellors not just through the period of setting up a business, but through the early years as well. The clients of Enterprise Agencies are twice as likely to survive as those who go it alone without formal guidance. Although these Agencies are of variable quality, we would hope that Government funding will not just continue for the most obviously successful of them. It will need to take special note of the difficulty of raising private local funds for this work in rural areas because of the lack of larger businesses there, even though the role of the major banks has often been an important factor in enabling rural agencies to be created at all.

5.26. As the problems of the 20-49 employees size band suggest (see 5.17.), it is of particular importance that advice continues to be available as small firms expand.

5.27. We have noted the role of Business in the Community (BItC) in advancing this work, encouraging partnerships between local authorities and business and attempting to obtain better liaison between the different public sector agencies concentrating on the encouragement of small businesses. But BItC has recognised that the range of schemes applicable to inner cities and towns are not necessarily working for rural areas. A high powered target team involving senior civil servants, landowners and representatives of rural business has been established under the chairmanship of the Duke of Westminster to investigate the specific needs for encouraging enterprise in rural areas. It is focusing initially on Cumbria, Northumberland and Shropshire and its report on creating suitable rural networks and partnerships is due in 1990.

5.28. Small firms are subject to a high failure rate, although there is some evidence that in times of deep recession, owner-managers dig in and the failure rate does not rise correspondingly. Evidence on profitability is mixed, but because of low capital backing, and therefore low productivity per worker, they often pay lower wages. Although it is true that the 'hi- tech' businesses which are attracted to rural areas tend to pay higher wages, at least to their skilled employees, the low-wage ethos which is typical of small businesses in general is reinforced by the low-wage agricultural milieu (see 5.70.)

Scale

5.29. The RDC has consistently championed the cause of jobs in rural areas, concentrating on the opportunities to be offered by small businesses. In conjunction with English Estates it has promoted the siting of business premises within truly rural areas, enabling businesses to start and continue locally where private investment has not been prepared to take the risk of speculative building. In doing so they have challenged the trend for rural areas to become exclusively residential. This has not always been a popular stance with conservationists, quick to fight against allowing businesses to develop in rural areas. Traditional rural sites have often been unsightly with old cars, equipment, and other eyesores lying around. As with the smells from farms, these have become unpopular with some new residents, and have led to conflict and still do, with those who have long worked in the countryside feeling threatened by what they feel is an unreal and aggressive attempt to create a sanitised, picture-book countryside, unrelated to genuine rural life.

5.30. What is significant now is that rural employment and the need to maintain a living rural economy is being accepted as desirable and necessary by a range of rural interest and heritage bodies (such as the

RDC, National Trust, CLA, Rural Voice and Countryside Commission amongst others) who would not necessarily be expected to agree with each other. Separately, they seem to be probing not only the ingredients necessary for successful rural life, but also the sense of scale they feel is appropriate for creating jobs within a rural setting by achieving the elusive balance between development and conservation. In the Peak District National Park we saw some excellent examples of sensitive architecture which had achieved this, enabling new businesses to develop within a highly protected environment. However, we urge that the drive for environmentally acceptable jobs does not get out of hand, ignoring the skills and needs of rural people, and impinging unduly on the freedom of individuals.

5.31. The fact that a growing number of government agencies and voluntary bodies have arrived from different angles at something close to a consensus on this issue is powerful testimony to the need for successful small businesses in rural areas. However, it should not hide the shortcomings of small businesses in matters like training, financial control and marketing, where larger companies usually have a better record and from whom a training 'fall-out' occurs. If small scale becomes an exclusive norm for rural areas, it will perpetuate weaknesses in the rural economy which will be dependent on outside initiatives to counteract them. It is our view that a number of larger organisations will need to be sited in rural areas in order to counterbalance this danger, and to ensure a better balanced rural economy more capable of dealing with its apparent weaknesses from within.

Planning and business

5.32. The pressure for attracting inward investment on a large international scale was emphasised in his evidence to us by Professor Alan Budd. He felt that this would affect some rural areas very considerably, because the evidence of Japanese and other firms was that they wanted greenfield sites close to pools of suitable labour and to the main highway network. It is likely that when the national interest is to be served by such investment, pressure will be placed on the local authorities to make space available. Whether this trend will slow down after 1992 remains an important but open question.

5.33. The appearance of new business parks and factory units on the edge of small rural towns illustrated for us the commitment of many local authorities to encourage local enterprise, even if this has been concentrated on towns rather than villages. However, it was clear from the evidence of small businesses that there were often severe problems in obtaining planning permission for premises in rural areas. Farmers reported difficulties where diversification needed planning permission and where a business, successfully started, needed additional space to expand. We cannot overemphasise how important we feel it is for local authorities to enable rural enterprise to thrive without undue bureaucracy. Time and again people seeking to convert redundant buildings told of delays and frustration, due to what they felt was *a lack of vision and commitment to a working countryside* - a countryside no longer dominated by agricultural employment, but still capable of creating jobs which would enable people to live and work in it. Together with the forward-looking vision needed from district planning authorities, there is a real need for proper technical advice from officers, and perhaps outside consultants, which would facilitate a full appreciation by planning committees of the economic benefits likely to flow from development proposals. Too often in the past it is clear that innovative schemes have been considered by planning committees only from the viewpoint of their negative environmental impacts, and often little attempt has been made to weigh these against the positive contribution which might accrue to the local economy.

5.34. Although it seems that this trend in growing local prosperity is set to continue, the EC warns that in its judgement, rural areas across Europe should expect to see a decline in the number of new production units being set up as a result of outside investment, with new investors being more selective and fewer in number. The EC feels that rural development through the 1990s will depend more on the extent to which indigenous development potential can be mobilised.

5.35. If this trend develops in the UK, it will place even more emphasis on the need to encourage local enterprise by providing local incentives and encouragement. The streamlining of the provision of information, and the reduction of obstacles to job creation through as much deregulation as is consistent with a workable planning policy, will become increasingly important in the economic climate after 1992.

5.36. A major contribution to this improved situation could, we believe, be brought about by a coming together of the several agencies and strategic planning systems which have grown up piecemeal in recent years. Among the most important are the counties which have produced Structure Plans and, much more recently, are now beginning to bring forward Countryside Strategies, following the recommendations of the Countryside Commission Countryside Policy Review Panel. In addition, we note the existence in much of rural England of Rural Development Plans (RDPs), relating to the RDAs. There are also the emerging strategies produced by the Training and Enterprise Councils (TECs), where the rural component needs to be fully recognised. The 'green audits' now being undertaken by some innovative counties, mentioned earlier, would also have a key place in this dialogue. These, and other structures, must increasingly work together and not in isolation to produce what should be seen as integrated 'rural strategies', giving due recognition to the needs of both rural economic development and proper planning and environmental protection.

5.37. There are models which illustrate this crucial integration. The innovative Upland Management Experiments (UMEX) fostered by the Countryside Commission in the 1970s, the integrated Rural Development Project in the Peak District, and several others, have shown, albeit on a relatively small scale, that environmental and economic objectives can be fostered together, especially under the guidance of a gifted animateur. These small-scale experiments in integration now need to be expanded to a broader scale, certainly to county level, and perhaps even beyond to give a regional perspective and strategy. The function of SERPLAN, which was mentioned earlier, has to date concentrated largely upon a planning role, but it may provide a model for such a broad-based, integrated strategic view of a region's economic and environmental future.

Uniform business rate

5.38. The introduction of uniform business rate (UBR), at a time when the economy is growing more slowly, is causing concern to many small rural service businesses. Village shops have seen their rates increase by up to 300% when many are hitting increased competition from new out-of-town superstores. To many small businesses UBR is unwelcome and untimely, perceived as an attack on them in favour of large organisations and those in the manufacturing sector. Even though UBR was intended to help redistribute rates in favour of the north against the south, it has been from the northern region, with its lowest economic growth rate in England, that we have had the greatest concern about the impact of UBR on small service businesses. In tourist areas many businesses are service based and therefore vulnerable. The impact of UBR needs to be monitored and reviewed. 5.39. If it does lead to closures this will impact many of those who need local services in rural areas, and will force people to travel or to do without them. We are very concerned if public policy is having this effect, as once again it will be the poorest element of society who will be further disadvantaged, and some of the less affluent businesses which will be forced to close. Often these are run by rural people not expecting a high return for their efforts, but providing a valuable local service.

Agriculture

5.40. Even if agriculture employs fewer people than previously, it is still the single most important sector in rural areas. In visible terms it *is* the countryside with 90% of rural land farmed, and the familiar views of fields, hedges or walls all created by developments in farming over the centuries. It is the link between food production and the nature of the countryside which has produced growing tensions and debate over recent years.

Food production

5.41. The Agriculture Act 1947 confirmed the importance of the industry in post-war Britain. It was designed to give farmers and those who worked on the land a fair reward for their labours. It enabled farming to prosper and in so doing to reduce balance of trade difficulties. Productivity and production improved immensely and in some commodities self-sufficiency was attained. Up to entry into the EC, support for agriculture was based primarily on a subsidy to cover the difference between world market prices and a higher guaranteed price. On entry, the policy of cheap food was reversed, and farmers obtained most of their returns from the consumer within the managed market arrangements of the CAP. This policy came under great strain when surpluses began to build up and the cost of storage and subsidised sales to other countries such as Russia pushed the cost unacceptably high. There followed a combination of price and product restraint, including the use of quotas on milk, which have brought about a much greater degree of control. World farm prices have been high in 1988 and 1989 owing to drought in the USA and shortages in the USSR, but the evidence suggests that this is a lull and not a trend to be relied upon, and it may well be that to sustain farm incomes at a reasonable level, but with reduced quantities and yields, some extension of the quota system should not be ruled out.

5.42. For many years the CAP was the only policy common to all members of the Community. As a result it developed a sanctity and mystique which set it apart from all other aspects of policy. Not only were prices to be kept high, but the social implications of a decent standard of living in the rural areas were to be sustained by a guidance fund which would take up to 25% of the agricultural budget. In the event, only a small part of the budget has so far been made available for these more social purposes.

5.43. The advent of the single market in 1992 means that all distortions in prices caused by the value of the so-called 'green pound' have to be eliminated. With the decline in our currency in recent years this will mean considerably increased farm gate prices, and the first step in the readjustment was announced in April 1990.

5.44. The underlying trend is towards larger units, driven by the need for volume to offset lower unit prices. In a lecture given at the Bank of England in March 1990, George Jackson of the Royal Agricultural Society of England emphasised the view that the effects of the market place would increasingly prevail, causing both structures and systems to adapt in their response, and possibly leaving serious food production in the hands of as few as 60-70,000 highly professional farmers by the turn of the century. He felt that the balance of as many as 180,000 units would contribute little to output. He acknowledged, too, that Britain's current farming structure puts it at a serious disadvantage with the political and social emphasis focusing more sharply on the difficulties faced by the poorer countries like Portugal, Greece, and Spain. He supported the view that for Britain to attempt to maintain a small farm economy would be unacceptably expensive to the taxpayer. The regional impact of this trend will mean that whilst agricultural production will become concentrated towards the better land of the south and east, in the poorer farming areas of the north and west farm revenue will fall and production will become more extensive. It is in these remote and difficult areas, such as the north Pennines, that the diversification of farming and the rural economy will be of great importance to rural communities. Yet, although in many parts of the south and east the pressure to diversify the rural economy needs little encouragement, greater help and encouragement are needed in upland farming regions, if working communities are to be retained in areas which have a growing national importance for landscape conservation and public recreation.

Environmental aspects of farming

5.45. The incentives given to farmers, particularly to produce cereals and oil products, took little account of the environmental cost of such policies. Public policy did not protect hedges, heaths, wetlands and other natural features, with the result that farming developed at the expense of a serious depletion of indigenous flora, fauna and variety in landscape. Even if the areas disappearing under the plough were not wilderness, they often had a quality of wildness and natural freedom which was a significant aspect of the variety of habitat available in the English countryside.

5.46. There are gradual moves in public policy to address the environmental aspects of farming. In England, Environmentally Sensitive Areas now account for 2.5% of the land surface, and show a way forward. In order to support a policy of greater emphasis on environmentally sensitive farming practices, the National Trust in 1989 budgeted for a drop of £100,000 in its income as the cost in lower rents. Not all landowners can afford to do that without subsidy.

The farming community

5.47. We have noted that the number of people engaged in farming is dropping steadily and, with that, many of those with the deepest understanding of rural life are disappearing. This is changing the character of rural communities and rural churches.

5.48. Any general view, therefore, that farming means the ownership of land, a generous lifestyle, and guaranteed harvests is far from the truth. Of course large farmers have very considerable capital investment: it is not surprising that to many people they appear to be well off. But even with public support, farming for many is a precarious occupation, far more dependent on weather than most people would appreciate. Particularly in the north and west, many small farms of around 50 acres are worked by a farmer on his own or helped by his wife. Many of these are tenants who seem trapped, unable to retire because they have no prospect of local housing, maintaining a hard life well beyond conventional retirement age. For many small tenant farmers there has been a serious decline in income which has not been compensated for by social schemes or environmental support. These farms add much to the beauty of the upland areas. It would be a national tragedy if they or the people who work them were lost to the nation. One man drove to a meeting with the Commission in North Yorkshire on his tractor because he could no longer afford a car as well. Another in Derbyshire acted as a part-time postman, aware that his children were unwilling to follow in the family farm. He accepted the inevitability of this under existing agricultural policy, but he regretted that the wholeness of his way of life would not be inherited by his children.

5.49. Whereas farmers had been seen as the producers of the nation's food and the traditional custodians of the countryside, a growing body of opinion began to see in farming production practices a great and continuing threat to conservation. As more people with urban origins have moved into the countryside, so has the criticism of farmers grown. With this growing protest coming at a time of increasing financial pressure, many farmers reported to us that they felt that their standing in the community had fallen.

> **One man and his wife in Coventry diocese farmed the 200 acres which had been in their family since 1650. During their time the number of people they employed had been reduced from four to none. In their own eyes, their standing in the community had fallen, even though their output had grown in line with national policy. They found that farming and food production were the subject of local criticism and even abuse, leaving them feeling strangers in the church in which they and their ancestors had worshipped for centuries. Their experience was not unique.**

5.50. To many members of the Commission, this issue was given a human face when they were given breakfasts, lunches, teas and coffees in a wide range of rural and farming homes. Everywhere we met the same apprehension and uncertainty for the future. Amongst the agricultural and older rural community, morale is often low, family continuity queried and in the saddest cases suicide has occurred. The pressure under which the farming community is currently living should not be under-estimated.

Questions for the Church

5.51. The pressure to increase size of agricultural holdings is asking serious questions about the traditional role of farming in rural areas with pressure mounting on the viability of family farms. Statistics show that the number of farms at either end of the size spectrum are growing, with medium sized ones under the greatest pressure.

> **Where a similar trend is emerging in the USA, many of the churches are actively supporting family farms, seeing in them a vital component in the structure of rural life. Families also reflected a style of contact and continuity with the land which was felt to be theologically important. The churches in the USA felt strongly enough about this to make representations to GATT over the effect of free trade on the nature of American farming.**

5.52. We had evidence of the continuing importance of the farming community for the Church in many areas, but usually it was within the context of a dwindling and ageing group, often being squeezed out by the twin effects of public policy and growing productivity.

5.53. Amongst these people we found those who acted as churchwardens, held prayer meetings in their homes, played the organ in church, helped to clear church gutters and do other small pieces of maintenance work. In many different ways, they have been deeply involved in their community, giving their service as a matter of course in ways not necessarily appreciated or followed by newcomers.

5.54. Our judgement is that, where it holds agricultural land, the Church of England could well see itself coming under pressure to review the nature of its tenancies to reflect theological insights rather than a slavish acceptance of growing intensification and the move to larger units. In doing so, it would be asking questions which were raised with us:

— Is there a human scale that is appropriate for agriculture?

— Do humans have a special relationship with and responsibility for the land?

— How is stewardship to be interpreted within the context of modern agriculture?

The future of agriculture in the rural economy

5.55. Throughout our visits to dioceses and parishes in rural England, and in much of the evidence presented to us, the future of agriculture and of the upstream and downstream industries dependent upon it has figured prominently. In summary, the situation as it has been described to the Commission is as follows:-

(1) In the face of surplus production capacity within the agricultural sector at present, the European Community and the UK Government have embarked on a policy of cutting price support for agriculture as a means of bringing supply and demand into better balance.

(2) A central tenet of this policy is that we currently have too much land in agricultural production. A policy of price pressure would therefore not only seek to reduce production, but would do so by driving land and the farmers and their employees out of agriculture. The extent to which this will occur is currently a matter of some conjecture. Estimates of potential land surplus vary according to source, assumptions and the time scale over which projections are made, and range from 1.3 million hectares by 1999 to somewhere between 5.5 and 5.75 million hectares by the year 2015. The most recent estimates of the impact on labour suggest that at current rates the agricultural industry could shed up to 90,000 workers (both farmers and employees) over the next decade.

(3) To compensate for this process, farmers are being offered a number of incentives to develop alternative activities/enterprises on their farms which (it is hoped) will allow them to remain in business and hence maintain the rural socio-economic structure and the environment which are so valued by the UK population. These incentives range from schemes to develop new enterprises on farms through to initiatives to encourage farmers to farm in a less productive but more environmentally friendly manner.

(4) Some farmers will leave farming through the lucrative option of developing their land. Since 1987, planning policies automatically protect only the better grades of agricultural land, thus removing the 'agricultural objection' from development projects on the majority of agricultural land in the country.

5.56. Serious questions surround the policy approach which is attempting to tackle the current agricultural production problems by means of price pressure. Whilst we understand the need to achieve a better balance between supply and demand in food production, the price mechanism may not be the best means of tackling that problem. Not only will it drive more farmers and workers off the land, but we believe that its main impact will be to increase pressure for intensification in some favoured areas whilst creating problems of dereliction elsewhere. In that context, we have serious reservations about the current perception of agriculture's problem as being one of surplus land.

5.57. Our concerns about the use of the price mechanism and the surplus land argument are heightened by our doubt about the effectiveness of policies aimed at diverting farming into new businesses such as woodlands or farm diversification. We recognise that whilst some farmers will benefit from these schemes, not all farmers are in a position to develop new enterprises. The location of the farm relative to sources of demand, the nature of the farm resources, the level of indebtedness, the tenure status of the holding and the business management skills of the farmer are factors which alone, or in combination, can seriously reduce the potential for developing successful new businesses on many holdings. Even where this is not a problem, we are aware that external factors such as local planning and/or highway policies can sometimes inhibit the development of new businesses.

5.58. The most appropriate form of diversification is the take-up of the Farm Woodlands Scheme. At present the incentives are inadequate to bring about the scale of tree planting which is needed on upland farms. New hardwood plantations are needed there (a) to support farm incomes, (b) to enhance the landscape quality and (c) to provide screening for additional enterprises that could develop, and which we argue are needed to sustain a viable rural economy. We are not referring to blanket afforestation, but to small-scale, environmentally beneficial plantations. It is therefore to be regretted that because large-scale planting has made an unwelcome impact on some upland landscapes new planting through the Farm Woodlands Scheme has not been encouraged. Yet the form of planting envisaged by the Scheme will be of greater landscape benefit than any other as the decision to plant will be determined by considerations relating to shelter, land quality, and topography - choices which are grounded in an order and purpose which has ever been the most satisfying aspect of human influence on the landscape.

5.59. We are also concerned that some diversification enterprises can be divisive for the farming community. The farmer who successfully diversifies by changing his redundant farm buildings complex into holiday accommodation can create considerable problems for his neighbouring farmers, especially if they are livestock producers. The vulnerable position of tenants when landlords gain planning approval for diversified activities on tenanted land is another matter of great concern to us.

5.60. In a wider context, we are concerned to note that, to date, government policy to assist agriculture has been targetted on the farmer, with nothing being specifically allocated for the assistance of the agricultural workers who also lose jobs as a result of current policies. Although some farm workers are themselves diversifying and/or may find new employment in the diversified businesses on some farms, we are persuaded by the arguments of the RDC that the workers' employment problems will not be solved by the creation of on-farm employment.

5.61. In this context we are increasingly concerned that Set Aside, one of the current solutions to the agricultural problems of over-production (see 5.13.), may indeed be exacerbating the socio-economic problems in rural areas by creating redundancies. There seems every likelihood that this trend will accelerate, especially if subsidies drop in real terms. We have been made aware of cases where the decision to enter the whole farm into the Set Aside scheme has resulted in the loss of jobs for employed labour.

5.62. In some parts of rural England, the concerns about the future prospects for agriculture are heightened by the decisions of some farmers to solve their problems by moving out of a commodity that is in surplus, into one where they think there is room for expansion. The most accepted moves are currently out of wheat into sheep. At present this trend is resulting in a significant increase in the sheep population of some parts of lowland England, such as East Anglia. We see this trend creating a significant problem not just for the farming community, but also for those, essentially upland areas, where the sheep economy is the key element in the maintenance of the fragile balance between the socio-economic needs of the community and the environment. Even if the UK is able to capture a long-term increase in its market share of the European sheepmeat market, which was felt to be essential following 1992, the competition within regions will cause problems for the poorer areas, which have no serious farming alternatives and where resources for diversification are often scarce. We believe that this issue of knock-on effects is now a major item of policy concern to which agricultural policy makers must give greater priority than has been apparent to date.

5.63. Concerns about the future of the rural economy, however, are not confined to the uncertainties surrounding the agricultural industry. In some of the more accessible areas of the countryside we were made aware of increasing conflicts of interest between different groups in rural society over the issue of job creation in the countryside. For a significant percentage of the rural population the countryside has become a place to live and not to work. For them the creation of premises for new jobs is often perceived as a threat to amenity and/or property values, with the result that opposition to such proposals is often articulate, well-organised and effective. By contrast, the potential beneficiaries of such proposals are seldom so well-organised, or have their case articulated so effectively in order to present a balanced argument.

5.64. Whilst more localised examples of such conflict are commonplace, we are aware of the existence of more significant conflicts involving major development proposals of national significance, in which local people often feel that their impact on the economy and local prosperity is perhaps not being given sufficient weighting. The cogency of such arguments is heightened when development proposals arise in more remote areas where the opportunities for alternative employment are limited. At the same time, fundamental questions must be asked about the strength of local commitment to revive the economy of some rural areas. Whilst the policy rhetoric is frequently incontestable, the realities of policy implementation are often a different story. The balance between socio-economic needs and environmental qualities can often be solved by development of the appropriate scale and character. The achievements of the RDC are adequate testimony to this fact. In some parts of the countryside now, however, the stakes are too high to render the problems soluble by the skills of the architect.

The current employment situation

Unemployment

5.65. From the preceding analysis of recent employment trends in rural areas, it could easily be imagined that unemployment is not a problem in rural Britain. Whilst the available evidence confirms that in general, unemployment in rural areas is lower than in the more urbanised parts of the same region, this pattern is not consistent across all regions. Only in the South East and South West were the rural unemployment figures higher than the regional average in July 1988 and of these two, it would appear that only in the South West (especially Devon and Cornwall) has the in-migration of people into rural areas not been balanced by a comparable growth in jobs, hence leaving a higher unemployment rate than the regional average.

5.66. However, the problem of specific areas that break the trend is best illustrated by those industrial villages which often owed their development, if not their origin, to the growth of one major employer or industry. Boots and shoes across the East Midlands provide one example, while the dependence of villages round Ministry of Defence installations is another.

> **Military establishments have existed for most of this century and sometimes longer, contributing greatly to the local economy and shaping patterns of employment for civilians both at the base and as suppliers to it. Concern was expressed to Commissioners through Lincolnshire, East Anglia and Salisbury plain, as well as round Catterick in North Yorkshire, at the serious vacuum which would be created if changes in defence policy led to severe reductions or closures.**

5.67. The most notable current example is, however, coal mining. Between 1947 and 1970 coal mining employment across the UK as a whole dropped from 703,900 by 59% to 287,200; and then between 1980 and 1990 it dropped further, with the figure for England alone falling from 226,000 to only 80,000, a drop of 65% spread remarkably evenly in percentage terms across the regions. Such figures are serious nationally and regionally, but the effect on small, often isolated, communities has been devastating. It was reflected in the fact that the lowest priced housing we encountered was £8,000 for a terrace house in a Durham mining village. Even where pits have not been closed, unemployment has grown, with the older people being the first to go. In one Nottingham village we were told that nobody over 50 now worked in the pit.

5.68. Although these two examples involve the public sector, a similar problem arises when a major private employer reduces jobs on a large scale or closes a plant outright. Pilkington's showed how sensitively such problems could be handled in St. Helen's, but in truly rural areas alternative jobs on the scale needed are difficult to create. Our experience suggests that where a reduction of jobs occurs on a scale that is significant for the area concerned, something close to temporary RDA status needs to be granted, involving the local authority, the RDC, the Ministry concerned (if appropriate) and the local TEC. Belatedly, in January 1990, new measures were announced under the Rural Coalfield Partnership Area Scheme. To date, one in North Nottinghamshire has been approved. This special aid to a rural coalfield has not, however, attracted additional funding from the Department of Employment. It could be interpreted, therefore, that this special assistance is being provided at the expense of programmes in existing RDAs which are predominantly agricultural. We are also concerned that the original 1984 criteria have been applied in a rather bureaucratic way by the Department, creating anomalies and leaving people damaged for longer than should have been the case. Although the Department produces unemployment figures on a 'travel to work' basis, this may mask high levels of local unemployment and prevent action being taken under RDA provisions. Such unemployed people are doubly disadvantaged because of their distance from possible available jobs: this is why inward investment initiatives are required.

5.69. Such regional data, however, conceal a number of issues of concern about rural employment which have been repeated to Commissioners both in formal evidence and during regional and diocesan visits. These concerns relate to a number of specific issues:

(1) Although employment rates in rural areas are high, the statistics conceal problems concerning the quality of many rural jobs, especially but not exclusively the level of pay and conditions.

(2) Problems of access to jobs especially in terms of gender, qualifications and physical distance.

(3) The question of training (or lack of it) in rural areas and the particular problems attendant upon changes in Government policy.

(4) The future of rural economies in the face of known and anticipated changes in agriculture and the knock-on effects of contraction in the agricultural industry.

Quality of employment

5.70. Although statistics tend to create a comparatively rosy picture for rural employment, there remain serious questions about the quality of many of the jobs available to the rural labour force. It is widely recognised for example that incomes in many rural areas are generally lower than elsewhere. In his report to the DoE on Deprivation in Rural Areas, McLaughlin (1985) identified that some 25% of male manual workers and over 77% of female manual workers in selected study areas earned below the low pay thresholds. In April 1988, the average hourly earnings of full-time male workers in Lincolnshire were 464.7 pence, and in Norfolk 485.4 pence, compared with 577.8 pence in Oxfordshire and 577.2 pence in Avon, while the national average was 579.0 pence.

At our regional meeting in Worcester, the Chief Executive of Bridgnorth District Council drew our attention to their analysis in forming a housing strategy for 1990/91, which illustrated the problem for lower paid local people. While the price of an average three bedroomed semi-detached house in Bridgnorth had more than doubled from £29,000 to £60,000 in three years, relatively low weekly pay had now made house purchase impossible. Average weekly earnings of men in Shropshire at £211.60 per week were £37 lower than those in England as a whole and £14 less than in the West Midlands region. For women the corresponding figures were £141.60, £25 and £7. On the basis of a mortgage of three times earnings, the average Shropshire man could fund a capital sum of £33,000, while he and his wife together could cover £40,000 if the second income was valued at only one year's earnings. A mortgage had just been possible in 1986 for them, but was impossible by 1990. These figures showed not only the lower level of rural earnings, but also how their buying

> power in terms of housing had withered in three years.
> And these figures are based on average earnings, not
> those of the most poorly paid.
>
> As for rented accommodation, the Housing Corporation
> position highlighted the continuing problems for the
> poorest section of the community. Their allocation to the
> whole of Shropshire in 89/90 allowed for 36 new units of
> accommodation, while the Housing Survey showed a need
> for 606 affordable dwellings in the Bridgnorth District
> alone.

5.71. What is equally important to consider is the length of the working week that is often necessary in order to derive incomes that are still below the national average, especially for manual employees. McLaughlin (1985) calculated that in five rural survey areas, 15% of male manual employees and 50% of female manual employees needed to work at least 50 hours per week in order to earn £80 per week. The corresponding national proportions were 2.5% and 30% respectively. Nor can it be assumed that deficiencies in rural wage levels are somehow counterbalanced by the ready availability of fringe benefits for rural workers. On the contrary, data from McLaughlin's survey confirm that the distribution of fringe benefits amongst the rural labour force tends to favour the higher paid workers and, as such, exacerbates the gap between them and the lower paid.

5.72. Within this general picture of low wage economies, the plight of women is particularly notable. Low paid and/or seasonal labour tends to characterise the labour market for many rural women. This problem has tended to be readily dismissed hitherto as many women were perceived to be working for 'pin-money'. Increasingly however, as the price of living in rural areas increases, joint incomes are often the only means by which young couples can aspire to gaining a foothold on the rural housing ladder. Of more fundamental importance perhaps is the implication that whatever progress has been made in recognising the principles of equal opportunities elsewhere, such progress is still not readily apparent in rural labour markets.

Enterprise Cumbria was set up by the four Cumbrian Enterprise Agencies as an umbrella body which brings together each quarter all the bodies within the county which offer advice to small businesses. The purpose of these regular meetings is to co-ordinate the activities of government departments, agencies and the voluntary sector so as to reduce duplication and concentrate the service to the benefit of small enterprises and the economy. Those who participate include: the four enterprise agencies, DTI, Department of Employment, County Council, the Small Firms Service, TEC, RDC, and MAFF, and these meetings are the only occasions at which they meet.

A useful testing ground for people considering marketing their craft or food producing skills is the WI market. There are 555 of these trading in villages and country towns, mostly on a one day a week basis. Quality checks are rigorous. The producers need not necessarily be Women's Institute members - indeed, quite a few of the shareholders are men. To become a shareholder one pays the sum of 5p for life membership of one of the 92 Market Societies which are registered as Friendly Societies. As a result of selling garden produce, baked goods, preserves, crafts of all kinds and many more items, the annual turnover countrywide is in excess of £8,919,000 of which £8,139,000 is returned to the producers, the rest being taken up by overheads. For at least some of these producers, this provides an important part of family income.

5.73. The Commission recognises the strength of the work ethic in rural communities and greatly admires the ingenuity and resourcefulness which many rural people use in order to gain access to paid employment. We remain concerned, however, that rural workers should not be disadvantaged compared with their equivalent elsewhere in the country. The perpetuation of a low wage economy in rural Britain in the 1980s is in danger of doing just that. We became aware, too, that rural isolation could lead to long term unemployment with the problem often being tied to housing as well as to transport.

In Fenland Lincolnshire we were shown another perspective in the cycle of becoming long-term unemployed when we met people in isolated council housing, hardly even in a village, which had originally been provided for farm workers. With the downturn in agricultural employment these had either moved away or been left unemployed. The local authority had filled the empty housing with people from the local towns who had no experience of rural life, but had fallen into arrears on payment and had possibly also offended or been provocative in other ways. The Council had done this, it seems, to remove them from sight. Local clergy told us of very serious deprivation within this group, with nobody obviously interested in helping. The housing issue may have been temporarily solved but at the cost of long-term social and economic difficulties. The stigma of parental unemployment was causing acute difficulties at school for the younger generation. Prospects for so marginalised a group of people looked grim.

Problems of accessibility: physical distance and qualifications

5.74. Although accessibility problems are almost synonymous with rural areas, we have identified a number of key issues in the context of access to employment in the countryside which are a cause of some concern.

5.75. It has long been recognised that the price of getting to many rural jobs is access to personal transport. Repeated surveys have shown that over time public transport has featured less prominently as a means of getting to work in the countryside, and we have no reason to believe that this situation has altered to any great extent since privatisation: the evidence given to us has been mixed. Rural populations and employers have adapted to these circumstances over time and, by a combination of works buses, car sharing, giving lifts, etc, have usually overcome many of these difficulties.

5.76. We are aware, however, of a residual population for whom personal mobility is not an option, such as those who are at pre-driving age, those who do not hold a driving licence and/or those whose income does not allow them to buy and run a vehicle of any kind. In the absence of works transport or any type of lift giving, these people depend on public transport. But we have had reported to us instances where local employers are sufficiently jaded about the unreliability of public transport (especially in winter) for them to avoid recruiting people who rely on it for journeys to work. A related reason has been the inflexibility created by a worker whose availability is dictated by bus time-tables. Such schedules are a barrier to the flexible hours upon which many rural firms depend.

> **In Northamptonshire rural magistrates confirmed the incidence of poorly maintained vehicles and those run without proper tax and insurance because the owners felt that keeping a vehicle was crucial if they were to remain at work or to have a hope of re-entering the job market. The action of the owners was illegal and was dealt with as such, but it reflected the pressure on the poorest section of rural society to secure transport. The magistrates also felt that it illustrated the spirit of desperation and a resignation that other assistance was not forthcoming.**

5.77. An important corollary is that of cost. The cost of using public transport often takes a disproportionate share of the income of many who depend upon it, especially young people. In Norfolk examples were given to us where up to 40% of a person's net earnings went on transport to and from work. Dependence upon public transport also dramatically reduces the choice of jobs for which many rural people feel able to apply.

5.78. For rural populations over generations, the answer to the problems of rural employment has been the pursuit of academic and/or professional qualifications. Such credentials allowed them to compete in a wider labour market and often resulted in their out-migration from the countryside. Although this trend continues, we have been made aware of an interesting variant of this problem in some of the more accessible areas of the countryside today.

5.79. The continuing movement into rural areas of hi-tech, highly skilled jobs should mean in theory that highly qualified locals need no longer move away from home. In practice it would appear that the relationship between availability of jobs and appropriate local skills is less clear cut. Many new firms in rural areas are relocating there, often from an urban or suburban location. For reasons of continuity they are bringing much of their skilled labour with them so that the creation of new jobs as such is often more apparent than real.

5.80. There is also some evidence of a significant skills gap between the needs of new employers and the skills available in the local rural labour market. We were not able to uncover objective data on this complex relationship between new in-migrant firms into areas and their impact on local labour. In many areas, the best information was based on anecdotal evidence from sources whose knowledge was at worst incomplete and at best not totally objective. Given the importance of this issue in terms of both national and local policies for rural employment creation into the 1990s, and the need to avoid the application of misleading generalisations to what is clearly a wide range of local variations, this gap in knowledge is somewhat surprising and points toward the need for research.

5.81. The difficulties encountered owing to the mismatch of the skills available in the labour force and those required by the employers, and the shortcomings of the transport and housing infrastructures, are, of course, not solely problems for the employee. They create problems also for employers as they seek to recruit local labour and to make decisions about location or expansion. They are compounded by the fact that for a considerable number of employees, both husband and wife will need to find jobs in the same locality. We encountered this problem across a wide range of professions as well as in industry - and not least in the rural church.

> **In the urban parts of Southwark diocese it was represented to us that a clergy wife was usually able to find the work she wanted, appropriate to her skills: this was clearly not the case in more rural parishes and was felt in Lincoln to contribute to the near impossibility of**

filling rural posts - some positions had remained unfilled
for six years.

A North Yorkshire electronics firm told us that it and
other hi-tech businesses in the area were finding it hard to
expand because of a shortage of skilled and professional
labour. Recruitment was on a national scale and, even
though many people were attracted to live in a beautiful
area, the company was finding it increasingly difficult to
engage people unless a job for a spouse could be found.
The need for a second car and the rise in local house
prices were both cited as becoming increasingly a barrier
to recruitment if lower rates of pay had to be considered.

5.82. Where people do accept work for which they may be
over-qualified because of the wish to obtain work and to remain in a
rural area, others in competition with them, who feel that they have
adequate experience or a lower but acceptable qualification, find
themselves pushed further down the employment ladder. The problem
seems to affect those with GCSE or 'O' level qualifications, but varies
from area to area. As a result the relationship between academic
achievement and earnings in many rural areas is less clear cut than it is
in towns and cities.

Again in North Yorkshire a hi-tech firm told us that with
such attractive surroundings in which to live, some of
those who had moved up before the peak of the house
price boom had bought land around their houses for
recreational purposes - and did not want overtime or
promotion if it adversely affected their lifestyle.

Training

5.83. Evidence given to us suggested that professional training for work has not been a successful element in British life and this is reflected in rural areas. It is seen as an area of great importance if Britain is to maintain a position as a leading trading nation. However, in the UK in 1986, only 64% of 16-18 year olds were in full-time or part-time education or training, compared with 90% in West Germany, 80% in the USA and 79% in Japan. Also, British companies as a whole are seen as investing less in training their human capital than their competitors.

5.84. In rural areas the attitude towards training is as much entwined with the type and scale of industry, which are thought to be appropriate for rural areas, as it is with spatial difficulties. The public sector and larger firms are more committed to training, much of which is conducted in-house both formally and informally - but larger firms are rarely to be found in remoter rural areas. They will often be located in towns, and therefore only available to those who live near to them. In the deeper rural areas where employment is often in larger villages and small towns of well under 20,000 people the scale of business is likely to be much smaller. Many of these will be employing fewer than five people and operating from a small, perhaps precarious, capital base. For many of them, training is either too costly and/or involves a need to release existing staff for supervisory roles which they can ill-afford.

5.85. The disabled are often particularly disadvantaged, their rather special needs requiring a more sophisticated understanding of training than is usually apparent in rural areas. As for other disadvantaged groups, travel is a serious problem, as are opportunities for work in small units where a range of skills may be required. Nevertheless, good work was seen encouraged by the Shaw Trust in Melksham, Wiltshire.

From small beginnings in Wiltshire in 1982, the Shaw Trust has now grown into a national organisation, with more than sixty staff members. By 1990 their aim is to have helped to place over two thousand people with disabilities, many of whom live in rural areas, in jobs all over the country. Their objective is to find permanent employment for disabled people working individually alongside able-bodied workers. The trust is the major sponsor of the Department of Employment's Sheltered

Placement Scheme – the host employers pay a contribution towards the cost of wages and the Shaw Trust then collect from the Department a sum to make up the balance of wages and cover administration costs.

The trust also runs a work preparation centre in Hereford, a garden centre in Wiltshire, a garden and horticultural services team in Buckinghamshire and has embarked on a rehabilitation enterprise in partnership with the Department of Employment.

5.86. Access to off-the-job/formal training opportunities also remains a major problem for many rural employers. The location of courses at Colleges of Further/Higher Education, which are invariably located in distant urban centres, poses a challenge both to employer and employee. For the employer, the costs of enrolling an employee (including travel costs) together with the cost of his/her absence from work for a day are often too high. For the employee, the challenges posed by such training methods are often severe. Coping with the demands of a training course on top of a normal programme, together with problems of access to courses, means that training for the rural employee is the preserve of the committed.

5.87. Our concerns about the adequacy or inadequacy of training in the rural context have been heightened by our recognition of the need for a substantial programme of re-training for many of our rural workforce, if they are to compete in the new labour markets which are being created. Here again, the available evidence tends to suggest that much of the training of rural labour focuses upon the training needs of new employees, is geared towards managers or professional and supervisory staff, or consists of short up-dating skills seminars which are often determined by the need to meet external legislative requirements such as health and safety regulations.

5.88. We are more concerned by the recent changes in government policy in respect of its policies for training for employment from what was known as the Community Programme (CP) to the revised system of Employment Training (ET). In addition to the specific rural implications of the cessation of the CP scheme, especially in the context of environmental and social care projects, we are especially concerned that the structure of the current ET programme does not fit the needs of rural areas. Problems of cost and scale of provision, of access, and the adequacy (or not) of the skills available to provide training in rural areas remain a problem. We are particularly concerned by the fact that whilst the target audience of all government training initiatives is the unemployed, the problems of rural areas also extend to the under-employed, and the particular problems of the 'hidden unemployed', many of whom are working in family businesses which are economically stretched in order to absorb them at all. Current training initiatives do not appear to be accessible to this hidden market. Given the predictions which currently exist about possible future trends in agriculture, it is possible that our concerns about the adequacy of current ET Initiatives may even be understated. It is critical that the new TECs respond to these challenges.

5.89. Once again, we were made aware that the fragmentation of rural areas makes the delivery of services difficult. Nonetheless, we feel that the move by the more enterprising agricultural colleges, and those schools being developed as community colleges, to provide a broader range of courses, directed not just at adult education but at job skills and training, should be encouraged by the Department of Education and Science (DES). We should like to see more signs of a growing use of distance learning techniques which seem particularly appropriate for rural areas. They will often need more than just bridging help to get such schemes under way and public funds would seem to be necessary on a wider scale than is currently provided. But they are well-placed and well-known in the rural community to form the basis for a sustained initiative.

The Commission saw good examples at Bishop Burton in Yorkshire, Bishop's Castle in Shropshire, and the Lancashire College of Agriculture and Horticulture. These covered a range of full-time, day release, and evening classes. We particularly noted those helping women to re-enter the job market by bringing their office skills up to date. It was encouraging when these colleges had clearly developed courses to meet the needs of the local job market.

Cumbria is the second largest county in England, much of its area being sparsely populated uplands. The Cumbria Training and Enterprise Council was one of the first launched and faces the challenge of developing training and enterprise in a remote area with poor communications. To do this it has, under its Local Initiative Fund, introduced programmes which are tailored to meet the special needs of the locality. These include the Upland Cumbria Initiative which aims to sustain and enhance Cumbria's greatest economic asset - its unique environment - by providing with others, including the Church, core funding to encourage farmers and others to undertake contractually the maintenance and improvement of threatened upland landscapes.

A training voucher scheme for a wide range of jobs will be introduced to encourage young people leaving school to enhance their career prospects in a tighter labour market by obtaining training to recognised national standards. With the Tourist Board the TEC will introduce special training programmes for the tourism industry to increase professionalism and a career structure in Cumbria's fastest growing industry, which now employs twice as many young people as agriculture in the county. In order to encourage enterprise in a changing rural economy, the TEC is addressing the specifically rural problems of remoteness and access in a number of ways: it is paying a premium to young people in rural areas who undertake training; offering a freephone enterprise service for those wishing to start or develop a business so that they can obtain help through one contact point; setting up business development centres as 'one stop shops' at several key locations, and introducing telecanvassing to help introduce services to those in remoter areas. The TEC believes that local expertise, understanding the local dilemma, is more likely to put its finger on the pulse of what is needed to stimulate the local economy by

> **introducing programmes which are carefully tailored to meet the needs and difficulties of the community in rural Cumbria.**

The relationship between affordable housing and the economy

5.90. Whereas rural workers have often been provided with housing through farming, this is rarely the case with other forms of employment. Evidence given us locally has led us to appreciate that many rural businesses need local employees who require a continuing supply of affordable housing. This realisation of the social needs which have to be satisfied for the rural economy to thrive have led even the RDC (whose main emphasis is economic) to champion local affordable rural housing in its attempt to diagnose what is required for a continuing healthy economy - and one which during the 1990s and thereafter is likely to be even less underpinned by agriculture, which has traditionally had its own housing structure. While we deal with the issue of affordable housing more broadly in Chapter 6, we log here the fact that lack of it impacts the working of the local economy.

Conversion of buildings for new businesses

5.91. Traditional landowners reflect one group with a longstanding investment in, and concern for, rural life. The way they and others have converted redundant farm buildings into workshops and offices, rather than letting them be converted to homes, has helped numerous enterprises to start up and remain rural. In doing so, landowners will often have spurned a useful short-term capital gain and we respect their motivation.

> **The Commission has seen many good examples of schemes that have provided business premises or have been used to promote and develop tourist attractions. Lord Henniker's developments at Thornham, Suffolk, have done both. Dr John Farrer at Clapham, North Yorkshire, has increased employment there during 40 years of dedicated work. At Eaton in Cheshire more people now work within the boundaries of the estate than was the case in its halcyon days a century ago.**

5.92. We welcome the schemes with which the Church Commissioners have been involved on several of their agricultural estates, where redundant farm buildings have been converted to a variety of uses including an aviation museum, a wine warehouse and a furniture workshop/store. It is important that the Church, through its land-holdings and tenancies both at diocesan and national level, encourages this trend and does all it can to create rural jobs rather than rural executive homes, thus demonstrating itself, here as in other areas, to be a leader of good practice.

5.93. In most cases, the change of use required, the alterations to what may be a listed building, and the locating of suitable occupants have all absorbed more time, energy and finance than originally anticipated. Each landowner giving us evidence stressed the need to be persistent on the basis that, even on such a small scale, the bureaucratic procedures could be irritating and apparently designed to block local initiative - despite the DoE's circular 22/80 published as long ago as 1980.

> **A video produced by BItC gives helpful ideas to those wishing to involve themselves in converting redundant buildings and illustrates how long-term income can become a realistic objective for the landowner while helping small businesses to develop.**

5.94. The Commission would heartily encourage all such initiatives. It thinks that it is so important to encourage rural landowners to take the option of converting redundant farm buildings for business rather than residential use, that tax incentives should be developed to strengthen this movement.

Transport

5.95. Throughout this report transport recurs as a key theme for rural life. It is crucial for social life, the ability to reach services which more and more are being grouped in large villages and market towns, commuting to work, and for contact with the wider world. With the virtual collapse of a rural railway network transport depends on roads. This creates a profound dilemma for rural life. By definition it is dependent on a mode of transport which is a major contributor to the greenhouse effect through its exhaust emissions. While we accept the imperative of finding other, more benign, forms of transport, we have empirically to acknowledge that in the meantime there will continue to be a growth in demand for personal transport with all that that entails for the environment.

> **During our visit to St Albans diocese the Chief Planning Officer for Hertfordshire outlined his concern at the growing number of rural journeys being made, not just commuting to work but for general living. He felt that the road system would not cope without increasing frustration and danger of accidents and that the cost of maintaining and improving rural roads was disproportionately high for the number of people living there. This growth in use is an inevitable effect of the population movement to rural areas and is one reason why a body of opinion, led by the CPRE, wants all types of planning consent reduced for rural areas.**

5.96. As the network of motorways and major trunk roads has been extended to link the main conurbations, so there has been a major impact on those rural areas placed within longer distance commuting range of larger towns and cities. Access is a two-edged sword: it is capable of bringing jobs and prosperity on one hand, but it disturbs the deeply rural culture of an area on the other. This was felt by those living in Shropshire with the construction of the M54 to Telford. Telford is now on a national network and will prosper more rapidly as a result. But it is not just Telford which is affected, people from the West Midlands can now commute from the environs of places like Shrewsbury and house prices in that area have moved rapidly upwards; pressure for development has grown on the surrounding villages whose rurality is threatened and in many cases will change irrevocably. Others saw this as opening up North Wales to those seeking recreation from the Midlands. The effects of major new roads are complex but appear to receive little detailed consideration.

5.97. As the Ministry of Transport informed us, their remit is trunk routes and motorways without thought for pressure on the villages in between the centres they wish to join up. We were surprised and concerned that there was not a more broad based assessment of the impact of motorway policy on the social, environmental and economic life of the areas through which a new or upgraded route was planned to pass. The recent inspector's report on parts of the M40 made minimal reference to the environment in spite of EC requirements to do so. Among these pressures will doubtless be those for more business premises which in turn will provide work within rural areas, but the strongest evidence is that the greatest pressure will be for more housing. We are deeply concerned at the apparent lack of co-ordinated planning and thinking between the Department of Transport and other bodies as part of the normal procedures for developing national transport policy.

5.98. The loss of the bulk of the rural railway network in the Beeching cuts of the 1960s may now seem to have been untimely as population continues to move back to the rural areas. This reawakening of demand has resulted in the reopening of 72 stations between 1982 and 1987. Good road or rail communications seem to be a key to new residential developments, as the recent pressure on the M40 corridor and the effect of the electrification of the main Eastern rail line north of London reveal. Insufficient consideration seems to have been given to these effects. They reveal how important integrated planning is, and how much strategic regional and county plans are needed, so that rural communities can contribute to the process of which they are so often the victim.

Recommendations

1. The Department of Employment should make special provision, in the funding of Training and Enterprise Councils (TECs), for rural areas with special difficulties, to provide for the training and retraining of the rural workforce. (5.13.)

2. The development potential of many small businesses is of crucial importance for the economies of many rural areas. The benefits of the Department of Trade & Industry's Enterprise Initiative, or similar schemes, need to be promoted as the take-up in many rural areas has been low. (5.17. - 5.28.)

3. The special problems of re-orientating the economies of many, primarily agricultural, rural areas should be recognised by Government, government agencies and local authorities in funding enterprise creation and expansion. (5.25.)

4. There is an increasing need to improve the quality of advice and professional support for very small rural businesses in the first stages of growth. (5.26.)

5. The Commission recognises the need to strengthen the changing rural economy in many areas. It also recognises the need to protect and sustain the countryside. The need to emphasise the interdependence of these purposes should be reflected in strategies for counties and regions. This means a more effective integration of, for example, county structure plans, National Park plans, countryside strategies, Rural Development Programmes, TEC Business Plans, and other statutory and non-statutory programmes, with the intention of bringing them together in integrated rural strategies. (5.30. and 5.36.) (See also Recommendation 6 in chapter 4.)

6. In RDAs, because a more integrated and complete approach is called for in the countryside, district council planning committees should be required to be advised by the appropriate economic agency, such as county economic development departments, the RDC, etc, as well as by planning officers. Such procedures within RDAs should be seen as an experiment, with a view to extending them to other rural areas. (5.33. and 5.63.)

7. The Commission strongly supports MAFF's Farm Woodlands Scheme. However, it regrets the low take-up in marginal and hill areas, and recommends a uniform rate of annual payment throughout the United Kingdom. (5.54.)

8. The threat to the hill sheep industry is serious in some of the most fragile rural economies where the landscape is of great national importance. MAFF should increase the headage rates of the Hill Livestock Compensatory Allowance. (5.62.)

9. Where the Countryside Commission or the Nature Conservancy Council consider overgrazing to be a threat, rates of the Hill Livestock Compensatory Allowance should be topped up to compensate adequately for voluntarily reduced stocking limits to achieve a desired botanical and ecological structure. (5.62.)

10. Many rural economies are particularly dependent on the employment provided by a single employer. In the event of such employment being substantially reduced, local authorities and the RDC should be empowered to declare a special status for the area in order to strengthen the rural economy and encourage new employment by providing advice, professional support, financial assistance and premises. (5.68.)

11. The owner or occupier of a redundant agricultural building should receive greater encouragement to convert such a building for business rather than residential use by increasing the 25% rate of grant available from MAFF under the Farm Diversification Scheme. (5.94.)

Chapter 6
The Rural Social
Condition

6.1. Thus far in this report we have tried to delineate some of the major structures which form the framework within which rural life is lived. The fluxes of population movement, of employment change and industrial development, interact with the systems of planning and of governmental administration to provide a dynamic situation far removed from the stable and unchanging view of rural life which is often assumed.

6.2. This chapter attempts to go beyond an understanding of these structures to outline something of the rural 'social condition'. By this we mean an understanding of some of the conditions of ordinary life in the countryside and the pressures and the opportunities which impact upon the lives of rural people, whether incomer or local born. The search for suitable housing, the need for transport to work, school or for leisure, requirements for education and health services, and for shops and other facilities, are all part of a multi-faceted picture which must be understood before we see, in later chapters, how the Church responds and relates to the lives of rural people.

6.3. This chapter therefore has three main objectives:

— First to specify certain key circumstances of rural people which are important for setting some of the parameters of their lives.

— Second to consider some of the major issues which have been made clear to us both in the written and verbal evidence which we received and which we saw for ourselves, especially in our regional and diocesan visits.

— Third to bring these circumstances and issues together to outline the picture of advantage and disadvantage in the countryside.

Rural circumstances

6.4. Chapter 1 outlined our view of England's rural areas as the arena for different expectations and objectives. This chapter continues that broad theme by emphasising the point that there are many different 'countrysides'. The rural idyll of the recently retired city worker, newly arrived in his chosen village complete with material comforts and an inflation-proofed pension, is a very different vision from that of the elderly lady, long resident in her village, who has daily to cope with the distance from the nearest shop and who has difficulty in living on her inadequate state pension. The countryside is not a neutral place but rather the raw material from which lifestyles are defined and constructed according to individual circumstances. Thus no rural issue picked up by the newspapers exists in isolation, but is always to be seen in the context of people.

6.5. Three particular elements define our countryside - age, gender and wealth. They interact with each other to give a variety of circumstance and reaction to normal country living. They are by no means the only variables which may be important in deciding how people live and how close to the 'good life' is their own particular rural experience. The strength of family connections and networks, or the articulacy and influence which education can give, are obvious other factors. These three elements are, however, of especial relevance.

Age

6.6. For two major groups in rural society, the old and the young, rural living can frequently be hard. Growing up in a rural area can often be a fine experience and one which many middle class parents are keen to offer their children. But for those young people who lack parental resources or who live away from the accessible countryside where urban facilities are but a short journey away, rural living can be narrow and confining. In particular, the growing teenager can find even the largest and most suburban of villages a backwater of experience where facilities for leisure time are confined to those for younger children only and where access to jobs and job training can present a special problem.

6.7. At the other end of the age spectrum, the elderly in the countryside can be equally trapped and restricted. For some, especially those who have retired from low-paid rural employment, it may be difficult even to provide food and clothing beyond a basic minimum. Older people, contented in their way perhaps, were concerned at rising prices which were not matched by pension levels and frightened at new incursions on their material lives like the community charge or increased prescription levels.

6.8. One aspect of the older age groups particularly struck us on our visits and in our evidence. The countryside has benefited enormously by the influx, noted in Chapter Two, of the 'young old', that is, those who in their fifties and sixties have come to villages and, from the strong point of their good health and relative wealth, give a great deal to rural communities. In some areas, it would not be an exaggeration to see the vibrancy of country life as being maintained and enhanced by these active and willing newcomers.

Gender

6.9. A second element which defines the nature of rural living is that of sexual division. As the rural researcher Dr Jo Little has argued, the place of women in rural areas is a key part of the whole image of the countryside.

6.10. For those women whose lives are based in the main upon the home, rural living can bring both rewards and costs. Some will benefit from a community life which is frequently more caring than that on the suburban estate or the tower block, and which is perhaps seen at its informal best when mothers meet at the school gate at the end of the day, but this is hardly a substitute for a full social life. For others, the countryside can be a limiting and narrow existence, especially for those who have no transport of their own, whose children have left the village or who live in inaccessible areas or in villages where the 'community spirit' is a hollow sham. For them, work opportunities, if they exist at all, may be poorly paid, boringly routine and unrewarding to the spirit. We have heard much of the economic opportunities which are provided by diversification from agriculture, but we have yet to be convinced that these opportunities will overcome the male dominance that has long been characteristic of farming.

Distribution of wealth

6.11. A major impression which we have gained from our visits to rural areas, particularly, but by no means exclusively, in the southern half of England, has been the incursion of visible wealth into the village. The material fabric of our villages and small towns, at least those parts which are in private hands, has probably never been in better state. This is most clearly seen, of course, in housing conditions. We have no estimate of the extent of private investment (albeit subsidised fiscally through the mortgage system) in rural housing, but it is extremely visible, with many properties being converted and extended. The rural house or cottage has, in the past twenty years or so, been the main vehicle for the import of wealth into the countryside.

6.12. Notwithstanding the prevailing image of affluence throughout much of rural England, we are concerned about the plight of that proportion of the rural population for whom the image of affluence represents the myth of the rural idyll. We are convinced by the arguments in the report to the Department of the Environment by McLaughlin (1985), which indicated that approximately 25% of households in rural areas were living in or on the margins of poverty. That proportion, which accounted for some 20% of the rural population, was consistent across a wide range of rural environments and was composed primarily of two groups - elderly people living alone dependent primarily on state pensions and households of low-paid workers.

6.13. It is this sector of the rural population for whom issues such as the availability of housing, jobs, transport and the decline of services are matters of key concern. The countryside is an expensive place in which to live. Despite modern modes of transport rural areas are still expensive to service. Shop prices for a more limited range of goods are frequently higher and the alternative of transport costs to a supermarket can add significantly to the weekly household bills.

6.14. Wealth in some sections of the rural community allows some people to exercise considerable choice over the goods they buy, the housing they can afford and the services which they need. But the exercise of that choice impacts upon those who do not have that freedom. The ability of some families to use urban shops with ease and frequency means that the rural shop often loses custom, with an effect on prices that is felt by the residual poorer user who cannot get to town. The choice by some parents of private education may mean the effective decline of the school roll irrespective of demographic change. The knock-on effect may be a poorer education service and eventual school closure.

6.15. We recognise that those choices, exercisable by some and not by others, have always existed and we are not arguing that this is a new circumstance. What has changed, however, is the scale. Whereas historically poverty was more prevalent in rural society and, as such, was a shared experience, today it affects a substantial minority who find themselves living amidst a better-off majority. In some ways, however, there have been changes in recent years which have made for new situations. First we are conscious of a new set of values which emphasise the acceptability and visibility of material wealth and the choices which flow from it. Those who have benefited from new wealth and from the increased opportunities to use it to enhance lifestyles have increasingly opted for rural living and their presence and influence has been felt accordingly. They have not necessarily felt any responsibility for those who are less fortunate; the interlocking of rural social needs and provision, often by individuals, has been severely weakened as a result. Where this is appreciated, individual initiative can do much to compensate.

6.16. A second recent change has, we believe, aggravated this polarisation. Hand in hand with the encouragement of personal wealth has come a clear and unequivocal winding down of the public sector and of the provision of statutory services. Consequently, the idea of a safety net for those poorer members of society, which for much of the twentieth century, and especially for the post-war period, has been seen as coming from state provision, has been seriously questioned and, many would argue, critically jeopardised. Evidence has shown that isolation has seriously impeded the way in which this safety net can reach those in need in rural areas. Work done by the Citizens Advice Bureau in Oakham and elsewhere has shown how difficult it is to explain entitlement to social security and to ensure that those who have a right to it first appreciate that fact and secondly feel able to apply for it without their peers being aware of it. Rural independence may appear obtuse to those in bureaucracy, but it is part of the rural tradition and as such needs to be understood and to be taken into account when implementing policy.

6.17. At the time of writing this report, it has not proved possible to up-date the findings of McLaughlin's earlier work in any systematic manner. Empirical evidence from a number of sources that we encountered in our programme of visits, however, suggests to us that the picture painted by McLaughlin's earlier study has not changed to any radical extent. Indeed we would suggest that since that survey was undertaken, the degree of relative deprivation in rural areas may well have increased. The on-going repopulation of the countryside by the more affluent has done little to improve the lot of the less well-off except perhaps to throw into sharper focus the housing dilemma faced by many low to middle income people.

6.18. Privatisation of public transport does not appear to have improved the cost, availability and reliability of rural services to the extent that was anticipated. Fundamental changes to education and health and welfare provision do not appear to confront the problems experienced in the consumption of those services by the less well off.

6.19. Nor can we see much on the horizon to suggest that matters will improve. The impact of the community charge for many rural households may be significant. For that sector of the rural employed which hitherto lived in tied acccommodation which was rent and rates free, it represents a new bill. As rural households are characterised by a high proportion of adults living at home, the cumulative costs of the charge on the total household budget could be significant. The uniform business rate could also take a heavy toll of rural services such as village shops which may well be unable to withstand the level of increase. In view of the degree of dependence on the local shop by the less well off in rural areas, this will be a further disadvantage.

6.20. In the longer term, despite assurances to the contrary, we cannot see how the market system will be able to deliver water services to rural areas which do not reflect the costs of providing that service over extensive areas to dispersed populations. If and when electricity services are privatised, we foresee similar difficulties there. Whilst many people will be able to afford such changes and may even consider them a small price to pay for the privilege of living in the countryside, a sector of the rural population will inevitably be disadvantaged.

6.21. In any process of resource allocation, it seems inevitable that there will always be winners and losers and the rural resource allocation process is no exception. Whilst not everyone can win, a Christian society will try to ensure that the impact on the losers can be cushioned so as to minimise the detrimental effects of the allocation process.

6.22. We already have enough experience of the 'unforeseen' effects of the privatisation of public services in rural areas to question whether enough attention has been paid to the detrimental impact of these policies on the rural deprived.

Key Services

6.23. The middle section of this chapter now looks at key services as they are found in our rural areas.

Housing

6.24. One issue above all others - housing - has been at the centre of the evidence which we have received, especially on our regional and diocesan visits. In part we recognise that our work took place just when rural housing moved into clear public and political focus. However, our reading of the evidence tells us that this problem is not simply an idea whose time has come. Concerns about the rising cost of rural housing, particularly in relation to the levels of rural incomes, have been voiced since at least the mid-1970s. Moreover, the interrelationship between housing and other rural issues, notably employment, has been increasingly recognised in both official policy statements and by rural entrepreneurs and administrators.

6.25. The problems posed for rural areas in respect of rural housing are now relatively well known. In brief, they can be summarised as a disparity between the availability of housing (and thereby its price,whether for purchase or for rent) and the resources available to a significant minority of people. This disparity is frequently expressed in the context of the problems of local people who, it is argued, are forced to leave their home rural area in their search for affordable housing and migrate to the town in the hope that prices will be lower, or remain in substandard or overcrowded housing.

6.26. This basic problem has been compounded over many years by other factors. One is a legislative system which, in its enthusiasm to protect the tenant, has effectively destroyed the private rented housing sector. Another is that a wealthy minority of the population are in a position to afford two homes, and thereby to inhabit a rural house for recreational purposes for just a very few weeks in the year. We have been made aware of the scale of this issue. In parts of Norfolk as many as 11% of houses are thus unoccupied by permanent residents. Elsewhere in some villages the ratio is very much higher. Community life can be severely damaged when the ratio of second homes rises above a small number.

6.27. The emasculation of a significant public housing sector took place with the privatisation of local authority housing under the 'right-to-buy' legislation of the Housing Act 1980 and continues to have controversial repercussions.

6.28. The sale of council houses has given the Government an electoral success. Equally importantly, it has given to a great many rural people an equity stake worth many tens of thousands of pounds, which in other circumstances they could never have expected to acquire. We welcome their good fortune, but remain profoundly disturbed at the social consequences for other rural dwellers who can never aspire to such opportunities. Because the stock is not being renewed, the opportunity to buy is not being extended to a new generation of lower income rural people. There has in effect been a one-off distribution of capital to council house occupants of the day with no serious thought being given to how that process can be continued in a consistent way and on a comparable scale. If the transfer of national capital assets in housing to less well-off private households was right once it should be continued.

6.29. We share the view that has been frequently expressed that the system of mortgage tax relief is unfair to those who are unable to benefit from it - the less well-off. Their need is for homes to rent, and the fiscal regime needs to be slanted to meet their needs.

6.30. During the time of our deliberations, we noted that the concern which we have found expressed was to some extent echoed by government action and ministerial comment. However the rhetoric is not being matched by the clearly needed programme of housebuilding. Government is by no means the only agency involved in the efforts to ensure good and affordable housing for our rural population. Local authorities, housing associations, voluntary agencies and the private sector all have a part to play and it is important to recognise their respective roles.

6.31. *Local authorities:* Local authorities developed particularly after the First World War as very significant providers of rented housing. While rural local authorities were often less active in the provision of council housing than their urban counterparts, they nonetheless built up over sixty years or more a valuable public housing sector, with many villages having their quota, albeit small, of homes for rent at reasonable levels. All this is now in process of major change. In every large village many council houses are now sold, while in many small villages virtually all the stock has ceased to be available as rented accommodation. The process is aggravated by the move to smaller households and the ageing of the population, with the need for yet more accommodation required for the elderly so that family-size housing is released. Every effort should be made by local authorities to encourage owners of empty property to make them available for rent, if not for sale. In the case of public property, particularly the Ministry of Defence, we are concerned that the time taken to make surplus property available to the public is too long. The Ministry of Defence should urgently examine ways of releasing more of its empty properties either for sale, or for management by housing associations or district councils. This re-allocation of property in the current review of defence requirements could make a significant contribution to public housing provision.

6.32. It is too early for us to judge just how useful local authorities can be in the new roles which have been given to them. We are assured that, as 'enablers', they will be able to encourage the provision of housing by the private sector and by the voluntary agencies. In the meantime, we wait with some scepticism to see whether local authorities will develop, and will be allowed to develop, their new role to the full. Do they have the expertise, energy and political will and resources to do so?

6.33. We have been encouraged by the way in which imaginative and hard-working parish councils have taken the initiative in carrying out housing needs surveys, sometimes as part of a wider village appraisal, which have identified local housing need. We welcome such initiatives and hope that they will be emulated, and we hope that district councils will take careful note of these local assessments.

We note the example of Ashford Borough Council in Kent where a rural housing officer (jointly funded by the Council and by the NACRT (see 6.39)) has been appointed specifically to work with parish councils and village communities to investigate the scale of need for affordable housing, and to influence the political process accordingly, so that the homes needed are built.

6.34. Local authorities exist not just as housing agents, but also as the guardians of the land use planning system. This system has, in the forty years or so since its inception, had major impacts upon housing in rural areas, not least by restricting development in the countryside. The benefits of this control to the landscape and the built fabric of our countryside have been enormous, but the price has to some extent been paid by those least able to afford it. Housing has been restricted and its price thereby increased in the face of rising demand from urban people. The disbenefit of the planning system is, of course, recognised not least by planners themselves. Indeed, we note that it has often been the planning profession which has tried, insofar as it has been able, to do something for affordable housing provision. The use of Section 52 agreements, often in the face of governmental opposition, provides a good example of willingness to act. While we remain convinced that these tactics alone are insufficient (and may even be counterproductive) we acknowledge the good intention behind the effort. In collaboration with a new category of 'social housing' as implied by ministerial statements in 1989, they could go far to provide housing for lower income households. We earnestly hope that the new circular PPG3 from the Department of the Environment will tackle these complex matters.

6.35. *The Housing Corporation and housing associations:* The gap created by the demise of council housing is, it is argued, to be filled by the private sector and by the voluntary housing movement. In this latter case, the activities of the Housing Corporation and the individual housing associations are critical.

6.36. While there have been more recent changes in the attitude and operations of the Housing Corporation with regard to rural housing, there is still a great need for a major initiative. There is still a massive underfunding of rural schemes with very little result to be seen on the ground. At the time of writing the crisis in the funding of the Housing Corporation is reflected in a collapse of confidence in those organisations dependent on the Corporation for their building programme. The intention of the Corporation to fund even a token rural housing programme now looks in doubt. The Corporation had intended to fund a programme of 1100 units in 1990 against early estimates of a need for 25,000 a year from ACRE (Action with Communities in Rural England). The failure to achieve even this target is a disgrace and requires immediate rectification.

6.37. In their turn, housing associations have a long way to go before they fulfil their potential in this area. We have seen and heard of many initiatives, some quite large and under the auspices of enlightened national or regional associations, others which only operate in one country or even one village. Activities in this regard in Wiltshire and in Gloucestershire come to mind, but we have seen them throughout rural England. These activities need continued support and more publicity.

Wiltshire Rural Housing Association was established by the Community Council for Wiltshire in 1984, supported by the NACRT. Nearly all of Wiltshire is rural, and there are 300 villages, many of which express a need for affordable housing. The unavoidably slow start is now turning into a period of some small successes, with 28 units in development in four villages, and 16 completed in other places. This meets 1% of the known need for housing for local people in Wiltshire's villages. There is a long way still to go.

6.38. A particular area which concerns us is the system whereby houses provided by housing associations may, if they operate on a 'shared equity' basis of part-ownership/part-rental, be lost to the community if tenants exercise their full right to 'staircase' their share to full ownership and thereby put the house on resale at a price which is out of reach of the next needy would-be resident. Although the Government have put forward proposals to enable housing associations to exercise a pre-emptive repurchase right we are not confident that the mechanism can work quickly enough in market conditions, nor that the resources will be adequate.

6.39. *The National Agricultural Centre Rural Trust (NACRT) and the voluntary agencies:* We have particularly noted the role played in this area of affordable rural housing by the NACRT and also some of the other voluntary agencies with which it has worked, notably the rural community councils (RCCs). Their efforts to encourage village communities to develop affordable housing, either in association with an established housing association or by creating their own association, are very much to be applauded, as are those of the Rural Development Commission (RDC) which provides finance for the NACRT.

The NACRT, established in 1975, is the only charity in England to specialise in the provision of affordable housing for village people. Since 1983, it has set up 15 rural housing associations to build homes for rent and, in 1988, the English Villages Housing Association to build shared ownership homes. Targetting the smaller villages

> **which often suffer the worst shortage of housing, the Trust's housing associations will have completed 400 homes by the end of 1990, and 1,500 by the end of 1993, in around 200 villages. Its expansion has been made possible by a grant from the Department of the Environment as well as generous donations by charitable trusts.**
>
> **The Trust actively works from the grass-roots with the villagers themselves through their parish councils. Its field staff welcome invitations to advise and assist villages on assessing and meeting housing need. In 1989, the Trust published *A Practical Guide to the Provision of Affordable Housing in Villages* - an essential manual for anyone involved in the provision of affordable rural housing.**

6.40. It should be noted that the achievements of the English Villages Housing Association (see box) will still leave those who cannot afford an equity share with no foothold in housing. For them there is no alternative to the provision of houses at affordable rents. We remain disturbed, moreover, at the general disparity between the size of the problem and the voluntary effort currently available to tackle it. The development of small rural housing schemes is labour intensive, and those who carry out this task need adequate funding to be able to see it through.

6.41. *Private housebuilders:* A major role in the provision of affordable housing has been given to the private sector. As the statutory housing sector is emasculated, so the private housebuilder is invited to meet the challenge. We note with cautious optimism (*Affordable Homes in the Countryside*, Housebuilders Federation, September 1988) the statements which have been made in this area, notably by the Housebuilders Federation. A very great responsibility lies with the private sector to replace what has been lost by the sale of council houses. We share the scepticism of many people who argue that some private builders have seized upon 'homes for locals' as a convenient 'sugar on the pill' for what would otherwise be unacceptable private housing development. At the present all we can say is that the case on both sides remains unproven and the onus of proof lies firmly with the developer and builder. Only when village communities have seen affordable housing built without a heavy price being paid in speculative development, will they be assured that the private builder is a worthy successor to the local authority. We welcome the *Builders' Guide on Affordable Homes* published in 1990 by the Housebuilders Federation. We welcome the work of those companies with partnership divisions which work in collaboration with local authorities or housing associations. Assurances from the Government that housing benefit will be raised to meet market rents are not secure enough to persuade providers of new homes to build for the vital rented sector.

6.42. *Mobile homes:* This is really a misnomer as these 150,000 units of accommodation spread on sites around the country with a wide variety of standards are hardly mobile. We are concerned at the way in which, in some cases, residents are harassed by rapidly changing site owners. While the Mobile Homes Act 1983 is felt to be adequate protection for residents, the application of the Act and its supervision leave residents with little effective protection.

6.43. At the time of writing we have been involved in discussions with the relevant minister in the House of Lords to clarify and correct injustices, and we are hopeful of new guidance to the local authorities who are the responsible enforcement body in law. The high cost of a modern and fully satisfactory mobile home rules them out as an alternative way of meeting the housing needs of low-income rural people. The majority of privately owned sites restrict occupancy to retired people, leaving local authority sites with the difficult responsibility for family provision.

6.44. *Private landowners:* Our evidence made clear to us the critical role which the provision of land plays in ensuring that affordable housing is built in rural areas. Around 40% of the finished price of a house is accounted for by the initial cost of the land, a figure noticeably higher than in other European countries. The reasons for this are confused, with landowners blaming housebuilders, housebuilders blaming landowners, and everyone blaming planners! While we are not equipped to enter far into this debate, we note the intense competition for rural houses in recent years, with the consequent rise in prices and must conclude that the high prices which housebuilders can get for the finished homes must inevitably bid up the price of land. Providing cheaper land thus becomes a priority if more affordable housing is to be assured.

6.45. Many landowners continue to provide some housing for rent at reasonable levels, as they have done for generations. However, landowners have now begun to realise their key role in the area of land provision for new housing and have begun in some areas to do something about it. The encouragement given to its members by the Country Landowners Association to provide small areas of land in villages for low cost housing is especially noteworthy as are other initiators such as the Devon Land Bank and the actions of a few private landowners.

> **The Community Council of Devon set up the Devon Land Bank Trust in 1989 to obtain from willing landowners an option lasting up to 10 years to receive land by gift or purchase. The trustees will be seeking to identify plots of land of up to an acre situated in or near the planning envelope of a village or town, and capable of housing development for six or more houses. They will only accept options on land on which they believe there is some prospect of planning permission being given, and only on condition that, when built, the housing remains available for local people in perpetuity. The success of this trust accounts for the relatively large number of schemes now in the pipeline in Devon.**

6.46. It is right to emphasise the altruism of a number of wealthy landowners who have felt it their responsibility to provide for those in greater need within their community. Without their initiative and persistence many schemes would not have been started. They deserve every encouragement. Where they have enlisted the early support of parish councils their proposals have often been quickly relayed by village news. Even so, misunderstandings can arise, which emphasises the wisdom of involving the community's representatives at an early stage.

6.47. These actions must be encouraged. It is important that landowners who are prepared to release cheap land are assured that there will be no fiscal handicap to their generosity and that planning authorities will respond positively with regard to planning permission. Equally, landowners need to be assured that 'staircasing' will not result in their gift being to the benefit of one individual rather than to a succession of households in need.

6.48. There is a very special place in this debate for the Church as the holder of glebe land. Very frequently the role of the Church as landowner has been impressed upon us in our evidence and we feel strongly that the Church must take a lead in this area. To do so will require it to review its land holdings in this light and to reflect on the nature of its purpose and trusteeship. We have been glad to learn of the interest being shown by a number of dioceses in making their land holdings available for the provision of affordable housing, particularly in rural areas. Collaboration with local authorities by the Diocese of Hereford, and with housing associations by the Diocese of Gloucester, suggest that much more could be done by imaginative diocesan glebe committees, without prejudicing the right and proper trusteeship they must exercise. It has been confirmed by the Charity Commission that the provision of social housing is itself an act of charity.

6.49. *Gypsies:* This group of nearly forgotten people, many of whom are a remnant of ancient European travellers, receive little sympathy from modern, settled communities. In recent times they have provided casual labour on farms particularly at harvesting time, but their economic contribution is now often seen to be limited to scrap-dealing. Their housing requirements are simple: somewhere to park their vans and maybe tether a horse.

6.50. County councils have been under a legal obligation since 1968 to provide sites for this transitory purpose, but to date only a handful have fulfilled their obligation. This failure is usually because of the political difficulty local committees face in persuading local people who are often resistant to such provision. We have seen cases of extreme violence against such provision, and we deplore the prejudice which fuels this reaction. We accept that not all travellers are pilgims behaving in socially acceptable ways, but they do have legal rights, and the rest of us have legal responsibilities to provide for their proper needs.

The County of Avon has only one official site for 15 of the 200 eligible traveller families, but has a policy of non-eviction from unauthorised encampments on its own land, and also helps by providing some basic amenities. A Traveller Liaison Officer has been appointed to help other local authority departments relate to the special

> **needs of this sector of the population. We welcome these moves.**

6.51. From the evidence we have received on rural housing, we are convinced that much can be done by many authorities and individuals to improve matters in this critical area. We feel strongly that there has not been proper recognition by the Government of the real value of council houses in rural areas as the major source of homes to rent by less well-off households. The right-to-buy has contributed substantially to the individual wealth of one generation of tenants - but nothing has been put in its place. Accordingly, we see a real need for a revival of the rural council house and an encouragement for local authorities to use their available resources to meet housing need. We welcome the moves being made by ACRE to involve the private sector in the provision of new homes for renting at affordable levels.

Education

6.52. For the purposes of our enquiry we have taken the concept of education to be as wide as is the provision of formal educational facilities, encompassing play-groups to adult education. The major constraint on those providing facilities in rural areas is sparsity of clients, and this affects educational provision as well as all other services. This has financial and other practical consequences which need to be appreciated by critics of the cost of rural service provision. The current climate of local choice and market forces may have little good to offer rural areas, where there is little opportunity to attract extra pupils and where small numbers may generate insufficient base funding.

6.53. There has been a long tradition of education being made available to rural people in village schools. Within the schools the village understood that its learning, culture and beliefs would be handed on to the next generation. Since the Second World War this has changed, with primary education usually the only component left in a village. And even this has been subject to significant change as grouping has caused local closures.

6.54. *Pre-school education:* Relative to many urban areas, pre-school education is often distant or non-existent in the countryside - just 10% of nursery and play-groups were paid for by public monies in 1985 as against 50% in the urban areas. Where play-groups exist they usually do so as fee-paying enterprises, often run on a shoestring by a group of mothers needing the service for their own children. Others are attracted to make up numbers. Our evidence was that these usually form an interest rather than a serious source of income for those who run them. Some are run on a break-even basis as a service to the community. Nonetheless, fees and transport are needed, which makes pre-school attendance difficult for some families. We were gratified, therefore, to come across examples of the Department of Social Security (DSS) covering the cost for some families sending their children to the local play-group. There needs to be a wider appreciation of this possibility, particularly since this may form the only regular social contact for some rural children. We were heartened when we saw village and church halls as well as spaces in churches being used for these activities and would like to encourage parochial church councils (PCCs) to do all they can to further pre-school activities.

6.55. *Primary education:* Common characteristics of many rural primary schools are that they are small, and that they are Church of England schools. We address these two complex areas of debate regarding church schools and small schools in Chapter 10. The three key implications of the discussion for the present chapter concern finance, teachers and governors.

6.56. We have noted the concern of the National Association for the Support of Small Schools (NASSS) that arguments about the quality of education may be used to mask financial issues. It is clearly understood that the cost of providing satisfactory education for small numbers of rural pupils is appreciably higher than the national average: as high as £1,000 per annum per pupil in Oxfordshire as against the national average of £400 per annum in 1985. There seems to be no clear evidence on grounds of quality that the education provided by small schools is inferior. Indeed, the NASSS argues that rural small schools have the potential to embody all that is desirable in education for the under-11s. It would be wrong to damage this quality in the cause of financial savings. (For a further discussion of the small schools issue, turn to 10.26 and subsequent paragraphs.)

6.57. It is important to recognize the strains on the staff of small schools in fulfilling the requirements of a wide curriculum, and we have noted the excellent arrangements that are possible with the clustering of small schools in many counties, particularly with the support of additional staff to implement the clustering model. This is a method of enabling schools to collaborate, without loss of independence, to deliver the full range of the curriculum. Pupils, and/or staff, move between schools for specialist lessons. Thus additional costs are incurred. It is with considerable concern that the future financial management of small schools will be faced. It is in this year (1990/91) that Education Support Grants come to an end. This raises the concern put to us most strongly by the Cumbria Director of Education who felt that many small schools would not be able to survive the financial squeeze for which the governors would by then be responsible. Clustering may be in part able to mitigate the effects of this squeeze but we would wish the Government to be clearer in its commitment to the ideal of the small rural primary school. This should be reflected in continuing to fund the additional costs of support for school clusters. Parents should be encouraged to see that clustering is possibly the best future for the small school and for the education of their children.

6.58. In many places we were told that there are difficulties in recruiting headteachers for posts because of the additional management responsibilities alongside the normal strains of being a full-time teacher as well as head. Guildford diocese was using its Diocesan Education Committee budget to pay for part-time secretarial and administrative assistance to the smaller schools.

6.59. We have been told in a number of areas of the difficulty in recruiting willing governors to undertake the new levels of responsibility. The training of school governors to carry out their new responsibilities is of the utmost importance, and we have noted the commitment of many dioceses to this training. It is one more demand being made on local people to carry more responsibility for managing their own affairs.

6.60. We were surprised not to hear anxieties about the primary school child getting to school along busy unlit roads. Perhaps local people are increasingly aware of their responsibilities to each other to ensure safe arrival; but it is likely that there are occasional problems in this area that need an appropriate community response.

6.61. Some parents, perhaps particularly the newcomers to rural living with sufficient resources, send their children to private schools. This loss of a potential child for the village school is felt sorely by those fighting to retain their school by means of numbers on roll. Parents are of course free to make such a choice, but it could be that educationally they would be better advised to enroll at the local school.

6.62. *Secondary education:* A major issue for county councils in this matter is that of school transport. Cumbria's bill for school transport in 1988 was £3 million. This was equal to the Rate Support Grant (RSG) from central government. For Norfolk the bill was twice the RSG. We agree with the Director of Education for Cumbria that it would be appropriate for central government to meet the entire cost of secondary school transport, to avoid disadvantage to the rural counties.

6.63. Transport is again an issue at the end of the school day when extra-curricular activities are planned. It is difficult for children of households without the daytime use of a car to participate in these important activities. It should be possible for alternative arrangements to be made to allow for such participation. The cost of these arrangements should not fall on households unable to bear them. It is important that each of the communities that forms the catchment area of a secondary school has its voice on the governors of the school. It is they who would voice the concern for the pupils for whom travel is a large part of their school day.

6.64. We were impressed by the innovative self-supported study programmes being developed in Northumberland for the over-16s as a way of combating distance and sparsity. It is a useful way of bringing high-quality educational materials with expert tuition before all who can make use of them, and of enhancing the choices that sixth forms can offer their pupils.

6.65. The education of the handicapped is a specialist subject in itself, and each individual has different needs. Special care and training are so labour-intensive and expensive that handicapped people are usually transported to schools located in a central town. The educational and financial advantages of this have to be offset against the fact that this removes the handicapped child from local contact with their peers, thus further isolating young people who are probably already isolated. On top of this the handicapped child who lives in a village often has to face a car/bus journey of up to an hour in each direction.

6.66. We wholeheartedly support those authorities which take such trouble to see that handicapped children receive specialist education. On the other hand we have seen a number of examples of handicapped children who have benefited greatly from the care offered by small village communities.

Among the good examples of integrating handicapped youngsters into the mainstream of life was the village of Lakeside in Cumbria where long-term support to the families of two handicapped children enabled them to cope; a play-group in Cirencester, Gloucestershire, which deliberately mixes 'normal' and 'handicapped' children; a spina bifida child in Sapperton, Gloucestershire, who with the help of a nursery assistant made excellent progress in the small village school; a unit for autistic children attached to the school at Chinnor, Oxfordshire, which is nationally famous; and a Riding for the Disabled holiday at Barton-Le-Clay, Bedfordshire, which involves many local enthusiastic teenagers.

In some cases what is needed is a sympathetic adult to be there in the background as teacher back-up. It does seem that village schools, with the right motivation and the right level of ancillary staffing, could be the best option for a number of rural handicapped children.

6.67. *Adult education:* The use of the considerable investment in the secondary school campus by the rest of the community is an important opportunity. We have seen some excellent examples of the community college idea as a way of providing for the educational needs of a whole area, for example at Bishop's Castle in Shropshire from which educational services are developed throughout the area, as well as more conventional adult education classes at the college itself. Here the mobile youth service is based. Two full time members of staff are responsible for the development of the college and for liaison with the daytime staff of the school. The evenings at this college are as fully populated with adults as the daytime is with children. We commend further developments of this kind.

6.68. *Further and higher education:* This provision is necessarily at a distance from many rural clients and while it is difficult to quantify it must be the case that there is a lower take-up of these educational opportunities because of the constraint on travelling time and cost. This will be to the disadvantage both of the individual, and also of the community which needs the development of skills. Some rural areas are dependent on what are effectively small colleges of higher education (eg Bishop Grosseteste College at Lincoln, and North

Riding College at Scarborough). These need protecting against the prevailing economic doctrine which would close them on grounds of size. The county agricultural colleges are responding rapidly to the challenge of a changing agriculture, and the needs for skills development in new areas. We saw good examples of positive developments in new courses, such as tourism, business, conservation, and equine studies, and in the marketing of those courses, at Bishop Burton College, Humberside. Other colleges are making similar adjustments, and these are necessary and welcome as the rural economy adapts to the new challenges.

6.69. *Redundant schools:* When a village school closes, the rural community is in danger of losing far more than the educational facility. Often the school has been the home of other community activities, and every opportunity should be given to allow for the continuation of these activities. The same principles apply whether it be a county or a church school. The Church of England, as a major provider of small rural schools, is often criticised by local people for seeking the highest possible price on the disposal of a redundant school. It has to be remembered that, like the secular education authority, it has a responsibility to provide and maintain many other schools in other parts of the diocese/county, but, unlike the local education authority (LEA), it normally has no means of raising the necessary resources to fulfil this responsibility. It is doubtful whether those who are to lose their school properly understand the wider responsibility of the diocesan board of education, and whether the diocesan authorities fully appreciate the feeling of ownership in the local community; that is, until there is a dispute. It is important that careful discussions between the diocese, the local church and the community take place at the earliest opportunity so that there may be as few misunderstandings as possible. We return to this topic in Chapter 11.

Transport
6.70. As has been seen above, the ability to get to things is a key freedom. For many people life and the opportunity to flourish are curtailed because of distance from desirable facilities. This problem has become more sharply focused as the majority of the population have become more affluent, and expressed that affluence in the use of

private cars. As more cars are used so the demand for public transport is reduced. As public transport is withdrawn so the lot of those without the ready use of a car is worsened. As those with cars use them to utilize more distant facilities so the viability of nearby facilities is weakened. As nearby facilities fail and disappear, so the lot of those without cars is further diminished. Thus to be without the use of a car at all times in today's countryside is to be considerably disadvantaged.

6.71. So we can see that children and young people below driving age, and those who cannot or are no longer able to drive, and those who cannot afford the considerable cost of buying and maintaining a car are unable in large measure to take part in the way of life enjoyed by the majority of Britons today. The National Travel Survey has revealed that in rural areas 22% of households have no car; but 44% of households have only one car, and that car will often not be available during the day for other members of the household. That car ownership is vital today is indicated by the greater distances travelled by rural people, averaging 9.6 miles per journey compared with 7.2 miles by urban people.

6.72. For those who are physically handicapped the problem of mobility is a double burden. Research by Buchanan for Berkshire County Council (1989) showed that a semi-scheduled, zonal, dial-a-ride system of designated transport would only cost 70p per head of the adult population a year if a reasonable proportion of the eligible population used it. It should be remembered that 11% of the population has some form of immobilising disability.

6.73. The effects of the Transport Act 1985 are now beginning to show more starkly. Initially there seemed to be little change in the quantity of public bus service provision in rural areas, but evening and weekend services are being reduced as the level of subsidy from county councils is cut in order to balance overall budgets. The number of journeys supported by the local authority as contracted services is being increased as private transport companies withdraw from loss-making services, as has been reported to us in a study in North Norfolk and East Hertfordshire. One effect of the Transport Act has been so to increase diversity that the information about public transport is confusing, and frequently non-existent.

6.74. It must be asked whether the provision of public service vehicles (PSVs) is necessarily the best way of moving small numbers of people when the journey requirements of those people are so variable.

6.75. Many communities have responded for several years to the occasional transport needs of their fellows by ad hoc social car schemes, which are organised networks of drivers who may be refunded for their mileage. These may be partially funded by the Women's Royal Voluntary Service (WRVS), whose social transport system travelled 1.2 million miles in 1989, helping nearly 100,000 people in this way. Shropshire County Council use their transport fund to pay volunteers 22p a mile (1989). These ad hoc arrangements can work well to provide for the occasional visit to the doctor or hospital, and can cover weekly shopping trips, although purely social visits to friends are not usually catered for. The evidence we have received has showed that amongst the range of good neighbourly support, assistance with transport is the most common. It is very difficult, however, to obtain volunteers to help those who need to travel on a regular basis. Routine journeys to work or college require something more solidly established, and targeted on the particular individuals who have this need. It has been brought to our attention that the vital journeys to certain centralised facilities are frequently difficult, and even impossible by public transport. There have been cases of defendants being unable to reach court in time to defend themselves and being penalised for late arrival. This is unjust. We have heard that Hereford and Worcester County Council is trying to remove the obligation to provide free school transport. New district hospitals are partly justified in terms of cost, but there is an additional cost of transport which is transferred to patients and visitors. Voluntary car schemes are often hard pressed to cover the multitude of diverse journeys which are needed.

6.76. The RDC Rural Transport Development Fund has been used in two main ways:

(a) To enable many counties to employ a rural transport broker whose work can include the co-ordination of the many passenger-carrying vehicles in the ownership of sundry agencies and authorities which are under-utilised. Their work is also likely to include liaison between service providers and the rural communities. There is certainly need for improvement here, as information about transport services is not always easily obtainable by those who need it most.

(b) To fund the purchase of vehicles suitable for rural community use as PSVs. Cornwall has been the most enthusiastic applicant to this fund, but for an example of local initiative we highlight the Gloucestershire example 'The Villager'.

Begun in 1982, the Villager Bus Scheme now services 58 villages in 300 square miles in the Cotswolds. Chairman Trevor Baxter secured funding from the county and district council and the RDC. Passengers carried have increased by 2,000 each year, with over 14,000 in 1988, when 16 volunteer drivers covered nearly 34,000 miles. The newest minibus has a tail-lift. The community arranges routes and schedules to serve local needs; the county council manages insurance, technical advice, driver training, vehicle servicing and publicity. Local groups may also hire the buses. Grants bring in twice the fare income, and 1988 saw a surplus of over £13,000, so this initiative looks set to continue its public service.

6.77. Many communities depend on volunteers to drive minibuses. It concerns us that post-1992 it may prove necessary for all such drivers to pass a PSV test to drive a vehicle with more than nine seats. Safety is an important issue, but such stringent requirements may deter many volunteers and prevent the arrangement of many important journeys. If such regulations are necessary, it would be important to phase their introduction and for adequate funds to be allocated for driver training.

Shops and post offices
6.78. In many villages the rural shop is perceived, along with the pub, hall, church or school, as a hub of community life. It fulfils roles which are much wider than just retailing, becoming involved in the provision of advice and information, a centre for notices, and a meeting point where village news is exchanged.

6.79. Where the entrepreneurial skill and vision of the shopkeeper has kept abreast of social and market developments, thriving enterprises continue to exist. But there are many villages where the shop is a more precarious enterprise surviving at the economic margins and as such vulnerable to even the lightest breeze of economic change. They often face major problems of supplies and margins as their level of operation seldom makes it economical for them to be serviced by wholesalers.

Additional problems arise, as for other very small service businesses, with the administration of VAT and the consequences of the community charge, together with the uniform business rate. These have been particularly worrying for those living on the same premises as the shop, as is being increasingly witnessed by ACRE and the RDC. The ACRE/RDC report *English Village Services in the Eighties* also highlights the pressure on marginal shops when the premises can be sold at a higher price if planning consent is obtained for a change to residential use.

6.80. Many small shops double as the post office, with this additional income making the difference between closure and survival. This feature is of particular importance to the elderly and those on social security who can obtain their benefits near to home without access problems and costs. Concern has been expressed to the Commission right across the country over the growing uncertainty of how the Post Office will respond to maintaining a considerable rural presence under the pressure of cost-effectiveness. The new status of 'community post office' provides opportunities for some areas once again to have a level of post office service, but established post office businesses have had their long term viability put in question by this development. The social value of post offices to the less well-off within society is as significant as their economic role. The matter has been carefully studied in the RDC publication *The Impact of 'Community Post Office' Status on Rural sub-Post Offices* and we would strongly urge the Government to see the rural post office in the context of service provision rather than looking for it to be a cost-effective business.

6.81. It is difficult to assess quite how far this pattern is being affected by large out-of-town shopping centres, with their wide range of low cost foodstuffs in particular. Although the environmental aspects of these centres have attracted some research and comment, we were not made aware of any socio-economic research, assessing the impact on rural areas and identifying the effects on those who have problems with access and those who run small village shops. Conventionally it would appear that both would suffer, especially if access through community buses and informal transport arrangements, as was particularly noted in Derbyshire, become widespread. Nonetheless there will still be a residual group who will rely on local facilities even if they are more expensive; their interests require local facilities to remain even if the move of the market is towards much larger units. Here again we encounter a circumstance the effect of which can be very different for those who can afford the choice offered by private transport and for those for whom such choices either do not exist or depend on lifts or a community scheme.

Health provision

6.82. *The general level of health care:* From the evidence which we have seen, we are not aware of any general circumstances which suggest that rural people are substantially disadvantaged with regard to the public provision of health care. The benefits of the National Health Service are carried deep into rural areas and, while rural patients may sometimes be inconvenienced, their welfare is seldom put in jeopardy. This is in part due to a commitment to blanket welfare care which has developed since the 1940s, but it is also very much dependent upon a close involvement of the voluntary sector, both formal and informal. We find the extent to which ordinary people are willing to commit themselves to helping others with hospital visiting schemes, prescription delivery systems and the like, especially noteworthy. While the churches in the rural areas often play a part in this activity, we recommend a much greater involvement.

6.83. This is not to say, however, that there are not aspects of health provision which cause us concern. There is no doubt that the distances over which patients, and also hospital visitors, have to travel are often long, tedious and expensive. The general centralisation of many hospital services in larger urban centres and the growing tendency for medical practices to increase in size and locate in larger villages and market towns is inevitably to the detriment of local people. For those who do not have private transport the position can be very difficult.

6.84. There are many instances when the area health authority as part of a plan to promote a district hospital centre will wish to close a long established local or cottage hospital on grounds of greater efficiency and economy. We question these economics, and believe that where the local hospital is well supported by the local population, as is the case in many places, keeping open the hospital becomes possible and meets local needs and wishes.

6.85. *General practitioner services:* As with other issues (transport, education) we were investigating health provision at a time when radical new proposals were emanating from the Government. The proposals made in 1989 for a greater involvement of market principles met with substantial opposition from doctors and it is obviously too early to assess their implication. We firmly believe, however, that any new proposals must take adequate account of the particular circumstances of rural areas. In particular, the payments to rural doctors made for travelling under the new contract system seem woefully inadequate and seem likely to imperil some rural practices. In particular, it is crucial that the 'rurality' factor is properly considered and that doctors' remuneration is not too narrowly based upon the number of patients which they have on their list.

> **We found on our visit to the north east of England a single-doctor medical practice serving just 1,400 patients - yet the doctor was travelling some 35,000 miles each year in their care. We have no doubt that, without adequate financial safeguards, that service would not remain viable and the medical care of those rural people would be jeopardised.**

6.86. *Hospital services:* In general, we found that hospital services have been subject to substantial centralisation in large urban centres, on the justification that economies of scale in what is an increasingly expensive service may be gained. In most areas, the old pattern of cottage hospitals has disappeared and with it the locally-based, responsive hospital service which was especially valuable for out-patient treatment, minor operations and recuperative care.

6.87. Paradoxically, we found that in the Exeter District Health Authority the cottage hospital network was in effect being recreated under the name of 'community hospitals', with attendant benefits to the more rural areas.

> **Norwich Health Authority tried to close the 14-bed hospital at Wells on the north Norfolk coast. Public resistance has kept this unit open, now functioning as an accident unit for this remote part, used extensively by summer visitors, and also as a four-day-a-week geriatric day hospital which is backed up by much voluntary support.**

6.88. We feel strongly that the arguments in favour of increased centralisation are worthy of more scrutiny and the supposed extra costs of providing a basic, rurally centred hospital service should be more fully investigated. In Shropshire a number of threatened local hospitals are to be transferred to a new trust organised under the umbrella of the Rural Target Team of Business in the Community. This approach offers an imaginative and innovative way forward in the search for ways of keeping health facilities local and accessible. Development in the hospital grounds will help to fund the reordering of a new 27-bed community nursing home in one case.

6.89. Proposals currently being made to allow competition between hospitals and to allow hospitals to opt out of direct control, seem likely to bring mixed blessings to rural dwellers. For many rural dwellers there will effectively be no choice since the 'local' hospital will already be far distant. Again, when hospitals opt out, there are fears that this will again disadvantage rural people if services are sold to others. Even more, if the community services (clinics, health visitors, community buses, etc) now attached to district hospitals are found to be too expensive for the new hospital 'business' and are effectively abolished, then rural communities will be very much the poorer.

6.90. *Dispensing services:* We received evidence from both the Dispensing Doctors' Association and the Royal Pharmaceutical Society, each vigorously arguing its case as to the desirability or otherwise of allowing doctors to dispense as well as prescribe in rural areas. The apparent antagonism between these two groups, in supposed pursuit of customer benefit is, we feel, unworthy of two professional groups and bodes ill for a medical system which will purportedly take greater account of market forces.

6.91. In some areas, especially the more remote ones, there is little alternative to doctor-dispensing. No pharmacy business could survive and the additional income probably ensures the survival of the doctors' practice. In more populous areas the argument is less clear, and it seems likely that the loss of the pharmacy, which will frequently follow doctor-dispensing, would often mean a net loss of service provision to the rural community. We believe that in general the Rural Dispensing Committee, which was set up in 1983 to adjudicate between competing dispensing claims, has done a good job. We feel strongly, however, that proper solutions in cases of dispute are more likely to be found in co-operative ventures between doctors and pharmacists, rather than in decisions which decide for one side or the other. We recommend that doctors in rural practices be normally permitted to dispense medicines.

6.92. *Care in the community:* As the programme to implement the Griffiths proposals gathers momentum, organisations, voluntary and statutory, are discovering ways of responding to the challenge to enable those who might once have stayed in institutional care for many years to return to or remain in their own home. Many rural areas now face the problem of a high proportion of elderly (over 75 years) needing support. Dominating themes are those of transport and mobility, and the need for coordination between the plurality of agencies and sources of information. After much delay by the Government following the Griffiths Report, there is now only a short time for plans to be drawn up for approval, although early implementation now looks doubtful. As much reliance is placed on the voluntary sector to deliver Care in the Community we are worried that many voluntary organisations may not be able to transform themselves into the new cultural model required. There seems to be little provision for training and yet voluntary bodies are suddenly expected to become expert at negotiating, tendering and contracting. Councils for Voluntary Service and Volunteer Bureaux are involved in the encouragement, support and training of caring volunteers, but too much of their staff time is having to be spent in seeking out those who will engage in fund-raising.

6.93. We note that funding for most Volunteer Bureaux comes from county or national sources. We regret the reversal of the recent decision in the House of Lords to 'ring-fence' local authority community care budgets as an essential step in ensuring that the policy of developing care in the community is adequately funded. The voluntary sector has an important part to play, but it cannot be regarded as a cheap option. It is equally vital that the voluntary sector is properly involved in the planning of the new arrangements in each locality. There is an added danger that some large national organisations will be powerful enough to dominate the local delivery of services. This is a real challenge to statutory organisations which will involve many of them in seeing the voluntary movement in a new constructive light. In view of the fact that there are an estimated 6 million people who carry out a caring role at home the enormity of the task for the rest of society in supporting them in a systematic and effective way is alarming. In Chapter 11 we refer to some examples of Church involvement in this work, but there can be few challenges more important to any society than the way it cares for its elderly and disadvantaged. The quality of life for all can be measured by the quality of care available for the weakest.

6.94. It is clear that local authority budgets are being squeezed between a constraint on raising income from central or local sources and a requirement to ensure an adequate quality of service delivery. Long established patterns of care, like meals on wheels and home helps, are having to be reduced or provided at additional cost. It must be the case that with a growing proportion of our population in some kind of need, more revenue will have to be allocated if we are to care for the needy in a dignified way. Care in the community is a noble ideal, but it will be more costly than the old institutions.

6.95. Another aspect of care in the community is the re-housing of long-stay mentally handicapped patients within the community. This can be a sensitive issue. Communal homes have been established in a number of market towns and local residents have welcomed those moving into them. We support the initiative of those local church congregations who have also welcomed these patients and integrated them into their worship. The acceptance of the handicapped into the normal life of congregations is of particular value and importance. The provision of respite care is of great importance, both to the handicapped, but also to their carers. The local church can do much to help with this provision.

Information and advice

6.96. Information about the availability of advice and counselling for problems, and about access to services etc, is particularly important for the rural dweller, particularly when more and more services are centralised and therefore not evidently available in the village. This need was recognised more than ten years ago (*The Right to Know,* NCSS 1978) and has since been re-emphasised by several groups. We need to recognise that there are both formal and informal information and advice systems and both have something to contribute.

6.97. *Formal advice systems:* Formal advice systems seldom exist in the more rural areas, although some formal services such as the Citizens Advice Bureaux, Samaritans, Age Concern and Relate can be found in the larger market towns. While some of these are specialist agencies dealing with particular types of problem, it is the Citizens Advice Bureaux which provide the general advice service for rural people. We have been impressed by the professionalism, breadth and quality of the service which is provided by the bureaux and by their recognition of the need to push their activities further into the rural areas. Their work is especially dependent upon statutory support, particularly from district councils, and we are disturbed to note that gaps in the service tend to be in the more rural areas where district councils have yet to be persuaded to provide support. We were glad to be able to see one or two rural bureaux in operation and endorse the need for the network to be able to provide its service more widely. We heard from them that lack of knowledge and difficulty in reaching an information centre leads to under-claiming of state benefits among rural people.

6.98. *Mobile information and advice services:* Some RCCs operate a mobile service with the assistance of the RDC. These, such as the Avon service, visit a wide range of small settlements on a scheduled timetable and carry information about leisure and local authority matters as well as benefits and employment. Such services ought to receive the full support of the district councils in which they operate, as many thousands of local people are associated in a wide variety of ways.

6.99. The imaginative development in the use of the county mobile library service is to be recommended, with the provision of computer-based data, as library staff are already trained in the provision of information. What is more difficult is dealing with the cautious enquirer who is reluctant initially to reveal the core problem, and may require confidentiality.

6.100. *Informal advice systems:* At the village level, particularly in those villages and rural areas where there is a strong community feeling and a point of focus such as a shop or post office, the informal network of advice and information can operate. There are, however, several handicaps to this system. Firstly, there is no doubt that the evident prosperity in many villages, consequent upon new people and new wealth, hides the needs of the less fortunate. Every village needs a 'signpost', often as part of the local newsletter or parish magazine, which ought to be widely available in public places including the church and pub. Ways should be explored of paying shopkeepers/publicans so that they can earn income as general as well as tourist information points.

6.101. Secondly, rural people, like others, are often unwilling to talk of their problems, even to those whom they know well. We were told of low paid people being unwilling to claim because the subsequent enquiry to the employer might be counterproductive. Similarly those in tied housing may still feel unwilling to make a claim for housing benefit because of possible repercussions. Their relative isolation contributes to the characteristic of 'making the best of things'. As in urban areas, to admit to a problem of ignorance is difficult for many people and especially so for those who feel intimidated by the articulation and apparent competence and wealth of others.

6.102. These informal advice systems are important, despite these difficulties, and they need to be furthered. The McLaughlin report of 1985 (see 6.12) revealed that formal advice services are used most by those who know how to use them, whereas those most in need tend to use sources of advice for which they have to pay. All advice agencies need to try to attend to this disparity. However successful the formal advice agencies are in reaching the more remote rural areas, they depend upon an initial contact and the willingnesss and ability to travel to advice centres, write letters or use the telephone. All these things may be difficult for some, particularly elderly people, and face-to-face contact, especially at the early diagnostic stage, is critical. It is not surprising that it is often the home help or district nurse who first takes up an enquiry. It is important for the leaders of the local church to be a trusted part of the supporting network.

Community development

6.103. The lack of central government attention to social problems in rural areas has been a major factor behind the upsurge of interest in rural community development during the 1970s and 1980s. There has been growing recognition on the part of organisations representing the various rural interest groups of the need to work together, both to provide self-help solutions to those problems not addressed by statutory organisations and to lobby for greater attention from central government and its agencies.

6.104. Local authorities' involvement in community development has increased in response to these new concerns. To some extent the lead has come from urban authorities, such as Oldham, although a recent research study shows that important initiatives are also being taken by a number of rural county councils, notably Hereford and Worcester. Such involvement in rural community development is still the exception, however, and at the local level the organisations most involved in the promotion of self-help initiatives are the RCCs and parish councils.

6.105. RCCs are independent county voluntary organisations with a particular concern for the welfare of rural communities. They aim to encourage community self-help, mainly through voluntary initiatives. The first RCC was established in 1921 and, with the creation of one in Norfolk in 1988, every shire county now has one. Members of RCCs include both statutory and voluntary organisations. In many counties church representatives played a formative role and this continues with membership of the RCC executive. Funding comes principally from the RDC (up to 50%), local authorities and voluntary subscriptions. RCCs typically have intimate knowledge of the rural communities they work with, acquired through contact with parish councils, village hall committees and other groups representing local interests. Some of this contact is on a formal basis; for example, it is usual for the RCC to provide the secretariat for the County Association of Local Councils. Other contacts are more informal, the result of intensive 'networking' by RCC officers who provide information, advice and practical help to parish councils and other groups, organise training courses, and convene meetings and conferences on countryside issues. The role of RCC countryside officers has been formative in rural development, ranging from representation on behalf of community interests to the now more normal practice of encouraging self-help by advice, training and information.

6.106. Village appraisals are a common result of more active community interest and work. These are questionnaires submitted to each household in the area. They are usually arranged by the parish council in order to test local opinion about many of the facilities which exist, or are deemed desirable for the village. They produce a more accurate assessment than any other system tried so far and can include questions requested by a number of village organisations, not least the church. They are increasingly valued by district authorities when creating local development plans and are a required procedure for an assessment of the need for low-cost housing. There is a danger, however, that each small community will seek to investigate social needs within it through a series of separate studies. Those villages which have undertaken village appraisals have found that gathering a wider range of information on such things as housing, transport, and household characteristics at one time has helped to unite the village and enabled it to focus on its integrated needs in a constructive way. We have seen excellent examples of this and we urge all rural communities to undertake one. (See also 11.27)

> **It is notable that Cotswold District Council with the help of the Gloucestershire RCC is using a standard format of village appraisal as the basic form of community involvement in the development of the District Plan. This is a practice which we would commend to other district councils.**

6.107. Parish councils are key actors in all these programmes and much RCC effort goes into encouraging parish councils to fulfil the tasks which lie within their remit. We have been impressed by the extent to which the National Association of Local Councils (parish and town councils) (NALC) have been promoting the idea of a local, trained, professional officer not just as clerk to the parish council, but also as someone available to the whole community as a point of secretarial and executive expertise. We believe that parish councils can be much more effective than many of them are in practice. There is a serious need for parish councils to take stock of their potential role if they are to fulfil the opportunities offered to them. If they do not, then truly local government loses a crucial voice. We welcome the renewed interest, shared by NALC and the Association of District Councils (ADC), in furthering the effectiveness of parish councils.

6.108. It is in keeping with the spirit of decentralisation that runs through this report that more responsibility should be devolved to parish councils. We have much to learn in these matters from our European partners, for whom parish government is more of a reality. This is not without risks, particularly in the early stages, as parish councils appear at present not to be representative of more than a small minority (based on electoral turnout and the actual need for elections). But, given responsibility, we believe that local people will be able to take more into their own hands than is currently the case. Local people are being expected to manage their school and voluntary caring in the community, and to be local hospital trustees. They already manage the parish church, churchyard and village hall. Why should they not have overall responsibility, within the district plan framework, of being the first line in housing and economic development policy? It works in Germany and France. We believe it can work here. Rural community development is a bottom-up approach. We have the bones of a framework with parish councils and RCCs, supported by the RCC national association, ACRE; it needs a concerted push to make them more effective.

6.109. The main lobby on behalf of rural people is Rural Voice, whose secretariat ACRE provides. The Churches are members of Rural Voice, in the form of the Arthur Rank Centre (see Chapter 11). Rural Voice was established in 1980 in response to growing pressures on rural communities and what is seen as a lack of sensitivity among policy makers towards the needs of rural areas.

6.110. As a result of the way in which RCCs across the country directed our attention to a wide range of community development activities during our local visits, the Commission endorses this positive view towards local rural activity. Commissioners saw for themselves the value of truly local initiatives and the essential role RCC staff were capable of playing in helping to establish contacts and funding. With the current political interest in self-help and local initiative it is to be hoped that every encouragement will be given to RCCs through the provision of adequate finance without their directors having to spend undue time in raising partnership finance. Thus the rural voluntary sector is well organised to press its case through parish councils, NALC, the RCCs and ACRE; we urge the Government to build on this network.

Representation

6.111. From time to time we have been approached by those who are concerned about how local government works politically, with particular reference to representative patterns in rural as opposed to urban areas. Young and Mills have drawn a helpful picture in Appendix G illustrating the nature of partisanship, and of officer power and the changes which have taken place since Victorian times. They have set this against the vesting of power in the old landowning classes and the challenge of the newly enfranchised ratepayers. Their study argues how, until the reforms of 1974, the pattern remained remarkably unchanged, with the local electorate supporting the natural leaders of the countryside.

6.112. Since the mid-seventies changes have been noted, with a greater trend towards party membership, reflecting larger local authorities, even if the behaviour of individual members was more likely to remain independent than would be the case in more urban local authorities. They note too that in rural areas local authority officers are less likely to give assistance to members than to act independently. What the study does not address are the questions of whom the councillors represent and which interests are most powerful in rural local government.

6.113. Keeping costs down and therefore taxes low has been a traditional element in rural policy at each level of rural local government. We are concerned that the introduction of the community charge will exacerbate this view, with the effect that because of their cost rural services will be further pruned. This may especially be the case where urban-dominated local authorities are looking for savings. We have already expressed our concern for the poorest sector of rural society who would be most damaged by such cuts. These people are rarely a majority in electoral terms and neither so visible nor so concentrated as their counterparts in the inner cities, where, at worst, riots have thrust their condition onto the national stage and consciousness. Often rural people are not articulate and demonstrative about their circumstances, perhaps because they have been dependent on others for many of the essentials of their lives: estates and farmers have offered employment and housing; schooling has been local; retirement housing has been available; and doctors used to visit, as did clergy. But the rest of society should not be content to benefit from their quiescence, especially where such people are elderly and infirm.

Conclusion: the rural dilemma

6.114. The scene, as we have noted, has been changing steadily and in one direction: local village employment has declined; housing has become more difficult; schooling has been grouped, with transport needed for it; local shops, post offices and halls have often been under the threat of closure or have actually closed; local transport has declined to a point of uselessness in many areas; most doctors are based in local towns, with only a few using village facilities; and ultimately even the Church seems to have followed the general pattern of withdrawal, with many rural clergy stating that they no longer had time to conduct a pattern of local visiting. Many of the people who are most affected by these changes are the least powerful and articulate - and yet they are the ones who most need public services and support. In all fields - welfare benefit, transport, access to shops, medical services, housing, jobs, training and education - they need a public budget to support them. The local political system may well be reflecting democratically the wishes and interests of the majority - but we as a Christian Commission strongly urge the majority to look much more carefully at the wholeness of their communities, seeking out ways (perhaps through networking and funding through voluntary bodies like local transport groups) to help the least advantaged. There is much goodwill in rural areas, but it needs to be focused politically and with an understanding that rural life needs a proper share of resources even if deprivation is hard to see and the lot of a minority. It emphasises the responsibility for government to govern in the interests of the whole community and not just for those who brought it to power.

Recommendations

1. Local authorities should be positively encouraged to provide once again some housing for affordable rent, which they would manage either directly or through agents. (6.32)

2. Restrictions which forbid local authorities to use much of the finance gained from house sales to provide new affordable low-cost housing in rural areas should be removed. (6.32)

3. Local authorities must actively explore their new role as 'housing enablers' and seek new and imaginative ways of working with parish councils, housing associations, and the private sector; in particular, they should, in conjunction with parishes and with the voluntary sector, look to produce district-level rural housing strategies with clear objectives and attainment targets. These should be monitored annually, and revised as appropriate, by the full district council. (6.32)

4. Preferably in the context of a village appraisal, every parish should carry out a housing needs survey, with the advice of its rural community council, to assess the local need for affordable housing. The results should be conveyed to the district council and interested housing associations. (6.33)

5. Where there is a right to buy, new tenants should be given the option of a rent that is closer to market levels with a right-to-buy attached, or a lower rent with no right-to-buy. There should always be some housing available in the second category. (6.38)

6. The Housing Corporation should:
   (a) encourage housing associations and other appropriate agencies to deliver social housing in rural areas;
   (b) make a consistent grant of 70% available to schemes;
   (c) increase the number of houses to be built in rural areas for which it will provide finance to not less than 5,000 a year by 1992, climbing substantially beyond that to clear targets to be specified by the Government for 1995 and 2000. This will

encourage effective planning preparation. We would welcome a multi-party commitment to support this to ensure long-term consistency. (6.36)

7. The Church, at both Church Commissioners and diocesan level, as owners of glebe and investment land, should take a lead in showing the responsibilities of landowners towards rural housing provision. They should invite district housing officers to inspect the register of Church land holdings to enable land suitable for affordable housing to be identified. The PCCs of those parishes where land is so identified should ensure that a housing needs survey, and land availability, should be drawn to the attention of appropriate housing associations. (6.48)

8. Strict limits should be set regarding the maximum amount of equity which an individual owner can accumulate in housing schemes where public subsidy is involved. Moreover, staircasing should not be possible where that is the wish of trustees when more than 50% of monies in a scheme are from private sources, even if public money is involved. (6.47)

9. The Government should develop a transport policy based on an integrated public service which should have the objective of providing accessible and well publicised services connecting all settlements with more than 1000 people. (6.73)

10. Organisations providing services which require attendance at a central location (eg hospital, law court, school) should consider the interests of those for whom access to those facilities is difficult and ensure that their 'clients' are not penalised by distance. (6.75)

11. Churches and local voluntary groups should encourage members to become voluntary car scheme drivers and should ensure in collaboration with the parish council (where one exists) that each parish has a designated person or group responsible for discovering mobility needs. (6.75)

12. Preferably within the context of a village appraisal, parish councils should regularly review the provision of public and voluntary transport in their area, and establish the travel needs of those without use of cars. A parish precept should be raised to provide for the training of drivers of minibuses in use by voluntary bodies for the benefit of the whole community. (6.75)

13. District councils should use their powers under the community charge mechanism to assist village shops/post offices as community facilities. (6.80)

14. Parish councils should encourage the development of new community post offices in appropriate locations. (6.80)

15. Programmes to close hospital services should be critically reviewed and particular account should be taken of the travel costs of rural patients and visitors. (6.83-6.84)

16. Remuneration for general practitioners should take full account of the needs of rural patients and due allowance should be made for distances travelled. (6.85)

17. Where arrangements are introduced for greater competition within hospitals guarantees will be needed to ensure that satisfactory levels of medical and community services are maintained for rural areas. (6.89)

18. Incentive payments for innovative services, running branch surgeries home visiting and the like should be incorporated into the payment schedule. (6.91)

19. Doctors in rural practices should normally be permitted to dispense medicines. (6.91)

20. The vital role of volunteer workers within the community and the importance of continuity should be more widely recognised, and positive support should be given to them by the provision of adequate finance and training. (6.93)

21. The Church should encourage and support programmes of care in the community, shaping its own network of care to include all sections of community, but especially the elderly. (6.93)

22. Local churches should be especially aware of rural dwellers' need for information, and should use established means (magazines, notice boards, church bookstalls etc) to provide the widest possible range of information. (6.102)

23. Church leaders should act as the 'eyes and ears' of their community and should develop clear links with local agencies and especially the local Citizens Advice Bureau. (6.102)

The previous chapters have shown the breadth and depth of the changes that have been affecting life in our rural areas in recent years. We now focus on the implications of this changed context for the rural church.

Of all the institutions active in England's countryside, the Church is that with the greatest single continuity of historical presence. Indeed, this presence is woven into the very fabric of rural community life. Hence it is not surprising that at a time of major change - affecting the balance of the rural population, patterns of communication, the rural economic structure, and public attitudes - the Church should also be experiencing strain. These new tensions, and the challenges they present to the organisation and mission of the rural church, are the focus of the chapters that follow.

Chapter 7
The Origins and Development of the Rural Church

7.1. By its nature, the history of the development of a village and its parish church is specific rather than general, for the history of no two villages is the same. However, some acknowledgement of this history is important, partly because so much in the current life of the rural church can only be satisfactorily explained by reference to the past, and partly because a major element in the decline in rural culture and community, which is so much regretted, lies in the decline in awareness of a common past. So dominant has been the tendency to write the history of the Church as if it were the history of its upper echelons, the bishops, cathedral dignitaries and dons, that there are few published works on the development of the country church.

The early history

7.2. The term 'parish' was unknown in pre-conquest England and does not occur in the Domesday Book. In the sense in which the historian Bede uses the term 'parish' it denotes the sphere of authority of a bishop; the term 'diocese' (which is derived from the secular nomenclature of the Roman Empire) came later. While the Celtic missionaries, who were essentially itinerant preachers, worked from monastic settlements in the northern and western parts of the country, the mission of Augustine landed in Kent in AD 597. By the mid seventh century, the kingdom of Kent had been parcelled out into parishes (as we understand them today) by Archbishop Honorius, but it was Archbishop Theodore who is usually credited with the creation of the parochial system. He encouraged Saxon landowners to erect churches on their estates and granted the right of perpetual patronage.

In areas away from the more populated south east, minsters were established, from which the clergy served a large rural hinterland. In these villages stone crosses marked the assembly point for religious services which were held in the open.

7.3. The status of the priest, who officiated in these early churches, was that of a private chaplain to the landlord; he was not infrequently one of the landowner's servants who had been sent to the bishop for instruction and ordination. Priests were in short supply and the rights and interests of the established minsters in some areas stood in the way of that village based ministry which Bede was among the first to call for, as early as the first decade of the eighth century. The local priest, in addition to his glebe (which literally means soil or 'clod of earth'), also received a range of dues payable at appropriate times and festivals. At first the tithe was a voluntary gift by the faithful, but the Church sought to have this regarded as an enforceable tax, though this was not achieved until the tenth century.

7.4. It can be seen that a number of features of the contemporary Church date from this early period. Among these are the primacy of the diocese; the significance of the local landowner and his right of patronage; the importance of a local ministry and the fact that it was supported financially by the local church.

7.5. On the eve of the Norman conquest many of the parochial clergy would have been local men, who, it is assumed, were similar in many ways to other members of the village. At this time the clergy were married, though already this was looked on with disapproval by reformers seeking different standards. The church itself was the property of the Saxon thegn and was both essential to his status and part of his capital worth; the village church could not exist outside his seigneurial jurisdiction. Not only did the builder of the church and his heirs retain the right to appoint the priest, but they also acquired an interest in the tithe and the offerings.

The early mediaeval period

7.6. In the early mediaeval period three processes of change can be identified; first, the continuing development of the parochial system as new rural settlements became parishes in their own right. The period of church building reached its zenith between 1150 and 1250; large numbers of churches were built and almost every church received some addition or improvements. The parochial system, with which we are familiar, was firmly established at this time and the network of parishes brought every member of the 2.5 million population into close relations with the church and the parish priest. Second, it was in this period that the clergy became an increasingly separate and independent group in English society. Gradually, the Church became a great feudal power and at the local level the parish priest was no longer the servant of the local landowner. Third, the development of monasticism in the twelfth and thirteenth centuries was in many ways a rural phenomenon. It had a particularly deleterious effect on parochial churches. In the early period, the village clergyman was styled 'rector'; he was appointed by the landowner, instituted by the bishop and enjoyed his benefice as a freehold. As the monasteries developed, many landowners desired to give their churches (and the income associated with them) to a monastic house to ensure that prayers were said for themselves and their families. In this way the monasteries were able to acquire considerable wealth from the rectorial income of the parishes, and they themselves appointed a vicar. It is not uncommon in the countryside today to find that the market towns and larger villages have vicarages while the smaller hamlets and villages have rectories.

7.7. Fourteenth century rural England was increasingly polarised between the landless poor and vagrants, and the wealthy farmers, landowners, wool merchants and staplers. It seems that much of the new money which came from the development of sheep farming was used to build, not only country houses, but also magnificent parish churches in the perpendicular gothic style that originated at Westminster and was perfected after 1331 at Gloucester. The largest churches are to be found in Norfolk, the richest county in England in the fourteenth and fifteenth centuries, and in those areas such as the Cotswolds which benefited most from the wool trade.

The late mediaeval period

7.8. In the late mediaeval period, the villages suffered from disease, civil war and the debilitating effects of weak government and heavy taxation. After the splendours of 'the age of faith' the Church seemed to fall into a malaise. Certainly, the black death caused high mortality among the clergy, who, in the course of their duties, were inevitably brought into contact with the dead and dying. Some authorities suggest that up to 60% of the parish clergy perished in this way. In the fourteenth and fifteenth centuries, inflation, high taxation and oppressive legislation provoked a variety of outbursts of revolt. Although Protestant apologists have concentrated attention on the gross superstitions of the late mediaeval church and their 'purification' in the post-Reformation period, the literature of the period provides many examples of idle absentee clergy and rich worldly monks, which, although they may not all individually be true, point to a commonly accepted view of the church. At another level, the relative income of the parish clergy was falling and the situation of many poorer clergy was certainly deteriorating at this time. By the early 16th century it was reckoned that an income of £16 would be necessary to meet the expenses of a parish clergyman, yet only a quarter of the parishes in England provided an income of this size.

7.9. In the second and third decades of the sixteenth century, anti-clerical feeling in England had been transformed in scale, temper and conviction. Wolsey's reforming legislation of 1518 made little difference, and even the subsequent legislation of 1529, aimed at curtailing clerical absenteeism, trading and farming and introducing high standards for ordination, failed to improve the situation radically. Anti-clericalism played a large part in the English reformation. The breach with Rome in 1533/4 was principally a constitutional change; but the temper of the times was more clearly indicated in a Bill of 1535 which opened with these words: "For as much as manifest sin, vicious carnal and abominable living is daily used and committed among the great and small abbeys, priories......". At Evesham Abbey, where the monastery was suppressed on 30th January 1540, the monks in choir were not allowed to complete the psalm they were singing at Evensong. It is reputed that local people, after years of oppression from the monastery (which was the major local landowner) tore down many of the buildings, grateful for a free supply of superior building materials. A vast acreage of monastic land was confiscated and sold to lay owners. The modest wealth of the Cromwell family came from church land which had belonged to the monks at Ely. The roots of the English squirearchy tradition lie in the subsequent dispersal of monastic lands by the Crown.

7.10. On 28th January 1547 Edward VI came to the throne; within a few months Royal injunctions were published ordering that such images in the church as might lead to superstition be removed; the number of candles on the high altar were to be reduced to two; the ringing of bells during Mass was to cease, and a copy of the book of homilies and the paraphrases of Erasmus were to be placed in every parish church. In 1540 Cranmer's new prayer book was ready and was imposed as a schedule to the Act of Uniformity; all clergy were obliged to use the new book on pain of imprisonment. In a relatively short period, the old religion had become proscribed; the practice of generations and the devotions associated with them were supplanted. It is hard to imagine that the suddenness and the ruthlessness of these changes did not affront the conscience of many people. Certainly, 'the German doctrine', as Protestantism was known, remained virtually unknown to the conservative people in rural areas, and even in the towns of the more sophisticated south east, passionate Protestants often complained that they were treated as madmen. It is hard to imagine that the suppression of much mediaeval spirituality and particularly the vast cult of prayers for the dead, which had worked its way deep into the hearts of many country people, was not profoundly offensive to many. Some commentators have suggested that its suppression has had a permanent effect on popular religion in rural areas.

7.11. Certainly, the selling of church land, which continued during the reign of Edward VI, proved a financial disaster for the rural church. No serious thought was given to the problems of clergy incomes, which were further depressed in a period of inflation. In some measure the conservatism of the reformers is reflected in their preservation of the tithe and the profits from glebe land as the principal basis of the parish economy. Thus the ministry was poorly rewarded; graduates remained in very short supply; and the prestige of the clergy was persistently low. At the beginning of James I's reign there were approximately ten thousand parish clergy, approximately the same number as there are today.

7.12. The effects of the Civil War and the long period of turbulence which followed was brought to an end with the arrival of Charles II in London on 29th May 1660. The Book of Common Prayer was used in the King's Chapel; Anglican bishops were appointed and they set out, with the vigour of men long kept waiting, for the task of revitalising the Church. Within a few months, seven hundred Puritan clergymen had been ejected from their livings and St Bartholomew's Day (24th August) 1662, the day the Act of Uniformity became law, marks the beginning of the modern history of the Church of England. In 1666 the Five Mile Act further forbade all non-Conformist clergy to live or visit within six miles of any place where they had previously ministered. Such legislation led to a further one thousand clergy being expelled and had the effect of permanently dividing England between Conformists and non-Conformists.

The recent history

7.13. The Church in the eighteenth century is customarily seen through the eyes of Victorian writers who have portrayed it as uniformly decadent and lethargic. Certainly, there was an acute shortage of suitably qualified candidates for ministry; clergy stipends were low; many vicarages and rectories had fallen into disrepair. In 1704 the establishment of Queen Anne's Bounty was a means by which some of the Church revenues were used to create a fund for the relief of the ill-housed and poorly paid clergy. This followed a survey which revealed that half of the benefices were worth less than £80 a year and that many of the curacies were worth less than £20 a year.

7.14. In many rural areas, clergy were largely non-resident and curates served as many churches as they could on a Sunday for a fee of half a guinea. Dr George Horne (later Bishop of Norwich) wrote in 1787 of his visit to a country church. Having described the dilapidated state of the church and churchyard, he continued:

> "The minister of this noble edifice was answerable to it in dress and manner. Having entered the church he made the best of his way to the chancel where he changed his wig; put on a dirty, iron-moulded, ragged surplice; and after a short angry dialogue with the clerk, entered his desk and began immediately without looking into the book. He read as if he had ten other churches to serve that day, at as many miles distance from each other. The clerk sang a melancholy solo - neither tune nor words of which I have ever heard before."

7.15. The principal changes that transformed the Anglican rural ministry in the mid and late eighteenth century were not theological in nature. The rise in the price of agricultural commodities and the enclosure movement produced a situation in which many clergy found themselves in positions of modest wealth. It was possible to borrow money against the value of the benefice from Queen Anne's Bounty and in this way many of the country rectories of that period were built. It was at this time that many clergy were appointed as magistrates, particularly in rural areas, where there was an absence of suitably qualified people.

7.16. However, the prevalence of pluralism and non-residence continued to be a prominent feature of the Church in rural areas, where 50% of the churches had only one service and even this would be cancelled when the weather was bad, or when, 'Parson Woodforde' being ill or away, a substitute could not be found. Clergy who took the university disputations as their model were unlikely to engage the attention of a rural congregation, and Hogarth's cartoon of the sleeping congregation recalls an experience with which many could identify. A large part of the appeal of non-Conformity lay in the more energetic and colloquial preaching of its ministers, whose social and educational situation more closely approximated that of the congregation. In thousands of villages there sprang up chapels, which were the religious expression of other divisions and stratifications which were becoming increasingly evident in eighteenth century society. It is hard to overestimate the contribution of these chapels to village life, for it gave to the village that sense of solidarity which took pride in independence and honest poverty, but had a horror of destitution and charity. The thrift, sobriety, hard work and earnestness of much of Victorian life had its origins in Wesley's preaching and the chapels that he and his followers established.

7.17. The mid nineteenth century residence legislation meant that in many country parishes there arrived, for the first time, a resident clergyman, trained at one of the new theological colleges and determined to introduce higher standards into parish life. Country life at that time was often portrayed as boorish and uncultured, if not wild, savage and brutal. It must have appeared the more so to a newly ordained clergyman, and he, along with his colleagues, frequently sought to address these problems by founding a range of parochial institutions which included provident clubs, penny readings, lantern lecture shows and most important of all, a village school. Village schools are the most enduring monument to the work of the parochial clergy in the mid nineteenth century, for neither their scheme of provident institutions or their elaborate restoration of the church have survived subsequent changes in taste and local demand. However, the scheme of parochial primary education, which was largely established through their efforts, and, in many cases, financed from their private resources, has remained unchanged in many of its essential features. The village primary school, with its separate entrance for boys and girls, its prominent foundation stone (in all probability bearing a date between 1840 and 1870) and the schoolmaster's house attached, was considered an essential part of the parochial ministry in the mid and late nineteenth century, and many incumbents considered that their most important work was done within its walls. Between 1811 and 1842 seventeen thousand schools were built or assisted by the National Society (the Church's organisation for financing schools).

7.18. The last decade of the nineteenth century and the early years of the twentieth century, before the first World War, are often portrayed as the golden age of the Anglican rural church. Certainly, in many rectories, where the income was sufficient to employ servants, the clergy were able to sustain a style of life which, though less grand, approximated to that of the manor and the hall. However, the residence legislation, which had done so much to awaken the clergy to the nature of their duties, had settled many in parishes that were too small and too poorly endowed. The decline in agricultural prices in the last two decades of the nineteenth century had resulted in a sharp decline in clerical incomes, particularly for those dependent on letting their glebe; in certain areas some clergy had to face a number of years when their fields were untenanted. One incumbent saw the value of his benefice fall from £1,500 per annum in the high farming years of the 1860s to £300 per annum in the depressed 1880s. By the early years of the twentieth century the practice of making the Easter offering as a gift to the incumbent had already become widespread throughout the Church. Less income led directly to the dismissal of the curate, more modest contributions to village charities and organisations and less support for the school.

7.19. However, poverty may have been easier to bear than the vague presentiment of a life passing by, which many rural clergy were beginning to feel. Richard Jefferies provides a touching vignette of a country parson in the 1870s, as seen through the eyes of his wife:

> "But the work, the parish, the people, all seemed to have slipped out of her husband's hands ..... But surely his good intentions, his way of life, his gentle kindness should carry sway. Instead of which the parish seemed to have quite left the Church, and the parson was outside the real modern life of the village."

7.20. Many parishes with populations of about one hundred had resident incumbents at that time, and it is no coincidence that the first criticisms of the patronage and freehold system should date from that period, when H Rider Haggard, a Suffolk landowner, wrote:

> "In the future, although it may be distant, I believe that all will be changed; priests will not be pitchforked into livings by the arbitrary decision of the owners of the advowsons, which in practice often means their own decisions, but will be selected by proper authorities in consultation maybe with representatives of the parishioners, for their quality and nothing else. Also, perhaps, the revenues of the Church will be paid into a general fund and

portioned out according to its local need, to be supplemented, if need be, by the contributions of the laity ..... Of one thing I am certain - if the Church does not, or cannot, reform itself ere long, the laity will lose patience and take matters into their own hands."

7.21. It is from this period that the general perception of the rural ministry as being the Church's second eleven, and a backwater suitable for the less energetic and able, began to establish itself. Dr A Jessop, Vicar of Scarning in Norfolk, wrote in 1890:

"When the rector on his induction takes the key of the church, locks himself in and tolls the bell, it is his own passing bell he is ringing. He is shutting himself out from all hope of a future career on earth. He is a man transported for life, to whom there will be no reprieve ... for the day he accepts a country benefice he is a shelved man ... once a country parson, always a country parson."

7.22. The first World War was a crucial period for the Church of England in particular, and for the countryside in general, and it marked a period of abrupt change. It saw the erosion of many social conventions which had previously sustained church attendance, notably 'the English Sunday', and in the village the clergy became aware of the competition of other leisure activities. Archbishop Randall Davidson devoted part of his charge to his clergy at the Diocese of Winchester in 1899 to observing that the bicycle was having a particularly deleterious effect on Sunday church attendance.

7.23. In the last quarter of the nineteenth century the number of clergy continued to rise until it reached a peak of 25,235 in 1901. In 1873 there were 429 parochial clergy in the Hereford Diocese in addition to 20 full time clergy on the cathedral staff. In the Diocese of Norwich in 1880 there were 1,140 priests ministering to 600,000 people. From the turn of the century the number of clergy began to decline and almost every rural area which now comprises a rural deanery has lost approximately one clergyman every 15 years during this century. By 1931 the total number of Anglican clergy had already fallen by over 6,000. For a short time in the late nineteenth century it appeared possible to provide one clergyman for almost every parish, no matter how small, but already by the 1920s it was acknowledged that this policy had to be abandoned and neighbouring parishes linked together under the charge of one clergyman. Pluralities, one of the abuses of the eighteenth century, became again a common feature of rural church life.

7.24. A survey in 1943 of a group of villages in North Oxfordshire undertaken by C S Orwin of the Agricultural Economics Research Institute in Oxford (*Country Planning; A Study of Rural Problems*, Oxford 1949) commented on the isolation, demoralisation and inadequate stipends of the clergy, and the poverty of many villages in North Oxfordshire (which at that time had significant numbers of derelict and unoccupied cottages). The Report's suggestion was in effect the creation of a deanery team ministry with salaries paid out of pooled endowments. It recommended also the use of retired clergy, and arrangements for the laity to be much more heavily involved in parochial work. This far-sighted report anticipated many of the changes that have taken place in the rural church in recent years.

Changes in recent years

7.25 In 1985, reviewing a report of the church in Suffolk, the religious affairs correspondent of *The Times* wrote (7th June 1985): "The Church of England faces extinction in the countryside in the next twenty years ... it is a picture of almost unmitigated hopelessness." The predominant feature of the rural church in recent years has been its adjustment to the decline in the number of clergy. In 1961 there were 15,488 full-time clergy in the Church of England. Leslie Paul, in his report of 1964, predicted that there would be 18,940 clergy in 1971; in fact, there were only 15,223. In the next ten years there was a further sharp reduction of 4,000 clergy to 10,922.

7.26. The decline, however, has been spread unevenly across the country. Leslie Paul pointed out that, at that time, a larger proportion of the clergy worked in rural areas, that whereas there was one Anglican clergyman per thousand of the population in rural areas, there was one per six thousand in urban areas. He pointed out that half the benefices of the Church of England contained only 10% of the population (the rural areas) whilst less than one tenth of the benefices contained one third of the population.

7.27. In 1974 the Church looked for ways to rectify this imbalance between urban and rural areas, and the Sheffield Report of that year suggested a formula for the deployment of clergy which would result in a significant redistribution in favour of urban ministry. The Sheffield Commission took four factors into account: total population; places of worship; size of area; and electoral roll. After testing over 80 variations of a formula which gave different weightings to the four factors, they chose one which clearly placed the greatest emphasis on population, thus:

8 points for total population
3   „   „   places of worship
1   „   „   size of area
3   „   „   electoral roll

This formula was accepted unanimously by the dioceses and the General Synod and thereafter annual target figures of stipendiary clergy were allocated to each diocese based on the agreed formula. Despite minor modifications the system still controls clergy numbers across the country on a diocesan basis. The result has been the significant shift of a number of stipendiary clergy to the urban and suburban areas of England. Furthermore, the formula has served to halt the drift of clergy to dioceses in the southern half of the country.

> **In the Diocese of Hereford between 1956 and 1986 the total number of clergy fell by 43%, but this overall decline masked the fact that rural clergy declined in number by 57% while market town clergy (places with populations over 1,500) actually increased by 36%.**

7.28. The pastoral reorganisation of rural benefices which has taken place to implement the recommendations of Sheffield (the methodology of which is discussed in the following chapter) has resulted in the rapid and widespread development of the multi-parish benefice, the name given to the unit in which parishes are clustered together under the care of a single clergyman. Although simultaneously there have been a variety of experiments in collaborative ministry and non-stipendiary ministry, the multi-parish benefice is the predominant pattern of rural ministry in the Church of England today.

7.29. The present number of clergy stands at approximately 10,500 but the number of ordinations and the age structure of the present clergy suggest that there will be a 10% decline in the next 15 years. There is also evidence to suggest that if present policies continue, this will be translated into a 20% decline in most rural areas.

Chapter 8
Ministry

8.1. The purpose of this chapter is to examine the way that the Church's ministry is pursued in rural areas and the ways in which it has changed in recent years. These changes have been caused partly by changes in the Church itself, and partly by the recent developments in rural society which have been described earlier.

8.2. Within the Church's structure we consider the effect of declining clergy numbers, the growth of multi-parish benefices and the serious questions they are posing for the laity as well as for the clergy. We reflect on new patterns of ministry which are emerging, and the preparation and training which they require.

8.3. Since the Church is working within a rapidly changing rural context, we consider pastoral re-organisation and the need for parishes to relate to a variety of communities which are not necessarily coterminous with villages. We also consider the roles which clergy and laity are being asked to perform within a pluralist rural society and the factors which need to be taken into account in planning.

8.4. The evidence we received during our visits was often apologetic and nostalgic, looking back at the days when there were more clergy in rural areas, and too rarely looking at the strengths of the present and seeing the opportunities they offered. Many of the people we met, equated the Church's ministry with the work of an ordained person. However, it was where we saw a combination of leadership by a parish priest and a growing understanding of personal ministry on the part of the laity that we found the most inspired churches. These have often been quite small, but they have led to our concern that the emphasis which has been placed on the full-time stipendiary clergy has overshadowed every Christian's vocation to discover their own ministry at work, in the community and in the Church.

8.5. It was from this beginning that we decided to reflect on the aims of the Church and how it should achieve its mission through ministry.

Aims of ministry

8.6. What is the Church for? When the Revd Bruce Reed, Director of the Grubb Institute, spoke to the Commission, he asked whether any church could live fully if it had not struggled to answer this question for itself in its own place. A good starting point for this self-questioning is the following definition:-

> "The Church is called to proclaim and prefigure the Kingdom of God. It accomplishes this by announcing the Gospel to the world and by its very existence as the Body of Christ.
> Living in this communion with God, all members of the Church are called to confess their faith and give account of their hope. They are to identify with the joys and sufferings of all people as they seek to witness in caring love. The members of Christ's body are to struggle with the oppressed towards that freedom and dignity promised with the coming of the Kingdom. This mission needs to be carried out in varying political, social and cultural contexts. In order to fulfil its mission faithfully, they will seek relevant forms of witness and service in each situation. In so doing they bring to the world a foretaste of the joy and glory of God's Kingdom."
>
> *(Baptism, Eucharist and Ministry*, page 20, para 4
> WCC Faith & Order Paper No 111, 1982)

The Lambeth Conference of 1988 echoed this statement in its final report:

> "This means that lay people must take hold of their ministerial responsibility for doing their Christian living out in the world. And only when their Church requires of them that they see their sharing of the life of the streets and shops, of wrestling with the land, of feeding, housing and transportation, of business and unemployment, as their Christian vocation of ministry, will they begin to be effective. For then through the Holy Spirit they will bring blessing, forgiveness and the sacrifice of the Lord Jesus for the world."
>
> *(The Truth Shall Make You Free*, page 52, para 106
> Report of the Lambeth Conference 1988)

8.7. We endorse the vision of J Moltmann which inspired Canon John Tiller's *A Strategy for the Church's Mission:*

> "The Church always belongs within the context of the world, whether it likes it or not. Even if the clergy and the laity are only

concerned with themselves and their own internal problems in the Church, the world still has its word to say. If some people don't notice this, it is only because they represent the world's interests themselves, in pious guise. The Church is sure to be most misused politically at the very moment when it wants to be totally 'non-political'. This means that it is quite simply essential for the Church, every minister and every congregation to see themselves as far as possible in context, and to become involved, with all their minds and capacities, in the conditions, powers and potentialities of the society they are living in. But the context is not the text, and we must never allow it to become so. The Church's context is society. But its text is the Gospel of Jesus Christ."

8.8. The evidence presented to us demonstrated the wide variation in how people see the purposes of the ministry of the Church. At one level there has been great concern for the continuance of a local ministry which is primarily for the benefit of a small group within the general population. At another level there has been a vision of the Church as salt and leaven in the world and the local church as a means toward that end rather than as an end in itself. The Church ought to be both a local presence as well as a stimulus to mission in the world, but much of the evidence was weighted towards the former rather than the latter. The Industrial Christian Fellowship, for example, spoke of the needs of people who work within the structures of the world at large, but who feel that their needs are not met by the local church because its emphasis is too parochial.

8.9. It is clear from what has been said earlier in this report that the focus and arena of the Church's work and ministry should be the world and not just the institutional church. This has important implications for the ways in which ministry is understood. Since much of the evidence about the Church was taken from committed church members, it would be easy to conclude that the Church is the arena of God's activity, leaving the world to pick up any crumbs which fall from the Church's table. The Church's internal ministry is much better understood than its missionary task in the world.

We recommend that dioceses should pay particular attention to the need for the Church's mission and ministry to be focused in the world as well as within the Church.

8.10. Although we wish to affirm the parochial structure of the Church of England, and encourage it to respond to the needs of the present day, we are concerned that the Church should not fall into the trap of seeing the maintenance of the parish system as its sole object of mission. The structure must serve the main purposes of the Church and not vice versa.

We recommend that dioceses should affirm the parochial pattern of ministry and regard it as a base which is designed to equip the people of God for their ministry within the world.

8.11. The mission of the Church is the responsibility of the whole people of God. The general aim was summarised by the 1988 Lambeth Conference:

"1. To proclaim the Good News of the Kingdom.

2. To teach, baptize, and nurture new believers.

3. To respond to human need by loving service.

4. To transform unjust structures in society."

Even though the Lambeth Conference considered environmental issues, it is significant that these four headings concentrate on human issues. Mission is not only concerned with the structures of human society, but with the nature of the universe itself. The ecological debate is at heart a theological one and needs to be accepted as such by the Church at large, and not just by those in rural areas or with a particular environmental concern. A fifth aim might be added:

5. To assert the cosmic significance of the Gospel.

8.12. These short statements capture the breadth of the Church's mission and point to the types of ministry which are needed to achieve it. The proclamation of the Gospel, together with the teaching and nurturing of all believers, are essentially 'priestly' tasks. The response to human need is essentially 'pastoral', and the transformation of unjust structures and the assertion of the cosmic significance of the Gospel involve a 'prophetic' role. Yet as soon as one has said this one sees the overlap between the ministries, just as one sees that there is a corporate ministry of the whole body. The gifts of particular lay people may well be employed in some of the 'priestly' tasks, just as some priests will be involved in pastoral work and prophetic roles. Who actually carries out the different kinds of ministry is not as important as the fact that all aspects are represented within the local church. Evidence presented to the Commission confirms the impression of the bishops gathered at the Lambeth Conference that in this country there is a strong emphasis on pastoral work and also on teaching and nurturing the faithful. The proclamation of the Gospel and the transforming of unjust structures within society receive very much less attention, and this has serious implications for the integrity of the

Church's mission. The priestly, pastoral and prophetic aspects of mission are interdependent, and if any one of them is unrepresented within the body then it undermines the whole. Mission is a corporate responsibility shared by the people of God, which includes the ordained.

The role of the priest

8.13. Over-arching much of the detail of ministry in rural areas is the single point that the life of the Church in the countryside has over the generations become sharply focused in the person of the incumbent. Many of those parishes which do not have a resident incumbent, or parishes from which the incumbent has been withdrawn, feel that there is a 'parson-shaped hole' in the centre of their church. In contrast to this feeling there was also a considerable amount of evidence that some of the most self-sufficient and forward-looking parishes were those in which the incumbent did not live. One group of parishes indicated to its parent diocese that it did not want the appointment of a new resident clergyman, but would like access to the services of a clergyman for ten hours per week. This was a particularly interesting example, since the parishes were not just looking for liturgical functions, but for a priest in a consultancy role in teaching, pastoral care and general guidance within the group.

8.14. A number of parishes testified to a common experience that the life of the church was enhanced rather than diminished during a period of vacancy. One churchwarden near Bath said that "we all slowed down again" after the arrival of a new incumbent. There is clear evidence that while rural clergy may be trained to serve a parish they may also unconsciously be restricting its growth and the potentiality of its leadership. During a vacancy congregations can often break out of patterns of deference and dependence, but when a new appointment is made these patterns reassert themselves. This raises some important questions about selection and training and the style of ministry for which clergy are trained.

8.15. Since the second world war the role of the parish priest has been increasingly under question. Many pastoral tasks have been taken over by other professions within an expanded state sector and by new voluntary bodies dealing with social welfare and counselling. It should be noted, however, that many of the workers in these agencies are active lay Christians whose ministry is largely unrecognized by the Church for what it is. Within the community of the Church itself many of the tasks previously done by the clergy are now performed by the laity, with bishops granting authority for preaching, teaching, administering the sacrament, visiting the sick, and burying the dead. With this welcome development of the liturgical and pastoral work of the laity, there has come also a questioning of the role of the ordained ministry.

> **"Within the lifetime of some of the people in this place, the vicar has changed from being the person who distributed money to those who were the chief charge on the community, to now being the chief charge on the community himself!"**

8.16. Various attempts have been made to redefine this role, either theologically or in terms of the practical tasks to be performed. For many rural clergy, the principal problems of their ministry arise from the fact that they find themselves trapped between the realities of modern multi-parish ministry, the traditional expectations of the laity formed possibly as much as two generations ago, and a perception of priesthood which was formed during the period of their own training. In essence, the model of ministry by which many rural clergy operate is inappropriate for the structures in which they are required to work. It has become quite clear that in such benefices the clergy can no longer tackle all the tasks which were carried out by their predecessors with a smaller number of parishes.

8.17. What then is the specific role of the ordained priest? Much of the evidence presented to the Commission still assumed that the priest is the person who should be an exemplary performer of all kinds of ministry, and to be a model of perfection. Whether the expectations are implied or made explicit, they are a recipe for disaster and many clergy have suffered seriously from their attempts to meet them.

8.18. Ordained ministers, like lay people, have their own particular gifts and abilities, so it would not make sense to create a restrictive list of the priest's tasks. Each priest will be able to offer particular skills just as each lay person is able to offer theirs. But the key role of the priest is to bring into focus and enable the total mission and ministry of the Church. The priest should be the one who is trained to hold the breadth of the vision and to share in it with the whole body committed to his charge. This is particularly vital when the corporate nature of mission and ministry has to be worked out in a multi-parish situation, where the priest cannot feasibly be present in all parishes at all times.

8.19. The role of the priest in relation to the parish is:

1. To be aware of the full breadth of the mission of the Church in its priestly, pastoral and prophetic aspects.
2. To share in this vision with the corporate body of the people of God in the parish, coming together in worship.
3. To focus with others on what can and should be done in ministry, using the gifts of all members of the body.

8.20. In practical terms, this points to guiding and enabling people to minister within the broad vision of mission, without falling into the trap of feeling responsible for doing everything themselves. A large part of the priest's task will be reaffirming the vision and helping others to focus on it.

8.21. Other types of ordained and lay ministry will need to be brought into this overall pattern. In some cases, it will be a matter of using skills, abilities and ministries which are already available; in others it will be a question of identifying and calling out what is needed.

8.22. The focal role of the priest at a parish level reflects the role of the bishop, who is the focus of ministry at a diocesan level. Both bishop and parish priest have the responsibility of holding a vision for the Church and sharing it with their people. What is done at a local parish level needs to reflect the vision of the diocese. One diocese gave evidence of the way in which its bishop and diocesan synod had become conscious of the need to respond to the problems of rural homelessness. The synod passed a resolution in support of making glebe land available, within the legal constraints, for charitable housing associations. Parishes were encouraged to identify areas of need and possible building sites, and clergy were part of the practical as well as the theological working through of the overall vision. The same process needs to take place in relation to a series of other issues, not least the practice of extended communion, over which the national episcopal view seems to be very different from local practice.

8.23. There are others who share in this process, but at an intermediate level. The rural dean is a key figure and the deanery lay co-chairman is emerging as a potentially influential role. The work of the rural dean will include support for the clergy, relating to other Christian churches in the area, representing the Church in civic affairs and with other public bodies as well as facilitating relationships with the diocese.

8.24. The rural dean will have a considerable responsibility which will require a person of some experience, personality and competence. In our view this is a position requiring both administrative and pastoral skills, with a good understanding of communications, team building and what is required to relate the Church to the world. In many senses this ministry is episcopal in character, and gifts and skills appropriate to that kind of ministry need to be sought and developed.

8.25. In order to develop a vision of what is required as part of mission and ministry at parish, deanery and diocesan level, the diocese will need to draw on the insights of those whose responsibilities reach beyond narrow ecclesiastical boundaries and embrace area, county and regional concerns. These will include diocesan education teams, social responsibility officers, industrial missioners and others.

8.26. A number of dioceses have appointed rural officers or agricultural chaplains, whose task it is to work across parochial and secular boundaries to help people explore, from a theological point of view, the wider issues which surround the environment, the agricultural industry and the future of rural communities. Some of this will be done with committed church members, but much of it will be with those with no particular church allegiance, but with a shared concern about the issues. The insights from this kind of work need to be taken into account by dioceses in setting their aims in ministry. Evidence from Kent described the way in which chaplaincy work has increasingly become county-based rather than diocesan-based and ecumenical rather than Anglican.

The Hereford diocese and the Hereford & Worcester Rural Community Council sponsored a study of farmers and farm workers displaced from agriculture. No organisation or official department has a list of such people, with the consequence that their needs are unknown. The study, which traced fifty farming families, revealed a disturbing level of stress and a serious inability of caring and advice-giving organisations to reach those in need. It is hoped that the outcome will be an improved system of pastoral care in which church and secular agencies will join.

We recommend that dioceses should affirm and use the insights emerging from the ministry of rural officers and agricultural chaplains in developing a theological understanding and critique of issues which over-arch parish and diocesan organisation.

Training and induction

8.27. Following on from what has been said above, it is clearly essential that clergy who are to work in rural areas should receive the right kind of training to prepare them for present day rural ministry. A century ago most clergy either came from a rural background or had close acquaintance with the circumstances of rural communities. Nowadays the vast majority of clergy come from urban or suburban backgrounds and have little knowledge or first-hand experience of rural life. Theological colleges, which have been subject to the same influences, do not appear to present rural ministry to their ordinands as challenging and exciting.

8.28. As a result, many clergy approach rural ministry with an out-dated understanding of the recent changes which have been taking place in rural society and with an out-moded style of ministry to offer, particularly in large multi-parish benefices. The fact that urban ministry tends to be seen as being the more exciting and demanding sphere of work means that rural experience is often seriously under-rated. Two prospective ordinands from one rural diocese were not thought suitable for training because "they only had experience of rural life". It was suggested to the Commission that many ordinands perceive rural ministry to be second rate or a soft option. Coupled to the fact that there are only a handful of training posts for first curates in rural areas, there is a problem bringing new young blood into rural ministry.

We recommend that dioceses should review their provision of rural first curacies.

8.29. Evidence to the Commission suggests that part of the problem lies in the confusion which exists as to which bodies take responsibility for the different parts of the training and induction process. Ordinands go through a selection and training 'pipeline' which begins with their home diocese, followed by contact with the Advisory Council on the Church's Ministry (ACCM), which is the body charged to advise bishops on selection and training. The ordinand then goes forward to a training course or college before coming back, usually to the home diocese. This can be represented as follows:

DIOCESE - ACCM - COLLEGE/COURSE - DIOCESE

8.30. It is within this pipeline that communication breaks down. Some dioceses seem to expect to have priests ready for all situations rolling off the college production lines and complain that colleges are failing to give comprehensive training. Colleges and training courses have complained that they are hard pressed to complete the basic academic requirements, let alone provide total coverage in pastoral studies together with experience of different pastoral situations in practice. There is also confusion about whether placements and pastoral study experiences are designed to give experience of different kinds of ministry, or whether the primary purpose is to provide an opportunity to try out skills in analysis and theological thinking.

8.31. ACCM sets out its thinking and criteria in a series of occasional papers which either lay down the policies which have been agreed by the bishops and General Synod, or offer advice and guidance on good practice. Occasional Paper 22 *Education for the Church's Ministry* is a good guide to what ACCM feels is required in training for the ordained ministry, and it has been used by the Commission as a basis for what has been said earlier in this chapter about the role of the priest in relation to parochial ministry.

8.32. Traditionally, the full-time stipendiary clergy have been trained in residential theological colleges, where ordinands could be prepared on a quasi-monastic basis. The colleges work on the assumption that their students will go forward on ordination to a single parish benefice and be part of a parish staff, which is what in fact usually happens, since most training parishes are in urban settings. But, as already described, the situation for rural ministry is very different. The multi-parish benefice, comprising up to a dozen parishes or more, presents a different challenge to anything which was known in this country prior to 1970. Most theological college training is not geared to the needs of rural ministry.

8.33. The colleges have countered this criticism by saying that their task is not to prepare students for specific kinds of ministry and that this is the responsibility of dioceses as part of induction into a particular post. The Commission felt that considerable confusion existed around the question of induction and to what extent colleges and courses should be concerned with preparing ordinands for particular types of ministry. The Commission feels that dioceses should recognise as a matter of urgency their responsibility for induction of clergy into new posts and new spheres of ministry. The evidence suggests that some dioceses run their own courses for induction into rural ministry while a number reported that they make use of the courses run by the Arthur Rank Centre at Stoneleigh. The Commission was concerned by the number of dioceses which were extremely vague about their arrangements for induction and seemingly regarded it as a personal option rather than a normal provision.

We recommend that dioceses should recognise their responsibility for induction of clergy into rural ministry and either set up their own courses, link with other dioceses to develop them, or use those which are available nationally.

8.34. Following the publication of *Faith in the City* (The Report of the Archbishop's Commission on Urban Priority Areas (ACUPA) published in 1985) there was a rapid growth in the number of pastoral studies units (PSUs) which were made available for theological students to experience life in Urban Priority Areas. The Commission encountered some ambivalence on the part of colleges and courses as to whether these units were designed to give an insight into particular kinds of ministry, or whether they were opportunities to try out skills in analysis and theological method. The evidence from ACCM and from those who run such units is that the purpose is clearly the latter, though there is inevitably some overlap. Evidence was received on a number of PSUs, including one run jointly by the Carlisle Diocesan Training Institute and Cranmer Hall, Durham. The Revd Ian Cundy wrote: "In common with many other PSUs we have sought not to train people for rural ministry, but to explore the theological issues raised for ministry in this particular context." The Commission wishes to encourage the development of further rural PSUs, but is concerned that dioceses do not confuse them with courses for induction into rural ministry. This is a grey area, since a few people do take part in PSUs in order to explore the possibility of rural ministry for their own future. This is to be encouraged, provided that the original aim of the units is not obscured.

We recommend that dioceses and other bodies should be encouraged to develop rural Pastoral Studies Units as well as supporting and using those which already exist, but may not be well known beyond their immediate area.

8.35. A number of colleges and dioceses co-operate in arranging placements for students so that ministry in various contexts can be experienced. The Commission was unable to estimate how many rural placements are made available each year, but would wish to encourage more. The evidence showed that placements vary widely, and while some are closely linked to the clergy and the congregation and parochial matters, others involve working on farms and exploring the nature of rural society with a range of local people and organisations. One trainee spent a day helping with a milk round and was amazed to discover how many people live outside gathered settlements, even in caravans in the corners of fields.

We recommend that dioceses and colleges should establish further rural placements with the aim of learning about rural society as a whole, as well as the operation of the Church.

8.36. The Commission accepts that there are severe limits on what can be accommodated in syllabuses which are already bursting at the seams, and does not want to put further pressure on the colleges and courses to add yet more. But it was felt that there are three particular ingredients of clergy training which should be given greater emphasis and which are especially relevant to rural ministry. The first is to do with learning a collaborative style of ministry, the second involves expertise in contextual theology, and the third relates to skills in management.

8.37. A collaborative style of ministry may be presented as desirable in any form of ordained ministry, but in the opinion of the Commission it is a fundamental necessity in rural ministry. Clergy need to be skilled in working with others and to recognise that their role involves working with a large number of volunteers. There has been some discussion as to whether the dioceses or the theological colleges and courses should be responsible for developing a style of ministry in ordinands, and some have suggested that this is a question of personal preference or a task for the dioceses. We feel that a collaborative style should be part and parcel of the teaching of any training programme and should influence the style of teaching itself. We are therefore particularly concerned that candidates for stipendiary ministry are still to a very large extent trained separately from candidates for other ministries. Similar reservations were expressed by ACUPA (*Faith in the City*, pages 119-122). If the Commission is right in its opinion that rural ministry increasingly involves bringing together a whole variety of ministries, then it is essential that the people who are responsible for this process at a local level are trained in an appropriate way.

8.38. It appears that theological training is still dominated, particularly in the residential colleges, by the teaching of theology as an academic subject in order to meet the demands of examinations. This was commented on by ACUPA and is echoed by this Commission, which feels that there is little evidence that the colleges have progressed very far in equipping students to develop what ACUPA called "habits of reflection and social awareness such that they can draw creatively on their resources of theology and spirituality in the face of new realities" (*Faith in the City*, page 119). Once again, the Commission recognises the very real pressures on colleges and courses to make sure that academic qualifications or standards are achieved. But there are important questions which have to be faced about the consequences of this for the ministry of the Church, which needs clergy who are skilled in theological reflection which is rooted and grounded in the daily experience of life, and who are able to work with others in developing what is a local and contextual theology. This need is as great for the rural areas as it is for inner cities and this Commission joins with ACUPA in urging that this must be allowed to influence priorities in basic theological training. The task of reviewing the content and style of training lies with ACCM, and it may well be that developments have to be initially tried out on an experimental basis. The Commission is conscious that, if any of its recommendations in this respect are to be carried forward, then ACCM will need the necessary encouragement and funding.

Following similar recommendations by ACUPA, we recommend that ACCM should review its priorities in theological training and development, taking into account the needs of rural ministry in terms of contextual theology, collaborative ministry, and management skills.

We recommend that ACCM should be adequately funded to promote and monitor experiments in theological education.

We recommend that dioceses should review what they offer in terms of theological development in Continuing Ministerial Education (CME) and in lay training.

8.39. We then come to the question of management; a concept which is resented in some clerical circles, but which we believe is crucial in the context of multi-parish benefices. The responsibility for training in the management of multi-parish situations seems to lie most appropriately with dioceses, but the evidence suggests that this has not been widely accepted or understood. Clergy are trained to approach parish ministry on the basis of consensus and mutual agreement, and often find the managing of conflict in face-to-face situations among small numbers of people in different communities among the most difficult and demanding tasks in rural ministry. In urban areas the immediacy and direct nature of these conflicts is to some extent cushioned, whereas in small rural communities they can be inescapable and may envelop the incumbent and his wife and family.

8.40. Good management is difficult to achieve and improvements are constantly being sought throughout secular life - often by Christians in their daily work. It seems to us that the needs of many secular organisations are similar to those of the rural church. We therefore urge bishops and dioceses to discuss the whole question of development training with local secular organisations. Where we have raised this with a number of such bodies, they have confirmed that they would welcome the opportunity to include clergy in courses, feeling that their own representatives would benefit from the clergy experience as well as vice versa.

In Peterborough diocese for over 20 years a lay body, the Centurions, has been in existence to support new initiatives agreed with the bishop. The lay people concerned, not all of whom are members of the Church of England, give support both financially and through their professional expertise. In recent years this has included help with clergy reviews and assessment, training programmes, and a report on industrial mission.

We recommend that dioceses explore the opportunities of working with secular organisations to develop skills in management.

8.41. In the light of what has been said above, it does seem that non-residential training courses are particularly appropriate for the kind of training which is envisaged. Such courses could accommodate students training for different ministries, and could develop the style of ministry and the theological methods which the Commission feels are essential for present day rural ministry. Evidence to support this came from most regional training courses and also from the Aston Scheme. With this in mind, the Commission is very concerned about the proposals in ACCM Occasional Paper 30, *Ordination Training on Courses*, which proposes a number of conditions for such courses, including a limit on the minimum number of students. The Commission received evidence from Cumbria, Durham and the West Midlands which demonstrated that these proposals would seriously disadvantage the most deeply rural areas. As has been seen in the first part of this report, the key rural problems are small numbers, distance and the cost of travel, and the Church must recognise these factors in any proposals for training. We recognise that any recommendation for the development of courses will be seen as a threat to residential colleges, and the Commission has no wish to undermine their position or to under-value their contribution. However, there can be few things which are more important than the provision of appropriate training for those who will play key roles in the development of rural ministry.

We recommend that the role of non-residential training courses should be developed further.

Clergy numbers and deployment

8.42. As we have implied, our deliberations have convinced us that the decline in clergy numbers in rural areas is opening the way to a new and more cohesive vision of the Church's ministry. We believe this to be the work of the Holy Spirit. This has not, however, been achieved without profound and in some cases harrowing effects. We indicated in the previous chapter that the forecast is for a continuing fall in the numbers of full-time stipendiary clergy over the next fifteen years with this being a higher than average decline in the numbers for rural areas, should present deployment policies be pursued. While standing ready to adapt to this decline, we are concerned that there has not been any serious research by ACCM into the causes of this state of affairs: whether these be the perception of the job as it compares with other vocational work, the conditions of employment, financial considerations, methods of preferment, or simply that the Church of England is seen to be increasingly marginal to contemporary secular and spiritual life. There is some evidence emerging of clergy leaving for work outside the Church, but the scale and causes of this need to be examined.

We recommend that research is urgently undertaken to get a clearer view of the causes underlying the reduction in numbers available for the ordained ministry.

8.43. Taking the present position with the predicted numbers for the coming years, how then, within the vision that we offer, should these be allocated? To decide this we needed to examine in detail the working of the Sheffield formula, which continues to dictate the allocation of clergy to dioceses. (See 7.25-29)

8.44. The Commission found, during its visits that, although the formula had been accepted by all dioceses, some had wittingly or unwittingly worked on a different formula of deployment within the diocese by giving certain factors a heavier weighting. We found, for example, that some imposed a maximum number of church buildings or a maximum geographical area per incumbent. This therefore meant that, although they had accepted the national formula for their total diocesan allocation, they found that its application at a local level proved unsatisfactory if an adequate rural ministry was to be maintained. In effect two formulae were being applied: the national one according to Sheffield and a local one according to the perceived pastoral needs and constraints of rural circumstances which did not fit into Sheffield's statistical framework. This was the evidence from several rural dioceses which claimed that their rural ministry was in danger of breaking down if clergy numbers were futher reduced.

8.45. This discovery bore out the argument put to us by the Rural Theology Association (RTA) in its evidence that the Church of England, in its acceptance of the Sheffield formula, had failed to appreciate the rural factors of space and scattered population and seriously underestimated the time required to serve a group of churches.

8.46. The RTA made a further criticism of the formula inasmuch as it failed to address the ecumenical dimension. The calculations underpinning the formula disregarded both the numbers of non-Anglican ministers, principally based in urban situations, and the numbers of adherents of other denominations in urban areas. Both considerations reduce considerably the proportion of the population for which an Anglican clergyman might reasonably be expected to be responsible.

8.47. The Sheffield Report did in fact devote considerable time and space to ecumenical considerations and, in an appendix, effectively conceded one of the above points, namely that if ministers of the other main Christian churches were taken into account then Christian ministerial coverage in urban areas was much heavier than their report assumed. Indeed, had this approach been taken in 1973, it would have led to a flow of clergy from the province of York to that of Canterbury and from the urban to the rural dioceses. This would be even more true today in that the other main Christian denominations have in recent times pursued conscious policies of centring their ministry on towns. The corollary of this is that the Anglican Church in rural areas increasingly embraces people of other denominations with all the implications for styles of worship and questions on the validity of membership and confirmation that this brings. Such considerations bring another dimension and responsibility to rural ministry.

8.48. We found both the RTA's arguments persuasive and, in particular, were left firmly with the impression, from our reading of the Sheffield Report, that the ecumenical approach was rejected because it did not assist those who wanted a more urban Anglican priesthood rather than because it presented insurmountable difficulties. These were inconvenient statistics which argued against the goal that was desired. This is made explicit in a report by the Ministry Co-ordinating Group in 1981, reviewing Sheffield:

> "Present strengths of Anglican and non-Anglican clergy in town and country made it inevitable that any method of ecumenical deployment is bound to result in urban dioceses losing and rural dioceses gaining a number of Anglican clergy, thus reversing the intention of the Sheffield formula."

8.49. Thus, in this later report, ecumenical considerations were again discounted although it was requested that these be given consideration by dioceses when making decisions about pastoral reorganisation. We have received no evidence that this has ever been done in any systematic way; indeed we seriously question how often reports commissioned by the Church of England are reviewed to reassess their messages. We feel that the percentage of the population which professes an active church-going faith is so small, that denominational unilateralism in such matters as developing a deployment strategy is a luxury which the Church in its broadest sense can ill afford. The point needs emphasising that to be Christian is more important than to be Anglican and the Church of England should affirm this in a more determined way. Although there has been little significant formal ecumenical progress since 1973, we would strongly urge all churches to discuss together their ministerial deployment strategies, both nationally and locally. For the Church of England this would mean each diocesan pastoral committee establishing a framework for consultation with the other main denominations represented in its area on all relevant matters of pastoral reorganisation.

8.50. To sum up, we are persuaded that the formula used by the Church for deploying its clergy has unfairly disadvantaged the rural church. However, we believe that the principles which lie behind clergy distribution in urban and rural areas are, in many ways, incompatible, which means that any national formula is bound to be flawed. The geographical problems of the rural church, complicated as they are by the number of worship centres, are difficult to reconcile with a statistical framework based principally on ratios between clergy and the total population. These, together with the ecumenical factors, seem important to us in a way which did not influence Sheffield. Although we argue for a ministry which is not dependent wholly on the ordained members, we feel strongly that present numbers must be held while a stronger lay ministry is trained and developed. This will mean an adjustment to the Sheffield formula in the short term with clergy losses coming from the urban and suburban areas.

8.51. The possible effects of new approaches to ministry which the Commission has seen and would wish to encourage and of more creative ecumenical cooperation, would enable future reductions in numbers to be applied more evenly across the board.

We recommend that dioceses review their pastoral reorganisation proposals with the other main Christian denominations.

We recommend that the General Synod reviews the Sheffield formula to protect the number of clergy in rural areas while new schemes for local and lay ministry are developed.

Pastoral reorganisation

8.52. A mixture of declining clergy numbers and the effects of the redistribution as a result of the Sheffield formula has led to the multi-parish benefice, where a number of parishes are grouped together under the care of a single incumbent. This is the usual pattern of rural ministry in the English countryside today. It has occurred through circumstances rather than as a result of a new understanding of the needs of ministry followed by systematic planning. No new theology has prompted it; the stipendiary clergy have not been trained for it, and the laity have been suspicious of it, seeing yet a further attack on the integrity of their rural community. The Bishop of Grantham echoes the feelings of many when he writes:-

"Every parish is different.....Just as each person has his or her own history with God, so' too does each parish. When pastoral reorganisation began, that factor was not, I believe, acknowledged or taken into account."

8.53. While some dioceses have given careful attention to the criteria for pastoral planning, in others parishes have been joined together with little rationale. Often new benefices have been formed when convenient vacancies have occurred and parishes have been bundled together without proper planning. Some consultation will have taken place, but too often this has been through offering a solution for comment rather than by involving local churches in a broad-based, open-minded consultation. The parishes may have been told that much will be the same, but it has not been. There is a lack of awareness among church leaders of the subtleties of rural society and the way it differs from urban situations. The result is that many still feel bitter about how pastoral reorganisation has been handled - and with some justification. We encountered some deeply held views reflecting a desperation close to anger on the part of some disaffected laity.

8.54. The fundamental problem has been the starting point from which much pastoral planning has begun. The original impetus which set off the first stage of parish amalgamations was the shortage of stipendiary clergy, and consequently dioceses originally began putting parishes together on a clergy-orientated basis. Most dioceses began by using a rough rule of thumb to share stipendiary clergy out over the population. The evidence presented to the Commission indicates in the majority of dioceses that ratios for most rural clergy varied between one to 1,500 people and one to 3,000. Other factors began to be incorporated and the dioceses of Norwich and Southwell among others gave evidence of using social indicators in pastoral planning. The aim throughout has been the same, namely to find a fair and acceptable way of spreading a smaller number of stipendiary clergy more evenly.

8.55. A stage of more sophisticated pastoral planning is under way, but only in a limited number of dioceses. The Diocese of Liverpool, to choose a more urban example, gave evidence of its recent re-organisation which was primarily concerned with creating a new deanery pattern. The diocese established a set of criteria which included the need to have units which:-

1) Provide proper pastoral care for clergy and licensed lay workers.

2) Are viable in terms of synodical structure.

3) Are coherent geographical areas.

4) Take account of co-operation with other churches.

5) Relate to civic boundaries.

The Pastoral Measure 1983 lays down that diocesan pastoral committees shall pay particular attention to "the traditions, needs and characteristics of individual parishes" and adds that sociological factors, the "make-up" of congregations, and differences in forms of churchmanship need to be assessed and balanced. The Code of Recommended Practice advises pastoral committees to be in regular informal contact with local planning authorities, with the object mainly of spotting where new housing developments are likely to be. In the early 1980s this was a step forward in laying down criteria for pastoral planning, but it is now time for new guidelines to be worked out. This is particularly important for rural areas in which communities have become far more complex and are not necessarily coterminous with parishes or villages.

8.56. The Commission was concerned that the presence of other denominations did not figure more prominently in diocesan planning. Evidence from other Churches which are largely withdrawing from rural areas suggests that wider consultation would be both helpful and appreciated.

8.57. A large amount of material is available to help dioceses in their planning. County structure plans and the proposals of health authorities and education authorities are available as background information. Sometimes, for example, the building of new roads, with their dramatic effect on local communications, may need to be brought into the picture.

8.58. However, even when an outline pastoral plan becomes clear, there is still the question of the internal structure of multi-parish benefices. There may be little to be gained by clustering parishes together if the new incumbent has to manage a large number of individual PCCs. The Ripon Diocese gave evidence of its attempts to resolve this problem as a matter of policy by uniting parishes within the area of a benefice so that there was only one PCC for the whole benefice, although individual churches continued to have their own church councils. This went some way towards solving the problems of what had been very small parishes which frequently expressed frustration at having to cope with all the legal trappings required of a parish, but with very few people to shoulder the burden. The Ripon Pastoral Committee argued its case on theological as well as pastoral grounds, and maintained that a united parish gave an added element of security. As the Archdeacon of Richmond commented, "it's very difficult to chip bits off a united parish!"

8.59. The rural situation differs from the urban one in that the number of parishes involved in any one piece of reorganisation may be so large that dioceses may have to wait many years for the necessary vacancies to occur, and evidence was given of schemes which had taken over twenty years to complete. Reorganisation is often a slow process which requires much patience. Evidence given to us at Market Bosworth, among other places, described the slow and demanding process of bringing parishes together, which requires vision as well as patience and persuasion. The incumbent, Canon John Seymour, felt that the trust and sense of unity which had developed depended in part on the fact that he had been there for ten years, and in part on the increasing lay participation in the tasks required for the benefice to grow in mission. This is illustrated in his activity chart entitled *The Care of all the Churches*. (See Appendix I)

8.60. The Church of England faces two particular problems in relation to its structure which other organisations do not face. The first is private patronage, often complex in rural benefices, which can make pastoral planning extraordinarily difficult. The Patronage (Benefices) Measure 1986 has eased some problems but created others. In its attempt to give a more effective voice to lay parish representatives, it allows the appointment of a particular priest to be effectively vetoed by one representative of any one parish. Although such a blocking move can only be exercised for a limited period before patronage passes to the Archbishop, it can be effective in preventing the appointment of someone who might introduce change. In addition, evidence suggests that the new procedures are proving cumbersome and that appointments are taking longer than before. It is difficult to believe that those who framed the legislation ever seriously considered what it would entail for large multi-parish benefices. In certain circumstances the required meetings may involve over 70 people and the periods of time allowed for arranging meetings may be adequate in an urban setting, but raise considerable problems for multiple small rural parishes.

We recommend that the operation of the Patronage (Benefices) Measure 1986, particularly in rural areas, be reviewed.

8.61. The second problem is the parson's freehold, which legally entitles an incumbent to remain in his current post for the remainder of his working life, and can be a serious inhibition to effective pastoral planning in the long or short term. Because of this, much of what passes for pastoral strategy is often the reactive management of situations as they arise, since diocesan pastoral committees are unable to plan ahead with any certainty. The Pastoral Measures have established the principle of licences for terms of years for Team Rectors and Team Vicars and the evidence suggests that these are working well. Many previous reports have questioned the principle of the parson's freehold.

We recommend that the parson's freehold system should be re-examined and a method of time-limited contractual employment be explored.

8.62. A particular plea was made in the Lichfield Diocese that schemes should not be formalised too quickly and that flexibility and time should be available to worshipping communities to discover how they might relate to one another. This highlighted the fact that judgements about the grouping of parishes have to be made against the background of several different factors which include history, social factors, geography and church life. In the light of its travels to almost every diocese in England, the Commission did not find any schemes which suggested a blueprint which would be applicable across the country. In fact, the reverse was the case and there was a strong feeling that strength lies in the diversity, particularly if it means that all the background and local factors are being taken into account. The rural context itself varies enormously across England and requires different responses in different places. Added to this, dioceses have developed varied patterns of ministry which will be described in the next section and which defy a simple summary. The Commission encourages dioceses to continue with their exploration, but is concerned that communication between dioceses should be improved and that experience should be brought together and shared on a national basis.

We recommend greater collaboration between dioceses in sharing their experience of pastoral planning and see some national co-ordination of this as being essential.

8.63. There is always a danger that a review of structures will be seen to be an end in itself. It is crucial that this review is prefaced by probing the purpose of the Church in the diocese, its vision and how it intends to progress towards it. In other words, a diocesan strategy needs to be articulated in terms of faith and the Gospel and shared with the parishes.

8.64. In dioceses and parishes, clear aims and strategies need to be worked out. Positive aims need to be identified, assessed and adopted as priorities, rather than making do with inherited corporate cultures which may be stultifying. Thus, in drawing up strategies and plans, the ultimate mission and purpose of the Church must be in the forefront of thinking.

We recommend that dioceses should draw up a statement of aims which can be shared with parishes as part of corporate pastoral planning.

The rural deanery

8.65. Having felt that the parish would be our principal focal point, with the diocese a second, we have become increasingly aware of the gap between the two. The principal lines of communication are essentially between bishop and incumbent on one hand, and diocesan boards and committees with parishes on the other. The evidence showed that the role of any intervening structure between benefice and diocese needs to be carefully worked out if it is to be effective. In this category, the deanery and the office of rural dean have become incorporated into the synodical structure, but their roles have frequently not been explored in practical terms, with the result that the deanery structure in some dioceses has become more of a burden than a means of support. Although we saw that deaneries appeared to be irrelevant for many parishes, we also saw good examples of the way in which they can give parishes both support and a wider vision.

8.66. The deanery is the unit which is capable of linking the benefice with the diocese and the wider church as well as being the means for parishes to relate more effectively to the rural questions within their own area. A single rural parish cannot normally build the necessary network of support which individual parishioners may need, but a deanery can provide a forum in which parishes can share their concerns and seek solutions. The Commission was grateful for the information supplied by organisations such as Parish and People, Partners, and Administry, all of which produce excellent supporting material for deanery synods and provide communication links across the country so that synods can learn from each other. The evidence showed that some deaneries have produced directories of members who will help or advise on certain subjects; they have enabled parishes to share their problems and they have supported deanery projects ranging from local youth work to overseas community development. This potential for supporting and enabling parishes needs to be used more effectively, and we commend those dioceses which are reviewing deanery boundaries to give careful thought to their aims and criteria. This seems to the Commission to be another area in which communication between dioceses is essential, since no one particular scheme suggested itself as a blueprint. The dioceses of Ripon and Liverpool both gave evidence of extensive deanery re-organisation from which other dioceses should be able to learn. Ripon reduced the number of deaneries and made their units larger, while Liverpool increased the number of deaneries using the criteria already quoted in 8.55. It is clearly not an easy task to create deaneries which possess a sense of cohesion and relate effectively to synodical as well as secular structures, but failure to make the effort will result in deaneries which serve neither the Church nor the world.

In the Ripon diocese the Bishop's Council has been restructured to include all rural deans and lay co-chairmen of deanery synods. In this way, the synodical structure, the deanery organisation and the diocesan structure have been brought together.

8.67. Of all the activities of a deanery it is the deanery synod which has attracted most criticism. Evidence from many representatives complained that it was little more than a talking shop, and that it is ineffective as an executive body. The evidence presented to the Commission supports the view that the effectiveness of synods is directly related to the responsibility and authority which they are given. Deaneries themselves can give authority to their synods by agreeing that, in certain instances, they will act on a deanery basis and in the name of the constituent parishes. In this way, a deanery can relate directly to health or education authorities as well as making representation to the diocese on matters of deanery concern. Dioceses can also give authority to deaneries, and this has been seen to be particularly effective where they have the responsibility for allocating diocesan quota to parishes and where they are fully involved in pastoral organisation. Some dioceses were examining the possibility of specialist ministries such as youth work being anchored at deanery level, and some felt that lay and clergy training were both more effective at a deanery rather than a parish or diocesan level. Both pastoral reorganisation and training have ecumenical implications, and these contacts are more likely to emerge satisfactorily at deanery level.

8.68. In the evidence given to us it seemed clear that deanery synods often had insufficient work and responsibility to operate as effective bodies. If this continues they are likely to wither and the system will weaken further. We strongly urge dioceses to pass decision making to a more local level on both quotas and pastoral reorganisation, and we urge deaneries to develop their networks and contacts with other bodies in furthering the needs of local communities and the area as a whole. (See 12.80 and subsequent paragraphs.)

We recommend that dioceses review the working of their rural deaneries, the tasks given to them, and the selection, support and training of rural deans (see also 8.97 and 8.98).

Patterns of ministry

8.69. It is interesting to note that many of the experiments in ministry have first been attempted in rural areas and they have then been adopted elsewhere. In 1949 the first collaborative ministry in a recognisably modern form was established in rural Lincolnshire, involving twelve small parishes with a total population of 1,100 in approximately 75 square miles. These parishes, previously served by six elderly clergy, were welded together to form a single group served by a rector and two assistants. In 1961 nine parishes in West Norfolk were formed into the Hilborough group. In the next ten years 17 groups were established in Norfolk and by 1970, when Bishop Launcelot Fleming retired, approximately a third of the parishes and a third of the clergy in that diocese were involved in this pattern of ministry. In operation these groups varied considerably as did their nomenclature. However, each group sought to provide for a wide area a pastoral ministry which combined on the spot pastoral care with centralised planning of services and other activities such as youth and children's work, adult education and confirmation classes. These ministries, which pre-dated the Pastoral Measure 1968, were based on the availability of manpower and relatively cheap transport costs. A number of these group ministries still continue, though with reduced manpower. However, the Commission has been aware during its visits that this style of ministry is not widely regarded as providing a pattern for the future. It is sad to record that, whilst many group ministries flourished under their initial leadership, it appears to have been difficult to maintain the same momentum and vision into a second and third generation. Other dioceses, notably Salisbury, Hereford and Exeter have taken this process much further, with Salisbury in 1988 having 15% of benefices as teams and 18% in groups. While evidence at ground level suggests relationship difficulties, it would be helpful if further research were conducted to establish how successful these systems are in terms of ministry and mission. We acknowledge the valuable report on *Team and Group Ministries* by the Ministry Co-ordinating Group, published in 1985 (GS 660), but we believe further research is needed, particularly relating to teamwork in rural areas.

We recommend that research is carried out into the effectiveness of rural groups and teams and into other patterns of collaborative ministry in the countryside.

8.70. Much of the evidence from clergy has concentrated on the problems of reconciling the expectations of villagers which were formed in the days of one clergyman to one church and parish, with the realities of the present situation. Many clergy find that they are effectively asked to be the individual vicar of four or more separate communities that often have little inter-relationship. The central problem in most multi-parish benefices is the tension between the demand of people in the constituent parishes that the fullness of church life should be available in each parish and the time constraints that this places upon a clergyman which encourage him to centralise planning and programmes within the benefice. The Commission met one clergyman who participated one year in 34 harvest occasions within a single large benefice.

8.71. An inevitable consequence is that clergy are less able to be involved in the wider community activities to which their predecessors made such notable contributions, and this is borne out by the RCP statistics detailed in paragraph 11.29. This is almost universally regretted, and many clergy themselves felt that they had become as one said "a chaplain to a string of congregations". Conversely there is much frustration in rural villages that the clergy are being constrained by the time spent servicing the congregations to the neglect of the needs of the wider community.

8.72. The Church's realisation of this situation has given urgency to the search for those who could strengthen the ministry of the Church in rural areas. The Bishops' Regulations in 1970 established auxiliary pastoral ministry which it was hoped would supplement the contracting number of stipendiary clergy in urban and rural areas. The number of auxiliary pastoral ministers (now called non-stipendiary ministers) who have been recruited from rural areas has been small. In fact, most of those who now work in rural areas have moved there from the towns, and are people with an essentially urban background.

8.73. The original thrust for the development of this ministry occurred for a number of reasons. For some it was an attempt to provide more ordained priests at a time when clergy numbers were falling. For others it was a conscious attempt to recruit into the priesthood from those parts of society which had produced few priests in the past. Yet others wished to encourage an Anglican equivalent of the French worker-priest. The experience of non-stipendiary ministry in rural areas has been varied, with some notable examples of faithful and imaginative local service by those who have been ordained under this scheme. The experiment has been particularly successful in the Diocese of Chester, where NSMs are made priests-in-charge of rural benefices and are permitted to occupy the benefice house. The Commission was persuaded that there was further scope for extending this experiment in other dioceses.

8.74. In recent years a number of dioceses (particularly Lincoln) have initiated or are at the final stages of discussing, a scheme for the recruitment of priests to work in a local area (variously called Local Ordained Ministers or Local Non-Stipendiary Ministers). The evidence presented to the Commission indicates that there is a wide variety of views about local ordained ministry and that it lies at the intersection of a range of theological and practical considerations regarding the ministry and the nature of the Church. In essence, the call to such ministry is seen as coming from the local congregation, with the people concerned being approached in a number of different ways rather than volunteering themselves. The candidate is trained in a way which takes greater account of the local context and his/her ministry will be exercised only in a restricted area.

8.75. In effect, there are four main streams to contemporary pastoral strategy in rural areas. It should be noted that these do not occur in isolation, but in varying degrees of combination.

(a) There are many who believe that the need in the countryside is for more *stipendiary clergy* and that the Church should make this its principal effort. The evidence of the RCP indicates that many parishioners would prefer a full-time stipendiary minister looking after a cluster of parishes, even if that minister lived at some distance, to a part-time minister living in the parish. There is some evidence that in certain areas an increased number of stipendiary clergy are being deployed in rural areas as dioceses acknowledge that the withdrawal of clergy in the 1970s/80s proceeded too far, and too fast.

(b) There are in some places strong advocates for the widespread recruitment of *non-stipendiary ministers* (NSMs), trained to the same standard as stipendiary clergy, who satisfy the requirements for some degree of localness and yet are clearly within the traditional Catholic ordering of the priesthood. NSMs are often found in a situation where there is a ministry team of clergy and lay people, who together serve the needs of the local churches. However, the distribution of NSMs is such that they occur principally in the larger market town parishes.

(c) A significantly different view is that of those who advocate a pattern of church life based on *local ordained ministers* (LOMs). Whilst some see LOMs working within a team, for others the main emphasis is that each local community should specifically have its own ordained minister. The onus would be upon the community finding a suitable person and encouraging him to offer himself for ordination, after which his ministry would be limited by licence to the communities from which he came. This pattern has been very successful in some overseas dioceses, but there is some concern about the degree to which this would encourage the growth of congregationalism, and continuing reliance on one person to 'do it all'.

(d) The fourth approach advocates the widespread deployment of *lay ministers* within ministerial teams who share with the ordained clergy the ministerial tasks of the Church. Such a view sees the corporate priesthood of the Church conferred by baptism as effected by a group of lay people within a parish, supported by the stipendiary clergy.

8.76. The Commission was unable to estimate to what extent patterns of ministry are determined by attempts to meet the demands of a eucharistic pattern of worship. It has been suggested in some quarters that greater use could be made of retired clergy. To base a strategy for ministry on the retired is a recipe for further decline, despite the positive contribution that some retired clergy make. In the model for collaborative ministry which we are promoting, the retired clergy may have a role if the incumbent and PCC wish it so. There has, however, been some evidence that retired clergy may inhibit the development of lay ministry. A useful way of involving them may be as a licensed curate so that both bishop and incumbent retain the necessary authority. We note that in many areas, high house prices make it less likely that clergy will be able to afford to retire into villages, and in the spirit of preferring someone local to lead worship, it would be better for retired clergy to find a ministry (if they want one) in their own locality. This raises questions about the Church's ability to maintain the cycle of communion services, which is discussed in the next chapter.

8.77. The Commission was impressed by the variety of patterns of ministry and the extent of new thinking in many rural areas. It wishes to encourage this varied exploration, but is concerned that it should be monitored and that dioceses should be able to share openly what they have learned, both in their successes and their failures.

8.78. A number of these approaches have interesting echoes in the writings of the Anglican missionary, Roland Allen, whose books written over 50 years ago advocated a system of local ministry and leadership, which has been more influential in the Episcopal Church of the USA than it has been in his own country. More recently Canon John Tiller has built a vision for future ministry around teams of both clergy and laity. The Commission feels that Tiller's ideas need continuing study and application: there is great experience and insight in much of his Report which has obvious relevance for the contemporary rural Church.

8.79. The multi-parish benefice is a fact of life for the time being in rural areas, whether it is staffed in practice by a sole incumbent or by an extensive ministry team of one kind or another. A key problem for clergy is the sense of professional isolation, since rural clergy can be so many miles apart, unless encouragement is received through ministry teams and chapters.

8.80. Some dioceses have tried to solve this problem of isolation by forming team ministries based on market towns. The Bishop of Sherborne gave evidence which supported the idea of following a minster pattern in which clergy would live in or close to a focal market town and would minister to the town and its hinterland. The need for a focal person in each parish would be provided by a locally ordained diaconate. The Bishop of Chelmsford's Commission on Diocesan

Strategy (1988) suggested the possibility of establishing a minster church tradition rather than a parish church tradition and so building on church centres already noted for their strength and possibly making them focal centres of rural deaneries.

8.81. There seem to be two points at issue: firstly the mutual support of the clergy and secondly the sense of belonging, or alienation, felt by the rural parishes. The minster pattern can work well in providing mutual support for the clergy, but tends to make rural parishes feel marginalised. The alternative of having a team member living away from the centre in rural parts has the opposite advantages and disadvantages. As the stipendiary clergy become fewer on the ground, it is important that priority is given to the mutual support of the clergy, but the Commission is concerned that this might mean the further withdrawal of stipendiary clergy from residence in genuinely rural locations. Most schemes which have been put to the Commission would meet this concern by proposing that each parish would have its own focal person in the form of a lay leader or locally ordained deacon or priest.

8.82. The Commission recognises the force of such arguments, but is concerned about the proliferation of further ordained ministers. It seems clear that the future lies in a collaborative approach which provides mutual support for the ministers as well as enabling all to feel part of something bigger. The key point which remains unresolved is the best way of enabling parishes to develop a local focus. The future seems to lie in a variety of ministerial teams. The Commission has seen a wide range, stretching from heavily clerical to almost entirely lay. It seems right that experiments should continue which relate to local needs and perceptions of individual situations. But there does need to be more effective communication in sharing what is going on, together with monitoring, assessment and co-ordination of ideas.

We recommend that dioceses should continue to experiment with different patterns of ministry, but that there needs to be some centralised monitoring and assessment of what is being done and more openness about what is actually taking place. The new Board for Ministry should be responsible for this.

Lay ministry

8.83. At first sight lay ministry would not appear to be a specifically rural concern and might be assumed to be the same whether the context is urban or rural. However, the role of the laity in recent years has often been understood in the context of a declining number of clergy, and the greatest reduction has been in the rural rather than the urban church. The result has been that the lay role has been frequently conceived in terms of filling the gaps left by the clergy shortage. This has produced some imaginative and far-reaching schemes, but has left an uncertainty about the nature of lay ministry for those who are not trained or commissioned to carry out specified tasks in the parish.

8.84. The Commission identifies three distinct but related spheres of ministry for the laity:-

(a) The first is within the institutional life of the Church. It is with this type of ministry that most existing lay skills are concerned.

(b) The second area is the ministry exercised by laity within the community. This is often unrelated to church activities and could be in the form of parish councillors, school governors, running meals-on-wheels, etc.

(c) The third, which we believe is the primary and normative ministry of the laity, is exercised in the world of work, which includes not only paid employment but also the roles exercised by those whose major concern is the creation and maintenance of the home.

It is not within the scope of this Commission to be able to develop this concept of ministry in detail, but it forms the necessary background to our understanding of the ministry of the whole Church and the role of the clergy. This ministry may be exercised by individuals or by organised groups such as the Mothers Union.

8.85. Lay ministry should not be conceived as a series of domestic functions concerned primarily with compensating for the loss of ordained clergy, nor should the Church forget that, although the parish structure is a vital vehicle for its mission, it is not the sole or even the primary sphere of work. There are issues and concerns which are of fundamental importance to rural areas and rural people, which cannot be addressed solely on a parish basis.

8.86. Much consideration has been given by dioceses to the development of new lay ministry teams, and to the training and commissioning of individual people in pastoral and liturgical skills. Less attention seems to have been given to the lay ministry teams which already exist in every parish in the form of churchwardens, treasurers, PCC secretaries and other parish officers. The Commission was concerned that such officers were seldom considered to be a ministry team, although individual officers frequently played a key role in the life of a parish. Churchwardens in particular are required to lead worship under certain circumstances and most officers also exercise some kind of pastoral ministry. Evidence from the Salop Archdeaconry of Lichfield diocese demonstrated what can be done through training days which involve parish officers and clergy and which set the duties of such officers in the context of the whole mission of the Church. It has already been noted that the parish officers of small rural parishes carry a proportionately greater responsibility than most of their urban counterparts. In many cases the responsibility devolves effectively onto as few as half a dozen people, and yet the financial and organisational demands are frequently no less than would be carried by a far greater number of people in an urban or suburban parish supported by a resident incumbent.

8.87. The Commission feels that much more attention and support should be given to elected parish officers, and that they should be considered first and foremost as part of a local ministerial team.

We recommend that dioceses and parochial clergy should be more aware of the part played by the elected parish officers and should see them as potentially part of the local ministry team and recognise this in training plans and programmes.

Readers

8.88. Readers were originally introduced to preside at Mattins and Evensong and to offer a teaching and preaching ministry. The Commission received a considerable amount of evidence from individual Readers and the Central Readers' Conference, and it seems that there are valiant efforts being made to maintain the tradition. Many Readers have a bi-focal role which is partly focused in an active ministry within their own home parish, but equally in a kind of roving ministry filling in gaps. Whether such a split ministry proves satisfactory depends on the way in which Readers are treated and organised. At worst the Reader may be seen as a gap-filling dogsbody, while at best the Reader is valued as a member of a local ministry team. The problem seems to be that the original reasons for introducing Readers have largely disappeared, and a number of other authorised ministries have been developed in recent years which cut across the Reader's role. The result is that in some places the Reader is not necessarily assumed to be part of the local ministry team; for instance in the Diocese of Lincoln a Reader's licence is revoked the day before being commissioned into a Lay Ministry Team. Other dioceses are exploring the possibilities of the permanent diaconate and whether would-be Readers should be ordained as deacons.

8.89. The Commission is conscious of the valuable service which is being offered by Readers, but that in rural areas they are often not integrated into local parish ministry teams. There are signs that Reader training will become less centralised and may be more closely linked with local and regional ministerial training courses which are also training people for other ministries including full-time stipendiary priests. The Commission encourages this development as a means towards the proper integration of Readers into local ministry; it is likely that their role will change and this needs to be acknowledged locally. This integration is essential if the wealth of ability and dedication represented by the ministry of Readers is to be fully realised.

We recommend that dioceses should work towards the incorporation of Readers into local ministry teams and recognise the Readers' needs of affirmation and support.

8.90. Lay ministry teams have been established in a number of dioceses, but Lincoln's are amongst the most developed. In that diocese names are put forward by a PCC and are then checked out by the incumbent before formal nominations are made. The local bishop is usually much involved at this stage helping the benefice to understand what is happening and to guide it. The same process is used to nominate potential local non-stipendiary ministers (LNSMs) and at the time of the Commission's visit 16 people were being trained for LNSM out of 120 on the basic diocesan course. The scheme is specifically not designed to prop up the parish system, but in practice the team members are trained in pastoral and liturgical skills, which contribute greatly to the maintenance of parish life. The Commission was impressed by the scale of the Lincoln exercises and the contribution which lay ministry teams are clearly making. However, there was some concern that lay ministry might be perceived as being solely pastoral and liturgical and that diocesan training schemes may not be helping lay people to make full use of their experience in assisting other people to grow in ministry in the world at large. This is not intended as a criticism of Lincoln, but rather a question to the Church about its general perceptions of lay ministry. The Commission applauds the work being done in Lincoln and feels that the Church needs to pay more attention to the development of lay ministry both within the parish and in the world.

It is a matter of concern to the Commission that no one Board in the General Synod structure has been given specific responsibility for the oversight of lay ministry.

We recommend that in affirming its commitment to training for lay ministry the General Synod should clarify where within its new board structures responsibility for lay training will lie.

We recommend that dioceses should review their aims in training for lay ministry and where responsibility for such training lies within their own structures.

Support for clergy and their families

8.91. At one level there is little difference between the situation faced by clergy families and that faced by many other families in the countryside. The higher cost of living and the shortage of services are common to all, though, as we have seen earlier in the report, some are affected to a greater extent than others. However, clergy families can be caught between two stools. On the one hand they probably enjoy a reasonably high standard of accommodation without the worries of maintenance, but on the other hand they face the limitations imposed by the lack of local services and protected by only a modest level of income. In addition, clergy families are often expected to live as their predecessors did when areas of responsibility were smaller and incomes were relatively better. The predicament can be characterised as a tension between high expectations and limited resources.

8.92. It makes an enormous difference if the clergy spouse is in paid employment, since this not only adds to the family income, but also provides a separate role outside the parish. This is more significant for wives of clergy since they are usually expected to play a particular parish role. The RCP found that 71% of rural church people felt that clergy wives have or should have a significant supportive role to play in the parish. Even in the general population the survey found that 56% of people felt the same. Perhaps more surprising was the survey of clergy themselves which found that although a significant number were keen not to assign a role to their spouses, a greater number did expect or prescribe certain roles. The dominant theme was that clergy wives should have a background, supportive or 'wifely' role. There is less evidence of what is expected of clergy husbands, though one woman deacon told us that she was asked why her husband should join her in the vicarage rather than provide her with her own home!

8.93. Evidence suggests that clergy wives in rural parishes may be particularly vulnerable. Some younger clergy wives have been taken by surprise at the level of personal hostility which can be directed towards them when their husbands pursue an unpopular course of action. On the other hand, wives may be approached by people with problems who want to talk to a woman. This can be a very positive role for those who are happy to accept it, but it puts great strain on those who feel unable to respond, or who do not want to be used as an alternative to their husbands.

8.94. The same general points could be made in relation to all clergy, but the point about rural ministry is that clergy and their spouses have a much higher profile. Single clergy, particularly men, may feel that their sexuality is under question and some have given evidence that they have been asked specific questions on the subject when being interviewed for a post by parish representatives.

8.95. In the same way that lack of rural public transport afflicts other families, so it affects clergy families which have only one car. The suggestion that married rural clergy may need two cars has been met with derision in some quarters, but the fact remains that multi-parish situations require mobility and the lack of transport may impose severe limitations. A significant number of clergy say that they can only remain in rural ministry up to the point at which their children reach secondary school age, when they need greater flexibility of movement to cope with extra curricular and other activities. The problem is more serious in the remoter rural areas and seriously affects the availability for rural ministry of clergy with teenage families.

8.96. Dioceses vary greatly in the support which they provide for families and spouses and the degree to which preparation is available for those coming to a rural area for the first time. Most wives we met had had no preparation at all, but would have welcomed it. A number of bishop's wives have made a particular point of caring for clergy wives and often rural deans make this a high priority in their deaneries. Many dioceses produce handbooks which are aimed either at families or wives, and which give information on most things from housing, expenses and sources of help, to practical advice if the husband dies in office. The quality and coverage of these handbooks varies and much of the basic information is common to all and indicates that much could be gained by collaboration across the country. The Commission did not see any handbook which covered specifically rural matters, although at least one urban diocese provided detailed advice on dealing with vagrants, including telephone numbers for local advice and day centres. Some handbooks appeared to be thinly disguised parsonage house regulations and yet were aimed at wives. We discuss in Chapter 12 some problems related to the parsonage. The variety of publications illustrates the way in which support for families can become muddled with matters which are more akin to conditions of employment. Obviously there is overlap, but wives in particular are often treated by implication as being adjuncts to their husband's job rather than people in their own right. It is sometimes assumed that a wife's commitment to her husband and family, which is freely given and frequently makes a difficult job possible, also automatically extends to commitment to the Church.

8.97. The clergy chapter has probably been the group which has been most often cited as providing the best support for clergy. Here clergy have drawn strength from each other by meeting for prayer, study and general support. It is a point at which stress can be detected, initiatives considered and morale encouraged. We cannot over-emphasise how important this is felt to be for clergy with multi-parish benefices, but the size of chapters can be problematic. There was a plea during the visit to Gloucester diocese that chapters should be no bigger than the number who can sit conveniently round a table for a meal. Visits to other dioceses have suggested that larger chapters can be valuable if they provide a good mix of skills, experience and churchmanship, but much rests on the way in which individual members get together and on the leadership of the rural dean. Once again, the Commission is persuaded that there is much to be said for the variety which exists in practice, provided that chapters are aware of the importance of their role and that they receive proper support and encouragement from the archdeacon and diocese.

8.98. The Commission received evidence from rural deans up and down the country that the proper responsibility for a deanery was impossible with a full-time parochial post. Few wanted to surrender their parochial responsibility and therefore felt that the job they were doing as rural dean was inadequate, often failing to create the vision and give the leadership which they felt was necessary. From the evidence, we conclude that the support they need is as follows. First, the support of the bishop and archdeacon, with whom the rural dean will work closely, is necessary in order to obtain a clear view of his role and that of the deanery, to make sure that he receives whatever training he needs, and to support him through a regular review of his ministry.

Secondly, it must be recognised by all that the rural dean will not be able to run his own benefice as before, and therefore it is desirable either that a small benefice should be identified as the deanery benefice, or that an assistant curate should be allocated to the rural dean's benefice during his occupancy of the office. It is possible that in a benefice with well-organised lay pastors and support, a lay team could fill this role. But the importance of well-defined support cannot be exaggerated.

Assessments and reviews

8.99. Most dioceses have developed some kind of assessment programme through which clergy can review their progress in ministry and set objectives for the future. Many systems are in an early stage of development and some of the more complicated seem to have hit problems. ACUPA noted that clergy exhaustion was twice as serious in UPAs than in other areas of ministry, but that otherwise clergy in all types of ministry need similar kinds of support. ACUPA was especially concerned by the number of clergy who had not had a 'personal talk' in the previous twelve months with someone having direct pastoral responsibility for them. We share this concern and would underline ACUPA's recommendation that dioceses and deaneries should undertake a re-appraisal of their clergy support systems.

8.100. With the pressures of modern life affecting so many people, it was not surprising that a considerable amount of evidence was submitted to the Commission on clergy stress. *Stress in the Ministry* (United Reformed Church 1987) and *Clergy Stress* by Mary Ann Coate (SPCK 1989) address this issue, much of it common to all types of ordained ministry. Some evidence has focused attention on the internal causes which surround the concepts and attitudes which clergy themselves have of the ordained ministry and the tensions which these can bring. This underlines the need for regular contact with a personal counsellor or director, not least because the person suffering is often unaware of the level of stress in the early stages.

8.101. Other evidence has concentrated on the external causes of stress, such as workloads, lack of support and financial and other pressures. Clergy are not immune to normal human frailties, nor to problems in their married and family life. Opportunities need to be provided for them to be able to explore and process their particular situation. There is a considerable literature on the subject and the task of the

Commission has been to draw out those aspects which are specifically rural. Some have already been alluded to, and include the higher cost of living in rural areas, the pressures of a high profile role in several communities and the frequent lack of privacy. *Stress in the Ministry* highlights the problem of isolation which was a recurring note which rang through the evidence which was gathered. This can be exacerbated by the lack of readily available independent counselling, though a number of dioceses have set up helplines or have provided lists of counsellors who offer assistance on a confidential and independent basis.

We recommend that courses to increase self-awareness and group experience are a routine part of in-service training.

Recommendations

1. Dioceses should pay particular attention to the need for the Church's mission and ministry to be focused in the world as well as within the Church. (8.9.)

2. Dioceses should affirm the parochial pattern of ministry and regard it as a base which is designed to equip the people of God for their ministry within the world. (8.10.)

3. Dioceses should affirm and use the insights emerging from the ministry of rural officers and agricultural chaplains in developing a theological understanding and critique of environmental and rural issues which over-arch parish and diocesan organisation. (8.26.)

4. Dioceses should review their provision of rural first curacies. (8.28.)

5. Dioceses should recognise their responsibility for induction of clergy into rural ministry and either set up their own courses, link with other dioceses to develop them, or use those which are available nationally. (8.33)

6. Dioceses and other bodies should be encouraged to develop rural Pastoral Studies Units as well as supporting and using those which already exist, but may not be well known beyond their immediate area. (8.34.)

7. Dioceses and colleges should establish further rural placements with the aim of learning about rural society as a whole, as well as about the operation of the Church. (8.35.)

8. Following similar recommendations by ACUPA, we recommend that ACCM should review its priorities in theological training and development, taking into account the needs of rural ministry in terms

of contextual theology, collaborative ministry and management skills. (8.36.-38.)

9. ACCM should be adequately funded to promote and monitor experiments in theological education. (8.38.)

10. Dioceses should review what they offer in terms of theological development in CME and in lay training. (8.38.)

11. Dioceses should explore the opportunities of working with secular organisations to develop skills in management. (8.40.)

12. The role of non-residential training courses should be developed further. (8.41.)

13. Research should be urgently undertaken to get a clearer view of the causes underlying the reduction in numbers available for the ordained ministry. (8.42.)

14. Dioceses should review their pastoral reorganisation proposals with the other main Christian denominations. (8.51)

15. The General Synod should review the Sheffield formula to protect the number of clergy in rural areas while new schemes for local and lay ministry are developed. (8.51)

16. The operation of the Patronage (Benefices) Measure 1986, particularly as it affects rural areas, should be reviewed. (8.60.)

17. The parson's freehold system should be re-examined and a method of time-limited contractual employment be explored. (8.61.)

18. There should be greater collaboration between dioceses in sharing their experience of pastoral planning and some national co-ordination of this would be essential. (8.62.)

19. Dioceses should draw up a statement of aims which can be shared with parishes as part of corporate pastoral planning. (8.64.)

20. Dioceses should review the working of their rural deaneries, the tasks given to them, and the selection, support and training of rural deans. (8.68: see also 8.97 and 8.98.)

21. Research should be carried out into the effectiveness of rural groups and teams and into other patterns of collaborative ministry in the countryside. (8.69.)

22. Dioceses should continue to experiment with different patterns of ministry, but there needs to be some centralised monitoring and assessment of what is being done and more openness about what is actually taking place. The new Board for Ministry should be responsible for this. (8.82.)

23. Dioceses and parochial clergy should be more aware of the part played by the elected parish officers and should see them as potentially

part of the local ministry team and recognise this in training plans and programmes. (8.87.)

24. Dioceses should work towards the incorporation of Readers into local ministry teams and recognise Readers' needs of affirmation and support. (8.89.)

25. In affirming its commitment to training for lay ministry the General Synod should clarify where, within its new board structures, responsibility for lay training will lie. (8.90.)

26. Dioceses should review what their aims are in training for lay ministry and where responsibility for such training lies within their own structures. (8.90.)

27. Courses to increase self-awareness and group experience should be a routine part of in-service training. (8.101.)

Chapter 9
Spirituality and Worship

Spirituality

9.1. Sir Laurens van der Post spoke to the Commission of the religious significance of 'wilderness' as the place where the individual is assured of a place and a purpose in the order of creation. The Alister Hardy Research Centre at Oxford has catalogued the religious experiences of tens of thousands of the general public, and found that many of these experiences happened in the great outdoors. *Pilgrim at Tinker's Creek* by Annie Dillard is one of a number of modern chronicles of wonder and awe before creation in the tradition of Wordsworth and Francis Kilvert.

9.2. We believe that the link between religious experience and the countryside is real for many urban and rural people alike. The Church has always found it difficult to categorize such religious experience theologically. But such experiences need to be reflected and celebrated at the centre of the Church's worship.

9.3. The Rural Theology Association (RTA) has for 25 years tried to articulate Martin Thornton's idea of a specifically rural contribution to theology. In its publication *The Rural Church towards 2000*, Mervyn Wilson draws parallels between the rhythm of the seasons and the rhythm of disciplined prayer; between the planning of a garden or landscape and the coming of the Kingdom on earth; between the wholesomeness of digging the garden and the theology of work.

9.4. Edward Bailey, founder of the Centre for the Study of Implicit Religion, helps us to come to grips with 'natural religious experience'. He has explored the insight that many people express religious fervour implicitly rather than explicitly in numerous papers as diverse as *The Implicit Religion of the Pub,* and *The Implicit Religion of the National Anthem. (Workbook in Popular Religion,* Partners 1986)

9.5. This chapter will focus on credal Christian worship and spirituality, but it should be recognised that this explicit worship and spirituality takes place in a context of widespread implicit religion, not least - if Christians are honest - within themselves. We believe that Christian worship should not stifle implicit religion. On the contrary Christians are challenged to articulate and make explicit in public worship what many people feel implicitly outside the setting of formal worship. Thus the Church should respond to the hunger for spiritual expression, which is at times outside the limited range of its authorised liturgical offering.

> **In Dovedale we found a small Methodist chapel on a well used footpath which was kept open to offer spiritual refreshment for walkers and holiday makers. Inside there was an open Bible and a welcome for visitors.**

The spirituality of the laity

9.6. It was encouraging to see signs of growth in the spirituality of the laity in so many places we visited. While saluting the faithful, dutiful, painstaking witness of those Christians whose loyalty has kept open village churches for the rest of us, it was good to see so many of them beginning to move from heroism to hope.

9.7. Nevertheless, for many churchgoing people, their work and their life in a wider society seem frequently at odds with the faith proclaimed in church. If the ministry of the laity is primarily to be God's people in the world, then they need help in understanding their vocation. They need to be able to share with each other, for mutual support, the ways in which the Christian faith confronts the ways of the world, and the difficulties this brings. They should be encouraged to pray for and about the matters of daily life, and spirituality will find its hardest test, maybe, in the work place, in the places where decisions are made which affect the lives of others. All too often spirituality has been felt to be confined to the home and leisure time. What is needed is a spirituality of the market place, the shop, the office and the traffic lights.

9.8. Amongst today's rural population are frequently to be found senior managers and decision-makers. The Church needs to explore ways of discussing the issues of the work-place and supporting those who carry particular responsibility in this area. Industrial and agricultural chaplains are well versed in assisting in this way.

We recommend that churches establish a forum for discussion of work-related issues and that parish clergy make fuller use of the diocesan resources in this area in the form of industrial and agricultural chaplains.

9.9. An increasing number of lay people find strength and support from participation in the growing number of parish groups. These groups are sometimes ecumenical in composition and may focus on study, prayer, discussion, Bible study, healing or worship or any combination of these possibilities. Those parishes which have begun such groups have frequently found them to be a source of new spiritual energy. It is important that the benefits which flow from group work are widely shared to prevent division among the faithful. In small country parishes a group might come together from across the benefice and beyond. Those Christians who have found new stimulation from participation in groups need to realise that spiritual needs will be met from a wide set of circumstances and should be tolerant of those who seem more cautious in the expression of their spirituality.

9.10. Many people have found inspiration from involvement in a week-end at a Christian conference centre such as Scargill, Lee Abbey or one of the many diocesan or religious residential centres. In some areas there has been a steady stream of people, singly and in groups whose faith has been rejuvenated by such experience with great benefit to the whole Church in the area.

For the past seven years a party from the Cotswold deaneries have gone for a Christian discovery weekend to Lee Abbey on the North Devon coast. There is never any lack of applicants because so many people want to go again.

"When we first joined up as a benefice the Vicar took us for a parish day to Ampleforth. It really sorted us out and got us working together."

9.11. One result of this heightened spiritual awareness has been the growth in the number of lay people trying to be more disciplined in their own prayer life. In some villages lay spirituality is developing around the saying of the daily office - either together, or on a rota basis. We found a number of rural prayer groups who use silence and contemplative methods of prayer. The Fellowship of Contemplative Prayer was founded by Robert Coulson in 1949 and has groups all over the country. Youth officers told us that they are finding that young people particularly understand and relate to silent prayer.

In Childswickham near Evesham a rota of lay people say evensong daily in the parish church.

At Eyethorne in Kent a simple form of office is in use which can be used by lay people for both private and public prayer: "The word has got round that every morning and evening those who need our prayers are brought in love and faith to God, and those who now take their share in the daily readings and prayers have translated that new found confidence back into Sunday worship."

9.12. A further result of spiritual development amongst the laity has been the desire for a greater say in the preparation and planning of worship. Many parishes have established 'worship groups' - some take responsibility only for certain services, such as the monthly Parish Worship, others plan the major part of the worship in the parish, including the weekly services. Besides the obvious practical value of such groups, to which we refer again later, they give expression to the theological insight that worship is the response of the whole of God's family to His mighty work.

We heard of one NSM in Rochester diocese who is away on business all week and gets home on Friday to find the Sunday service planned for him by the local worship group.

9.13. We were frequently told that the tension between locals and newcomers can surface in spiritual matters. Christians with experience of larger, perhaps suburban churches, often hanker after newer music, close-knit study groups and a clear-cut commitment which was the pattern in their former church. The locals often have a different sense of what is and is not possible with small numbers in a close-knit community and are suspicious of a spiritual 'in-group'. Leaders of the local church need sensitivity and training to handle such conflict effectively. We were particularly impressed that the Church of England Evangelical Council in their submission encouraged rural evangelicals to stick with the local church.

9.14. Local radio and television stations, as well as providing opportunities for churches to project their message, can also be a spiritual feeding point for many, particularly the housebound. Local broadcasts will complement the national slots like *Thought for the day* and *Daily Service* on Radio 4. Television's *This is the Day,* which unites watchers by a simple shared action, is particularly noteworthy, and *Songs of Praise* and *Highway* remain very popular.

> **The parish of Bathford in Bath and Wells diocese records the parish morning service and takes tapes to several housebound people. With commonly used sound systems this is a practice that could be widely copied.**

9.15. With the laity becoming more spiritually active there is a great need for the clergy to keep up with them.

The spirituality of the clergy

9.16. In Chapter 8 we expressed concern about the way the rural clergy are trained and cared for; there are spiritual repercussions. While we met many rural clergy who were fulfilled, cheerful and extremely positive, we met others, often young, who were bewildered, frustrated, and disillusioned. The transition from a spirituality centred in regular prayer shared with others to the clerical isolation of the multi-parish benefice is often traumatic, particularly if no spiritual rapport develops between clergy and laity.

9.17. The weight of our evidence suggest that in a fast changing situation lay people still look to the clergy for leadership and expect them to be people of prayer and wisdom. What lay people must realise is that this means that clergy need ample time for study and prayer. In the view of a number of groups we met, this means at least an hour a day allocated in the diary. It also means setting aside a week a year for a time of special spiritual focus (like a retreat). The financial cost should be a routine part of every parish budget. It was good to find that many dioceses are developing systems of pastoral support and oversight for clergy which may include offering spiritual advice.

> **In his triennial visitation in Truro diocese the Bishop asks specific questions of the clergy about their spiritual life.**

9.18. It was encouraging that a number of clergy spoke of a lay group in the benefice as their major source of spiritual support. Learning to share even this very personal part of ministry with lay people is perhaps the key to an effective spirituality for today's multi-parish incumbent. Others named sources of spiritual advice outside the parish such as the Third Order Franciscans, and the Servants of Christ the King. It remains true however, according to a survey in 1985, that for many rural clergy their spouse is their main source of spiritual counsel and support. And who is the spiritual counsellor to the spouse?

9.19. Regular study, like the life of prayer, can suffer by neglect. The Rural Church Project (RCP) showed that the clergy surveyed spent only 3.2 hours a week in private study. We recommend that all clergy give attention to their continuing study needs and to make full use of the diocesan officer for continuing ministerial education (CME) in assessing courses which can meet these.

> **Salisbury diocese runs Reading Weeks where participants read a book in the morning and share their insights in an evening session. The cost of these residential weeks is met from the CME budget.**
>
> **The Banbury Clerical Society (founded in 1852) meets regularly to study the Bible and receive papers on a variety of subjects. In many dioceses deanery chapters serve a similar purpose.**

> *The Epworth Review,* published by the Methodist Church, provides a regular section on sabbaticals, enabling clergy to publicize the results of their sabbaticals.

9.20. It is strange how spirituality is assessed in rural areas, being sometimes based on practical matters including life in The Vicarage, the way the garden is kept, or the way the vicar drives! Clergy coming into the rural ministry from an urban experience may expect to find their spirituality assessed on the way they take services. They will find that other matters come into it. Because the private life of the clergy is so public, regular days off and proper holidays are important. Most dioceses encourage their clergy to take six weeks holiday a year, with four sundays included. It should be the task of a churchwarden to ensure that the minister does indeed get this level of proper refreshment, so that the work may more enthusiastically be done. We found that many clergy did not take the recommended time off. In a survey of rural clergy in Gloucester diocese in 1985, 40% did not have a regular day off. It is often the case that finance stands in the way of proper holidays and churchwardens should know of the various local and national charities that can help. Another reason for not taking holidays is the difficulty of finding anyone to take services. Rural deans should help clergy with this problem. Where clergy do not take adequate time off, there are sad repercussions all around them. This is not a good example of stewardship.

Public worship

9.21. One rural clergyman has written:

"Christians are called by God to be His people in their particular corner of the world - and it is a high and glorious calling. We are called, not just to a private devotion, but to join with others to give God glory. Worship is primarily a corporate activity. It has structure and ritual, but these are a means to help us celebrate the deepest and most important aspects of our selves. Worship is the natural response to the encounter with God and we should expect to be moved in every part of our being by our involvement in worship; but not on each occasion, for we cannot remain on a spiritual high and the memory will often suffice. Those who organise and lead worship have as their task nothing less than making possible the continuing revelation of God."

9.22. Before we suggest how this might happen in practice there are a series of organisational issues related to the future shape of the rural ministry which need to be examined. It has become clear to us as we have taken evidence that one of the casualties of pastoral reorganisation has been Sunday worship. The following points have been made to us:

(a) Many churches no longer have a weekly service.

(b) Rural congregations no longer have a variety of services to choose from.

(c) In many churches services are not at a regular time each week and often at 'difficult' times (eg 9.00am is possibly not the best time for young families).

(d) Clergy rarely have time after the service to meet the congregation socially, because they have to hurry off to another service.

(e) Because the incumbent cannot cover all the services, worship in villages is often led by an 'outsider' who has little personal contact with the congregation.

9.23. The Commission recognises that each benefice must decide for itself what is needed and what it can achieve. But there is, we believe, a need for radical re-appraisal.

9.24. Adequate preparation for worship will involve time, and the Sunday gallop by clergy trying to lead acts of worship in several churches in a limited space of time is unseemly and counter productive. It is not possible for clergy to give of their best when under this sort of pressure. The person leading worship needs to be able to meet the congregation in the relaxed social time after the service.

We recommend that clergy lead no more than two major services, in addition to an early said service, in any Sunday morning.

9.25. Virtually every settlement in England has a church. This suggests that our ancestors believed that God should be worshipped in every settlement every Sunday. It also reflects their theological assumption that the priest and congregation should offer prayer daily on behalf of the whole village. Although we recognise the force of the counter-arguments, that people should have the chance to go to a big well-attended service and that there can be value in a joint-benefice service, particularly in areas of sparse population, we endorse the aspiration for prayer and worship in the local church on a daily and weekly basis. We have been repeatedly told that the great majority of church members do not travel (and do not wish to travel) to other churches to worship. It is probable therefore that by cutting down the number of services beyond a basic minimum the Church is not building up but undermining its local witness.

> On Easter Day 1990 in the Queen Thorne benefice near Sherborne, Dorset, there was a service in five of the six churches at 10.00am. Almost twice as many people came to church as in 1989, when there was a more variable timetable to enable the Rector to take more services. It may be that on major feast days getting the time of the service right is more important than whether the incumbent is taking the service.

9.26. The RCP shows how successful the Parish Communion movement has been. Communion services formed well over half of the total services held in all the benefices surveyed over a four-week period. This is not surprising for it is precisely suited to the small band of the faithful needing to affirm the validity of their call to be God's people in that place. By comparison all other services have come to seem second class to many. The disadvantage is that the so-called 'parish communion' is the exact opposite: it *excludes* half the parish. And this exclusion is often deeply felt by adults who are not confirmed (and even by unconfirmed children). Where, as is so often the case, the Anglican church is the only place of worship left open in the village, it is likely that a significant number of the congregation will be non-conformist by upbringing. In their tradition too frequent (and casual) reception of the sacrament is reckoned very irreverent. If the Church of England is sincere in its desire for ecumenism it must surely listen carefully to what others are saying.

We recommend that each church discusses the frequency of its communion services and that it reviews this from time to time in the light of the needs of the people it exists to serve.

> In the RCP, while one third of a sample who attended Anglican services named the Parish Communion amongst their favourite services, Mattins and Evensong between them were mentioned as frequently. Interestingly, as

> **many as 11% who attended communion services did not always receive the sacrament.**

Extended communion

9.27. If a parish decides that it does want frequent Holy Communion, this will probably only be possible in many areas by the use of 'extended communion'. This is the name given to the practice whereby the consecrated elements from one service presided over by a priest are taken to another service presided over by a licensed person, so that the faithful may receive the sacrament in the absence of a priest. The recently re-affirmed official policy of the House of Bishops is to discourage this practice, but in several dioceses where there are insufficient clergy to maintain the desired pattern of communion services there is a tendency to allow it. It should be noted that extended communion is already widely used by the Roman Catholic Church here and in France to shore up the chronic lack of priests and it is also official practice in the Church in Wales where women deacons are in charge of rural parishes.

9.28. Support for the practice of extended communion arises from the shortage of clergy coupled with the preference of many to receive communion at the hands of someone who knows and cares for them. The use of clergy, who have no other involvement, for this purpose is not as appealing to those who feel this way as the authorising of someone local, a deacon or Reader, to administer communion from the reserved sacrament.

9.29. The fundamental theological objection to extended communion is that while Christ is present in the Sacrament and gives Himself to us in bread and wine - it is theologically and spiritually unhealthy to think of Him as 'welded' into the bread and wine outside the context of the service.

9.30. *We recommend that, in the light of the prevailing situation, discussion on extended communion be urgently reopened in the House of Bishops.*

The role of the laity in worship

9.31. As we asserted in the previous chapter we believe the rediscovery of the laity is of the Spirit, and we welcome it and the opportunity it offers to the clergy to share in a new way with the faithful in each place. The diminishing number of clergy has meant that where a church has wished to continue with frequent services of whatever form, it has fallen to the laity to plan them and lead them.

9.32. We have already mentioned in 9.12. the development in some places of worship groups who play a role in the planning of services and these will need to be widely emulated if there is to be weekly worship in every church. Such groups will need support and resources from outside and opportunities to exchange experiences and ideas with others involved in the same field. This will be an important role for stipendiary clergy and diocesan advisers.

> **The RTA has a number of local groups comprising both clerical and lay members, which meet regularly to exchange experiences of all aspects of rural ministry, including worship. The Standing Conference on Rural Ministry in Northumberland is another forum for this.**
>
> **The Federation for Rural Evangelism has an annual day conference where members from all denominations share news about good ideas that have worked in experimental worship settings.**

9.33. The leadership of worship by laity is also a possibility for every parish but each needs to decide for itself whether it will only make use of Readers for this task or whether it will encourage other local lay people to exercise this ministry. Our evidence leads us to conclude that what is most important in the nomination of people who might lead worship is that they are local and recognised figures, aware of the dynamics and vibrations of the local community. Belonging is a vital element in the ministry of leading worship which may be more effectively performed by local lay people than by an ordained person, who has to be brought in from outside.

9.34. We believe that many parishes have committed Christian laity who can share the responsibility of leading worship. There is an educated, capable population throughout rural England, many of whom have experience in public speaking through Women's Institutes, Young Farmers Clubs, parish councils, village hall committees etc, as well as the many new villagers who have responsible jobs in nearby towns and cities or recently retired from them. Furthermore, there is among the laity much rich life experience which can be drawn on, and we have experienced in many places a willingness to play a part in the organisation and leadership of public worship.

9.35. This increasing emphasis on the role of the laity in worship in the Church of England mirrors a similar development in the Roman Catholic Church. As in some Anglican parishes, the Roman Catholic Church has for some time allowed the communion of the sick to be administered by duly authorised lay people; and on mainland Europe in some Roman Catholic dioceses the parish priest assists teams of lay people in planning the worship they will lead. The English non-conformist tradition has always been much less dependent on clergy, and if Christians from those traditions are becoming involved in the church in the village then there may well be skills ready to hand. We acknowledge the contribution other Churches have made to the training of the laity.

> **In the parish of St Mary Bitton in the diocese of Bristol the priest-in-charge, who lives in a nearby parish, has delegated the planning and leadership of much of the worship to an able team of lay people under the leadership of the Reader. Church attendance has increased as a result of this involvement of the laity.**

9.36. A vision of how the future pattern might look is given by the Bishop of Norwich in his 1989 Strategy for the Diocese, *Moving Forward*:

> "These acts of worship, these weekly times of prayer, would have to be led by ordinary lay men and women from the congregations. In order to do that they would need some simple form of training.... My expectation is that sometimes a priest would come and there would be a celebration of Holy Communion.... But the continuity, the regular worshipping life of the church in that place, would depend not on a priest or a lay Reader, but on local people who pray and lead their neighbours in prayer faithfully week by week."

9.37. There are exciting possibilities as well as dangers in 'handing worship over to the laity'. But we believe that the future of the rural church will depend not least on whether some parishes and dioceses are prepared to take the risk and experiment with lay-led worship so that the rest of us can learn from their successes and their failures.

We recommend that dioceses establish and monitor pilot projects of lay leadership of worship in their parishes.

Practical considerations for worship

9.38. We were often asked on our travels about how to make small congregational worship effective. As a result of our visits we have come to believe that attitudes are as important as practical hints. First and foremost small congregations need to regain confidence in their own worth. The small church is not a failed large church. Indeed, the RCP found that although some clergy find small congregations difficult or dispiriting, many more are either not discouraged or feel it is not so much a question of absolute numbers as their relativity to the population or usual sizes of congregation. Ten is either twice five or half of twenty. Ten in some villages is 10% of the total population. If the tiny congregation can come to see itself through God's confident eyes worship will 'happen'.

9.39 Confidence, however, must be tempered with realism. Small congregational worship is most effective when it does not attempt what clearly cannot be achieved.

An experienced country clergyman suggests things to be avoided:

Overambitious ceremony

Majestic preaching

Singing of psalms to Anglican chant

Excessively long hymns and complicated tunes

New forms of service which have not been properly introduced

9.40. The small congregation needs first to be aware of the advantages which its size and setting bring. One such advantage is that those planning the worship will be able to do so in some knowledge of the spiritual needs of those who will be taking part. Small numbers mean that there is a job for everyone that wants one and this is a real opportunity for drawing on the talents, at whatever level, of the whole church community. Small numbers mean that shy people will not be too frightened to do something. A service with few attenders can be intimate and supportive if it is allowed to be and this can be helped if people are encouraged to sit closer together rather than dispersed around the church. Intercessions too can be more personal. Humour and the human touch are easier in the small congregation and can be as deeply moving as weighty solemnity. The most 'religious' aspect about many village churches is the quality of their silence. This could be incorporated in worship.

> **At Coates in Gloucestershire, individuals who have been somewhere or done something which is relevant and interesting (eg Oberammergau/diocesan synod/worked for the Church elsewhere) are sometimes interviewed in place of the sermon.**

9.41. This is a time of liturgical experiment, and has occasioned much reordering of the church building. We note with admiration the positive contribution which diocesan liturgical committees and diocesan advisory committees (DACs) can make to the difficult matter of liturgical reordering. Discussions with the archdeacon should begin at a very early stage in this process. This matter is covered at greater length in 11.13.-11.17.

9.42. Whatever goes on inside a church building, be it musical or spoken, it will be lost for those who are hard of hearing. Few rural churches we visited had installed amplification systems, but with an ageing population these may be needed in the future. Where they are installed, consideration should also be given to the incorporation of a sound induction loop to be used in conjunction with suitable hearing-aids. This need not be a major additional investment but it will enable the deaf to participate in a way they have hitherto been unable to in many places. The Royal National Institute for the Deaf and the Church of England's Council for the Deaf can give guidance about the practicalities and costs of this. DACs could also help by giving guidance on this matter.

We recommend that serious consideration should be given by every PCC to the possibility of installing amplification equipment including a sound induction loop in its church and that DACs should be in a position to give guidance on this.

Forms of service

9.43. While it is likely that no one form of service will entirely please everyone, the village that has only one service a Sunday is challenged to agree on an act of worship in which all are prepared at least to join. Most small parishes most weeks should try to cater for all ages. The RCP shows a significant percentage among the laity prefer the services of the Book of Common Prayer (BCP) and the *Children in the Way* survey shows that the smaller the parish the more likely it is that communion services using older language will be used. These surveys also show that a significant number of laity value the modern language services. There should be room for compromise among Christians in so fundamental a matter. A number of rural parishes have found that the Rite B service in the Alternative Services Book (ASB) can provide this common ground. It is worth noting that the older form of the Lord's Prayer can now be found alongside the new form in up-to-date versions of the ASB Rite A.

9.44. We are concerned that many younger clergy have had no experience or training in the taking of BCP services, which are still widely used (and not just in the rural church).

Resources for successful small group worship
2nd Workbook on Rural Evangelism - **particularly section II (Partners 1984)**
Ten Rural Churches, **edited John Richardson (Kingsway 1988)**
Grove Booklet: No 108 in the Worship Series - *Worship with small congregations*

9.45. The RCP shows that 90% of the lay people interviewed wanted children to come to services and *Children in the Way* challenges us to recognise children as fellow pilgrims. Where the numbers are small, as is often the case in rural areas, it is even more important that the congregation is sensitive to the needs of all its members. This can be demonstrated by adapting worship to suit all ages and by making all decisions affecting the church and its worship with regard to the younger members as well as the adults. In particular, those who do bring their young children to church need to be encouraged.

At Stilton in Cambridgeshire the children's bible story books are attractively displayed at child-high level and not stacked away six feet out of reach.

In several churches we found that records are kept of the dates of children's baptism anniversaries (or birthdays). These are marked by a candle ceremony during the main service.

"If there are four hymns, the children deserve at least one for themselves."

In a village in Gloucestershire the village school was encouraged to display the children's paintings, models and project work in church. At Christmas this included carrying the school's crib scene into church at the end of term.

9.46. Many parishes have experimented with new forms of service to provide for the 90% of the population who do not join in the set patterns of Anglican worship. In the RCP 76% of Anglicans who regularly attended said their church held a family service of some sort once a month. The aim of these services is to cater for all ages, rather than specifically for families and for this reason many may wish to use a less exclusive title such as Parish Worship.

9.47. Our evidence shows that such Parish Worship takes a wide variety of forms:

a) The Communion service is shortened and an illustrated talk rather than a traditional sermon given. Hymns sung at the local school are used.

b) The first part of the ASB Communion service is adapted (*Come and Worship*, Mowbrays 1987).

c) The BCP Mattins is adapted (*Family Worship*, CPAS 1971).

d) The ASB Morning Prayer is adapted (*Church Family Worship*, Hodder and Stoughton 1986).

All of these adaptations are intended for a regular monthly slot.

9.48. It is important, of course, that the theme underlying such services is comprehensible to the whole congregation but behind the idea, too.

must lie a longing to communicate the mighty acts of God. The preparation of the Parish Worship may thus require even more planning than the communion service with its structured liturgy. Worship groups may wish to invite the assistance of someone particularly to help with these services but, in any event, there will be an even greater need when preparing these services to draw on available resources and the experience of others.

9.49. It is particularly important, however, that where Parish Worship takes the form of a non-communion service it is not perceived in any way as an inferior form of worship. The Free Churches regard a non-communion service as 'the breaking of the Word':

> "Here, as in the Lord's Supper, there is a rehearsal of the story of God's mighty acts. Worship is a time and place of recollection as the story is re-told through hymns and prayers, bible readings and preaching...We need to recover a sense of the dynamic relationship between word and sacrament, if we are to renew our worship." (*Let the People Worship*, Report to the 1988 Methodist Conference of The Commission on Worship)

Moreover, the recent report of the Liturgical Commission, *Patterns for Worship*, reminds us that "actions speak louder than words". The lighting of a candle, the blessing of an animal, walking around the church, a pilgrimage, holding hands: these and many other actions (a piece of dance, drama or music) are things which rightly done and rightly interpreted will help the family service to be a true eucharist.

9.50. While most forms of Parish Worship are successful, we have been told that there is now a need for a fresh impetus to the movement and a supply of new resources. The introductory chapter to *Patterns for Worship* charts the problems and we welcome the many good ideas they suggest.

We recommend that those responsible for lay training in dioceses give particular attention to the training needs of the laity involved in the planning and leading of worship, and establish workshops and other resources to meet these needs.

Special services

9.51. Numerous special services are a particular feature of the rural church. These are services which celebrate special occasions, perhaps Christian festivals, such as Mothering Sunday, Advent, Christingle, and Christmas or the different stages in the farming year: Rogation, Lammas, Harvest, and Plough Sunday. Local community events, such as anniversaries, celebrations of work, festivals, school activities or local traditions, even those with pre-Christian roots, such as well dressing or beating the bounds may also be marked with a church service. Such services are suitable for every age group and many newcomers find these a way of getting the feel of rural life and taking part in the community. Local schools also may use them as pegs on which to hang the broad curriculum.

Recommended resource books for parish worship and special services
Together magazine (CIO) is a mine of good ideas
Patterns for Worship (CIO-GS 898) - Report of the Church of England Liturgical Commission (published 1990)
Making Contact - Leslie J Francis - Collins 1986
The various Wadderton Group Publications (CIO)
Readings for School Assemblies - Blandford Press - an excellent range of non-biblical readings
100 School Assembly Stories - F Carr - Foulsham 1973
Church Family Worship - Hodder & Stoughton 1986
Partners in Learning - National Christian Education Council
Church Services for the Farming Year - Arthur Rank Centre

9.52. Other types of special services may be those held for particular groups, such as pony club rallies, sportsmen's services and gardeners' festivals. These do not have to be long, but a few minutes in church with well-chosen readings and hymns and prayers help to demonstrate that God is Lord of all life.

9.53. All these special services, marking as they do events which cut across the lives of the whole community, offer an enormous evangelistic opportunity. They present the Church with a chance to show all members of the parish that they are welcome in a church which not only has a human face, but which can also be fun, and, most importantly, that God is concerned with every aspect of their life.

> **Other examples of services we have seen:**
>
> **A Rose Service in Cornwall.**
>
> **A Church Clipping Service at Painswick in Gloucestershire, where the whole congregation surrounds the church to 'clip' or embrace her.**
>
> **An annual pilgrimage service with the congregation travelling from church to church in the benefice.**
>
> **Children's services focusing on pets or toys in the context of a Festival of Creation.**
>
> **An All Saints Service centred on the ancestors of the village and featuring a pageant of village history.**

Baptisms, marriages, funerals

9.54. These three life events are still the Church's main point of contact with those who are not regular churchgoers. In the RCP, 75% said they had been to church for such an occasion in the previous year. For many parochial clergy, these are among the high points of rural ministry. The depth and length of the pastoral contact with the people most involved is a powerful way of demonstrating God's love in word and deed; often a major part of the community turns out for a funeral.

9.55. Baptisms and weddings, however, can involve questions of church discipline and regulations as to who can and cannot be baptised and married in church. While such regulations are increasingly common in an urban situation, the issue can be much more sensitive in rural areas where there is a blurred distinction between those who regularly attend church and the rest of the local community. The arguments for and against a 'strict' baptism policy have been raised again recently by Mark Dalby in his book *Open Baptism* (SPCK 1989). The evidence from our visits is that a clergyman who seeks to enforce a 'strict' baptism policy in a village is invariably misunderstood. It is significant that in its submission, the Movement for the Reform of Infant Baptism (MORIB), which promotes a strict line on baptism, admitted that to refuse to baptise a child in a village parish was usually counter-productive.

9.56. With regard to weddings, the increasing incidence of requests for the re-marriage of divorced persons in church can involve particularly the rural incumbent in difficult decisions, since he is likely to be well acquainted with the parties concerned and his decisions will be public knowledge. It should be noted that the official rules of the Church of England state that a marriage may not take place where either partner has been divorced, with the former husband or wife still living. However, such marriages, if performed in church, are lawful according to the law of the land. This means, on the one hand, that bishops are not able to give their permission for such marriages to take place and, on the other hand, that clergy who do so in defiance of the Church's regulations, are nevertheless acting within the law. Some clergy conscientiously believe that it is right, in certain circumstances, to conduct second marriages. In view, therefore, of the exposure of the rural incumbent, we feel that it is important that he seeks the support of the PCC in his decisions.

9.57. Funerals are often a major village occasion. It is the privilege of the minister to articulate the village's feelings for the dead and their family. A number of newcomers to rural life told us how moving they had found village funerals, demonstrating as they did neighbourly support in times of trouble. Many idiosyncracies will be forgiven the minister who empathises with the bereaved family.

9.58. However, a further point about funerals was made time and again during our visits and this was that the time involved in the ceremonies surrounding a funeral has multiplied as a result of the increasing preference for cremation. This commonly consists of a service in church, followed by a journey of up to an hour to a crematorium, followed by a funeral tea, followed a week later by a service for the interment of ashes in the churchyard - a good five hours work.

Music

9.59. According to the RCP, music was one area which was felt to constitute a problem for the small congregation. Music can play an important part in worship by providing in a special way for the expression of joy in praising God, and unifying those taking part. However, it is not absolutely essential - spoken services have their place and will be more uplifting spiritually than services where the music is so poor as to detract from the content of the service.

9.60. Few churches should have to go without some form of music in their worship. Where the music does prove to be unsatisfactory, the fault often lies in a misconception of what is called for. What is appropriate for cathedrals and for large parish churches is seldom appropriate for a small church with small numbers and yet all too often the cathedral format is seen as the norm at which to aim by even the smallest church. Instead, the small church should attempt a musical framework within its own capabilities.

9.61. Music does not have to be complicated or difficult to be uplifting. If a church does not have a good organ and a choir large enough to cope with leading four-part singing it should aim for something more simple. Hymns can be two-part or even just one-part, although in this case, it will be important to use good melodies that are easily singable and tuneful. Rounds are another possibility.

Hymns appropriate for small churches may be found in *Hymns for Today's Church* (Second Edition, Hodder & Stoughton) or *200 Hymns for Today* (Hymns Ancient and Modern).

A survey of church music in Oxfordshire showed a wide use of *Mission Praise* by village churches.

9.62. Chanting the psalms may be ineffective for a few voices and it may be better to say them. The Royal School of Church Music (RSCM) suggested the alternatives of using simple plainsong or, if there is someone who can lead, singing them responsorially, and recommended various books with good examples for this. Similarly, for communion services it may be inappropriate to use some of the more well-known settings, such as Merbecke or Appleford, but there are a number of alternatives which are more suitable for smaller numbers.

Alternative Psalm Books

***Psalms for Singers*, RSCM**
***Psalms for Sundays*, Mayhew McCrimmon**
***Psalms for the Eucharist*, 3 vols, Mayhew McCrimmon**

Alternative settings for sung communion services

Rite A
Norfolk Setting - Martin How, RSCM
Addington Setting - Richard Shephard, RSCM
Music for the Parish Communion - Martin How, RSCM
The Unison Communion - Herbert Sumsion, RSCM
The King of Glory - Betty Pulkingham, RSCM
The Mass of All Saints - Alan Wilson, Weinberger
A Parish Mass - Dom Gregory Murray

Rite B
Rite B Communion - Grayston Ives
Folk Mass - Martin Shaw

9.63. Pre-recorded tapes have their use, too, as a resource for learning new hymns or to give a lead to the singing. Some cathedral choirs have recorded tapes specifically for this purpose.

9.64. Turning to the question of instruments, there is a common assumption that the pipe organ is an unquestionable must for music in church. Many have found that an electronic organ or an electronic piano makes a good substitute. We have also heard good reports of the use of other instruments and we suggest that any instrumentalist who is available and willing should be welcomed and encouraged. Even percussion instruments, if sensibly used, will help: the tiniest tinkle on a triangle can add a sense of occasion. It is not essential that the instrumentalist is at a high standard provided that the player does not attempt something beyond his or her capabilities.

The Royal School of Church Music (RSCM) offers the following help:
a) **A Churches Without Choirs Scheme - this helps small churches and shows them they need not be churches without music.**
b) **A Reluctant Organists Scheme - this is designed to help pianists learn to play the organ at least competently enough to play for a church service. (This scheme has a limited geographical coverage.)**

c)   A series of handbooks.

The Music in Worship Trust seeks to help churches looking for assistance in coming to terms with the explosion of material now available; it runs workshops, seminars and training weekends, publishes a magazine, offers an instrumental and vocal arrangements service and gives advice on the purchase of instruments.

9.65. In this area, the talents of children should be encouraged as much as possible. Many churches told us of young people playing their recorders as a first contribution to the church's music. We have heard other examples of youngsters playing the organ before, after and during a service. Percussion is a particularly good way of involving children. Children's bands have an important role in family services.

9.66. We felt it important to mention here the question of remuneration and recognition for regular church musicians. Our experience is that rural congregations tend to take for granted those who lead them in music. The faithful witness of the unpaid weekly organist needs to be recognised and applauded, but this level of commitment should not be assumed and churches should be prepared to pay properly (including travelling expenses) a regular organist/musician. The provision of music and other items should be a PCC expense.

9.67. We feel that music is one area in particular in which the small church needs to draw on the resources of the benefice or the deanery. Either of these may be large enough to supply the musical talent which is lacking at parish level.

At Chichester, and Melton Mowbray in Leicestershire, we heard of choirs drawn from all the parishes in the benefice, which visited each parish in turn.

At Market Bosworth, Leicestershire, the mother church choir "goes on safari" to the villages once a month.

9.68. We look forward to the report of the Archbishops' Commission on Church Music, which is due to be published early in 1991. We hope they will make specific recommendations for the use of music in small rural churches.

Bellringing

9.69. This particularly English practice is carried out, a sample survey indicates, by some 36,000 people of all ages, in some 3,500 towers, with another 2,000 towers where the bells are not usually rung or are not in full working order. The purpose of ringing was, and is, to summon people to prayer and worship although bells have also traditionally been rung to celebrate local or national events. In rural areas, it is usually the shortage of ringers which leads to village towers becoming unringable. Bellringing as an activity is a popular way of involving young people and leads to a high level of group commitment: further, over 50% of all bellringers are regular worshippers. We recommend that the clergy give full recognition of the worth of this activity, and where possible, conduct prayers in the belfry before or after ringing.

9.70. Some people complain of the noise invasion of bellringing, particularly on practice night, but we would advise that, like some of the other traditions of village life, it is an older custom which merits rediscovery and support. We have been told by someone totally deaf that he appreciated the ringing, as he could feel the vibrations and that this meant a lot to him.

Cathedrals and the countryside

9.71. Part of our journeyings included asking deans and provosts of cathedrals how they saw the role of the cathedral in relation to (a) rural issues and (b) rural churches.

9.72. A number of cathedrals hold what are often spectacular festivals of various aspects of rural life. We point to Coventry's Festival of Creation, Truro's Young Farmers' Carol Service, and Peterborough's planned Festival of Rural Life in 1990. Others focus on work with children and young people. Salisbury has an annual diocesan children's festival attracting 1500 children; Wells and others have special events for older teenagers. Cathedral chapters should consider with the diocesan rural adviser ways in which rural issues could be brought into focus in what the dean of Salisbury described as the "laboratory of the spirit which the cathedral offers".

9.73. Points of contact include a broad and imaginative range of links with local churches, with cathedral staff providing expertise which is directed towards supporting the work in the parishes; this may include study, teaching, preaching, prayer, personal support, patronage responsibility, but most commonly the musical excellence of the cathedral choir and organist. It is common for rural choirs to combine for a cathedral evensong, and for cathedral choirs to go on tours of the diocese. Worcester has a touring second choir.

9.74. Cathedrals as a focus for tourists could well signpost visitors to the many other beautiful churches in the diocese which were prepared to receive them. Those dioceses that do not have a tourism officer (see 11.62.) should take advice from the tourist board about developing the potential of this link with the parishes, for the good of the whole rural community.

9.75. Blackburn diocese was planning for 1990 special services with a deanery focus, hoping to make a great occasion for a whole deanery with the visit to the cathedral. Several deans were sensitive to the need not to dominate or patronize parishes, but to encourage them to 'be themselves' on a cathedral visit. Contact with the cathedral can be uplifting for a small congregation, but may set standards which are impossible and therefore inappropriate for the home parish. It is important for parishes to see the cathedral and its staff as an additional resource in their own work, and, as with other diocesan resources, full use should be made of what is on offer.

We recommend that cathedrals should review their resources and the potential that lies in these for supporting youth work, tourism, and parish worship, particularly in rural areas, for example by:

    (1) appointing a member of the chapter to have special responsibilities for the cathedral's involvement with youth work in the diocese;

    (2) using the cathedral's tourist facilities to signpost visitors to other churches in the diocese;

    (3) keeping in closer touch with parish clergy about what the cathedral can offer them in terms of resources.

Recommendations

1. Churches should establish some forum for discussion of work-related issues and parish clergy should make fuller use of industrial and agricultural chaplains. (9.8.)

2. PCCs should make provision for the costs of at least one retreat for their incumbent in their annual budget. (9.17.)

3. All clergy should give serious attention to their continuing study needs and make full use of the diocesan CME officer in assessing suitable courses. (9.19.)

4. Churchwardens and PCCs should ensure that clergy take the amount of holiday recommended by the diocese and that they are adequately financed to do so. Rural deans also need to help in ensuring that there is adequate clerical coverage for holidays. (9.20.)

5. Clergy should lead no more than two major services, in addition to an early said service, in any Sunday morning. (9.24.)

6. Each church should discuss the frequency of its communion services, reviewing its decision at intervals, in the light of the needs of the people it exists to serve. (9.26.)

7. Discussion on extended communion should be urgently reopened in the House of Bishops. (9.30.)

8. Those responsible for lay training in dioceses should give particular attention to the training needs of the laity involved in planning and leading of worship and establish workshops and other resources to meet these needs. (9.32. and 9.50.)

9. Dioceses should establish and monitor pilot projects for lay leadership of worship in their parishes. (9.37.)

10. Each PCC should give serious consideration to the possibility of installing sound amplification including an induction loop in its church(es). Diocesan Advisory Committees should ensure that they can give guidance on this matter. (9.42.)

11. PCCs should be prepared to remunerate and pay all expenses of their regular musicians. (9.66.)

12. Cathedrals should review their resources and the potential that lies in these for supporting youth work, tourism, and parish worship, particularly in rural areas, for example by:

    (1) appointing a member of the chapter to have special responsibilities for the cathedral's involvement with youth work in the diocese;

    (2) using the cathedral's tourist facilities to signpost visitors to other churches in the diocese;

    (3) keeping in closer touch with parish clergy about what the cathedral can offer them in terms of resources.
       (9.71-75.)

Chapter 10
Education and
Young People

Introduction

10.1. The Church's concern with education is very broad. Chapter 6 has already explored key aspects of the social context of rural education as they relate to pre-school, primary, secondary, tertiary and adult education. The present chapter focuses on two topics in which the church is directly engaged in the education of children and young people in rural areas. Part one examines the Church of England's close involvement in statutory education through the provision of church voluntary aided and voluntary controlled primary schools. Various scenarios are explored for the possible future of church schools in rural areas. This section also discusses the viability and effectiveness of small schools. Part two examines the Church of England's domestic ministry among children and youth. Particular attention is given to the relevance of the recent report commissioned by the General Synod Board of Education, *Children in the Way*, for fostering a realistic approach to children's ministry and to all-age learning and worship in rural parishes.

Church schools

Historical perspective

10.2. The Church of England's involvement in rural church schools needs to be seen in the context of a long history.[1] The original initiative to build schools came not from the state, but from the Churches through the National Society (1811) and the British and Foreign School Society (1814). While government monies were voted to these societies from 1833 onwards, state machinery did not exist to build schools until the Education Act 1870.

10.3. The dual system of church and county schools as we know it today was shaped by the 1902 and 1944 Education Acts. The Education Act 1944 secured the future of church schools by giving them the choice between controlled and aided status. The voluntary controlled school is controlled by the local education authority. The Church is absolved from ongoing financial responsibility, but retains the right to provide denominational worship and to appoint a minority of governors. The voluntary aided school is aided by the local education authority. In return for ongoing financial responsibility, the Church retains the right to provide denominational religious education throughout the school, as well as denominational worship, and to appoint a majority of governors.

10.4. At the same time the Churches secured two further key religious provisions in the Education Act 1944. The act made religious instruction obligatory in all county schools and gave the Churches an influential voice in defining the nature of this instruction through their role in the process of creating agreed syllabuses. The Act made daily collective worship obligatory in all state maintained schools. The parliamentary debate surrounding the Education Act 1944 illustrates that the assumptions behind religious instruction and worship were Christian in character.[2]

10.5. The various denominations responded differently to the opportunities of the Education Act 1944. The Free Churches generally felt confident about the religious provision in county schools and withdrew from the church school system. The Roman Catholic Church felt strongly that nothing less than voluntary aided status would serve the needs of the Roman Catholic community. The Church of England's response varied from diocese to diocese. Some dioceses, like London, Southwark and Blackburn, favoured striving for aided status; some preferred controlled status; others agreed with the Free Church view that the religious future was secured through county schools and Christian teachers. In the course of its diocesan visits the Commission noted how decisions taken at the time of the Education Act 1944 continue to shape the differences in diocesan policy towards church schools, as reflected, for example, by the continued commitment to a strong presence of aided schools in the Diocese of Blackburn.

10.6. Since 1944 the overall stake of the Church of England in the state maintained system of schools has decreased. In 1953 35% of primary schools in England and Wales were Anglican, in 1963 31.1% and in 1973 25.6%. In other words, during the period 1953-1973 the number of Anglican primary schools was reduced from 8,251 to 5,860. Since 1973 on average 55 Anglican primary schools have been closed each year. Many of these closures have been in rural areas and resulted in the sale of the school building. Today Anglican schools account for 24% of primary school buildings and 16.8% of primary school places. In 1953 Anglican schools provided 3.7% of secondary places, and in 1973 3.2%. Today Anglican schools provide 4.6% of secondary school places.

10.7. Since 1944 the overall stake of the Roman Catholic Church in the state maintained system of schools has increased. In 1953 Roman Catholic schools provided 8.3% of primary places in England and Wales, in 1963 10.4% and in 1973 9.6%. In 1953 Roman Catholic schools provided 3.3% of secondary places, and in 1973 8.1%. Today Roman Catholic schools provide 9.6% of primary places and 9.2% of secondary places.[3]

10.8. Because of these historical roots, today there is a much higher proportion of Church of England schools in rural areas than elsewhere and the emphasis is on primary provision. While nationally 24% of all primary schools are Church of England schools, in some rural local education authorities the proportion is much higher. In Oxfordshire, Shropshire, Somerset and Wiltshire as many as half of the primary schools are Church of England related. Moreover, within local education authorities the church schools tend to be in the villages rather than in the towns. In Gloucestershire, for example, 65% of the remaining village schools are Church of England, compared with 43% of the town schools and 25% of the suburban schools.[4]

10.9. The Education Reform Act 1988 reaffirmed the religious provisions of the Education Act 1944, safeguarding both the role of voluntary aided and voluntary controlled schools and the statutory place of school worship and religious education throughout the state maintained sector. At the same time the 1988 Act went beyond earlier legislation by specifying the central place of Christianity in school worship and religious education. Currently professional educationalists are exploring the interpretation of these clauses and their fuller implications for the Churches.[5]

Philosophical perspective

10.10. The Church of England's involvement in rural church schools needs to take into account informed educational debate on the relationships between Church and school and between theology and education. This debate focuses on five key complex issues.

10.11. The emergence of education during the 1960s as a self-conscious and autonomous discipline began to question, on grounds of logic, the right of the Churches to determine educational theory or practice. This view reaches its strongest expression in two papers by Professor Paul Hirst, *Christian Education: a contradiction in terms* (1972)[6] and *Education, catechesis and the church school* (1981).[7]

10.12. Professional debate regarding the nature of religious education began to draw a sharp distinction between the Church's function in catechesis or Christian nurture of engendering faith, and the schools' function in religious education of teaching about religious phenomena. This view reached clear expression in the formative Schools Council Working Paper 36, *Religious Education in Secondary Schools* (1971).[8]

10.13. Professional debate regarding school worship has begun to draw a sharp distinction between the nature of education which is committed to critical enquiry and the nature of worship which is committed to and pre-supposes belief. In particular, Professor John Hull's seminal book, *School Worship: an obituary* (1975)[9] argues that these are fundamentally different objectives and logically incompatible.

10.14. A main strand in secularisation theory argues that the social significance of the Christian Churches has declined considerably since 1944. The case is argued, for example, by Brian Wilson in *Religion and Secular Society* (1966)[10] and *Religion in Sociological Perspective* (1982).[11] Such a view raises sociological questions about the appropriateness of the Church's contribution to the state maintained system of schools.

10.15. Since 1944 cultural and religious pluralism has developed significantly in England. The educational implications of these developments are brought into particularly sharp perspective by the Swann Report, *Education for All* (1985)[12], the findings of the committee of inquiry into the education of children from ethnic minority groups. The majority recommendation of the Swann committee is against the development of denominational voluntary aided schools for Muslims or other faith groups and calls into question the continued appropriateness of the provision for the Christian Churches.

Theological perspective

10.16. The Church of England's involvement in rural church schools needs to be theologically grounded and to take into account the range of theological motivation underpinning church schools. This motivation varies from denomination to denomination.

10.17. A key statement on the Roman Catholic theology of church schools is the report of the bishops of England and Wales *Signposts and Homecoming* (1981)[13] which recognises that Catholic education should be confined neither to the years of compulsory schooling nor to Catholic schools, but also reaffirms the identity of Catholic schools as "a believing and integrated Christian community", the aim of which is to "encourage personal commitment to Jesus Christ". Roman Catholic schools generally serve church members rather than local neighbourhoods.

10.18. A key statement on the Anglican theology of church schools is the Durham Report (1970)[14] which distinguishes between the Church of England's domestic and general functions in education. The domestic function is "to equip the children of the Church to take their place in the worshipping community". The general function is "to serve the nation through its children". The Durham Report recognises that while historically these two functions were indistinguishable, "nowadays no one would pretend to claim that nation and Church are coextensive", and recommends that "religious education, even in a church aided school, should not be seen in domestic terms". Church of England schools generally serve local neighbourhoods rather than church members.

10.19. The Green Paper, *A Future in Partnership*,[15] published by the National Society in 1984, accepts the distinction between the Church's domestic and general functions in education and agrees that partnership and the voluntary aspects of church schools should be stressed in preference to denominationalism. At the same time this report includes a central chapter which reflects theologically "on the nature of a church school community and the Christian education that should be conducted within it". This chapter defines ten key features of the church school, including:

– a house of the gospel in which, starting at governor and staff level, there is a deliberate attempt to link the concerns of Christ's gospel with the life of the school, but to do this in educational terms.

211

- a beacon signalling the transcendent by the development of awe, mystery and wonder through the curriculum, exemplified in acts of corporate worship including contact with the Christian calendar and sacraments.

Research perspective

10.20. During the past decade a limited number of educational research studies have investigated aspects of rural church schools. It is important that future policy regarding the Church of England's involvement in rural schools should take these empirical data into account.

10.21. A study of the attitudes of teachers in church schools in Suffolk[16] found that many teachers believe that church schools should be religiously distinctive, in ways contrary to the recommendations of the Durham Report. The study also demonstrates that older teachers hold a more favourable attitude towards the church school system and tend to give more emphasis to the distinctiveness of church schools. The implication of these findings is that rural church schools may become less distinctive as older teachers are replaced by a younger generation of men and women.

10.22. These findings were confirmed by a second detailed study comparing church schools and county schools in Gloucestershire.[17] This study reported that younger head teachers in both county and church schools are less likely to promote a Christian presence in education. This study also demonstrated the many ways in which church schools continue to express more signs of church-relatedness than county schools in Gloucestershire. Church of England schools encourage more contact with the clergy and with the local church. They hold more explicitly Christian assemblies and give more emphasis to the church-related aspects of religious education.

10.23. Another aspect of this study has explored the impact of church schools on pupil attitudes in Gloucestershire. These data indicate that Church of England voluntary aided schools have the same impact on their pupils' attitudes as county schools, while Roman Catholic voluntary aided schools have a positive impact.

10.24. A study of the attitudes of the governors of voluntary aided schools in the Diocese of Oxford[18] demonstrated that the foundation governors were committed "to preserve the ethos of the voluntary aided school", while "in contrast parents of children in the school tend to value the Christian ethos of the school less". The authors conclude that "since this is a group that we can expect to see increasing in numbers and influence, this is potentially a worrying situation for those who value the distinctiveness of the church school".

10.25. A study of the impact of church schools on a range of indices of village church life[19] in a sample of 1,637 communities ranging in size from 250 to 1,250 inhabitants showed that church schools augment slightly the village churches' usual Sunday contact both with six to nine year olds and with adults, although not with other age groups. This suggests that children who attend village church schools are more likely to go to church on a Sunday and to take their parents with them. The presence of a church school was also shown to have some positive influence on the number of infant baptisms, the number of six to thirteen year olds in village church choirs, and the number of young confirmands under the age of fourteen years.

The small school

10.26. The small school question is a complex area of debate, of equal relevance to county and church schools. Current perspectives on this debate have their origin in the Plowden Report, *Children and their Primary Schools*,[20] published in 1967. Here the case against small schools was being advanced in educational terms, suggesting that small schools can restrict their pupils' social, emotional and intellectual development. Small schools, it is argued, limit the pupils' social opportunities to mix with their peers, deprive them of the benefit of working with the range of teachers needed to offer different skills, and restrict their acquaintance with educational resources, curriculum materials and extra-curricular activities. In its section on education in rural areas, the Plowden Report defines a small school not in terms of pupil numbers, but in terms of staff size. It recommends that schools with an age range of 5-11 should have at least three classes, each covering two age groups. In the same period, the Gittins Report, *Primary Education in Wales*,[21] recommends a minimum size of 60 pupils.

10.27. The 1970s, however, saw a change of emphasis on the small school question. A number of specialist research projects, like the Rural Education Research Unit in the Department of Education at Bangor, the study of *The Social Effects of Rural Primary School Reorganisation in England* in the University of Aston,[22] and the project on *The Rural Community and the Small School* at the University of Aberdeen,[23] all began to question the truth of the educational claims made against the small school. Counter arguments also began to emerge concentrating on the positive implications of the links between home and school, the detrimental effects of bussing and of long days away from home on young children, and the wider social consequences of community disintegration stemming from the closure of community schools.

10.28. In 1978 the National Association for the Support of Small Schools was formed. In 1979 the Advisory Centre for Education produced its booklet, *Schools Under Threat: a handbook on closure*,[24] giving guidelines on how to fight a school closure. By 1981 the Cambridge Policy Group had produced *A Positive Approach to Rural Primary Schools*.[25] At the same time, lessons were being learnt from the Organisation for Economic Co-operation and Development's Education in Sparsely Populated Areas Project, from the re-opening of small schools in Norway and Finland and from the reversal of the policy to close small schools in New Zealand.

10.29. During the 1980s the mood of the debate again moved against the small school. In 1981 the Department of Education and Science's circular *Falling Rolls and Surplus Places* advised a minimum primary school size of 100 pupils. In 1985 the White Paper, *Better Schools*,[26] states that it is the duty of local education authorities to ensure that schools are large enough to justify sufficient teachers to meet certain recommendations for the curriculum. This White Paper recommends that 5-11 schools should have at least one form of entry. Looking in greater detail at the small school question itself, the White Paper argues that:

> "the number of pupils in a primary school should not in general fall below the level at which a complement of three teachers is justified, since it is inherently difficult for a very small school to be educationally satisfactory. But geographical and social factors need to be given their full weight. In isolated communities it is often right, given appropriate augmentation of resources, to retain a small school."

10.30. At the same time the White Paper issues the clear warning that such small schools can only be maintained at the expense of the larger schools from which they divert resources. Educational and economic issues became intrinsically linked in this debate.

10.31. More recently the educational argument against the small school has been further fuelled by the requirements of the national curriculum and the introduction of clearly assessed attainment targets.

Such requirements seem to have been framed on assumptions consistent with larger schools.

10.32. Ultimately, informed decisions about the effectiveness of small schools remain hampered by a lack of consistent investment in educational research in this area and by equivocal conclusions from existing studies. For example, in their recent book, *Curriculum Provision in the Small Primary School*,[27] Maurice Galton and Helen Patrick claim that:

> "pupils in small schools do not necessarily get a better deal than pupils in larger schools and that small is not always beautiful".

On the other hand, Adrian Bell and Alan Sigsworth in their study, *The Small Rural Primary School: a matter of quality*,[28] were impressed by small schools for:

> "providing a stimulating, if sometimes idiosyncratic, education of their children, the warm social climates they often contained and the many different ways in which they and their local communities interrelated".

10.33. Clearly the question of the educational effectiveness of small schools remains an urgent subject for educational research, if small school closures are not to be determined solely on the bases of rhetoric and economic criteria.

The Commission's perspective

10.34. Certain recurrent themes have emerged as the Commission has visited rural church schools, held discussions with those involved with church schools as local clergy, teachers, governors, parents and pupils, and studied the range of written submissions.

10.35. The Commission has been impressed by the overall image generated by church schools in rural areas and by the commitment of teachers, clergy and governors to delivering a high quality of education appropriate to local needs. This is often in the face of mounting pressures and difficulties, as they respond to falling rolls, changes brought about by the new education acts, and financial stringency. We have seen that the small school can deliver excellent education. Within this overall context the Commission has noted the wide diversity of approaches adopted by rural church schools. Some church schools, emphasising their domestic function, have very close links with the local church, invite the incumbent to lead assemblies and to take religious education lessons, hold school eucharists, and make the building available for church based children's groups, youth groups and other parish activities. Other church schools, emphasising their general function, appear indistinguishable from county schools.

> A vicar in Oxfordshire describes how there is considerable cross-reference between the aided school and the parish church. He takes an assembly in school once a fortnight and the school makes good use of the church for educational activities. The school also helps to prepare for the Family Service in church on the first Sunday in the month.

10.36. Some clergy enjoy and welcome their contact with the parish's church school, develop their professional competence in the classroom, commit considerable time to the responsibilities of being a school governor, and offer a valuable service of support, counselling and friendship to the school staff. Other clergy minimise their contact with the school, resent the demands made by the responsibilities of being a school governor, and feel uncomfortable with contact with children in the classroom. Many of the clergy met by the Commission in the more rural areas felt that their work in local church schools gave them their best contact with the children in the parish. In some cases they considered that the local church school took the place of Sunday school activities. We encourage the rural church to recognise the current diversity of practice in church schools and to value the local historical and contemporary factors which underpin these variations.

10.37. The Commission recognises that the majority of Church of England schools in rural areas are neighbourhood schools. At the same time, the extent to which these schools are influenced by their church foundation varies greatly from place to place. Sometimes the local community feels that the church is too closely involved with the school. Sometimes the local community regrets that the church is not more closely involved with the school.

We recommend that dioceses help individual schools continually to evaluate and assess their relationship with the local community.

10.38. Many local churches value their church schools as a focal point in the community, as a key means of contact with parents and children, and as a way of bringing the Christian gospel to the attention of children who do not attend church, and they value the building as one which is available for other church and community functions. We recommend that local churches are encouraged to foster and develop the potential of their church schools, wherever this potential is appropriate and consistent with the wishes of the local community.

10.39. Some submissions expressed reservation about the competence of local clergy to lead assemblies and to teach religious education in church schools. One diocesan submission reported that the quality of response of incumbents to church schools varies greatly, some very good and some very bad.

> **We observed one rural clergyman in the Wakefield diocese, clearly an excellent teacher, conducting an assembly in the infant school. He had both children and teachers 'eating out of his hand'.**

10.40. *We recommend that the interest of individual clergy in education be taken into account when making appointments to rural parishes which include church schools.* We also feel that this important area is not given sufficient time and emphasis at theological colleges.

We recommend, therefore, that more use should be made of the Anglican Colleges of Higher Education, both to contribute to the initial training of clergy in educational matters, and to provide in-service training for clergy who teach and lead worship in church schools.

10.41. Some teachers, especially in controlled schools, expressed uncertainty regarding the nature of their school's relationship with the church. Sometimes teachers were confusing the legal status and privileges of controlled and aided schools. In particular, some teachers expressed uncertainty regarding the appropriate provision for religious education and school assemblies in church schools.

We recommend that dioceses strengthen wherever possible their advisory service to church schools and their provision of in-service training to teachers in church schools.

We recommend that initial teacher training courses should include more specific reference both to small rural schools in general and to church schools in particular. We note with interest the module on teaching in church schools offered by Chester College and welcome the new initiative of the College of St Mark and St John, Plymouth, to develop an in-service BPhil/MEd qualification on church-related education for teachers in Church of England schools. We would hope that other Anglican Colleges of Higher Education should continue exploring this area of work.

10.42. Many village churches face uncertainty over the future viability of their church schools, and are confused by the range of conflicting opinion on the advantages and disadvantages of small rural schools. Problems attendant on the closure of church schools discussed in 11.17. On our diocesan visits we were particularly impressed by the benefits accruing to some small schools from various experiments in clustering. *We recommend that dioceses, in consultation with local education authorities, draw up guidelines to help local churches evaluate the pros and cons of the closure of small church schools, and to enable them to be fully aware of the development of strategies like clustering.*

A meeting of teachers and governors of very small schools was called in Bourton-on-the-Water by the Diocese of Gloucester and the Gloucestershire RCC in 1987. As a result an informal consultative group was formed in the area.

10.43. Village churches are experiencing difficulty in identifying local people with the appropriate time and skills to undertake the growing responsibilities of school governorship under the new education acts. We welcome the range of initiatives being taken for the further training of church school governors and draw particular attention to the training videos produced by the College of St Mark and St John, Plymouth, to the joint training undertaken by the Diocese of Blackburn and St Martin's College, Lancaster, and to the appointment of an officer with specific responsibility for church school governors by the Salisbury Diocesan Board of Education.

We recommend that dioceses provide help for local churches by offering varied training opportunities for church school governors, and that where feasible this should be achieved in co-operation with the local education authority.

10.44. Some local clergy, especially in multi-parish benefices, are finding the increasing responsibility devolving on school governors to be over-stretching the time and energy they have available for this aspect of their ministry.

We recommend that dioceses explore ways of equipping local churches to meet the added responsibilities of the new education act without overburdening the local clergy. This may include appointing suitable laity to fill roles previously held by clergy.

10.45. Some dioceses operate a system of bishop's visitors to church schools in order to strengthen the link between local schools and the diocese. The effectiveness of this system varies greatly from place to place, but where it works well it is a valuable experience.

We recommend that dioceses explore the benefits of such a system and develop ways to equip visitors to church schools to work effectively.

10.46. Some submissions draw attention to difficulties which arise when the areas served by schools and the boundaries of multi-parish benefices fail to coincide. In some situations the same church school draws children from two or more benefices, while children within one benefice attend two or more church schools. Some clergy report difficulties in having contact with children from their benefice who attend a church school in a neighbouring benefice. Other clergy have spoken of their reluctance to develop close links between their parish church and the church school when a significant proportion of the pupils relate to parish churches within the care of another priest.

10.47. *We recommend that, wherever possible, the areas served by church schools are taken into account when structuring multi-parish benefices.*

We also recommend that church schools should fully involve clergy from all benefices within the area served by the school, as well as ministers of other denominations.

10.48. In the course of our diocesan visits we enjoyed opportunities to meet with a number of diocesan directors of education and other diocesan schools officers. We were greatly impressed by the thoughtful, caring and informed work undertaken by these individuals. We recognised the way in which the heavy demands of church schools were being balanced in some dioceses alongside the equally heavy demands of the Church's concern with all levels of voluntary education.

We recommend that dioceses should ensure that their diocesan director of education is adequately supported and resourced and that clear provision is made within the education budget for the adequate supervision of church schools and for curriculum development within these schools.

10.49. Commissioners visited a number of diocesan resource centres and recognised the importance of their potential contribution for resourcing church schools. At the same time, schools geographically distant from these centres remain reluctant to make good use of them. *We recommend that dioceses continue to explore the development of resource centres, and also consider the usefulness of resource packs which can be deposited in rural church schools for a month or so and then moved on to another school.*

> **The Diocese of St Albans has adapted a caravan as a travelling resource centre, stocked with audio-visual aids, books, tape cassette and video recorder. This is moved from parish to parish, spending a month at each.**

10.50. We listened to the apprehension expressed by some governors and teachers about the possible implications of local management of schools, the national curriculum, attainment targets and assessment for the small school with fewer than three teachers. At the same time we were impressed by the creative energy invested by many teachers in small schools in demonstrating their commitment to develop and deliver the national curriculum effectively and efficiently.
We recommend that every effort should be made to help small schools in these areas.

10.51. In a number of places we recognised confusion and tension between the Church of England's twin aims in education, the domestic and general functions. Some submissions, assuming the domestic model, questioned the effectiveness of church schools as a means of spreading the gospel among young people. Other submissions, assuming the general model, argued that it is not the proper purpose of church schools to seek to influence their pupils in favour of the church.
We recommend that dioceses continue to encourage churches and church schools to explore the theological bases of the Church's involvement in education and to test their current practice against these theological issues.

Ways ahead

10.52. There are five basic options open to the rural church regarding the use of church schools and involvement in county schools.

10.53. A first option follows the view of the Durham Report (1970)[29] that, especially in single school areas where parents have no real choice of school, the Church of England should see its involvement primarily as a way of expressing its concern for the general education of all children and should not emphasise denominational or Christian distinctiveness.

10.54. A second option follows the view that parents in rural areas are in basic sympathy with the Christian moral and religious ethos and want the local church to be closely involved with schools, whether they themselves happen to be churchgoers or not. This understanding reckons that by promoting a school's church-related identity, the church is performing a valuable and appreciated service to the community.

10.55. A third option follows the view that church schools are anachronistic and would encourage the church to withdraw wherever possible from church schools (particularly of aided status) and to concentrate its specific work of nurture and catechesis within voluntary church activities.

10.56. A fourth option follows the view of the 1971 working party in the Diocese of Truro that the Church of England should gradually withdraw from single area village schools and develop a system of church schools in larger centres of conurbation into which parents from the neighbouring villages can opt if they desire a specifically Anglican education for their children. The experience in the Diocese of Truro is that nine new deanery aided schools have opened since 1971 and the tenth is due for completion during 1990, but that it has been more difficult to withdraw from the village schools.

10.57. A fifth option follows the view of Leslie Francis's study *Religion in the Primary School* (1987)[30], which builds on the Truro model with the significant development of proposing area ecumenical Christian schools, on the grounds that the choice confronting parents in rural areas in the 21st century may be more realistically understood to be between secular and Christian, rather than between Roman Catholic, Anglican and Free Church.

10.58. The choice between these options hinges on perceptions of the relationship between the Anglican church and rural society, but is also constrained by the legal specifications of the Education Act 1944. Many submissions from the dioceses, together with our experience of visiting church schools and talking with local clergy and people, persuade us that the community model of church schools envisaged in option two is still significant and practicable within most rural areas. We encourage the Church to do all it can to maintain a local focus for schools and to develop creative links between school and church through the involvement where appropriate of clergy and lay people in assemblies and religious education and through the constructive support of the foundation governors. At the same time we recognise that, if rural society and educational theory and practice were to develop in more secular directions, it would be wise for the rural church to be able to effect a positive transition from the model outlined in option two to the model of area ecumenical schools outlined in option five in order to provide a lively option of Christian education for those parents who positively request this for their children.

The Church's nurture of children

Theoretical perspective

10.59. The Church's ministry among children under the age of fourteen was the subject of a recent working party constituted by the General Synod Board of Education and leading to the report *Children in the Way*[31] debated by General Synod during 1988. We welcome this initiative and recognise that the theory and recommendations in this report provide an informed background against which to locate the specific problems, needs and opportunities of the rural church in its work among children and young people. This work needs to take into account the situation of children already "in the way" through the encouragement and example of church-going parents and of those "on the edge" of the Christian community. Each of the five main chapters of *Children in the Way* addresses a specific topic.

10.60. Chapter 1 argues that the Church should take as the starting point for its ministry among children and young people a clear consideration of the ways in which "the child's world is changing and the place of the child in the world is changing". Realistic work with children and young people must be informed by an accurate view of how children perceive themselves in society and of the factors which shape this perception. In particular attention is drawn to the influence of changing patterns of family life, changing patterns in secular education and changing standards in society in general and the media in particular. *Children in the Way* recommends that the Church should investigate local pressures on children and be ready to learn from those professionally involved in work among children in a secular context. The rural church needs to be alert to the implications for its work of local secular debates on educational and welfare issues related to pre-schoolers and primary school children, particularly as these debates involve issues of deprivation, distance and resources.

10.61. Chapter 2 stresses that the Church has a responsibility to serve the needs of children outside its membership and to evaluate strategies for bringing the claims of the Church to their attention. *Children in the Way* recommends that the Church should actively support the efforts of uniformed groups to evaluate the moral and spiritual aspects of their work with children, and concentrate on family involvement. The rural church needs to explore ways of encouraging families on the edge to relate to the local church with their children and of helping uniformed groups to benefit from contact with the local church.

10.62. Chapter 3 evaluates three different models for the Church's work among children already "in the way". It characterises these approaches as the school, family and pilgrim models, and argues convincingly in favour of the pilgrim model. While the school model can all too easily be interpreted as teacher and taught and the family model may feel too restricted, the pilgrim community comprises a band of people all sharing in and learning from common experience. In line with this emphasis, *Children in the Way* recommends that parishes should plan special ventures in which adults and children can be involved together in learning and exploring what it means to be followers or pilgrims "in the way" and should develop a continuing pattern for learning together. Good examples of this approach working in rural parishes are provided in *Making Contact*[32] and further helpful ideas are offered by *Signposts on the Way*[33] and *Springboard to Worship*[34]. The rural church needs to explore how such events can be organised across parish and benefice boundaries.

For the past three years a parish in Oxfordshire has set aside Good Friday for a children's workshop. This started as a children-only event, but is growing in vision and turning into an all-age workshop event.

10.63. Chapter 4 explores the contribution of recent research in the theology and psychology of faith development towards an understanding of the Church's task of Christian nurture. In this context *Children in the Way* makes two key recommendations, which are of crucial importance for the rural church. First, a resolution of the issue of communion before confirmation is required as a matter of urgency. Secondly, the Church should commission an appraisal of the research into faith development and its implications for Christian nurture, and encourage further research into the crucial stages of transition and growth in a child's spiritual development. The rural Church needs to ensure that this work in faith development takes into account the realities of child experience and church life in the countryside.

10.64. Chapter 5 discusses what is involved in "leadership worthy of children", including the roles of clergy and laity. *Children in the Way* recommends that ministerial initial and in-service training should include adequate reference to work among children and suggests the possibility of liaison with professionals involved in teacher training. *Children in the Way* also recommends that parishes should support the lay leaders of their educational work with realistic financial resources, with regular training and with personal support and development. The rural Church needs to pay particular attention to assessing the physical environments available for conducting work among children and young people and to the key role of distance learning in the training of lay people for this area of work. In this connection we wish to draw attention to and commend the distance learning programme *Called to Teach*[35] developed by the Diocese of Truro and adopted by some other dioceses.

The Commission's perspective

10.65. A number of recurrent themes emerged as the Commission visited rural parishes and discussed the Church's work among children with clergy and laity.

10.66. The Commission has been impressed by the way in which many rural parishes have already studied *Children in the Way* and are exploring means of responding to the recommendations made by this report. Such exploration is crossing a number of traditional boundaries, those between the generations, between neighbouring parishes, and between different denominational groups. Successful ministry among children seems to be characterised by co-operation.

We recommend that rural parishes should make opportunities to continue to discuss the implications of Children in the Way, draw upon the resources of their diocesan children's adviser, and share stories of successful ventures as widely as possible.

10.67. The Commission has noted the ways in which diocesan and national organisations can help and foster experimentation and development in individual parishes. For example, in the Diocese of Truro the Mothers' Union is undertaking work in deaneries, initiated by the Diocesan Executive Committee of the Mothers' Union and the Diocesan Children's Adviser. This work involves planning all age-events, group work, special services, looking at the work of Sunday schools, and so on. We commend these initiatives and recommend the model to other dioceses.

10.68. The Commission has listened to accounts of all-day projects arranged in parishes, benefices or deaneries with children, families and all-age groups in mind. These days have combined opportunities for learning, fellowship and worship. Some project days held on a Saturday encouraged children and adults to work together to prepare for the Sunday Eucharist. Occasions like Harvest Festival and Pentecost lend themselves well to this project day approach. The key for success in such days seems to be the recognition of local interests and the harnessing of local skills. We would wish to encourage more rural churches to experiment with project days for all-age learning and worship.

10.69. Some rural parishes hold an annual summer holiday club to which they invite every child in the village as well as those attending Sunday school. Such events help to widen the number of local children who have some form of contact with the village church. We would encourage churches to be alert to the skills and resources available for such work in their neighbourhood.

Parishes in Lincolnshire and Norfolk reported how parents and other church members not usually involved with children's work help to run a regular holiday club. Another parish draws heavily on the leadership skills of older teenage churchgoers, while yet another invites students from a college Christian Union to come to stay in the village to help run the club.

> **In a parish in North Devon the Anglican Church and the Methodist Church pooled resources to employ a professional leader to train and co-ordinate local volunteers.**

10.70. We have noted the wide provision of children's work taking the place of the traditional Sunday school. One parish in Cornwall holds a mid-week session in the parish hall immediately after school, while another parish uses the local church school once a week. A group in Northumberland meets in the pub opposite the church. While some groups meet every week, others meet only during school term time, while others will meet for a six week session to explore a particular theme with one group of leaders and then take several weeks off before meeting again with another group of leaders for a further session of four weeks.

> **A number of brewers are prepared to encourage the use of pub rooms away from bars for youth work, even relating the activity to non-alcoholic drinks.**

> **In Limber in Lincolnshire the 'Sunday School' meets after school on a Friday afternoon in the vicarage. More children come on a Friday than on a Sunday. They remind each other at school and drift along together. Links are made between the Friday Club and the Sunday services by summing up a month's work, or sometimes even a whole term's work, in worship at the Family Communion. The children present the Ministry of the Word and display their creative work.**

10.71. Other churches arrange events for special occasions. We would encourage churches to adapt the timing of their work among children to suit local needs and resources.

> **A parish church in Cornwall held a Praise Party last October 31st as a positive alternative to Halloween activities, and this attracted a number of children who might have been out knocking on doors and frightening elderly people.**

10.72. We recognise that children's work can be hampered in rural parishes by the difficulty of finding an appropriate meeting place. A village in Suffolk, for example, pointed to the fact that until five years ago the parish church had use of both the church school and the vicarage as centres for work with children and families. Falling rolls led to the closure and sale of the school, while pastoral reorganisation has led to the removal of the resident priest and the vicarage too has been sold. The large medieval church is cold and an unsuitable environment for working with children. The parishioners who are willing to undertake children's work in this parish are now unable to provide an appropriate environment in which to work.

We recommend that the rural Church should urgently review the resources needed for undertaking a realistic ministry among children and families and keep these factors in mind when disposing of village schools and parsonages.

The Church and youth

Research perspective

10.73. From a research perspective, the Church's work among teenagers is a particularly neglected area of study. The most recent published study in the area *Teenagers and the Church*[36] was commissioned to underpin the British Council of Churches working party report *Young People and the Church*[37] published in 1981. This research was based on a survey of over 1,300 teenagers who attend Anglican, Roman Catholic or Free Churches. The findings of this study contain both good and bad news for the Church of England. The good news was that the Church of England possessed greater ability than the other denominations to contact teenagers who do not already

227

belong to church-going families. The bad news was that the rate at which teenagers lapse during teenage years was higher for young Anglicans than for members of other Churches. The statistics suggested that 74% of the fourteen-year olds who attend an Anglican church would have stopped doing so by the age of eighteen, compared with 55% in the Roman Catholic Church and 49% in the Free Churches.

10.74. Closer scrutiny of the age structure of those who come into contact with the rural Church throughout one diocese[38] confirmed that there is a sharp decline in Sunday contact during the teenage years and that very many rural churches have no contact with teenagers during the week. This research also indicates that after Sunday school attendances drop off around the age of nine, church choirs play a crucial part in involving young people in the life of the rural Church until around the age of thirteen. Those parishes which have servers continue to recruit teenage servers after church choirs lose their attractiveness. Serving is an important point of contact with fourteen to seventeen-year olds in the rural Church, but seems to lose adherents very quickly after the school-leaving age. Bell-ringing, too, is an important point of contact with fourteen to seventeen-year olds and maintains commitment more readily into the early twenties. This research also draws attention to the important role of the uniformed organisations in bringing ten to thirteen-year olds into contact with the rural Church.

The Commission's perspective

10.75. A number of recurrent themes emerged as the Commission visited rural parishes, discussed youth work with clergy and laity and met with young people themselves.

10.76. First, the Commission noted that frequent concern was expressed by clergy and laity at the lack of involvement of young people of secondary school age and over in rural church life. We recognise that this was a particular area of anxiety and sometimes of feelings of guilt. At the same time, little evidence was gathered of imaginative responses to that situation.

10.77. Nevertheless, those examples of good practice which were shown gave the Commission good reason to be hopeful that this situation could be redressed. We note the significant and growing impact of the report *Children in the Way* on rural parish work among children.

We recommend that a similar initiative should be undertaken by the Church of England to explore and promote the place of teenagers in the life of the Church and such a study should be informed by careful empirical research comparable to the research initiated by the working party on the Church's work among children[39].

Meanwhile, we welcome the initiative currently undertaken by the Board of Education in association with the Department of Education and Science to develop techniques for the objective evaluation of Church-related youth work, which currently involves some dioceses with commitments to rural areas.

10.78. Secondly, we listened to rural parishes which claimed to "have no young people", while turning a blind eye to the queues for the local school bus. When pressed to identify the teenagers living within the parish, some rural churches have been surprised by their number, although it has to be recognised that a proportion of these young people are away from the parish at independent schools, colleges or universities. Frequently, rural churches expressed feelings of discouragement because there were insufficient numbers of young people in the community to make a youth programme viable - subsequent conversation revealing that they were often pre-supposing a traditional urban youth club model and overlooking the very different possibilities available to rural churches to work with their young people in creating small groups tailored to local needs - groups more likely to be fluid in format and membership and therefore able to respond to peaks and troughs of numbers in particular age-bands, and the changing interests of their members. Work has already been done to create material designed to help rural churches assess what is appropriate to their local situation. *Stepping Forward*[40] - a kit to enable rural churches to take positive steps towards meeting young people's needs - is one excellent example, available from the United Reformed Church - the formation of a small group of concerned individuals from within a church to consider opportunities which might emerge from working through such material is seen as a positive beginning.

We recommend that parishes make a careful audit of the ages and situations of the young people within their area and review the most appropriate ways for relating to these young people.

10.79. Thirdly, we listened to young people themselves. Many young people talked of the lack of relevance of worship and church life to their own lives, though they appeared to retain a keen interest in the spiritual dimension. Other young adults, who may be called upon to take on responsibility and be fully involved in decision-making processes in their domestic and working lives, say that within the Church they are frequently de-skilled and excluded from leadership positions. Local churches should make opportunities to hear carefully the views of their young members and those young people living on the fringes of the Church, however uncomfortable this may be.

10.80. Where youth work has died out, the joys, rewards and challenges of working alongside young people seem to have been forgotten and replaced by a fear of doing the wrong thing; a concern that youth work inevitably means problems; and a lack of confidence based on a false notion that in order to work successfully with questioning young people a youth worker needs to know all the answers. Consequently the Commission has endeavoured to seek out examples of good practice and offers a model by means of which responsibility for youth work can be anchored in the local church, while gaining encouragement from a network of local and regional links. This model requires each church to nominate a person to be responsible for the church's work with young people, with this person then becoming part of a network with others involved in this field from other churches and youth organisations. The following diagram shows the extent of support available within such a network. Indeed, the network offers more than support – it offers a model of how youth work in an area might be co-ordinated. See 12.23-12.29 for an explanation of how such a network system might be used for other areas of the church's work.

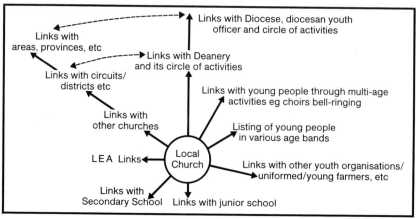

10.81. In general, churchpeople should not be inhibited by fear of doing the wrong thing. We heard of very successful groups meeting informally in homes, where all that had been needed was a comfortable relaxed atmosphere, a group meeting place, a willing ear and an openness to discuss and use ideas coming from the youngsters. Even here there was a tendency for the church to apologise that they were not doing other more organised activities, rather than rejoicing and affirming the work which was taking place.

> **The Diocese of Truro has launched a particularly imaginative programme called 'Challengers', which is capable of involving both individual isolated youngsters and small groups, linked to an adult, embarking on a programme which is almost a spiritual Duke of Edinburgh Scheme, with wide-ranging challenges appropriate to different age groups. The scheme registered 140 enrolments in its first few months.**

10.82. Several dioceses reported that church people were involved on management committees of village youth clubs and that there was a significant involvement, both directly and indirectly, in uniformed organisations, Young Farmers groups etc. Such involvement is to be commended, particularly where organisations are making special efforts to respond appropriately to rural situations as, for example, the Scouts, through their 'Scoutreach' development programme. It is also valuable to develop links with local LEA youth workers and make good use of their services and resources.

10.83. The Commission was also shown excellent examples of centres which had been established to enable groups of young people (and sometimes adults as well) to share in residential experiences in rural areas, familiarising themselves with the area in which the centre is set and engaging in stimulating activities involving challenging physical activities and developmental groupwork. The YMCA Centre at Lakeside near Windermere was one such centre, developed on a large scale, but we were also impressed with Anglican centres at Marrick Priory and at Askrigg in North Yorkshire (which had been adapted to give opportunities to handicapped as well as able-bodied youngsters). Not all such centres impinge on the lives of local young people, but the centre at Askrigg was developed with the full co-operation of local people, who continue to manage the scheme through the Askrigg Foundation and local youngsters are fully able to take advantage of all the facilities offered by the centre and its professional staff through their weekly youth club.

10.84. The importance of special events, celebrations, holiday clubs etc was frequently mentioned as a central element of a rural church's evangelical outreach to unattached or isolated youngsters, and it was found easier to attract leadership for annual rather than weekly events, though one can lead to the other. Holiday clubs seem to be of particular significance in working with younger children, but can involve older teenagers in leadership roles.

Truro Diocese report a successful club led "by our Sunday School team, youth group members and a gifted lay reader". A village church in Lincoln Diocese similarly reports a summer Holiday Club "to which we invite every child in the village" and where they aim "to communicate the love and friendship of Jesus and the joy of the Christian life in a way children can understand - through games, songs, stories, drama, films, videos, quizzes and practical activity, and most of all through the example of the helpers by sharing their love, care and enthusiasm".

A club in North Devon included a barbecue to which parents of the children attending were invited - "Every child brought a parent with them, the events of that evening led to a number of parents having a change of attitude to the Church in the local area." The ecumenical possibilities of such activities were stressed: one club was said to have "enabled Christians to see what can be achieved when we pool our resources, forget individual church/chapel allegiances and all work together for God's kingdom".

10.85. For older teenagers the possibilities offered by the cathedral for special events seemed to provide a draw: "Occasional diocesan-wide youth events held in Wells Cathedral and led by the two diocesan youth officers, with the involvement of one or both bishops, act as a real stimulus to the young from the rural areas and seem to reduce their feelings of isolation." Similar successes were reported from Blackburn, Canterbury and elsewhere.

10.86. Overall there is general evidence that young people who may exist in very small numbers in any particular church gain considerable benefit from mixing with other young Christians at events organised at deanery, diocesan, national and interdenominational levels, and that the local church could do much more to publicise such events, providing transport to them and where necessary finance, thus identifying themselves with the young people's need to broaden their horizons, rather than fearing its consequences.

10.87. It is felt that it would be an advantage if one bishop from within each diocese could take a special interest in youth work. However, the prime responsibility for youth provision still remains in the local situation, with stimulation, support and training being made available through the diocesan youth officer, whose own training should include consideration of the particular needs of rural young people and rural churches.

10.88. Although the Commission has been shown some examples of good practice (such as an open club in Derbyshire which attracts 100 teenagers over the age of 13 from a total population of 2,000 and through its programme is able to engage them in discussion of relevant moral issues), and although work with younger children can sometimes involve well over 50% of a small village's children (eg St Chad's, Great Habton, North Yorkshire), the general response of the Church to the needs of the older age group is poor. Furness Deanery is typical of very many, if not all, in reporting confirmation of young people as a 'graduation out' rather than a 'graduation in'.

10.89. It is worth considering the way in which other denominations try to draw young people into more active participation in church life at this stage in their development - for example, the young people of the United Reformed Church are afforded a significant role in the Church's decision-making processes at all levels of church life, and through involvement in FURY (Fellowship of United Reformed Youth) they are encouraged to develop their skills. A recent HMI report noted of the young people's assembly: "The level of responsible and informed debate is impressive, informative material is available and the atmosphere is one of serious endeavour laced with good humour and sensitive understanding for those who speak for the first time in a large assembly. It provides education in the mechanics of political discussion and democratic decision-making. Resolutions are formed which go forward to the General Assembly, and because of the place accorded to young people in the church constitution they are able to speak directly to them and to vote on them on that occasion."

10.90. The Commission did indeed find evidence of a growing awareness on the part of the Church of the need to recognise the social issues affecting older teenagers and young adults, eg The North Wilts Rural Churches group has been attempting to tackle some of these issues at a parish level. In Bristol Diocese young people are being encouraged by their diocesan youth officer, through two Youth Working Parties in the Chippenham Deanery and Malmesbury Deanery, to examine what is being done for youth in the two areas and what the youngsters themselves would like to see available. In being invited to put their results to their deanery synods these young people are being encouraged to feel that they have a place in the institutional structure of the Church and are not alienated from it. The Youth Council of Carlisle Diocese has similarly considered specific issues of rural youth work and produced recommendations very much in line with those of the Commission.

10.91. There is no clear division between the developmental needs of rural and urban youngsters during the all-important adolescent period. They are subject to the same cultural influences through the media and school life. They are passing through the same period of developing physical maturity, and are similarly engaged in taking important decisions with regard to curriculum, careers and relationships. However, the facilities and support mechanisms which are, or are not, available to them at this time are likely to play a key role in their development, and it is here that rural youngsters can lose out in comparison with their urban counterparts.

10.92. Generalisations are difficult since the remoteness of the area, the sex and social class of the youngster, and access to transport are all important, but a picture emerges of young people with few choices – of type of social activity; of developing relationships with a wide range of young people of the same age outside school, or with adults outside their immediate circle; of developing independence; of testing out new ideas; or of gaining a balanced picture of the urban life which many of them will inevitably move into in the search for jobs and housing. There is evidence that girls in particular can find village life very restrictive during the teenage years.

10.93. Submissions from churches of various denominations, as well as from uniformed organisations and secular groups concerned for young people, indicate problems of small numbers, lack of leadership, training and support, few resources, and unsuitable premises, coupled with a feeling that more could be done, and more should be done - but not by the Church or any other group in isolation. It is recognised that where specific Christian nurture is involved the Churches have a key role to play, though not a narrowly denominational one. A submission from the Girl Guides Association stressed the need to be open in approach and ecumenical: "There is no room for denominational barriers in small villages. Thinking youngsters cannot understand the divisions in Christian churches." Similarly, a survey of the Roman Catholic youth service in rural Wiltshire picks up a key theme from many denominational submissions: "One of the more encouraging aspects covered in the survey was the amount of ecumenical activity that seemed to be going on. Many of the smaller rural parishes look not towards the larger Catholic parishes found in nearby towns but the local Christian communities."

10.94. That locality rather than denomination should be the norm for organising young people's work is a recurrent theme in submissions. Sometimes locality relates to a village, but other localities such as school catchment area need to be explored. Successful work has been done in this way by Crusaders in Swaffham, East Anglia.

10.95. Another recurrent theme is the need for appropriate training and real and practical support and care for youth workers. In this respect, *Spectrum*, a new inter-church basic training course for youthworkers launched this year jointly by eight denominations, including the Church of England, would seem particularly appropriate to the needs of rural youthworkers. In commending *Spectrum*, Paul Battersby, National Youth Officer, notes that:-

1. It is a fine example of ecumenical co-operation in a specific area of work where what the denominations hold in common far outweighs what keeps us apart. As Cardinal Basil Hume said in his speech at the *Spectrum* launch in May 1989: "*Spectrum* has pre-Swanicked Swanick."

2. The Church of England has been heavily involved in the writing, editing and field-testing of material throughout (through diocesan

youth officers) and managing the project (through the National Youth Officers of the Board of Education).

3. The course is delivered locally through tutors from different denominations and received by volunteer youth workers from different denominations.

4. The course is group-work based and thus is of particular use in rural areas in providing support for isolated workers and giving the opportunity for isolated workers to keep in touch with each other (and collaborate) after the course has finished.

5. The sessions on 'Church and Community' and 'Support' should be of particular relevance to volunteer workers in rural areas.

Recommendations

1. Dioceses should help individual schools to evaluate and assess their relationship with the local community. (10.37)

2. The interest of individual clergy in education should be taken into account when appointments are made to rural parishes which include church schools. (10.40)

3. The Anglican Colleges of Higher Education should be used to assist in the initial training of clergy in educational matters, and to provide in-service training for clergy who teach or lead worship in church schools. (10.40)

4. Dioceses should strengthen wherever possible their advisory service to church schools and their provision of in-service training to teachers in church schools. (10.41)

5. Initial teacher training courses should include more specific reference both to small rural schools and to church schools in particular. (10.41)

6. Dioceses should draw up guidelines, in consultation with local education authorities, to help local churches evaluate the pros and cons of the closure of small church schools, and to ensure that local churches are aware of strategies such as clustering. (10.42)

7. Dioceses should offer varied training opportunities for church school governors, where feasible with the co-operation of the local education authority. (10.43)

8. Dioceses should explore ways of equipping local churches to meet the added responsibilities imposed on school governors by the new education act without overburdening the clergy. This may involve appointing suitable laity to fill roles previously held by clergy. (10.44)

9. Dioceses should explore the benefits of having bishop's visitors appointed to church schools to strengthen the links between school and diocese, and should develop ways to equip such visitors to work effectively. (10.45)

10. Wherever possible, the areas served by church schools should be taken into account when structuring multi-parish benefices. (10.47)

11. Church schools should develop ways of fullyinvolving clergy from all the benefices in the area served by the school, as well as ministers of other denominations. (10.47)

12. Dioceses should ensure that their diocesan director of education is adequately supported and resourced, and that clear provision is made within the education budget for the adequate supervision of church schools and for curriculum development within those schools. (10.48)

13. Dioceses should continue to explore the development of diocesan educational resource centres for the use of rural schools, and should also consider the usefulness of educational resource packs which individual rural schools can use for a month or so before passing them to other schools. (10.49)

14. Dioceses should make every effort to help the smallest schools to cope with the varying demands of local management of schools, the national curriculum and attainment targets and assessment. (10.50)

15. Dioceses should encourage churches and church schools to explore the theological bases of the Church's involvement in education and to test their current practice against them. (10.51)

16. Parishes should continue to discuess the implications of *Children in the Way* making use of the diocesan children's adviser. (10.66)

17. Dioceses should review urgently the resources needed by rural churches to undertake an effective ministry among children and families, and should keep these factors in mind when framing policies which involve disposing of village schools and parsonages. (10.72)

18. The Church of England should explore and promote the place of teenagers in the life of the Church by means of an initiative comparable with *Children in the Way*, backed by empirical research. (10.77)

19. Each church should have a member elected or nominated as the person who will lead the youth initiative, liaise with similar representatives of nearby churches and organisations, and report regularly to the parent church (in the case of the Anglican church to the PCC). (10.80)

20. Individual churches should, alongside young people, assess exactly the ages and situations of young people in their own locality, and what is available to them, what gaps in provision need to be filled and how they can co-operate with others to bridge gaps and make most effective use of resources. (10.78)

21. Partnerships should be developed with churches of other denominations or neighbouring parishes so that resources can be shared, encouragement and support given and training opportunities made viable. (10.93)

22. Individual members of churches should as far as possible support existing youth work in the community - uniformed organisations etc. (10.82)

23. The role of young people in the ongoing life of the Church should be examined to seek ways of enabling them to participate fully at all levels of Church life according to their individual skills and talents. (10.89)

24. It should not be assumed that any particular form of youth work or group meeting should go on for ever, but the situation should be regularly reviewed and young people given the opportunity to express their needs and the kind of activity they seek. (10.78-82)

25. The church fellowship itself should be comprehensive and have the full age range in mind in preparing its regular worship; young people should be encouraged to take responsibility for some elements of worship from time to time. (See 9.43)

26. The programme offered to young people as they approach confirmation should be carefully considered, ensuring that it is relevant to the world in which they live and they should be encouraged to see confirmation as a commitment involving a continuing relationship with the Church, rather than as an end product. (10.88)

27. The Church should make full use of opportunities offered by information technology to capture the imagination of the young, particularly those who live in isolated areas. (10.91)

28. The Church should be outward looking in its approach to young people, seeking ways of being of service to young people outside the immediate fellowship of the Church, and offering an appropriate programme of formal and informal opportunities for Christian nurture and education in an increasingly secular society.

29. The Church should make full use of all those members within individual congregations who have skills and talents to share with young people and encourage them to have confidence to take positive

steps towards instituting an appropriate programme, knowing that they have the full backing and support of the Church behind them. (10.80-82)

30. Churches should encourage the growth of activities in which all age groups can share together - Bible studies, social activities, outings, choirs, bell-ringing etc.

31. Churches should make better use of opportunities to advertise events and regular activities through notice boards, leaflets, school buses etc.

32. In order to encourage such local development it is felt important:

(1) for cathedrals to accept the challenge of offering stimulating and exciting events for young people; (10.85) and

(2) that diocesan youth officers should be sensitive to the needs of young people in rural parishes and that they should be encouraged to consider appropriate responses as an important part of their own training. (10.87)

End notes

1. M Cruickshank, *Church and State in English Education*, London, Macmillan, 1963; J Murphy, *Church, State and Schools in Britain 1800-1970*, London Routledge and Kegan Paul, 1971.

2. P C Souper and W K Kay, *The School Assembly Debate: 1942-1982*, Southampton, University Department of Education, 1982.

3. From statistics provided by the Department of Education and Science and the Welsh Office.

4. L J Francis, *Religion in the Primary School*, London, Collins, 1987.

5. John M Hull, *The Act Unpacked*, Derby, Christian Education Movement, 1989.

6. P H Hirst, *'Christian education: a contradiction in terms,'* *Learning for Living*, vol 11, part 4, pp 6-11, 1972.

7. P. H Hirst, *'Education, catechesis and the church school'*, British *Journal of Religious Education*, vol 3, pp 85-93, 1981.

8. Schools Council, *Religious Education in Secondary Schools*, London, Evans Brothers and Methuen Educational, 1971.

9. J M Hull, *School Worship: an obituary*, London, SCM, 1975.

10. B Wilson, *Religion in Secular Society*, London, Watts, 1966.

11. B Wilson, *Religion in Sociological Perspective*, Oxford, Oxford University Press.

12. Swann Report, *Education For All*, London, HMSO, 1985.
13. Report to the Bishops of England and Wales, *Signposts and Homecomings: the educative task of the Catholic community*, Middlegreen, St Paul Publications, 1981.
14. Durham Report, *The Fourth R: the report of the Commission on Religious Education in Schools*, London, National Society and SPCK, 1970.
15. *A Future in Partnership*, London, National Society, 1984.
16. L J Francis, *Partnership in Rural Education*, London, Collins, 1986.
17. L J Francis, *Religion in the Primary School*, London, Collins, 1987.
18. B W Kay, H S Piper and J D Gay, *Managing the Church Schools*, Abingdon, Culham College Institute Occasional Paper number 10, 1988.
19. L J Francis and D W Lankshear, '*The impact of church schools on village church life*', *Educational Studies*, vol. 16, 1990.
20. Plowden Report, *Children and their Primary Schools*, London, HMSO, 1967.
21. Gittins Report, *Primary Education in Wales*, Cardiff, HMSO, 1967.
22. L C Comber, F E Joyce, R J Meyenn, C W Sinclaire, M A Small, M J Tricker and R C Whitfield, *The Social Effects of Rural Primary School Reorganisation in England*, Birmingham, University of Aston, 1981.
23. D Forsythe, et al, *The Rural Community and the Small School*, Aberdeen, Aberdeen University Press, 1983.
24. R Rogers, *Schools Under Threat: a handbook on closure*, London, Advisory Centre for Education, 1979.
25. Cambridge Policy Study in Education, *A Positive Approach to Rural Primary Schools*, Cambridge, Institute of Education, 1981.
26. Department of Education and Science, *Better Schools*, London, HMSO, 1985.
27. M Galton and H Patrick (eds), *Curriculum Provision in the Small Primary School*, London, Routledge, 1990.
28. A Bell and A Sigsworth, *The Small Rural Primary School: a matter of quality*, Barcombe, Falmer, 1987.
29. See note 14 above.
30. See note 17 above.

31. *Children in the Way,* London, National Society and Church House Publishing, 1988.
32. *Making Contact,* London, Collins, 1986.
33. Marjorie Allen, et al, *Signposts on the Way,* Derby, Derby Church House, 1989.
34. Susan Sayers, *Springboard to Worship,* Rattlesden, Kevin Mayhew, 1989.
35. Tony Neal, Barry Kinsmen, Jenny Rolph and Paul Rolph, *Called to Teach: a distance learning course for Sunday School Teachers,* Plymouth, College of St Mark and St John.
36. Leslie J Francis, *Teenagers and the Church,* London, Collins, 1984.
37. *Young People and the Church,* London, British Council of Churches, 1981.
38. Leslie J Francis, *Rural Anglicanism: a future for young Christians?* London, Collins, 1985.
39. See 1 above, especially chapter 7.
40. *Stepping Forward,* London, United Reformed Church, 1986.

Chapter 11
Mission, Evangelism and Community

11.1. The opportunities available to the Church, which is at the centre of many rural communities, offers it the chance of challenging the conception of it as a wealthy, irrelevant anachronism. In many rural areas the church building stands as an ancient focus and is that which gives identity to the community. The Church's task is to ensure that what happens in that building and community in the name of God is worthy of allegiance, and is relevant to the lives of the local people.

11.2. In rural areas it is often wise to avoid too clear a distinction between the Christian life as lived in the Church and the Christian life as lived in society. This point was well put to us by the Revd Nicholas Beddow, Vicar of Escomb and Witton Park in Co Durham. He was writing about the part the Church played in preventing the destruction of the village by planning policy, and in its further reclamation. Now, with 600 inhabitants, there is a strong community life and 15% of them will gather for worship on Sunday...

> "When you pose the question as to the role of the Church in this process.. you are in danger of trying to unstitch a seamless garment, and of opening up divisions which in the normal course of events function in a kind of natural creative tension."

11.3. Thus the division between Church and Community is necessarily blurred. The difficult question is how one can live an openly Christian life in a way that does not alienate those who do not share the faith, but attracts through interest into commitment to Christ. Many Christians are unhappy about wearing their faith on their sleeve, particularly in small communities, where one's weaknesses as well as strengths are known. Many people claim the description 'Christian' but infrequently, if ever, attend church. The challenge of evangelism is how to develop the faith of those whose response is behavioural and not yet worshipful.

11.4. A further question for the Church is how to recognise, affirm and celebrate what the people of God are already doing in His Name. We have met many Christian people who are doing marvellous things, in their work and free time, but the gathered Church does nothing to support and encourage their Christian contribution.

11.5. Many new villagers are welcomed by neighbours and probably the vicar in their first week; a number of rural clergy take this opportunity to explain the dynamics of the community to such newcomers, and give them a copy of the community information sheet. We have evidence from our diocesan visits (Worcester and Chester for example) of this visit being accompanied by an invitation to a meal at the Vicarage. This will not be the only invitation from churchpeople to the newcomers. Such welcomes are a powerful social oil at least, and also effective pre-evangelism.

At the village of Stapleford near Cambridge the Vicar used to chair a 'Newcomers Evening' every six months or so to which all recent newcomers were invited along with the existing villagers. Local organisations and individuals made brief presentations, thus unravelling the full panoply of village life. A slide show offered a potted history of the village and the church. The living history of the village and its oral tradition was rehearsed before the newcomers in an entirely informal way, but one that had a profound effect on the newcomers. The Vicar commented: "The upshot of this exercise is that every newcomer has a sense of being known, and their presence noted and felt - even appreciated. For some this is a strange experience, having come from urban or suburban environs. I suppose the village is telling them that living in a village makes it difficult to be anonymous, even if you want to be."

We sadly record the death of the Vicar, the Revd Colin Hay Davidson soon after our visit.

11.6. If one of the attractions of rural life is the apparent closeness of the fellowship, then the church is on trial when visitors take a step into the Sunday worship. The Rural Church Project (RCP) revealed a very high level of support for the idea that the church is a social place, giving the opportunity to get to know people. This was the view of 95% of the church electoral roll sample, and 82% of the overall parish sample.

11.7. The pressure on local churches to raise money for their own and for diocesan purposes quickly changes a perception of the Church as wealthy to one of the Church as "always after your money". It is important for local churches to have a clear explanation about church finances available, as the Church *is* capital rich while being more stretched in the current account. The Church Commissioners' leaflets help provide such an explanation, and should be used by all parishes for both internal and external education.

11.8. The accusation of irrelevancy is likely to be countered by a church which is looking increasingly to the laity for leadership. A pattern of worship which is led by local people will touch and reflect the life of the local community. Many parishes arrange special occasions to which a very high percentage of the village come and are helped to realize that the church is for them even if they choose not to get involved very often.

11.9. The RCP revealed a high level of preparedness both to accept and to offer ministry among the laity, ranging from 57% prepared to conduct pastoral visits to 11% prepared to lead worship. The message is clear. The further development of skills among the laity will be well received.

11.10. Various research such as that conducted by the BBC and the Alister Hardy Research Centre at Oxford indicates that religious experience is widespread, and that official religious organisations touch only a small fraction of those who might be thought to be open to, at least, conversation about religious matters. Religion, then, is not a matter reserved for the clergy or churchgoers; it is potentially common to all humans and in fact experienced by most. The question is, how does organised religion touch and help seekers who are not attracted enough to test it for themselves? A seeker in a small rural church cannot test the service without being obvious. In rural areas an anonymous local presence is virtually impossible.

11.11. The Church at a local level is encountered by people in a number of different ways. The noticeboard, magazine, PCC, church school, parsonage, hall, graveyard and the church building itself all give out messages about our faith. We have seen many examples of positive uses of these.

Church-owned buildings

11.12. The church building in the middle of a group of houses is what makes an English village a village in the eyes of many people. It is a totem, a focus of identity, even to those who hardly ever cross its threshold. It may serve this purpose even more strongly in widely dispersed areas that may have no other focus. This feeling may be developed into a loyalty if its continuation is threatened. Even those who may feel indifferent to the Christian religion will often support fundraising to carry out an important repair to the parish church. It is quite common for locals to declare that the church building is more important than the parson if there is a choice to be made. The church building gives added dimensions: historical, vertical, spiritual. The care and presentation of the building, its environs and notice boards are therefore of prime importance in the mission of the Church to both locals and visitors.

11.13. A growing number of church people are actively trying to rearrange their church building through some process of reordering. We were impressed by those churches which did not leave this at the worship level but reviewed the use of the church building in broader community terms. Where reordering for worship involves an attempt to make the church structure and furniture more helpful for the needs of worship today, the altar is frequently brought forward and obstacles separating priest from people removed. We have seen parts of larger churches partitioned off to enable the worship to be more intimate and warmer, while carpeting, moveable seating, as well as modern heating, lighting and toilets have all been added in an attempt to create a contemporary setting within an ancient building. When reordering has only the purpose of allowing for modern styles of worship it may be that due regard should be paid to the possible transitoriness of such approaches. We warmed to the advice given by the Provost of Bury St Edmunds, as Chairman of the St Edmundsbury and Ipswich Diocesan Advisory Committee, that this type of reordering should be of a reversible nature.

11.14. Some of the most successful schemes we saw had clearly been designed so that the church could be used for a number of more secular activities. The best took into account the fact that the needs of the young, aged and handicapped are the same in social activities as well as in worship. This approach is particularly important where a community lacks other adequate public meeting places. Successful arrangements have been seen on our visits, which allow for youth work, meetings in comfort, a playgroup area, kitchen facilities and a church office. For all of these, the provision of toilets is crucial.

11.15 In some ancient buildings these adaptations are difficult and expensive to achieve, not least because of opposition from conservationists. In the end an agreement has to be made, and we urge churches to discuss their objectives with conservationists at an early stage; equally we remind conservationists that the church building needs to fulfil its original purpose and therefore must not become fossilised. The whole question of reordering is a sensitive and important matter, but we urge local churches to reflect on their buildings, using imagination to see how they can best serve the community at large.

The Victorian church at Neston near Chippenham in the Diocese of Bristol was adapted by building a two-storey suite of rooms at the west end of the church providing a large meeting room used by the school assembly for 120 children, Churchmen's Dinners with speaker, and, for festival occasions, the screen is folded back and the gallery provides overflow for the nave seating. Downstairs the parish has a kitchen, toilets and office.

The church at Flax Bourton in the Diocese of Bath and Wells solved their dry rot problem, and the absence of a community building in the village, by creating an open space in the nave, with moveable seating for use throughout the week. The atmosphere of the ancient church was not adversely affected at all.

In the diocese of St Edmundsbury and Ipswich there are several examples of adaptation of churches to provide for social purposes: Ixworth, St Mary and Stutton, St Peter (where the north aisle now serves as a parish room) are particularly noteworthy.

The parish church at Riseley in the Diocese of St Albans has had the chancel converted into a soundproof room for the junior church, coffee etc. Further consideration is

---

> **being given to expansion of the church building to provide more meeting rooms since there is nothing suitable near the village.**

11.16. Objections may arise from those who resent any change in what is familiar to them; from those who have a narrow view of what constitutes holiness; or from those who see the church building primarily as an architectural feature. Many objectors fail to realise the many changes have probably already taken place to make the church the place of beauty they perceive it to be. They may also fail to realise that the mediaeval church was indeed used for the wide range of activities that are being attempted anew. It has always been the case that the nave "belonged to the people" while the choir and chancel were for the sacred activities. The link between the sacred and the secular is vital in incarnational Christianity. At the moment of Jesus' death the veil in the temple between the holy of holies and the rest of the temple was torn in two. The division between God and mankind is removed like the Berlin wall.

11.17. This symbolic destruction is a most important Christian discovery for it is a demonstration of the scriptural claim that "the world is the Lord's and all that is in it". There is nothing in human life in which God is not already involved. We do not go to church to get away from the world. We take the world into church with us to celebrate and confess it there. The nave is our world, the world is our nave. We need not feel bound or constrained in the ways we seek to use our churches; perhaps the more we go to church for things other than conventional prayer and worship, the more we will come to appreciate that God is involved in each aspect of our lives with no division in His eyes between them.

Former Church assets

11.18. We have frequently encountered strong feelings against the Church over the way local assets given to the Church in the distant past have been removed from local church ownership. Many older people, and certainly farmers, tell stories about tithing and glebe land, and may find it difficult to see the Church in an innocent light. The clergy of the past were to be feared (or respected) as they wielded considerable power in the community. With the squire and doctor they effectively controlled the life of all in the village. Dissenters were harshly dealt with. The organising of local charities was a small compensatory act. As part of a hierarchical view of the created order people knew their place. Today there is a more egalitarian philosophy abroad and the old ways are seen as patronising at best. The Church has to work hard to change the way it, and the gospel it purports to present, is encountered; although this is made easier by new generations, and new villagers unfamiliar with the traditions of the past. The transfer of glebe from benefice to diocesan ownership hit rural people hard, and may account for some reluctance to give generously to the work of the Church. We believe it to be most important that diocesan authorities now respond enthusiastically to the request arising in many rural areas that glebe land might be used as one means of providing for the housing needs of local people.

11.19. We noted a similar resentment over the question of the sale of church schools. Many of these were built in the Victorian period as part of the Christian mission to help the ignorant improve their lot by literacy and numeracy, as well as to improve the morals of the nation. Land for the school was often provided at no cost by a willing landowner, and sometimes other local leaders helped with the overall project. The present conflict focuses around the question of whether the founding of the school was to provide local education for the parish, or whether it was part of a wider programme of church mission which happened to be placed in a particular village. The assumption of the diocesan authorities that all assets belong to the centre should, we think, be tested further in law. Currently, the major part (usually eleven fourteenths) of the proceeds from the sale of closed church schools is redeployed by the diocesan schools account to maintain other existing church schools or to build new church schools elsewhere. A number of submissions drew attention to the way in which the sale of a church school deprives the village church of a key resource for the community, often at a time when the historic parsonage house has also been sold. Even after taking into account their three-fourteenths share from the sale of a closed school, many rural churches cannot afford to provide alternative accommodation for Sunday schools and other forms of church activities formerly housed in church schools or parsonages. Some submissions, like one received from the Diocese of Salisbury, drew attention to the suspicion that the capital realised from historic involvement in the countryside is being re-invested primarily in non-rural environments.

> **At Uldale in the Diocese of Carlisle a closed church school has been let as a field centre rather than sold off. The terms of the lease mean that the school will be maintained by the LEA and villagers will be allowed to use the facility occasionally for other purposes.**

> **In one diocese, the primary school in Village X was sold for conversion to a private residence. An oral promise was made that a share of the proceeds would come back to the village, but the DBF retracted this, offering a series of arguments that proved to be specious. The DBF then offered 3/14ths of the proceeds to the PCC for use in religious education: three years after the closure of the school, this had not been received.**
>
> **In Village Y in the same diocese, the primary school was closed, and without local consultation the DBF leased it for use as a nursery school for the children of servicemen. The Scheme of Closure embraced £1000 gilt-edged stock bequested in trust for the upkeep of the school.**

We recognise the wide variations in the wishes of original school trustees, but invite the authorities to be imaginative in interpreting those wishes for the benefit of local community needs as much as for the wider educational needs. Diocesan synods will need to become more aware of the difficult balancing act that their Board of Education is often asked to perform, and to give full consideration to the social needs of the rural communities from which assets are being removed. 11.20. In the meantime, it would be good sense for diocesan authorities to be much more sensitive to the aspirations of the local church and parish in providing for a continuing Christian mission in their area, and to support that by imaginative interpretation of the understanding of 'education' when deciding the allocation of resources. There should be a positive vetting of facilities within the village and in particular a study of how those activities carried out in the school building will be housed in the future. Having made that study the diocese would be right to help the parish in its attempts to provide itself with a new building that is necessary by using a significant part of the proceeds it has raised from the sale of the asset.

11.21. As we mention in 12.115. there has been a concerted programme of disposal of redundant parsonages, and also of older, larger houses that have been a maintenance headache for dioceses and clergy alike. Many, but not all, clergy prefer the smaller, more modern houses. However, a point of view that has been put to us is that this programme of disposal has at times been over-hasty, and that other options have not been explored; nor have the wider costs to the community from which a meeting facility may have been lost.

11.22. In view of the imaginative uses to which 'The Old Vicarage' is sometimes put by subsequent owners, it may be that dioceses should explore more fully the alternatives to disposal, although not at a loss. These include use by housing associations to meet local need, development of the site at profit, preferably including an element of affordable housing, use by Christian residential communities, which include both well-established religious orders and others more experimental. The important point to make is that the sale of the house should not be done too quickly. Christian groups in other parts of the country may not know of its availability, and perhaps there should be a central register of such properties, which would give time for discussion, not least at the local level, where feelings may be tender. This is likely to be the case where there has been a tradition of community use of part of the parsonage. We recognise the dilemma that such a community use may be a benefit to the parish but it is likely to be a burden, perhaps unwelcome, on the incumbent and family.

11.23. The diocese needs to see that the presence of the parsonage, indeed each asset, is part of the Church's overall missionary strategy, and very full consultations need to take place before the disposal of what are often irreplaceable assets. It may be foolish to leave the church without some flexibility in housing the future ministry which could develop. The wider Church needs to give strong indications that it is on the side of the small rural community, not against it. To retain a parsonage, even if rented out for some years, is a sign of commitment to the future. We recognise that there are costs involved in implementing these ideas and that these may well increase the need for current giving, and the issues need to be considered in that light. There needs to be a discussion on the policy for ministerial housing in each diocese as part of the missionary strategy.

Social projects

11.24. Many imaginative projects in recent times have owed their success to church people. We note in the fields of affordable housing, social transport, community care, economic development, and play group provision, for example, the remarkable contribution of Christian people in the village organisations. It is clear from the expectations of those outside the Church's network that the PCC ought to be active in considering the wellbeing of all the people in the parish.

11.25. It is vital that any Church initiative should be developed in conjunction with other agencies where they are willing. Councils for Voluntary Service, Volunteer Bureaux and Rural Community Councils (RCCs) are willing partners in the generalist voluntary sector. Other specialist agencies, such as Age Concern or the Pre-school Playgroups Association, will welcome Church interest and support. The same is increasingly true for the statutory sector which is looking for organisations which are able to help particularly in the delivery of care in the community.

11.26. We now illustrate some good examples of projects in which Church people play a key role. We are aware of the danger of looking for Church projects precisely because the rural Church does not think of itself as separate from the rest of the community. However, the projects outlined below are included to 'whet the appetite'. We believe that this Christian example is a demonstration of the love of God for all that He has made. Through it others may be brought to know that love.

The North Wiltshire Rural Churches Group, a group of laity and clergy drawn from churches in two dioceses and three denominations within the area of the North Wiltshire District Council has, with the Council for Voluntary Service, begun a Circle of Care providing training of a practical nature for Carers. Support for a full time post is now forthcoming from the Health Authority and a trust, as well as the Social Services Department and the Rural Development Commission.

The work of Canon Malcolm Grundy as Team Rector of Huntingdon is a good example of the Church's officers putting their weight behind collaborative ventures. As chairman of the local Volunteer Bureau he created good links which have resulted in holidays for the needy, a drop-in centre for the elderly and disabled, and a gardening service given by Duke of Edinburgh Award students. A weekend creche for families visiting the local prison, lifts to hospital and elsewhere involve other volunteers. "Aiming to work in such a way has given informal support and encouragement to local church members to become more deeply committed to community work," he writes, "I am sure that the co-operation of churches and church members in this volunteer work has allowed much more to be done than could ever have been achieved by any group working separately."

At Uffculme in Devon the local church over 20 years has created a network of local trusts to take initiatives to provide over 80 houses for local families, restored a redundant mill as a working museum with additional workspace for new businesses, provided a one mile footpath connecting the ends of the village, and taken a lease on a redundant brewery to provide an activity centre for the handicapped, adult education classes and DIY resources for the whole community. The Church is now run from the parish office above a social centre in the main square, and the church building has been re-ordered with the nave being open and carpeted for good traditional and contemporary worship.

The St Edmundsbury and Ipswich Diocesan Board for Social Responsibility have since 1985 run Mobile Family Centres as part of its Family Life Project. The caravans visit a wide range of villages as a focus for parents and toddlers, and a resource base for summer Family Playschemes. This is a good way of breaking down isolation in remote rural areas. Some quotes indicate this success:

"It has improved my relationship with my neighbours ..."

"I am beginning to feel part of the village."

"We continued to meet in each other's homes through the winter break."

"It is the most important piece of work done in this parish in 40 years."

The Dioceses of Portsmouth and Winchester have both worked with the Hampshire Council for Community Service over the years in the development of care in the community programmes. Each diocese has a part-time adviser who encourages the establishment of local groups which focus on practical neighbourliness. The most common request for help is with transport. Newcomers to the field find this is a good way of getting involved in the community.

The parish of Windlesham in Surrey has 41 volunteer drivers whose availability is co-ordinated by a member of the Church. Users of the car scheme contribute towards petrol costs on a voluntary basis. This scheme is typical of many round the country. In this case it is a Church based scheme, but there are many in which churchpeople play an anonymous part.

The parish of Fingringhoe in Essex was bequeathed an old stable-block. This has allowed the development of sheltered housing for the elderly and some small workshops for new businesses.

Job Centre information was regularly displayed on the notice boards of 12 rural North Essex parishes after a successful pilot scheme by the Revd Keith Lovell of Tollesbury. "On average one person a fortnight was helped in finding a job. We stopped the scheme when unemployment became less of a problem."

The Revd John Mason, priest-in-charge of Weston Subedge in Gloucester Diocese is leading his four villages in a bid to obtain a 22-year lease from the Diocese on six acres of glebe on which the newly formed Cotswold Edge Sports and Playing Fields Association will create a multi-use sports centre with Sports Council backing. Indoor and outdoor facilities will be created for the benefit of all the member sports clubs, and the whole community.

The Carlisle Diocesan Board for Social Responsibility took the lead in backing an initiative for increasing training and employment opportunity in upland Cumbria, related to improving and maintaining the landscape and footpaths so that visitors will find the countryside in good heart. The Church grant of £500 gave encouragement to other public bodies to put their backing behind this proposal.

Village appraisals

11.27. Many parishes have responded to the suggestion made in *Faith in the City* of holding a parish audit. PCCs should be alert to the parallel but larger exercise called a village appraisal which should involve the whole community. Such an appraisal can be instigated by any local group, but the parish council should be involved, and the advice of the local RCC should be sought. In rural areas there is a ·strong presumption for privacy which often makes an assessment difficult, but it is possible to arrange a village appraisal in such a way that it will be acceptable to the large majority.

When social issues emerge, they will confront the whole community. They will come out in questions like:
Who in our village has no car to use during the day?
Who lives on their own; with or without relatives?
How are neighbours aware of whether those people are unwell?
Are they always alone for meals?
How many people, and with what skills and at what age, are out of work?

> **How many younger people have stayed at school or are in higher education? What are their needs?**
> **Does the local community concern itself about young people's futures, their recreation and holiday jobs?**

11.28. We welcome the new Rural Social Partnership Fund (RSPF) of the Rural Development Commission and suggest that the Churches acting together should take the opportunity to work in collaboration with the Fund. The fund was established in 1990 to enable innovative work to begin across the whole range of rural social concerns. It is early days, but the size of the RSPF is clearly exploratory. We hope that there is scope for a considerable increase in the size of the Fund to meet the predictable demand it will generate. A wide range of socially concerned organisations are invited to consider becoming partners. It is further intended to enable national organisations to increase their commitment to rural areas by making officer appointments. This concept of partnership is an important one for the Church, as it is through partnership with others that much can be achieved.

11.29. By working in conjunction with secular agencies the Church will discover that it is not alone in seeking to do God's will, and that it has a particular contribution as a partner with others, sharing in both motivation and professional expertise. Too often it seems as if the Church is unwilling to work with others, ignorant of the desire of other bodies (including statutory authorities) to co-operate with it. Certainly the reduction in the number of parochial clergy may have contributed to the diminution in the response of the 'official' Church to a number of important rural issues. The RCP revealed that of the 572 clergy only 4 were Justices of the Peace, 18 parish councillors, 3 either district or county councillors, but 372 were school governors; 78 held another position of community responsibility which for some was a local charity or village hall trustee. This means that 16% held no public office outside Church affairs. Sixteen dioceses have rural officers/agricultural chaplains, part of whose task is to enable the official Church the better to formulate a relationship with the rest of society, and we are aware that a number of other dioceses are encouraging the person appointed as their link with this Commission to continue some kind of limited responsibility for rural matters, often by involvement with the RCC.

11.30. The twin metaphors that Jesus used of his followers, that they were to be the salt of the world and the light of the world, are tantalising opposites. The one - salt - operates by total absorption, becoming invisible as it draws out and enhances the flavour of that within which it is placed. The other - light - operates by being placed at a distance from that on which it casts its benefit. It is highly visible as it operates, and remains distinct. For the rural Church these opposites are expressed as the gathered church, a light to shine out for the Gospel; and alternatively as a community church, the salt within the whole life of the parish. It may often be more appropriate to use another analogy used by Jesus: the faithful as the leaven in the lump.

11.31. If it be true that we are in days that might be called post-Christian, and the statistical evidence of church activity is unequivocal, then it will be true that even a community church also functions as a gathered church. The Decade of Evangelism, indeed the Gospel itself, impels us to seek ways of sharing our faith that are appropriate to the community setting.

11.32. Earlier in this chapter we looked at different kinds of investment the Church had previously made to support its mission: redundant buildings of one kind or another. The Church is primarily the people, devoted to the Gospel of Jesus and God's mission. Buildings then are only relevant for the Church insofar as they serve that purpose.

A national focus for the Church's rural work

11.33. Over the years the Arthur Rank Centre (ARC) has offered an opportunity for partnership between the Church and others, and we would urge that the ARC become more widely accepted in the Church as the focus for advice and information on rural social involvement. The Arthur Rank Centre is an ecumenical chaplaincy centre situated at the National Agricultural Centre, Stoneleigh, Warwickshire. The National Agricultural Centre had been established by the Royal Agricultural Society of England in 1963 to provide a permanent site for the Royal Show and also (increasingly) for countryside matters in general. The ARC was the result of Lord Rank's vision of a permanent Christian presence in the midst of this rapidly growing development. Lord Rank died unexpectedly before the vision became a reality, but on completion in 1972 the Centre was named in his memory.

The purposes of the ARC were defined early on as:

(1) To develop an ecumenical chaplaincy centre and to consider

the ethical and theological issues raised by modern agricultural practice from a Christian standpoint.

(2)   To be a resource centre for the rural church nationally and to explore new patterns of ministry and mission in the countryside.

(3)   To analyse and comment on the changes taking place in rural communities and to become actively involved in response to those changes, especially in the areas of housing and employment.

(4)   To encourage town-country links and to identify the nature of the interrelationship between urban and rural communities.

(5)   To relate to rural communities overseas - especially those in developing countries - and to explore the relationships between European and Third World agriculture.

11.34. Over the years, in pursuance of these aims, the ARC has established the NAC Rural Trust (concerned with rural housing), the Rural Enterprise Unit (concerned with employment in the countryside), the Church and Conservation Project, the Farmers' Third World network and courses on rural ministry and mission for clergy and lay people. It provides a resource and information service for the rural church. The staff have a peripatetic teaching role throughout the country. It also has a varied conference programme on the Church and rural issues, and it provides a valuable shop window for the Church on the occasion of major events such as the Royal Show. Members of its staff represent the Churches nationally on Rural Voice, and have produced literature on all these various subjects.

11.35. The ARC also services and provides a focus for the work of agricultural chaplains in this country. It has been closely involved in the establishment of the Rural Theology Association (RTA) and the Federation for Rural Evangelism.

11.36. Financially it is supported by the Rank Foundation, the Churches (Methodist, Anglican, United Reformed, Baptist, Roman Catholic and the Free Church Federal Council) and the Royal Agricultural Society of England. Approximately a quarter of the income is raised by the Centre itself, with a total staff complement of ten.

11.37. *We recommend that the General Synod should budget for an officer and secretarial assistance to be based at the ARC, liaising with dioceses and the appropriate General Synod Boards, to carry on the work of this Commission and to progress our recommendations.* In so far as this officer needs to liaise with other Churches there would be ease of contact at the ARC, where staff from those other denominations already work.

The 'vicar'

11.38. There are more villages which have no resident 'vicar' than those which have. This is a consequence of the growth of multi-parish benefices in recent times. Canon John Tiller's work was largely a response to this change. Historically the combining of parishes is no new feature as has been well illustrated in chapter 7. For those communities which have lost their resident incumbent in recent times that loss is painful; yet another loss of 'facility' in post-war rural Britain. But the 'vicar' is still expected to be at the centre of a circle of care, available and willing to carry out sundry but important tasks of neighbourliness which the Christian faith encourages. The 'vicar' is a resident social worker, community development worker, friend-in-need, adviser, counsellor, as well as a person of prayer. The recognition of the changes in the 'vicar's' role and the need to free the laity for service in the world are explored more fully in chapter 8.

11.39. The combining of these different roles requires the grace of God's blessing, indeed the Church may be at fault in assuming that the administrative functions required of the 'vicar' are combined with the role of the priest. Seldom does the 'holy man' have the gifts of administration. This may explain why the clergy interviewed in the RCP felt that administration took too much of their time, although to an outsider the ratio was not too great. The desire to have a parson in each parish may have to do with a hidden desire to have a resident 'holy person' rather than to have a local administrator of the ecclesiastical machine. The increasing difficulty in contacting him or her, and the pressure on clergy time with the multi-parish benefice, may mean that there has been too little preparation of the whole church for the new styles of ministry.

11.40. There have been several positive features about the old-style rural model (one parish, one parson) which are difficult or impossible to replicate in the new model. In the multi-parish benefice the incumbent will be hard pressed to know everyone in the way that was one delight of the old model. However, it will still be possible to exercise the impartiality of the 'vicar' in local disputes, the opportunity to try new ways of doing things in church life, and to bring freshness from outside. Nevertheless, in many rural communities today it is the laity who are pressing for new ways as people with wider experience make their contribution. The new style clergy will need to be better equipped in public relations skills, and to work harder at relations with other agencies whose interests meet theirs in the local communities. The differences between urban clergy and those in the rural areas focus in the expectations of most village people that the parson's work is not confined to the care of the faithful, but of the wider community. That is a perception which offers the clergy the basic privilege of entry to most places and a right to engage in conversation with almost anyone about almost anything in the cause of the Christian gospel.

11.41. One understanding of parish is its very parochialness, its localness, resistant to outside influence and change. The incumbent in a multi-parish benefice learns at what speed the different communities will move and accept the change without which all goes stale. He is not, however, the only point of contact with the outside world. He has a task of sharing a vision with the faithful and the wider community and to lead others in the practical outworking of that vision. The RCP confirmed that the incumbent was likely to be better known by those who live in the village where the parsonage is situated than by those in the parishes where he is not resident, and a disturbing 23% reported never having met him at all.

The ecumenical dimension

11.42. From the outset we were aware that ecumenical collaboration would be an important issue. The members of the Commission were drawn from a number of denominations, and those denominations made a clear statement of hope that our report would be relevant, not just to the Anglican Church, but also to the other Churches in England. Our questionnaire to the dioceses asked about ecumenical co-operation, and on our visits we were able to obtain a good picture of it. The RCP indicates widespread support for ecumenical services and further development of them. It is not surprising therefore to find encouraging developments in the way in which local churches and individual Christians have often been striding ahead of what is official policy, although it is encouraging that the new Canons of the Church of England point in a similar direction of reducing the importance of denominational identity in favour of a Christian one.

11.43. There are many places where church and chapel both serve a relatively small population. Delicate discussions need to take place about the sharing of those resources in the common mission to be undertaken, particularly when pastoral reorganisation is being considered.

> **A vision of a new relationship is enthusing the clergy and laity of the Church in Nidderdale in North Yorkshire. Six full time clergy of four denominations serve 24 churches with a membership of 810 in a widely scattered population of 4800. They are developing a management plan which will enable them to co-operate in the use of resources of people, money, and property so that the primary tasks of mission and caring can be given greater priority. Natural geography defines the 'shape' of the vision, which some other areas could emulate. The shape of existing deaneries may not make any sense for the tasks which local churches wish to undertake together.**

11.44. It is vital that joint planning takes place between the denominations on a local and area basis. Anglicans particularly need to remember that local preachers are of fundamental importance in the free churches and that they are full and proper participants in joint worship.

11.45. It is also a fact that in many rural areas the parish church is the only centre for worship that remains, although there are significant parts of some counties where a chapel is more commonly found. At present Canon B15A requires of non-Anglicans that, if they attend and receive Holy Communion regularly in the parish church, they must consider becoming Anglicans, with all the initiation that this requires. This is an inappropriate attitude with which non-Anglicans should be met in a single church rural situation. There are many examples of full members of other denominations attending the parish church as their local church without forgoing their continuing loyalty to their parent denomination. Indeed we should acknowledge the positive encouragement given by one leading Methodist to people to support the parish church rather than commute to their 'own' church elsewhere. We have heard many times that what is now needed is the enthusiastic take-up of the possibility of single church rural Local Ecumenical Projects (LEPs).

11.46. Such a development has several strands:

(a) Canon B44 allows for further ecumenical developments in sharing ministry and we would be pleased to see more rural churches taking part in rural LEPs. The advantages of this move would be to make it clear that the one church in the area is indeed *the* church for all the people of whatever tradition, and that all ministers of the participating churches are properly available to the whole community.

(b) This could involve the Methodist Church extending to Anglican clergy 'authorised' or 'recognised' and 'regarded' status with proper safeguards. Further thought would have to be given to limiting their commitment to additional denominational structures. The purpose would be to ensure that congregations of Methodists had a pastor in the locality.

(c) The Church Representation Rules were amended in 1985 to allow Christians of a number of denominations up to a third of the places on the PCC. This position is most welcome and we urge further imaginative development in the enfranchising of all committed Christians.

11.47. We were told on a number of visits that all Christians were welcome at the parish church. While that is no doubt the case, we would recommend that those responsible for worship in such a place make efforts to draw on the best traditions, particularly the musical one, of other denominations, rather than achieve "ecumenism by erosion".

11.48. The Church of England, because of its relative strength in numbers and resources, as well as the fact of establishment, needs to be extra sensitive to the feelings of threat that may be felt by those of other denominations when ecumenical projects are being considered. It has been assumed by some that 'merger' means closure of the chapel. This assumption is wrong. It could well make sense to keep both buildings in use, for different purposes, or for the same use at different times of the year. A good example of this is to be found at Saltfleetby in Lincolnshire where the new united Church (Anglican and Methodist) uses both their former buildings alternately. Had they not come together both churches might have closed. It has been drawn to our attention on a number of occasions that the Anglican tendency to centre worship on the Holy Communion is a problem. This is given fuller treatment in Chapter 9. Anglican clergy need to be sensitive to the spiritual insights of other denominations when planning an ecumenical or, indeed, any service.

11.49. We quote with approval from a report on the ecumenical situation in Loddon in Norfolk, where Anglican and Methodist buildings were retained:

> "Of course we have made plenty of mistakes - but we have now been in existence as one unit within a large LEP for 13 years. For the whole of that time Anglicans and Methodists have done everything completely together: worship; witness; pastoral care; decision-making; and fund-raising. During the last four years the local Roman Catholic community has joined us. They share the same buildings; we frequently enjoy non-Communion worship together and, using the same general principles, we are gradually deepening and widening relationships with them."

The Loddon success story leads to ten guidelines which we reproduce with enthusiasm:

(1) Seize opportunities which present themselves *naturally*.

(2) Commitment *before* detailed planning.

(3) In detailed planning be guided by *sensitivity* and *commonsense*.

(4) Balance of denominational elements in worship.

(5) Provide 'safety-valves' (ie denominational 'conservation areas').

(6) Don't 'double-up' (on meetings/officers).

(7) Pastoral care should be *totally* shared.

(8) Cease to be *self-consciously* ecumenical.

(9) LEP staff (clergy and lay) should meet regularly on a social basis.

(10) There is *no* boss.

11.50. We noted that in the experience of many the implementation of pastoral reorganisation within a denomination had happened without reference to other churches, with the unfortunate occasional consequence that several denominations were carrying out reorganisation simultaneously. We would recommend that denominational heads consult each other at the beginning of any process of reorganisation so that best use is made of the resources that are being redeployed. The same principle of joint planning applies to other wider church resources, such as sector ministers whose work bears on rural areas. The new Rule 9(1B) on Church representation allows for non-Anglicans to be elected by the Annual Parochial Church

Meeting to be on the deanery synod if they are already members of the PCC.

11.51. Use of this provision would make collaboration across the deanery more likely, and should be taken up. It is understood that this does not give the right to vote in further elections to Diocesan or General Synod. Maybe this further barrier will soon be removed.

11.52. It would be in keeping with current ecumenical thinking if the Churches could establish an inter-church group that would monitor developments in the rural church in England. The Church in Rural Life Committee, which was established by the Methodist Church, but now includes representatives of other Churches, is a useful starting point and with goodwill could be adapted to serve the needs of all the denominations in this way. Again we note the positive contribution made over the years in this field by the Arthur Rank Centre. The time is ripe for the Church of England to make a significant contribution to the work of this Centre.

11.53. In the climate of growing ecumenical co-operation there will be many people who move house to an area where there is less collaboration than they have been used to. They share the difficulty that large numbers of people have, that of wondering why, in the face of the huge task that is before us, we indulge in the luxury of fragmenting the effort by continuing denominationalism. Not everywhere is there sufficient enthusiasm for the ecumenical cause but in the basic matter of the Church's mission there can be no excuse for failure to act together.

An appropriate evangelism

11.54. The Gospel, however, does not merely apply to people's individual needs of body, mind and spirit. As was affirmed in Chapter 2 it is also corporate. Indeed, while the Gospel is deeply personal, it is never individualistic. It recognises both the interrelatedness of all humanity and also the corporateness of human society which is as much in need of redemption and liberation as is the individual person. It is a proper Christian response therefore to engage with the political system which shapes our society. The dilemma facing many Christian charities today, is that by law they cannot be political, and yet they know that only by being political can they be truly charitable. Simply to ameliorate the needs of the poor, without tackling the system which creates the poverty in the first place is like treating the spots instead of the measles.

11.55. If it is agreed that our method of evangelism is to start where people are, then it can fairly be stated that many people, while holding a belief in God are not ready to declare themselves as 'card-carrying' Christians. The RCP revealed that 92% of the sample claimed some kind of religious allegiance and yet only 51% ever attended Sunday services. Perhaps the remaining 41% fall into the category of faith which some have called 'implicit religion' or 'folk religion'. Maybe for them God is not found in the sometimes narrow frame of Church Christianity. Those churches that move occasionally outside the traditional framework of authorised services with occasions that celebrate the natural world in a way that can be called folk religion, may find a greater than usual interest from the 41%. Some of these possibilities are given greater detail in Chapter 9. It is interesting here to note that, in the RCP, a surprising 78% of all who claimed to be Anglicans thought that the Church should be "involved in environmental issues". Perhaps there is a need for more frequent celebrations of creation, and occasions such as well dressing and animal blessing, as ways of beginning a response to this awareness.

11.56. These special services can be found in some rural areas as ancient (even pre-Christian) traditions. It is an old strategy to take on old ways and reshape them for new purposes. Most people will be more familiar with the same process in relation to Harvest Thanksgiving. Imagination in creating the opportunity for the Word to be heard in such ways is needed.

11.57. We were encouraged by the submission from the Church of England Evangelical Council which confirmed a different approach by ministers to be necessary in rural areas from one which may work in urban settings. This difference is perhaps most marked over baptism policy. There is a painful compromise to be made between those for whom baptism is a believer's way of entry into the wounds of God, and those for whom it is an initiation into the life of the local community. It is important to remind some readers at this point that baptism is entry into the whole Christian community, not into a particular denomination. The temptation is on us to know who is in and who is out, but if our task is to sow rather than to reap then we may have to leave that sort of judgement to God. Our main task is the preparation of the ground, and the means to that end is the loving care which those of the household of faith give to those who come looking for God's grace. We commend for further reading the essays published by the Church of England Evangelical Council, the Grove booklet *Strategies for Rural Evangelism,* and the *Second Workbook on Rural Evangelism 1985.* (See also 9.55)

11.58. It is generally agreed that evangelistic methods used in urban situations, which involve a degree of anonymity within the crowd, are not appropriate for rural areas. In the village, evangelism takes place through personal and family relationships rather than through crowded rallies. Furthermore, the character of the evangelist is as important as either the message or its presentation. In the village one is known and "no secrets are hid". Therefore integrity is the key, together with a slow, gradual, 'softly softly' approach. The weakness of much rural church witness to date is that it has been so 'slowly slowly' as to be virtually stationary, and there has been a marked reluctance to "name the Name". Responding to an invitation to make a public confession of faith is extremely difficult, although it would be wrong to say it was impossible. In fact it does happen - as it has happened during many evangelical revival meetings in the past in the countryside. Today, however, it is less likely to happen, and a different strategy needs to be devised. The Church's mission is often seen at its most effective in its work with children and young people. This chapter is headed *Mission, Evangelism and Community.* We are reminded that everything about the Church, its buildings, its worship, its publications, its people are all part of the mission, and need to be assessed, prepared and presented with evangelism in mind.

11.59. This does not mean that there is no place for traditional missions in rural areas. There is good evidence that rural people themselves can engage effectively in missions to other rural people. Such missions are ways of raising expectations and standards of worship, of enlivening housegroups and service in the community, as well as of bringing people to a new and a deeper faith. Such missions need careful preparation both by those to carry out, and those to receive the visitors.

> **The Diocese of Bath and Wells, which has 500 lay people with experience of village to village mission, and others, particularly Rural Sunrise, have much experience of this way of conducting mission.**

11.60. Not all Christians are called to be evangelists, but all are called to witness. In rural areas Christians have a unique opportunity to witness through their lives because of the close relationship between church and community. They are in touch with their neighbours in a way that the urban church cannot be. With so many new people moving into our rural areas they have a remarkable opportunity to draw many to know our Lord in a new way. All the evidence points to people becoming Christian as a consequence of contact with friends and neighbours so there is every opportunity for the rural Church.

Ministry to visitors

11.61. English Cathedrals draw millions of visitors to our ancient towns and cities. Likewise, many thousands of people visiting the countryside wish to visit the many beautiful churches there. They are often prevented from doing so by locked doors, inadequate information or poor signposting.

11.62 The RCP indicated that a high 67% of the sample had visited a church (as opposed to attending a service) in the previous 12 months. Of these visitors 33% were able to say that they had had a spiritual motive for making the visit, while 53% went out of "general interest". The challenge to PCCs is to make adequate allowance for the largely unmet needs of visitors. Clearly there are different levels of response required and possible and it is encouraging to note a rising level of commitment in dioceses to the opportunities of using our historic churches as part of a programme of evangelism. We were pleased to find some churches that invited visitors to leave requests for prayer, using those requests as part of the prayer of the Church on the following Sunday, or by local people praying those requests during their own prayers during the week. The Diocese of Gloucester has a member of staff who has the responsibility of helping parishes with their 'marketing' and presentation to visitors. A good level of collaboration with the Tourist Information Offices is an important strategy. In Lincoln Diocese the Tourism Development Award from the Ecclesiastical Insurance Group has facilitated further growth in good quality material presenting churches to a wider public. Many parishes, of course, make their own response, but marketing of rural churches is likely to be more successful where there is collaboration across a geographical area. For detailed advice on what arrangements to make for visitors once they have arrived, we recommend a booklet entitled *Helping the Stones to Speak*, by Moya Feehally (Tortoiseshell Publications).

> **The Diocese of Bradford continues to make the running in the promotion of the ministry to visitors. For 1991 they are planning a conference for the Northern Province to share experience, and to encourage more local churches to take the opportunity the church building affords.**

11.63. Our encouragement of this ministry is that, while it may have a positive financial outcome, the main motive must be one of effective evangelism. Our ancient churches are for us a part of the Gospel message. They demonstrate the faithfulness of previous generations, they make theological statements in their very architecture, they offer a chance of interpreting the faith anew in our own time. We suggest that every PCC looks with fresh hope at their own church buildings with the question: "What does our church say to those who come to, and through, its door?"

Recommendations

1. The local church should ensure that every newcomer is greeted on arrival and invited to participate in the life of the community and of the Church. Full details of local facilities should be offered. (11.5.)

2. Explanatory leaflets about church finances should be circulated annually with the local newsletter. (11.7.)

3. PCCs should discuss the impressions being given by their buildings and publications with a view to their improvement. (11.12.)

4. The Arthur Rank Centre should compile data about the social use of church buildings to assist others wishing to make adaptations. (11.13.)

5. Projected Charity legislation should amend Section 112 of the Education Reform Act 1988 to permit the Department of Education and Science on application by a diocese to allow a school to be sold for a sum lower than the market price to a charity whose activity serves the area originally covered by the school, or to allow part of the proceeds of sale to be used for other charitable purposes for the benefit of the locality. (11.19.-20.)

6. Each parish should initiate a village appraisal with the help of the RCC which will set the social programme for the community. The parish council should expect to set a precept with which to pay the RCC for its help and advice. (11.27.)

7. Each diocese with a significant rural area should appoint an officer with responsibility both to represent the rural interest within the Church and also to represent the Church to the wider rural constituency, particularly to the local RCC. (11.29.)

8. General Synod should budget for an officer and a secretarial assistant to be based at the Arthur Rank Centre to progress the recommendations of this report. (11.37.)

9. Canon B15A should be revised to take account of the particular situation of single church rural areas. (11.45.)

10. We recommend the extensive application of the possibilities now encoded in Canon B43, which gives wide-ranging permission for shared liturgy and ministry. (11.42 et seq)

11. Boards for Mission and Unity should initiate discussions in deanery synods about ways of carrying out evangelism in each deanery. (11.54.-11.60.)

12. Each diocese should, as a positive contribution to the Decade of Evangelism, appoint someone to help PCCs make better use of the church building as a place of evangelism. (11.63.)

Chapter 12
Structure and Assets

12.1. This chapter looks first at some problems of communication and morale that the Commission has encountered in rural parishes, and suggests that the structures already exist in which solutions may be found. It then considers in this context the role of bishops, diocesan administrations and synods. It goes on to review briefly the way financial responsibility is exercised, both nationally and in dioceses, and the disaffection felt in the parishes in this area; and it proposes a way forward before focusing more closely on stipends and the related question of parish expenses. Finally, it looks at the local church's physical assets - the church building (with particular reference to English Heritage), the churchyard and the parsonage.

12.2. Our visits to local churches and our discussions with rural clergy leave us with the impression that a large majority of rural churches do not find it easy to relate to the wider Church. Contacts with the diocese or with the synod structure seem to be minimal and attitudes either indifferent or hostile. Mistrust and frustration are often focused on the boards at diocesan level, even though these are staffed by conscientious people seeking to carry out the business of the Church in a decent way: making due allowance for local parochialism, there does seem to be on the part of dioceses a mixture of inadequate consultation and ineffective communication. At the same time, the preoccupations and debates that are seen to be occupying the Church's time at the national level seem simply irrelevant to those, whether in rural or urban situations, who are faced with the problems of everyday life.

12.3. The men and women in the pews, particularly in the small country church, are in fact feeling increasingly remote from the Church's centres of power and influence. The Bishop of Norwich has said in his diocesan strategy:

> "I am quite clear that we are unbalanced in favour of centralisation and the large-scale. I believe our present need is to find ways to put the focus firmly on the local community, the village, the neighbourhood, the parish, the congregation ..... We have become a top heavy Church, in which value and importance increase the nearer to the centre one gets ..... A reversal needs to take place. It is the parishes that are at the sharp end of mission."

12.4. This remoteness of the Church's central structures, diocesan and national, as seen from the parish, is, we believe, seriously affecting morale in local churches, especially in rural areas. If this decline in morale is to be reversed, the dioceses need to improve their communications with the parishes together with their responsiveness to local feelings. In our view, the men and women in the parishes would be more likely to feel they had an active role in the wider Church and were valued members of it, if:

(a) dioceses had greater powers than they do now, and some of the responsibilities at present exercised centrally and nationally in the Church were devolved to them; and

(b) dioceses sought more active participation by the laity in the parishes in shouldering the burdens of this increased responsibility.

12.5. We are encouraged in this view by the fact that there is currently a a growing recognition in the business world of the value of federalist structures with fewer tiers of management. In such a structure, rather than the centre dictating policy and delegating certain responsibilities to the branches, the local units delegate to the centre only such functions as can usefully be performed centrally. It is the responsibility of the centre to provide leadership, build morale and encourage a corporate ethos; while in the interests of efficiency in the use of both personnel and resources, executive power is exercised locally, with lines of communication shorter and decision-making speeded up.

12.6. The Church of England, with its influential bishops and dioceses, has historically possessed this federalist form. It is the Commission's view that the Church should recognise the true worth of the valuable structure it has, and build upon it.

The role of the bishop

12.7. Historically, the role of leader of the Church belongs to the bishop. He has a presence in every parish: the cure of souls is both his and the incumbent's, many chancels contain a bishop's chair, and at the Holy Communion service a bishop has both ordained the celebrant and confirmed the communicants.

12.8. The work of a diocesan bishop involves national as well as local responsibilities. The late Bishop of Hereford told us that he was out of his diocese for four months of the year, up to one of those being holidays, with the balance being split between General Synod, the House of Lords, and national committee work. Travelling was a significant component in each. This reflected the demands of a national Church on its leaders. Being a senior bishop in the Church of England is far from being just a diocesan job, and yet the diocese could use the whole of his time. Because of the pressure on their diaries, more and more bishops are feeling an urgent need to re-order their priorities. The Grubb Institute is actively working on this with the bishops in one diocese.

12.9. The majority of rural parishes the Commission has visited have looked to the bishop as the head of the diocese, have often dissociated him from the irritations caused by diocesan offices and officers, and have seen him as an object of loyalty and affection, but all too remote. Episcopal visits are rare, except for inductions and confirmations - and these are usually in the same larger churches of the area. Bishops maintain a tenuous contact by means ranging from forewords in diocesan magazines and news-sheets to a presidential role at diocesan synods.

12.10. None of this particularly helps the rural condition. Given that there is a serious wish to travel round the rural part of the diocese, the demands on episcopal diaries make visiting and the fulfilment of a pastoral and teaching ministry hard to achieve. But the rural areas of the Church are looking for leadership and for reassurance that they are a valued part of a wider worthwhile fellowship and such reassurance comes most strongly from contact with the diocesan bishop, the father in God. We appreciate the extent and the unrealistic nature of the demands on bishops and the tensions between the national and the local. Balancing them is a difficult matter of judgement.

12.11. If bishops wish to visit more, their diaries will need to be unencumbered, leaving them as free as possible to concentrate on those aspects of spiritual leadership, involving study, prayerful reflection, encouraging the clergy, and visiting, which would in fact be most beneficial for the rural church. At the same time, we suggest elsewhere that a certain amount of administration is a necessary aspect of the ministry of the incumbent at parish level, and we would not wish to imply that the bishop should not see it as forming some part of his own role. It is indeed an inescapable part of the functioning of the Church's leaders, in diocese and parish, as the servants of the men and women in the pew.

12.12. In the final analysis we believe that if bishops are to have a more active and personal relationship with local parishes, and with their clergy, more bishops will need to be created. The size and scale of dioceses vary greatly. The majority of diocesan bishops do, of course, have suffragan bishops to assist them and some of our larger dioceses have seen the introduction of area bishops. The latter have a specific geographical area of the diocese, within which area they exercise episcopal functions, while the diocesan bishop remains father in God to the whole diocese. We have heard a diocesan bishop speak warmly to us of the collegiality this system brings to the episcopal role: it also preserves a sense of fellowship and a desire for mutual support among church members over the wide area of a large diocese, which a break-up into smaller dioceses might prejudice.

12.13. The Commission would urge that if new dioceses are not to be created, there should be an extension of the system of area bishops, at least in the larger dioceses, and an increase in their number. It has been suggested to us, in the context of suffragan and area bishops, that one bishop to 80 clergy is about the correct balance. We should like to see an area bishop in each archdeaconry, together with a sustained effort to ensure that rural areas, and others, come to feel that such a bishop, close to their interests and preoccupations, is as acceptable as the diocesan.

> **The practice of a bishop spending a pastoral day with a single parish or group of parishes (depending on size), without the function of an induction or confirmation, is much appreciated. It can take the form of challenging encounters, as undertaken, for example, by the Bishop of Exeter, during which he hears what the people are doing and what they are planning: he celebrates the eucharist and spends the day within the benefice. It is a day of celebration and challenge, encouraging unity and understanding.**

Diocesan administration and communications

12.14. All too often the diocesan office is seen in the parishes as remote, as a source mainly of circulars and requests for information. We are aware that this sense of disconnection is appreciated by most diocesan secretaries, but we wish to underline strongly the importance of corrective measures. We would point out, for example, that for connections and communications to be effective they need to have a personal content. This is demanding, but modern systems exist to address communications personally and to keep systems and lists of office-holders up to date: personal signing of letters is worth the effort. If the parishes are to feel that they belong they will have to be courted. They are not directly represented at the diocesan synod, so it cannot be assumed that something said at synod has been communicated to the parishes. We look to diocesan offices to review their system of communications with benefices.

12.15. We have heard also in a number of dioceses that the practice is growing of direct personal contact with deaneries by the diocesan secretary, the chairman of the diocesan board of finance (DBF), or, where relevant, by other diocesan representatives. Diocesan budgets, for example, may be explained to deanery synods or meetings of parish treasurers by the DBF chairman, by one of his officers, or by a specially briefed DBF member. Such a commitment to travelling and local contact ensures a better and more direct flow of information between those at the sharp end and those at the centre. The information flows in both directions, with the diocesan representative listening as well as imparting information. This gives diocesan policy and correspondence a face, and it affirms that the ultimate purpose of the existence of a diocesan office is to support the mission of the deaneries and parishes.

> **The Diocesan Secretary of Sheffield makes an annual visit to each deanery and speaks to parish treasurers, and others who are interested, on the reasoning behind proposed budgets. He also holds himself ready to speak to individual parishes if they request it, but that may be something which can only be done in a diocese of 168 parishes. Even so, he will be out three nights a week, either doing this or attending diocesan boards and**

committees which are held after working hours in different locations round the diocese.
In the Diocese of Norwich in 1988, the DBF with the Board of Communications produced a video, explaining the financial situation in the diocese, with specific reference to the question raised in the title, *Who Pays the Parson?*

12.16. All this underlines the fact that there is a proper ministry in good administration. Without it, much good work can be damaged or nullified through misunderstanding and confusion. The responsibility and imagination required of diocesan secretaries also underlines the importance of this position, and the high calibre needed in those appointed to it.

12.17. But it must be emphasised that communication is a two-way matter, with parishes being properly required to help the centre with information. Administration is a function of ministry for the incumbent as well as for the diocesan office. Furthermore the RCP shows that administration does not in fact take up more than 10% of a rural incumbent's time. Even so, it has to be a basic principle of management that the centre moves to the margins in order to understand the problems and perspective of those at the edge. Unless they are made to feel connected with the centre, leadership will be ineffective and mistrust will grow. In the final analysis the effective working of the diocese and indeed the national Church requires that those in the parishes feel they can trust those at the centre with a reasonable confidence that their views and needs have been noted.

The synodical structure

12.18. Although the synodical structure (see Appendix H) is intended to be straightforward and representative of all clergy and laity, the Commission feels, on the basis of the evidence available to it, that the system is not working well. There appears to be a huge gulf between the perceptions of people at parish level and those at the centre in the General Synod. There is not the connection that exists in direct Parliamentary elections, which makes it very difficult for those in the parish to feel genuinely represented. The delineation between the authority of the bishops and that of the General Synod is unclear to most people, which leads to confusion. As mentioned in 12.2., the Church's priorities nationally appear ill-defined and often unrelated to the realities of life as they are experienced in the parishes. It is hardly surprising that local churches are critical of those at the centre and find it difficult to understand the relevance of the work being undertaken there.

12.19. Our concern at this gap is profound because it makes the creation of the loyalty and affection, upon which any organisation depends, difficult to achieve, and the problem is paralleled by the uneasy relationship we have observed existing between the parishes and the diocesan centres.

12.20. Within the synodical structure, membership at all levels comes only from those able to devote the necessary time. This in itself narrows sharply the number of laity offering themselves for election. Furthermore, many lay people believe the system to be ineffective and therefore choose not to participate. The upper strata of the system rest on the votes of the deanery synod, but the Commission has noted the difficulty encountered in many rural parishes of finding people willing to be elected to the deanery synod which carries this responsibility. We were told that it was often the case that volunteers had been sought, or sometimes people pressed into service, rather than any election process pursued; there were often vacancies.

12.21. The apathy thus often felt at parish level, particularly in the rural areas, regarding the synodical structure, and especially regarding the effectiveness of the deanery synods, indicates the need for a serious review of the system. The proposed review of synodical government is welcome and its brief should include the investigation of synodical government not just from a central but also from a local point of view, as well as the place of synods within the leadership of the Church of England and how they relate to the development of policy and executive action.

12.22. Existing hierarchical structures in general provide an effective channel of communication quite easily for the clergy if those at the top use a little imagination and drive. At deanery level, for example, clergy chapters are usually far more supportive to individuals, and more useful as a forum, than synods are for the laity. For the laity, we feel that changes to the system are necessary if truly representative lay participation in the life of the Church is to be real and effective.

Networks

12.23. It has been suggested to us that for the laity at the local level a networking system might enable them to make a more worthwhile contribution to the affairs of the Church. Thus, in larger parishes at least, various individuals would be appointed, each specialising in a certain subject - youth, or education, or transport, or finance (in this case probably the treasurer). Each person would be expected to cover his or her subject on the church's behalf in all fora, whether the debate related specifically to the church or to the local community as a whole. A local church would be free, if it wished, to appoint someone from another congregation, whether Anglican or not, or from some secular body or interest group, to be its representative in a particular subject.

12.24. The parish's specialist representatives would be expected to be aware of developments in their respective fields in the wider locality or deanery, and to take part in building a wider network of the representatives of the individual churches and, where relevant, of secular interests. This wider network would handle not only local affairs but also contacts, within its specialism, with the diocese and its sector ministries.

12.25. Such a system could provide a way of spreading the load so that one parish representative did not have to cope with every aspect of the business agenda. Something like this system is essential if those with the necessary skills but with less time to spend on church affairs are to become more actively involved.

12.26. Sometimes the specialists appointed by parishes would need to represent it on what would be ad hoc rather than continuing bodies. This would be particularly important for the smaller parishes, which, it has been suggested to us, might find it as difficult to recruit people for a networking system as for the present structure. Indeed, some ad hoc groups have already come into being and have involved other Christian churches and secular bodies, and the Anglican church at parish and deanery level should do all it can to encourage this. If it needs a budget, money should be allocated for this purpose from parish funds.

12.27. We have seen good examples of initiatives in the field of transport working in this co-operative way, normally as a result of one person's inspiration. They have not always had overt church participation, but the church has a good opportunity to engage in local issues through being part of such a network. Rural Community Councils have spoken of their desire to see churches more actively committed to local community projects at both benefice and deanery levels.

12.28. Networks could also work at diocesan level. A particular area of activity could be handled by laity who might be leaders of industry, commerce or civic life, as well as by a certain number of specialists elected by the relevant specialists in the deaneries. This would be an extension of what is in effect widely done in the social responsibility and industrial mission fields in dioceses. The diocesan budget could be discussed by financial appointees elected by the deaneries together with any centrally appointed diocesan representatives. The parishes or deaneries would still have direct representation at diocesan level in the diocesan synod which would meet, perhaps less often than at present, to discuss general church matters and to support the bishop's council.

12.29. For such a system to work, there might well be needed both in parishes and at diocesan level registers of the laity and their spheres of interest, using the modern systems mentioned in 12.14. above. It has been noted in 12.15. that some dioceses have already adopted the practice of calling meetings of parish treasurers at deanery level to discuss the diocesan budget and 'quotas' (ie the allocation to parishes of responsibility for a share in the cost of paying the clergy - after contributions from historic resources - of training ordinands and of financing diocesan administration and advisory boards). What we are suggesting is in effect an extension of this scheme.

Finance

12.30. All our work has shown the paramount need for the Church to raise additional funds. These are required for better stipends for existing clergy as well as the additional clergy we hope will be recruited; and to replace any loss of income from present resources occasioned by greater emphasis on the social and environmental aspects of investment policy.

12.31. The Church Commissioners for England were set up in 1948, inheriting both the assets and the functions of Queen Anne's Bounty and the Ecclesiastical Commissioners.

12.32. Queen Anne's Bounty was established in 1704, restoring certain taxes originally paid by the clergy to the Pope and annexed to the crown by Henry VIII. This revenue was to be used expressly "for the augmentation of the maintenance of the poor clergy". The Ecclesiastical Commissioners were originally set up under an act of 1836 and over the years took on an increasing range of duties. In connection with responsibility for reorganising dioceses, bishops' incomes and cathedral establishments they acquired large funds and property, and they came to be charged with augmenting the incomes of poor benefices and with the provision of parsonage houses and of stipends for assistant curates; they took on many administrative duties, particularly those concerned with the 'cure of souls'.

12.33. The Church Commissioners have virtually sole responsibility for the pensions of clergy and widows, contribute substantially towards the cost of both current and retirement housing, contribute a substantial proportion of the stipends of archdeacons, and the whole of the stipends (and some of the costs) of bishops, deans, provosts and two residentiary canons per cathedral, and pay, after these commitments have been met, large sums towards clergy stipends. In 1988 they covered about 40% of the costs of such stipends, a percentage which had come down from about 75% ten years earlier. The Church Commissioners operate a closed fund with no new injections of capital, and their massive contribution towards the expenses of the Church of England (estimated at one third of its day to day expenditure) has been made possible by improved investment performance, with the benefits of a long bull market and sharp increases in the value of development land. We acknowledge that this has been a considerable achievement.

12.34. In addition to their financial responsibilities, the Church Commissioners have a part in the administration of pastoral reorganisation in the dioceses. This is imposed on them by the Pastoral Measure 1983. The preparation and publication of pastoral schemes and orders may well be better carried out centrally, but we would like to see firm evidence of this. We hold that it is always better for work to be devolved to dioceses if possible; pastoral reorganisation is in only a small proportion of cases a matter for those outside the diocese concerned.

12.35. The Church Commissioners have a major role in relation to the settlement under Part III of the Measure of the future of churches that have been declared redundant. This role has been examined in depth in a report published in the spring of this year (*The Care of Redundant Churches*, Richard Wilding, HMSO, 1990) and we therefore do not examine it here.

12.36. In addition to the concentration of powers and responsibilities at national level in the Church Commissioners, the parishes have seen a loss of financial autonomy in favour of the dioceses. A policy of reducing inequalities of income between benefices culminated in the Endowments and Glebe Measure 1976, under which control of glebe lands and funds passed from parishes to dioceses. Diocesan control has resulted in substantial gains in capital values and incomes.

12.37. Not improperly, the executive staff of the Church Commissioners and the dioceses see their prime responsibility as providing financial undergirding for the Church's ministry. We heard this in oral evidence from a group from the Church Commissioners, and from the chairmen of diocesan boards of finance. In the case of the Commissioners, this is based on their interpretation of the wording of the Ecclesiastical Commissioners Act 1840, which instructs them to provide "for the cure of souls in parishes where....assistance is most required, in such manner as shall....be deemed most conducive to the efficiency of the Established Church".

12.38. This policy is, however, in practice already tempered by other considerations. Investments are for example not made by the Church Commissioners in companies whose main business is in armaments, gambling, alcohol, tobacco or newspapers, nor in any South African company or any company with more than a small part of its business in South Africa. In their land administration, the Church Commissioners' aim is to be model and compassionate landlords.

12.39. It may be noted also that the General Synod recently initiated legislation under which the Church Commissioners are currently providing £1 million per annum to the Church Urban Fund. In effect, the General Synod decreed that the historic funds of the Church should provide that much less (and by implication, current giving in the parishes should provide that much more) towards clergy stipends, in the light of the pressing needs of the inner cities.

12.40. Nevertheless, the Assets Committee, the group within the Church Commissioners which controls investments, whilst recognising that every investment decision has an ethical dimension, has not been provided with a framework which would relate their investment decisions to the mission of the Church. Apart from the specific considerations spelt out in 12.38., certain steps to avoid pollution and to protect the welfare of animals and some encouragement of its agents to favour low-cost housing, assets are deployed for income yield and growth in purely financial terms. In the context of present and prospective claims on income, financial performance is felt to be paramount. There is thus no mechanism for modifications of this criterion which would result in anything other than a marginal loss of revenue. We would like to see the episcopal members of the Board of Governors set up a small group to look at the moral implications of investments and, after a debate at Synod, to make recommendations to the Board. The work of the Church Commissioners is often perceived to be the work of the Church, and so environmental, social, welfare and general ethical policies must be scrutinised in the light of current Christian understanding of them. The way in which the Church Commissioners' activities reflected any overall guidance from the Board in this area could well, we suggest, form a regular separate section of the Commissioners' Annual Report.

12.41. Through its Board of Governors, chaired as it is by the Archbishop of Canterbury, the Church of England has the best possible vehicle for giving a lead in the evaluation and application of an explicitly Christian investment policy, taking into account general environmental considerations and the existence of specific local needs. However, the Church appears to have distanced itself from the opportunity thus provided, although we welcome the statement in July 1989 by the First Church Estates Commissioner that the Church Commissioners should not seek to be isolated from the national concern with environmental and green issues and must be seen as leaders of good practice in such things as conservation, reinstatement, high standards of farms and farm buildings and the like.

12.42. The Church Commissioners have not yet, for example, abated rent in order to secure more environmentally favourable farming practices which would cost the farmer a reduction in output and therefore a drop in profitability, and among dioceses, it is only in one or two that such a policy is beginning to emerge. In contrast, the chief agent of the National Trust informed us that in 1989 the Trust had budgeted £100,000 for rent reductions as a result of applying environmental conditions to their tenancies, which would directly reduce farm incomes. Any shortfall for the National Trust would need to be made up from members' subscriptions or other trading revenue. Although this could be justified as furthering the formal purposes of the National Trust, it could be argued that an interpretation of the doctrine of creation would demand similar action from the Church of England.

12.43. But no contemplation of a doctrine of creation and its implications for concepts such as sustainability has apparently affected investment policy in any noticeable way. Even though such a view would have been outside the interpretation of the legal liabilities of trusteeship as understood by the Church Commissioners, we would strongly argue that the Church has been in error by not pushing this further. In strictly financial terms, it may be inconvenient to reduce revenues for environmental reasons rather than as a result of market forces, but the Church must take a wider view. If politicians are urging people to show restraint about environmental issues from a sense of self-interest, how much more powerful would it not be for the Church to be proclaiming the same ends as a result of interpreting the word of God.

12.44. Again, land is a very visible investment which contains basic tensions within its ownership in addition to environmental considerations. People who hold large areas of land are thought to be rich: they also find themselves involved with clashes of interest when alternative land uses are considered. This is a dilemma which both the Church Commissioners and dioceses face when considering proposals brought to them by their land agents.

12.45. We were told by the First Estates Commissioner that individual partners within two firms of agents are appointed to manage the estates. We heard from several independent agents on other estates of the importance of the agent being fully committed to the social and economic well-being of the people as well as the land in question. We feel that the instructions to the Commissioners' agents could incorporate a more imaginative approach to job creation, new business formation and the appropriate training, by making full use of Training and Enterprise Councils and rural enterprise agencies, so that the Church is seen to have a wider and deeper interest in the community, rather than appearing merely a distant landlord.

12.46. Where the Church owns old rectories with large gardens or agricultural land in and around villages, it is drawn into a dilemma. Its wish to maximise returns requires it to take profits and to develop land irrespective of local feelings. Its local ministry in the form of a priest and congregation, and its position as the established national Church identifying with and serving the whole community, require it to listen to local views and needs. This rarely happens in a serious way that could lead to a significant change in the nature of the development, or to its being accepted that there should be no development at all. Where development has failed this has usually been due to its being turned down by a local planning authority, rather than through a change of heart by the Church authorities. The Church Commissioners have, not illogically, worked on the basis that the decision of the planning system is to be taken as the correct verdict of the democratic process. The effect has, however, been that the Church of England is often seen to be rich, grasping and unheeding of local views - and yet it depends for its support on the local people it so easily offends - and not just on those who form the core of its congregations. It does not seem to the Commission that sufficient heed has been taken of the injunction in the Ecclesiastical Commissioners Act of 1840 that "due consideration shall be had of the wants and circumstances of the locality".

12.47. We are concerned that the drive for financial returns means that all these matters can only be considered "at the margin", to quote the phrase used by the Church Commissioners during oral evidence to us. The application of revised standards would apply equally to dioceses and any other Christian body responsible for the investment of assets. It is not a simple issue and it is certainly one which, if taken up, will demand of the Church a significantly higher level of current giving to compensate for the lower returns which would come from operating a policy considered to be more sensitive in an ethical way.

12.48. There is indeed a real and difficult tension here between the financial need to pay the clergy so that they can undertake 'the cure of souls' and the way this need is met through conventional financial investment. There will always be an awkward balance to strike as ethical perceptions change, but it is one that needs constantly to be in the forefront of Christian debate. Those at the centre carry a great burden of decision-making, to which is added the need for Christian sensitivity. At the local end such policy affects church life and church discussion, but church members feel powerless to do anything about it.

The centre and the local task

12.49. In financial as well as administrative matters, we have become aware through our investigations of the very great gap that exists between the parishes and the central administration of the Church, whether at diocesan or at national level. There is in many parishes, particularly in rural areas, a sense of isolation, compounded with frustration, a feeling that those who make policy do not understand, or if they understand, do not heed, local feelings and experience.

12.50. Feelings of isolation may always have existed in remote rural areas, but the action of the Church of England towards its rural arm over the past twenty years has strengthened this view. Looking at things from the point of view of the villages, they have seen many changes and the loss of valued amenities with minimal consultation and no direct benefit to the village. Although this has resulted in more efficient use of resources centrally and the nationwide ministry of the Church has been preserved, the connection has often not been understood locally.

12.51. From its study of the rural Church, the Commission feels that the serious division between the administrative centres of the Church and its local operating arms, the parishes, is sufficiently serious for it to be adversely affecting morale and leading to confusion of objectives. We regard the building of morale as crucial. The Church is in danger of planning for mere maintenance, if not for decline, when it should be seeking the guidance of the Holy Spirit in looking for new ways of carrying out its mission, and seeking the structures which would further its exploration of these.

12.52. It should, furthermore, be stressed again that if the Church Commissioners and diocesan boards of finance take environmental and social considerations more fully into account in their investment policy, their contribution to the stipends of the clergy must be curtailed, and current giving in the parishes must increase accordingly. The Church Commissioners have, indeed, explicitly said that any further restrictions on their financial room for manoeuvre could easily damage financial performance. At parish level, it is often not appreciated how the historic assets of the Church have insulated the laity from the financial pressures involved in maintaining the Church's ministry. The increased demand on the laity will indeed be met only with difficulty - many have limited incomes - and only if it is seen not as a tax imposed by a central Church authority but as a challenge to cheerful giving in God's service.

12.53. It is the view of the Commission that if morale is to be rebuilt and the new challenge met, greater responsibility needs to be held as close as practicable to where the action takes place. It seems to us that this is likely to be at diocesan level.

12.54. We thus believe that it is very important that as many decisions are taken at diocesan or parish level as possible, and we also believe that there are a number of aspects of the Church Commissioners' work which might be devolved to the dioceses. We are aware that changing what are effectively management procedures is bound to be a delicate task. We believe it should be done in order to strengthen diocesan structures, and because it is in keeping with the federalist traditions of the Church of England. We recommend that the Archbishop of Canterbury should set up an inquiry to make recommendations, not later than the end of 1992, as to how this might come about.

12.55. We consider that greater freedom to fix maximum and minimum stipends should be given to the dioceses. It should be made plain to each parish what part of its quota is required for the payment of the stipend of their incumbent and their own responsibility to maintain and improve it. It is important to break down the complacent belief existing today that the Church Commissioners have a pot of gold out of which to pay the clergy. The parishes have a shared responsibility to raise the money to pay the clergy. The connection between diocese and parish, currently fairly weak, especially in rural areas, would be rebuilt and strengthened by parishes knowing their particular commitment for their minister's stipend.

Stipends

12.56. Despite printed information from diocesan boards of finance and the Church Commissioners, few parishes acknowledge their debt to income from historic resources or accept the need to fund the shortfall themselves to ensure a proper remuneration for their incumbent. Quota (see 12.29.) is usually seen as a tax rather than as a contribution towards the maintenance and support costs of their clergy. Frequently there seems to be an attitude that somehow the funds will be provided. This lack of realism seems unhealthy to the Commission, even if it has its origins in the payment system used for the clergy over the centuries, with endowments and glebe providing the money for many rural incumbents. The position was put dramatically by the Bishop of Norwich when he stated that only one benefice in his diocese was a net contributor - i.e. raising more money than was needed to pay for the gross costs of ministry within it.

12.57. The Commission argues that for this position to change there needs to be a far greater challenge to each benefice, evoking a sense of responsibility not only for working out its purpose and ministry, but for seeing the implications of these in financial terms as being a local requirement. Such a response would be encouraged if financial responsibility could be held as locally as possible, reducing the gap between fund-raising and expenditure. While we do not see parishes handling historic resources - the past experience of that was problematical at best - we do see merit in seeking to hold historic resources at diocesan level so that the inter-relationship of investment criteria and proceeds can mesh with the necessity to build on them through current giving. The evidence of the care that is taken of church buildings, suggesting that if a local community sees a specific need it will raise the funds required to meet it, prompts us to seek a similar approach towards the costs of ministry. The question remains how can the position be put in a winning way to parishes?

DIOCESE OF LINCOLN
A BENEFICE PROFIT AND LOSS ACCOUNT
(*or Where does the quota go to?*)

This is a simple way of seeing how diocesan finances work out from the standpoint of a typical diocesan benefice with one incumbent. If your benefice has a team of clergy, or a curate, or a deacon, or a stipendiary lay worker or a local ministry team trained and supported by the diocesan scheme, then you will need to change the figure because you will be getting more; perhaps for more quota. 1991 figures have been used.

COSTS		£
One Incumbent Stipend		12,000
Annualised Training Costs		900
One Maintained Parsonage		2,350
Direct Support Costs (Archdeacons, Rural Deans etc)		300
Specialist Support (Missioners, Parish Education Officers, Stewardship campaigns, Schools advice, Industrial, Agricultural, Ecumenical and others)		1,500
Central Administrative and Legal Services		1,200
TOTAL COSTS		**18,250**

EXTERNAL SUPPORT	
Church Commissioners	4,600
Diocesan Glebe	5,000
Income from Accumulated Diocesan Funds	950
TOTAL EXTERNAL SUPPORT	**10,550**

QUOTA	
Assuming Local Electoral Roll (adult population) of about 1600	7,700
	18,250

Postscript

In other words, the quota goes into the benefice. Most parishes receive more in external support than they contribute themselves as quota.

Most dioceses do not have anything like the glebe support that there is in Lincoln Diocese. They may have about £1,000 from glebe. So their quota has to be higher.

12.58. We like the presentation being made by the Diocese of Lincoln showing the total costs of supporting an incumbent and then the sources of income, emphasising to each benefice the modest nature of its contribution.

12.59. In the Diocese of Rochester, stipends have been divorced from quota altogether. Each parish fixes the stipend of its incumbent within the minimum and maximum limits prescribed by the diocese, and pays what is needed after the contribution from historic resources. Grants are made available for parishes which cannot afford the minimum. The diocese feels that more money is forthcoming from parishes when what is given is seen to be so directly related to the incumbent's stipend, and this is reflected in the position of Rochester at the head of the league table for clergy stipends. At the same time the diocesan quota is so much lower because it does not have to support stipends and is therefore psychologically and in practice less of a burden on parishes. The Diocese of Blackburn has operated a similar arrangement since 1965, and significantly occupies second place in the league table; other dioceses, such as Chester, are following this path.

12.60. The question of stipends raised itself periodically during our visits. It was when we were with those who did not have private incomes or benefactors, or whose wives were engaged with parish work or looking after families and felt that their vocation and duty lay there, that it became apparent that the level of stipend was an important factor not only in family life, but in the achievement of a satisfactory ministry.

12.61. In the definition of the Central Stipends Authority (CSA) a stipend should be "adequate for a clergyman (with no private means or a working wife) to do his job, without unnecessary anxiety about paying the bills, and to be able with his family to enjoy modest comforts".

12.62. In its annual consultation with the dioceses, the CSA lays out a number of factors which need to be taken into account. In January 1990, it noted that although since 1969 the value of the average stipend had shown a rise rather greater than that in the Retail Price Index, there had been a sharp deterioration in the relationship with the Average Earnings Index (AEI). In particular, the document noted that in 1989 a clergyman would have needed an increase of 63% to have been equal in terms of net disposable pay with a police inspector, 31% to equal a hospital registrar, or 4% to equal a senior teacher.

12.63. All this suggests that the CSA requirement in 12.61. is unlikely to be met, certainly in those instances where expenses are not being fully reimbursed. In these cases clergy are likely to suffer distress as individuals and will be distracted from doing their job properly. This analysis is in line with evidence we received from some of those who did not have other sources of income. Most were reluctant to raise their problems with those in authority, while the absence of a personnel function at diocesan level meant that no obvious alternative route was available.

12.64. There seem to us a number of different positions held within the Church of England, all of which have some merit. These cover attitudes to poverty, equality in pay, incremental increases and increases related to assessments. All of these (except, of course, poverty) assume that there is sufficient money to make the payments. We turn to this later.

12.65. There is an understandable tradition of the virtue of poverty within Christianity. Various orders insist on absolute poverty, but as a Church the Church of England has traditionally embraced a wide range of attitudes towards it. The statement that the intention of the clergy stipend is to enable the person to live modestly without financial worries is a vague one, and there will be variations from person to person and certainly from circumstance to circumstance in its validity and interpretation.

12.66. We encountered strongly held opinions that stipends should be equal, irrespective of seniority in the job, age, or the size of parish. Such views preferred not to consider need or achievement. We were told that stipend variations would lead the Church back to the idea of richer livings and therefore to the attraction of a well-paid job rather than the nature of the job itself.

12.67. A different view was presented by those who felt that a system of additional payments for length of service should be introduced. The CSA proposed such a scheme in its report GS 333 to the General Synod in 1977, proposing payments after 10 years in orders, with further ones at five yearly intervals thereafter; in its follow up report GS390 it quoted "a fairly heavy weight of evidence" amongst the dioceses supporting the recommendations. Those clergy who are employed as chaplains in the armed forces, prisons or hospitals, receive regular incremental increases.

A military chaplain will be paid on a scale similar to that used for officers from the rank of Captain to Lieutenant Colonel and like them he will be required to pay accommodation expenses out of these figures. On 1989 scales this would have been £16,184 on appointment, rising to £30,634 after 26 years' service.

Prison chaplains are paid (1.8.89) on a scale (outside London), which does not include accommodation, starting at £16,125 and moving to £20,404 after six years with possible further performance-related payments up to a maximum of £22,953.

Full-time hospital chaplains are paid (1.4.89) between £16,057 and £17,140, including an accommodation allowance, but excluding any London weighting or special payments for secure units. Their pay is governed by the Whitley Council.

12.68. With a growing movement towards a regular review of their ministry, clergy might expect some or all of any incremental payments to be related to performance. This would certainly be in line with much private sector pay review practice.

12.69. A major consideration is the fact that a large group of clergy remain parish priests for the whole of their ministry. With only 300 or so senior appointments, this is inevitable. It is easy for clergy to become stale and disaffected, which is a major challenge for bishops and others involved in clergy pastoral care. Personal contact can assist with stimulating, encouraging and opening windows, but it can be argued that there is a proper place for increased financial reward as well.

12.70. The Commission came to the view that a serious reappraisal of clergy remuneration needs to be made if those in rural areas are to be paid adequately. We have noted the costs of rural living, and we have seen enough homes where no private or second earned income applies to realise that this is an important issue. It is one which needs to be grasped and dealt with and it should not be allowed to disappear onto the bookshelves once this report has been read.

12.71. The Commission has made several costings, and feels that it is not so much the costs which will be in dispute, but the philosophy which lies behind the alternative methods of making payments. A fundamental starting point is that all proper parish/benefice expenses are paid promptly and in full. The example we give, based on 1990 prices, is of a new flat level stipend, relating to incumbents and assistants: we have not considered the pay of dignitaries as they are rarely rural. We accept that in order to produce a sound package for rural incumbents it is likely that the same one will apply to all clergy. Although our example is for a new level of universal stipend, we emphasise that this could easily be redistributed in favour of a lower starting point of say £12,000 and a series of incremental increases to a top level of between £16-17,000 based on length of service and satisfactory assessments. The latter would be more appropriate if freeholds disappeared, if continuing ministerial education became the force we seek it to be, and if clergy responsibility grew in the area of encouraging and enabling greater lay leadership. We believe it would also have a beneficial effect on recruitment, with something closer to a career pattern and with development being clearly identified through the stipend structure.

12.72. With their housing benefits taken into account, the parochial clergy would compare more favourably in pay and career structure with full-time chaplains.

Example (at 1990 prices)
Proposal:

National average stipend	£14,000
Housing benefit assessment	5,000
Total	£19,000

Cost:

(1)   Taking the estimated average national stipend for 1990/91 of £11,120 as a base, there would be a shortfall of £2,880 per head of the 8,381 clergy of incumbent status to meet the £14,000 figure. Allowing for National Health Insurance at 11% and a 16% pension contribution, the total required per head would be £3,658, giving a national total of £30.66 million.

(2)   On the basis that 80% of incumbents are married and half of those would warrant the full £2,000 payment suggested in 12.75., the cost of that without pension entitlement would be $2000 \times 3352 = £6.7$ million.

(3)   If the 2303 deacons and assistant staff received similar

awards in cash terms, the bill for them would be a further
2303 × 3658 = £8.42 million.

The total cost at 1990 prices would be £30.7 million

$$\begin{array}{r} 6.7 \\ 8.4 \\ \hline £45.8 \text{ million} \end{array}$$

Finding the money

12.73. We would recommend that these targets, increased by inflation and reference to the AEI, are met progressively over a three-year period. The historic assets of the Church will neither meet this extra cost nor make a contribution to it. The whole extra cost will need to come from current giving, which means that it will lie in the dioceses with the parishes. This will require carefully planned stewardship campaigns to assist in explaining the reasons and raising the funds, with publicity material prepared for widespread distribution within the parishes to outline the case for higher stipends. We look to the laity, presented with a clear case for helping to fund adequate incomes for those who have committed themselves to the full-time ministry, and been accepted by the Church in that capacity, to respond with sacrificial and generous-hearted giving.

12.74. To reduce this to a parochial scale the average weekly giving by Church members in 1988 was as low as £2.19. To raise the £46 million which in our view is needed the 1.16 million people who attend church regularly would need to give an additional £39.48 per annum or approximately 76p per week.

Clergy wives

12.75. The Commission would like to acknowledge the role played by many wives of parochial and senior clergy, as unpaid secretaries, receptionists and producers of refreshments. Many open their homes to meetings. We feel that this work should be acknowledged financially and recommend that each diocese reviews this aspect of ministry with the intention of paying up to £2,000 per annum to those wives who undertake these duties, with special emphasis on those who do not have other paid employment. This is not to ignore their invaluable pastoral and counselling role, not least in respect of their own husbands, but we do not feel that this can or should be measured for the purposes of this honorarium.

The clergy and parish expenses

12.76. The recommendations made each year by the Central Stipends Authority presuppose that approved expenses are fully met by parochial church councils.

12.77. The heaviest expenses in a rural parish relate to the incumbent's travelling costs - almost invariably car expenses. These vary widely, depending on the remoteness of the benefice, and the number of parishes in the benefice and their distance from each other. In remoter parishes, journeys of 70 miles to hospitals and 45 to a crematorium are not exceptional. In the north-eastern benefices of Carlisle diocese, some Ely and Lincoln fenland parishes and those of North Yorkshire, to name but a few, we were told of mileage on parish business of up to 14,000 miles per annum. One priest doing this sort of mileage felt that a contribution from his benefice of £1,000 was generous. Nobody had explained to him the cost of depreciation. Even at 30p a mile (see box) an annual mileage of 14,000 miles would justify expenses of £4,200.

The AA's April 1989 estimates of the cost per mile of a car, bought from new and well-maintained, allowing for depreciation over eight years but not including the interest-cost of the money used to buy the car or the cost of garaging it, are 29p for a car of 1001-1400cc capacity doing 10,000 miles a year, 34p for one of 1401-2000cc.

12.78. Many clergy do not allow for the fact that when a new car is purchased, inflation will mean that a higher cash sum will be required for its replacement. Evidence suggests that what usually happens is that the incumbent trades down to a less expensive vehicle, often second-hand. This in turn leads to greater unreliability and higher servicing costs. It is a downward spiral which leads to ever greater unreliability and more unsuitable cars.

12.79. The Church Commissioners' interest-free borrowing scheme helps to reduce the cost of funding a loan, but it does not remove the fact that capital has to be repaid.

12.80. Parishes are not always receptive to paying high travel expenses. It was said to us that, before the amalgamation of parishes and the confiscation of glebe, these costs were not necessary and that therefore the diocese should pay them from some of its rationalisation savings. It was thought that with the decline in clergy numbers huge sums had been received from the sale of surplus parsonages, none of which had come back to the parishes. Indeed, between 1986 and 1988 the rural dioceses made a net surplus of £16 million from the sale of parsonages. Local attitudes are thus often hostile towards paying expenses at a proper rate.

> **In one benefice we visited, the churches were most beautifully maintained, but when the diocese raised the mileage allowance to 30p the treasurer resigned when the incumbent confirmed that he would charge that rate.**

12.81. Other parish expenses include telephone and mail, stationery, secretarial assistance, office equipment, hospitality and provision of cover when on holiday or unwell. They may also include books and periodicals, in-service training not paid for by the diocese and the provision and repair of the furniture and furnishings in the official part of the parsonage. Once again, it was represented to us that the savings made out of reducing numbers needed to be offset against higher telephone costs, and the need for an answerphone, word processor and copier. These are less easily quantified in terms of parish amalgamations than car expenses.

12.82. Nevertheless, a commercial organisation would probably expect to cover the provision of answerphone, copier and word processor for an equivalent, independently-based, outworker. This support would help to ensure the most effective use of time and the necessary support to do the job properly. Should the Church expect less? We believe that it is the responsibility of the employer, the diocese, to ensure that these resources are provided. Provision by the diocese would also ensure that sofware packages were compatible throughout the diocese, and we would go further to suggest that the whole Church standardises on equipment and software which is nationally compatible.

12.83. When it came to claiming expenses, clergy attitudes were not consistent and ranged from those who kept good records and stood their ground, to others whose record-keeping was, in their own estimation, haphazard, and whose bargaining position was therefore weaker. Others again found facing up to the PCC such an ordeal that they preferred to understate the true costs they had incurred, feeling that their pastoral relationship was more important than proper financial reimbursement. They felt that contact between an incumbent and the PCC members who lived in a different village was sensitive enough for it to be essential that money matters should not come between them.

12.84. We are concerned that the voluntary and involuntary contributions made by the clergy towards expenses constitute a high degree of subsidy in rural areas.

12.85. The lack of understanding of the true costs of running a car have already been mentioned. In other instances, clergy seemed reluctant to install answerphones because of cost and because they felt that parishioners would be put off by them rather than feel relieved that their message had been left without repeated calls. This in part reflects an approach to the job as much as one towards expenses, but we wondered how much encouragement incumbents received, either from archdeacons or churchwardens, to incur costs which would make them more effective, especially when they were engaged in managing a multi-parish benefice. All through our study we have come up against the image of an amateur Church being run on the cheap and resisting the help that can be given through advanced technology. We would encourage clergy to grasp the benefits of modern information technology and not to feel guilty in the process.

12.86. A sense of guilt is never far from a sensitive priest. The nature of a vocation to share is often difficult to reconcile with the awareness of costs and costings that systems for claiming expenses pre-suppose. A more sympathetic attitude is required of the laity and particularly of its local leaders, the churchwardens, treasurers and secretaries. To obtain the fullest ministry from their priest, they need to encourage him and understand his predicament, the sketchiness of his training in matters of finance and equipment, and his natural reluctance to press for more. It is their job to be both imaginative and sensitive, so that providing and running the right office equipment and travel are seen as a proper part of the ministry of the whole Church. This degree of understanding needs to be promoted from diocesan bishops downwards, not just occasionally but as a regular concern and with a regular review of practice.

12.87. Discussing expenses in any detail in front of a PCC is an invidious experience. Wherever possible bills should be handled direct by the parish treasurer rather than via the incumbent. We strongly recommend that before a new incumbent is appointed, these matters and procedures are clearly discussed and agreed by the PCC and the archdeacon or rural dean, with a clear minute or letter being written to the incumbent to summarise them. We emphasise that parish expenses, like stipends, church repairs and other giving, are a basic part of ministry.

12.88. We recommend:

(1) that dioceses should provide such basic equipment as a word-processor and printer, a copier, and an answerphone, and the training necessary to enable an incumbent to use this equipment economically and efficiently.

(2) that at quinquennial visitations and upon any subsequent pastoral reorganisation a review of equipment should be automatically undertaken, with the intention of establishing suitable levels for the task in hand, together with a review of the incumbent's skills, which may reveal a need for further training.

(3) that the dioceses should seek to establish a common standard for computerised equipment, so that software, data and discs are interchangeable.

(4) that expenses not dealt with by the diocese should be passed by one person designated by the PCC to authorise them, and that these should be cleared on a monthly basis.

(5) that expenses should always be considered and referred to as parish expenses, not clergy expenses.

(6) that archdeacons should ensure that the clergy are fully briefed on expenses and are receiving reimbursement at proper and realistic levels.

The buildings

12.89. It has already been stressed (see 11.12.) that the church building has an important role in witnessing to the faith of the Church. It needs, first, to be kept in good repair, and this in itself can present a daunting challenge to the small congregation. We examine the role of public funds and of English Heritage in 12.95. to 12.112. below; and we commend the work of such bodies as the various county historic churches trusts and such diocesan initiatives as the Diocese of Rochester Church Repair Scheme.

> **The Diocese of Rochester Church Repair Scheme is essentially a savings scheme. Each church or other building accepted under the scheme is examined at diocesan expense, and the parish pays an agreed amount (the Repair Rate) half-yearly for five years into an interest-bearing fund. After five years, the building is again inspected, and a report made outlining necessary repairs. If the agreed savings are insufficient, an interest-free loan is made.**

12.90. We also urge congregations not to lose sight of the necessity to keep churches insured. The cost of premiums is, we know, burdensome to many small congregations. We welcome the considerable number of diocesan schemes for assisting in the payment of premiums and we strongly recommend that congregations should explore ways of reducing their premiums, such as limiting the total sum for which the building is insured (the Ecclesiastical Insurance Group helps greatly by not proportionalising any smaller claims), or raising the excess limit (ie the minimum sum which can be claimed under a policy). Any repairs or rebuilding should be put in hand speedily when damage occurs, because costs rise speedily and increases will usually have to be borne by the parish rather than by the policy. The Ecclesiastical Insurance Group, it may be noted, makes major grants to dioceses, out of its profits.

12.91. In addition to maintaining the fabric, the church building, if it is to be a witness to the faith, must have an atmosphere that is alive and welcoming. Keeping the church clean and tidy must be seen as Christian work of real value; occasional spring-cleans can be whole-day events for the congregation, with shared refreshments, fellowship and perhaps an evening meal or entertainment. This may happen at any time of the year: one parish used to do it on the last Sunday before Advent (or Stir-up Sunday, as it used to be known, after the opening words of the collect).

12.92. Sometimes structural alterations will increase a church's usefulness to the congregation generally, to its work more particularly among children, or more widely to the community as a whole. We discuss this in greater detail in 11.13. to 11.17., together with such matters as making the church welcoming to tourists and visitors and

reordering for changes in the forms of worship. We just note here the
advisability of seeking advice from the diocese or the archdeacon on
how to present plans in such a way that the implications can be fully
understood in the parish.

12.93. To be borne in mind also is the impact of environmental
considerations on the use of the church building. For example, is the
heating installation as efficient and economical as possible, and have
draughts been minimised consistently with adequate ventilation? A
useful booklet on the subject is *Heating the Church* by William Bordass
(Church House Publishing, 1984).

12.94. Finally, we commend the point made in the report mentioned in
12.35., *The Care of Redundant Churches* (particularly paragraphs 3.8
and 8.5) that where there is a redundant church in the care of the
Redundant Churches Fund, it is important that the living church in
that parish adopts a constructive attitude towards its possible use.

The role of English Heritage

12.95. Our ancient churches constitute one of the country's greatest
treasures, and there is generally free access to them. What help do the
churches receive, in recognition of this fact, from official sources, to
assist them in meeting the heavy cost of maintaining the fabric of these
old buildings? How does this country compare with, for example,
France, where the state recognises an obligation to maintain churches
built before 1905?

12.96. Churches do receive assistance from local authorities, but the
main source of official help, amounting recently to some £5 million a
year for churches of all denominations, is English Heritage.

12.97. English Heritage is the popular name for the Historic Buildings
and Monuments Commission for England, established under the
National Heritage Act 1983 to take over the responsibilities of the
Department of the Environment's Division of Historic Buildings and
Monuments.

12.98. Its primary objectives are:

(1) To secure the preservation of ancient monuments and
historic buildings situated in England.

(2) To promote the preservation and enhancement of the
character and appearance of conservation areas situated in
England.

(3) To promote the public's enjoyment, and advance their

knowledge of, ancient monuments and historic buildings situated in England and their preservation.

12.99. It is financed chiefly by means of Grant-in-Aid from the Department of the Environment; it also has income from trading activities, sponsorships and its membership charges.

12.100. When it came into existence, it assumed responsibility for, inter alia, the State Aid for Churches in Use Scheme, which had been set up in 1977 to provide funds from the Exchequer for the repair of important churches in regular use for public worship. The responsibilities of departments prior to that had not included churches, because they were not subject to statutory control, but by the early seventies considerable concern had arisen about the state of repair of our parish churches. The scheme is open to all denominations, but the Anglican Church, with its great number of old churches, is by far the chief beneficiary. The grants are discretionary, and may only be offered to buildings of outstanding architectural or historic interest.

12.101. The original total sum made available in 1977 was £1 million a year. This was the amount recommended by the Church of England itself in 1976, in a calculation based on 1973 prices. It also recommended that only 30% of its churches needed to apply for a grant on financial grounds: both this statement and the £1 million requirement have proved to be very serious underestimates. Unwillingness to pitch demand too high seems to have been a contributory factor. Because the base figure was inadequate, all subsequent allocations have similarly been too low, even though there have been annual increases to allow for, and sometimes exceeding, inflation. The total sum available has reached £6 million, but when the nature of the 13,000 listed churches of various denominations is considered, this is a small sum by national standards.

12.102. The amount available is being increased to £9 million in 1990 as a form of compensation for the impact on the Church of the introduction of the community charge, but even so this larger sum will still fall well short of what is required to keep all historic churches in acceptable order. Furthermore, for legal reasons, this sum is being administered under Section 10 of the Town and Country Planning (Amendment) Act 1972 and will go to churches in conservation areas in towns.

12.103. It will be noted that the additional money being given to the churches is effectively the Churches' own money; and some of this is then taken back by the state a second time in the form of VAT on repair bills. We consider that this anomaly should be corrected.

12.104. Even though it is empowered to make grants of up to 80%, English Heritage will normally not contribute more than 40% of the cost of an approved project, and will expect the parish to find the whole sum if the total cost does not exceed £5,000. It pleads shortage of funds for justifying this policy. Exceptions to both rulings are not impossible, and indeed the proportion of grants exceeding 40% is rising, but grants are only offered for major structural repairs of a fairly urgent nature. Grants for 'stitches in time' are not available, both because of the general shortage of funds and because it is thought that, in principle, churches should be responsible for their own ordinary maintenance work. During the last financial year, with more spent on churches than on all other buildings, shortage of funds led at one point to a complete halt on new offers of help.

12.105. In addition to the limitations on the funding at its disposal, for which the Church must take some responsibility, English Heritage was established with a small central staff, based on experience with grants for secular buildings, and reflecting also the prevalent restrictions on staffing levels. The resulting problems are at present compounded by stretched communications, with five separate buildings occupied in central London, and with outside architects working on commission, instead of in-house architects: both of these aspects of inefficient administration are under review, with attempts to recruit more staff and with a move out of London in prospect.

12.106. Notwithstanding the very valuable assistance which English Heritage has afforded hard-pressed churches, the way it goes about its work has attracted much criticism, and serious complaints have been made to the Commission.

12.107. Because of its terms of reference, its very raison d'etre being the preservation of buildings of outstanding architectural and historic interest, it will give grants only to churches which it regards as falling into that category, and is the sole judge of whether they do so. The value of a building to the local community as a place of worship, or its place in the local setting or landscape, do not come into consideration (although a church in a conservation area, like any other building similarly situated, could be entitled to receive Section 10 funds, and new money as mentioned above in 12.102. is being set aside for this). The specifications for the work which are acceptable to English Heritage may involve expensive traditional materials and methods, and sometimes the organisation seems so preoccupied with historical and architectural niceties that insufficient regard is paid to the practicalities of actually using a church for worship, let alone for any other communal purpose. In all these areas, misunderstandings arise and great bitterness may be caused, exacerbated by the failure of the overstretched administration of English Heritage to give adequate explanations, or even to keep open adequate lines of communication.

12.108. Indeed, delays of a quite inordinate nature arise, with replies to correspondence taking months rather than weeks. Although the lack of staff and stretched lines of communication already mentioned seem to be a frequent cause, it has to be admitted that frequently the church concerned, or the archdeacon involved, are at fault in not observing correct procedures, in spite of the very full briefing on procedures which is given by English Heritage to dioceses to disseminate to parishes.

12.109. At parish level in rural areas, the forms and questions are not readily understood as being necessary - there is a gap between rural commonsense and the bureaucratic need to record and justify action and expenditure. This leads to added correspondence and acrimony. The incumbent is often between the PCC and English Heritage, and where he has a number of ancient churches in his care he may well spend a lot of time on administration and learning the ropes. So far as English Heritage is concerned, the need for clear explanatory material for local churches seems to have been underestimated, but this has been recognised and work is in hand to fill the gap. So far as the Church is concerned, it would greatly help if there were at least one person appointed in each archdeaconry, who would be well-versed in English Heritage procedures and who would help parishes with their applications and monitor progress.

12.110. At national level, the delays, insensitivities and inefficiencies of English Heritage are probably best tackled by working on the existing structure. The staff of English Heritage are well aware of the organisation's shortcomings, and have devoted much time to frank and helpful discussion with us. It seems to us that their difficulties can be overcome only by an injection of funds and staff. We would be happier if in addition there was Church representation at a higher level than the organisation's Churches Advisory Committee.

12.111. To many in rural areas it is particularly ironic that the Department of the Environment's share of the funding of the Redundant Churches Fund is now 70%, but an open church, which a small congregation is struggling to keep alive, may receive much less for an essential structural repair to keep it safely in use!

12.112. To sum up, our recommendations for improving the present state of affairs are:

(1) In view of the fact that our ancient churches are one of the country's greatest treasures and there is generally free access to them, the Churches should press the Government to make sufficient funds available to enable English Heritage to function efficiently and to provide 70% grants towards major repairs on all Grade I and II* listed churches. In so doing, the Church of England should admit that the present problems are in large measure due to its own unwillingness to take the bull by the horns and claim the full amount needed in the 1970s.

(2) Repairs on all listed churches should be zero-rated for VAT.

(3) The terms under which grants are given to churches should respect their function as places actively used for worship and as communal meeting-places.

(4) The Historic Buildings and Monuments Commission should have on it two Church representatives nominated by the Archbishops.

(5) Each archdeaconry (or, at the very least, each diocese) should have an advisory secretary, fully versed in English Heritage procedures, appointed to help parishes with their applications and to monitor progress. We have in mind someone like a retired architect or surveyor.

(6) English Heritage should allow local congregations some freedom in the assessment of lighting positions, materials and style, ensuring that within a general practice of conservation, and subject to the advice of the diocesan advisory committee, local interpretation with its lack of uniformity should be permitted.

Churchyards

12.113. It should not be forgotten that the churchyard has a part to play in the witness of the Church. For many it can be a place that inspires, a peaceful place for reflection, often a place of beauty, and not least a place which reminds us of the transience of human life but equally of Christian hope. Churchyards can also be a source of valuable historical information.

12.114. We welcome the growing tendency to encourage the use of local stone and the employment of craftsmen in the production of memorials, and commend in this context a new initiative called 'Memorials by Artists'. We also welcome the increasing interest in the promotion of churchyards as conservation areas, and would mention in this context the Church and Conservation Project based at the Arthur Rank Centre (see 11.33.), which offers advice to any interested in pursuing this idea. We also recommend in the latter context *God's Acre* by Francesca Greenoak (Orbis 1985).

Parsonages

12.115. In many areas the parsonage has been almost as much a visible sign of the church's presence in a village as the church building itself and, like the church building, has assumed a symbolism over and above its immediate function. This situation has changed considerably, however, in recent years as a result of the formation of multi-parish benefices and the ensuing sales of surplus parsonages. The effect of that action has been compounded by the Church's policy of selling off its older and larger parsonages and replacing them with smaller, more modern houses. The prevailing situation is by no means uniform and the Commission has witnessed a wide diversity in the standard and style of rural parsonages in its travels around the country. In the Diocese of Durham we had warm hospitality and a useful discussion on local matters in a rectory situated in a modern row of houses facing the old rectory and having the interesting address, 'The Rectory, 1 Rectory View'.

12.116. The policy of disposing of many older parsonages is one that has now been pursued vigorously over two decades as a means of reducing the financial burden on dioceses of maintaining and heating old parsonages, many of which had fallen into serious disrepair or had become too large for the needs of the modern clergyman. The maintenance of unsuitable parsonages has been thought by those responsible to represent an unacceptable call on the limited resources of the church and a move towards smaller more economic houses was instituted. The policy is further justified by the argument that smaller more manageable houses are less of a burden in terms of upkeep for the incumbent and his family, particularly in an age where it is increasingly common for a clergy wife to work away from home.

12.117. In economic terms there is evidence that the policy has been successful. One diocesan parsonages secretary estimates that the annual budget for the maintenance of official parsonages and team vicars' houses is half what it would have been had the old houses been retained. The Church Commissioners cite another diocese, which has seen its maintenance budget drop from nearly £150,000 per annum to just £100,000 in the last four years.

12.118. The policy has, however, inspired heated emotion in some quarters, drawing the criticism that the church has sold off valuable assets or lowered the status of its clergy in society. In some cases the sale of the parsonage has been felt as yet another blow to a village which may have already lost its shop, post office and school and has been seen as the disappearance of yet another community facility. This is sometimes felt more strongly by parishioners than it is by the clergy themselves who are, after all, responsible for maintaining the house. Indeed our evidence is that the replacement policy has broadly been welcomed by the clergy.

12.119. The RCP showed that while many of the clergy interviewed were satisfied with the overall standard of their housing, the size was a particular cause for comment; many felt that the overall space was inadequate and that there were not enough large rooms. Indeed, there were some who unequivocally supported the retention of the few large old houses that remain in the ownership of the Church, feeling that although they might be too large and difficult to manage, by and large in the context of their ministry, the advantages of space outweighed the not inconsiderable problems of maintenance and heating. In some cases, special trust funds have been established by a parish in order to finance the upkeep of a large parsonage.

12.120. Since 1982, new parsonages have been built or selected according to a set of guidelines drawn up by the Church Commissioners. All new parsonages have to be approved by the Church Commissioners although the diocese has the main responsibility for the policy of replacement; in some circumstances, grants are made to meet all or some of the net cost.

12.121. The guidelines were revised in February 1990. Some attempt has been made to meet the criticism of size: the recommended dimensions for the overall size of the house, and in particular for the study, have been increased. Although some concessions have thus been made to the fact that many clergy still wish to use their home for hospitality and for meetings, the guidelines stress that the parsonage is not to be regarded as a substitute for a proper parish room.

12.122. Many clergy and parishes disagree. The RCP demonstrates that it is the view of many rural clergy that meetings should be held in the parsonage, either as a matter of course or because there is a lack of suitable alternative venues. At present, the practice of holding such meetings may be extremely difficult, and, where it does happen, may be burdensome and stressful for the family who are confined to the remaining space which may not even be well separated from the meeting room itself.

12.123. The Church Commissioners have occasionally agreed to build a parish room adjacent to a parsonage but do not favour this because it endangers the privacy of the incumbent's family, because subsequent incumbents may not like the arrangement, and because it could complicate any future disposal of the parsonage and utilisation of the sale proceeds. In general, they will only agree to this on the basis that the parish agree to be wholly responsible for the upkeep of the room.

12.124. While not wishing to return to the days of vastly overlarge houses, but considering that very few rural parishes have parish meeting rooms, we would encourage diocesan parsonage boards and the Church Commissioners to look more sympathetically at requests in rural areas for larger houses with additional rooms. The clergy family needs its privacy; equally, an incumbent may need to accommodate quite large meetings, especially in multi-parish benefices where an ordinary meeting of officers (churchwardens, PCC secretaries, treasurers) can comprise 30 people! Studies will need to be large enough to accommodate modern office equipment, but this is not peculiar to rural areas.

12.125. We welcome the inclusion in the new guide of the possibility of double garages and would urge dioceses to include this feature as a matter of course in their policy for rural parsonages.

12.126. Finally, the garden is an important feature of the rural parsonage and may be regarded as the last vestige of the days when the clergyman would have kept his own livestock and made his income from the glebe. A number of rural clergy have testified to being judged by the state of the garden, an important feature of rural life. For some the garden constitutes one of the joys of a rural living. Others recognise it as an important duty and consider it part of their week's work to give time to the garden. We suggest that prospective rural clergy should bear this in mind as another particular feature of rural ministry, and we commend the provisions of the parsonage guidelines that the garden should be easy to maintain. We also welcome the practice of some

PCCs of giving assistance towards the provision of machines or shrubs for the parsonage garden.

12.127. We end the main body of this report considering the quiet of a vicarage garden. To some this may have the air of an appendix, a postscript. But the theme of our report has been the ministry of the Church at the intersections of the spiritual and the secular, the holy and the humdrum; and many see such an intersection very clearly, albeit often in an undemanding and private context, in a garden. Furthermore, the biblical account of the human story begins in a garden. It is therefore not wholly inappropriate that in such a place we end our twentieth century Rural Ride.

Recommendations

1. There should be an area bishop in each archdeaconry at least in the larger dioceses. (12.13.)

2. Diocesan offices should review their arrangements for communications with benefices, and their use of modern information technology for this purpose. (12.14.)

3. Diocesan office staff and chairmen and representatives of diocesan boards should have as much personal contact as possible with deaneries. (12.15.)

4. The proposed commission to review synodical government should be given a broad brief to investigate this style of government not just from a central but also from a local point of view. The commission should also examine the position of synodical government within the leadership of the Church of England, and how it relates to the development of policy and executive action. (12.21.)

5. The episcopal members of the Board of Governors of the Church Commissioners should set up a small group to look at the moral and ethical implications of investments and (after a debate in Synod) make recommendations to the Board. The Church Commissioners should thereafter have a separate section in their Annual Report giving an account of how their activities have reflected these recommendations. (12.40.)

6. Instructions to the Church Commissioners' land agents should embody references to job creation, new business formation and the appropriate training, making full use of TECs and rural enterprise agencies. (12.45.)

7. In order to strengthen the responsibility required of the local Church, we propose that the Archbishop of Canterbury should set up

an inquiry to make recommendations on the extent to which the Church Commissioners' work could be devolved to dioceses, and that the inquiry should report by the end of 1992. (12.54.)

8. Greater freedom should be given to dioceses to fix maximum and minimum stipends. (12.55.)

9. A serious reappraisal should be made of clergy remuneration, with a view to the introduction of significant improvements to stipends. This reappraisal should include a reassessment of the arguments for and against length-of-service increments. It should be completed by the end of 1991. Its conclusions should be made widely available in popular form. (12.70.-12.73.)

10. Dioceses should review the measurable parish activities of clergy wives, and the parallel activities of the wives of senior clergy, particularly where they do not seek other paid employment, with a view to paying a wife undertaking these duties an annual honorarium. We suggest something up to £2,000. (12.75.)

11. Dioceses should provide such basic equipment as a word processor and printer, copier, and answerphone, and the training necessary to enable an incumbent to use this equipment economically and efficiently. (12.88.)

12. A review of equipment should be automatically undertaken at quinquennial visitations and upon any subsequent pastoral reorganisation with the intention of establishing suitable levels for the task in hand, together with a review of the incumbent's skills, which may reveal a need for further training. (12.88.)

13. Dioceses should seek to establish a common standard for computerised equipment, so that software, data and discs are interchangeable. (12.88.)

14. Expenses not dealt with by the diocese should be passed by one person designated by the PCC to authorise them, and these should be cleared on a monthly basis. (12.88.)

15. Expenses should always be considered and referred to as parish expenses, not clergy expenses. (12.88.)

16. Archdeacons should ensure that the clergy are fully briefed on expenses and are receiving reimbursement at proper and realistic levels. (12.88.)

17. In view of the fact that our ancient churches are one of the country's greatest treasures and there is generally free access to them, the Churches should press the Government to make sufficient funds available to enable English Heritage to function efficiently and to

provide 70% grants towards major repairs on all Grade I and II* listed churches as they do for redundant churches. (12.112.)

18. Repairs on all listed churches should be zero-rated for VAT. (12.112.)

19. The terms under which grants are given to churches should respect their function as places actively used for worship and as communal meeting-places. (12.112.)

20. The Historic Buildings and Monuments Commission should have on it two Church representatives nominated by the Archbishops. (12.112.)

21. Each archdeaconry (or, at the very least, each diocese) should have an advisory secretary, fully versed in English Heritage procedures, appointed to help parishes with their applications and to monitor progress. We have in mind someone like a retired architect or surveyor. (12.112.)

22. English Heritage should allow local congregations some freedom in the assessment of lighting positions, materials and style, ensuring that, within a general practice of conservation, and subject to the advice of the diocesan advisory committee, local interpretation with its lack of uniformity should be permitted. (12.112.)

23. Diocesan parsonage boards and the Church Commissioners should look more sympathetically at requests for larger parsonages, with additional rooms, in rural areas. (12.124.)

Conclusion

Our work has led us to see the Church as an integral part of the rural scene, not just through its history but as an active participant in contemporary life. The Church is in action in an arena in which not only local issues are focused, but also those of national and global significance. The mixture is compelling, but it is essential that the greater debates do not obscure the local issues which affect people daily, especially the less well-off.

The global environmental crisis is apparent in many local areas through pollution of different kinds on a disturbing scale. It requires new thinking in strategic policy on energy and transport as well as industry and agriculture, and has led us to reflect on the doctrines of creation and community. In both we have found sources for understanding the contemporary rural condition, and which point towards values which are the necessary basis for a renewed sense of responsibility towards our fellow human beings and the rest of creation. In reflecting on community we found an interpretation of person which transcends the individual and offers hope for a Christian view of corporate interdependence and activity. There is much more to be done by theologians, together with scientists, to help Christians and others to understand more clearly the relationships between the different aspects of creation, between human beings and other forms of life; to probe the continuing revelation of God through the process of creation, and to bring about a greater understanding of the role of humanity within it.

We have found that beneath a seemingly tranquil surface there are great changes, full of tension, occurring in most rural areas. Our studies have shown that population movements have brought new people with different perceptions and ambitions into rural life. The nature and style of work has changed, predominantly agricultural land-use has been questioned, and services have been withdrawn into local towns without the continued support of improved public transport. For many, these changes have been made acceptable, and even desirable, through having personal transport, but for a considerable minority rural life has become harder and remains so.

The rural areas are going through a period of change, the rhythms of which are long and deep, hidden from many observers. Agriculture, the dominant visible source of employment, has become almost insignificant in many areas as an employer, although its visible impact remains high, often exciting criticism of its methods, and not just from the uninformed. Most people still want to see a farmed landscape, but one which reflects the scale and patterns of former years. With overproduction on a European scale of some foods, there is likely to be growing pressure for agricultural subsidies to be directed towards environmental objectives. Jobs lost in agriculture have not easily been replaced. Many workers have migrated to towns, but there is still a need for both training and new jobs in rural areas suitable for those without hi-tech skills. Many rural people survive on a parlous mixture of casual and seasonal work, part-time jobs and relatively low-paid employment, often in service industries. With the high costs of rural living in terms of transport, shopping, and access to services, low pay is not balanced by a low cost economy. Many new jobs attract people from outside, stimulating a migration out of the towns, rather than satisfying local demands and skills. The need for local training and skill development is urgent, and requires initiatives which cope with the problems of accessibility.

Central to this discussion is the question of what type of society we expect find in the countryside of the future. The trend is towards a professional, wealthier group; but our judgement is that if this is the market trend, it is insufficient. Policies which provide local work, local homes and local communications for those who are less well-off, but who wish to remain in the country, are crucial if rural living is to retain the balance and cohesion which appear so attractive not only to those looking on from outside, but also to many of the people whom we met throughout the villages of England. This is a vision which places in the hands of the majority the responsibility to support action and policies which serve the needs of the weaker sections of society.

The village hall, the voluntary transport system, the Church, and the caring network all rely on people giving of their time and expertise: the local management of schools has added another responsibility, and maybe the cottage hospital will join the list of facilities that can only be maintained if local people provide the initiative and management. We have been warned by numerous national and local voluntary bodies that reliance on volunteers may be pushed to breaking point as a higher proportion of rural citizens joins the expanding labour force. Even if the volunteers needed are found, we are equally unsure whether the public sector will leave the buildings and other capital assets in place for them to use.

With all the changes in the provision of services brought about by the market economy, the weak, the poor and vulnerable, and the elderly have their choices further curtailed, since without readily available personal transport, access to basic facilities is restricted. Their future, if current policies continue, causes us serious concern.

Government at all levels, including the lowest but important parish council level, has responsibilities to provide what cannot be provided for themselves by individuals. We are concerned at the effect of housing and finance policies that have failed to supply the important sector of affordable housing, and particularly the rented sector in rural areas. We urge that more effort by all concerned is put into meeting this need, so that rural communities may remain a good mix of all social groups for the good of the whole community. Housing on its own is not enough. The interlocking needs of suitable work, transport and access to services are equally crucial if a balanced society is to remain in rural areas and if the interests of many of the more vulnerable people are to be safeguarded. The Church as landowner and landlord carries its share of this responsibility.

The fragmentation of policy in rural terms makes redress harder to achieve. But at national and local levels the rural implications of policy and the knock-on effect of seemingly independent decisions, like the routes for motorways, need far more careful consideration with closer contact of a meaningful nature between government departments. The European dimension of this is equally important.

The Church of England, together with the other main Christian denominations, has probably as great a stake, and certainly a more visible one, in England's rural areas as any other body. The life of the rural church has not been unaffected by the changes sweeping the country. These have coincided with radical change in the organisation of the rural church, with its smaller number of clergy, caused through a mixture of early retirement, a fall in recruitment and a reallocation of resources to the towns and cities. The Church has made errors, particularly by the way it has often failed to respect local understandings and needs. But that sad chapter in the Church's history is passing, and the rural Church is increasingly realising that it cannot live on either nostalgia or anger: it has to look forward.

The growth of universal education during this century and the new social mixes which are being formed in rural areas, mean that there is a great deal of potential for lay leadership in most areas. A growing partnership between ordained and lay Christians, based on the baptismal commission, can ensure that the public worship of the Church continues locally, as well as an effective involvement in the wider Church and community. For some this approach will involve a radical change of ideas, attitudes and prejudices, but we have witnessed in many places both faithfulness to this vision and an adventurous commitment to move forward. We accordingly feel optimistic that, with encouragement and a growing self-confidence, rural people will provide leadership, even in areas where they doubt their own skills and abilities. At the same time, these changes are posing questions about priesthood, ordination and the role of the laity which will force themselves onto the national agenda, affecting attitudes towards vocation, selection, and training, and certainly the role of the priest in the parish and his relationship with others.

We are clear that priority should be given to the local expression of community and worship, but growth will need a contribution of leadership from outside the local community. In secular life this will apply to significant landowners, including the Church and those companies with interests in rural supplies and markets: there is an urgent need for partnership and networking, bringing together people and organisations from disparate backgrounds. In this work, the role of rural community councils and other voluntary bodies could be crucial; but they will need well-planned support from the public purse, receiving a commitment that enables long-term roots to be put down. Bishops also are local leaders and we have examined their role, and urge a growing emphasis on their being seen at the furthest reaches of their areas of responsibility, affirming the local and linking it with the wider Church and society. The changes we observe taking place need to be thoroughly understood throughout the Church and represented at episcopal level.

For the Church to shift its course, every part of the Church structure will need to set clear aims and objectives for itself. When it knows what it is trying to do, it is more likely to attract the increased financial support necessary. We are proposing the devolution of responsibility nearer to the cutting edge of parish life, so that rural people may find it easier to identify with the aspirations of their local church. A majority of the population has some kind of religious faith, but the Church has generally failed to inspire them to active participation in its affairs. This remains a priority, and not just in the Decade of Evangelism.

Local churches for their part, amongst other initiatives, will need to assume greater financial responsibility as part of their growth in faith, and we have made suggestions which could have a radical impact on this. It is through facing local challenges of conscience and conflicts of interest that the Church is forced to probe its faith and to seek answers. Those answers need to relate to contemporary issues in contemporary language, while being set within the timeless relationship between human beings and God.

Principal Recommendations

1. In order to reduce the tensions relating to access to the countryside, local communities should be enabled to benefit directly when new housing developments are approved from, for example, the creation of new common land or increased free access to public areas of countryside, or from receiving a proportion of the planning gain to be used for their own named conservation purposes. (4.18.)

2. Payment should be made to farmers and other land owners, for example, on the lines of premiums in Environmentally Sensitive Areas, for facilitating the community's enjoyment of rural land, including the creation and maintenance of new rights of way. (4.22.)

3. The Government should commission a thoroughgoing review of transport facilities in the rural areas, in the context not only of social and economic needs but of environmental pressures and the greenhouse effect. This should include consideration of the adequacy of public transport, and of the accessibility of services. (4.31.)

4. The growing impacts of modern technology on the environment emphasise the need for more adequate debate and research, linked to Parliamentary processes, into how these can be evaluated. (4.33.)

5. Research should be undertaken into the scale and speed of development which small communities and the environment can assimilate without detriment.

6. The Department of Employment should make special provision, in the funding of Training and Enterprise Councils (TECs), for rural areas with special difficulties, to provide for the training and retraining of the rural workforce. (5.13.)

7. The Commission recognises the need to strengthen the changing rural economy in many areas. It also recognises the need to protect and sustain the countryside. The need to emphasise the interdependence of these purposes should be reflected in strategies for counties and regions. This means a more effective integration of, for example, county structure plans, National Park plans, countryside strategies, Rural Development Programmes, TEC Business Plans, and other statutory and non-statutory programmes, with the intention of bringing them together in integrated rural strategies. (5.30. and 5.36.)

8. In Rural Development Areas (RDAs), because a more integrated and complete approach is called for in the countryside, district council planning committees should be required to be advised by the appropriate economic agency, such as county economic development departments, the Rural Development Commission (RDC), etc, as well as by planning officers. Such procedures within RDAs should be seen as an experiment, with a view to extending them to other rural areas. (5.33. and 5.63.)

9. Where the Countryside Commission or the Nature Conservancy Council consider overgrazing to be a threat, rates of Hill Livestock Compensatory Allowance should be topped up to compensate adequately for voluntarily reduced stocking limits to achieve a desired botanical and ecological structure. (5.62.)

10. Many rural economies are particularly dependent on the employment provided by a single employer. In the event of such employment being substantially reduced, local authorities and the RDC should be empowered to declare a special status for the area in order to strengthen the rural economy and encourage new employment by providing advice, professional support, financial assistance and premises. (5.68.)

11. Restrictions which forbid local authorities to use much of the finance gained from house sales to provide new affordable low cost housing in rural areas should be removed. (6.32.)

12. Preferably in the context of a village appraisal, every parish should carry out a housing needs survey, with the advice of its rural community council (RCC) to assess the local need for affordable housing. The results should be conveyed to the district council and interested housing associations. (6.33.)

13. The Housing Corportation should:

    (1) encourage housing associations and other appropriate agencies to deliver social housing in rural areas;

(2) make a consistent grant of 70% available to schemes;

(3) increase the number of houses to be built in rural areas, for which it will provide finance, to not less than 5,000 a year by 1992, climbing substantially beyond that to clear targets to be specified by the Government for 1995 and 2000. This will encourage effective planning preparation. We would welcome a multi-party commitment to support this to ensure long-term consistency. (6.36.)

14. Strict limits should be set regarding the maximum amount of equity which an individual owner can accumulate in housing schemes where public subsidy is involved. Moreover, staircasing should not be possible where that is the wish of trustees when more than 50% of monies in a scheme are from private sources, even if public money is involved. (6.47.)

15. Churches and local voluntary groups should encourage members to become voluntary car scheme drivers and to ensure in collaboration with the parish council (where one exists) that each parish has a designated person or group responsible for discovering mobility needs. (6.76.)

16. The Church should encourage and support programmes of care in the community, shaping its own network of care to include all sections of community, but especially the elderly. (6.101.)

17. Programmes to close hospital services should be critically reviewed and particular account should be taken of the travel costs of rural patients and visitors. (6.84.- 6.85.)

18. The vital role of the volunteer workers within the community and the importance of continuity should be more widely recognised, and positive support should be given to them both financially and by the provision of training. (6.101.)

19. Dioceses should pay particular attention to the need for the Church's mission and ministry to be focused in the world as well as within the Church. (8.9.)

20. Following similar recommendations by the Arbhbishop's Commission on Urban Priority Areas (ACUPA), we recommend that the Advisory Council for the Church's Ministry (ACCM) should review its priorities in theological training and development. (8.36.- 38.)

21. Dioceses should explore the opportunities of working with secular organisations to develop skills in management. (8.41.)

22. The role of non-residential training courses should be developed further. (8.42.)

23. Research should be urgently undertaken to get a clearer view of the causes underlying the reduction in numbers available for the ordained ministry. (8.43.)

24. The parson's freehold system should be re-examined and a method of time-limited contractual employment be explored. (8.62.)

25. There should be greater collaboration between dioceses in sharing their experience of pastoral planning and some national co-ordination of this would be essential. (8.63.)

26. Dioceses should draw up a statement of aims which can be shared with parishes as part of corporate pastoral planning. (8.65.)

27. Dioceses should continue to experiment with different patterns of ministry, but there needs to be some centralised monitoring and assessment of what is being done and more openness about what is actually taking place. The new Board for Ministry should be responsible for this. (8.83.)

28. Dioceses should review their aims in training for lay ministry and where responsibility for such training lies within their own structures. (8.91.)

29. Clergy should lead no more than two major services, in addition to an early said service, in any Sunday morning. (9.24.)

30. Those responsible for lay training in dioceses should give particular attention to the training needs of the laity involved in planning and leading worship and establish workshops and other resources to meet these needs. (9.32. and 9.47.)

31. Cathedrals should review their resources and the potential that lies in these for supporting youth work, tourism, and parish worship, particularly in rural areas, for example by:

    (1)   appointing a member of the chapter to have special responsibilities for the cathedral's involvement with youth work in the diocese;

    (2)   using the cathedral's tourist facilities to signpost visitors to other churches in the diocese;

    (3)   keeping in closer touch with parish clergy about what the cathedral can offer them in terms of resources. (9.71.-9.75.)

32. The Church of England should explore and promote the place of teenagers in the life of the Church by means of an initiative comparable with *Children in the Way*, backed by empirical research. (10.77.)

33. Parishes or benefices as appropriate should examine the role of young people in the ongoing life of the Church to seek ways of enabling them to participate fully at all levels of Church life according to their individual skills and talents. This could be also a matter for deaneries.

34. Each diocese with a significant rural area should appoint an officer with responsibility both to represent the rural interest within the Church to the wider constituency and also to represent the Church to the wider rural constituency, particularly to the local RCC. (11.30.)

35. We recommend the extensive application of the possibilities now encoded in Canon B43, which gives wide-ranging permission for shared liturgy and ministry. (11.42. et seq)

36. The proposed commission to review synodical government should be given a broad brief to investigate this style of government not just from a central but also from a local point of view; the commission should also review the position of synodical government within the leadership of the Church of England, and how it relates to the development of policy and executive action. (12.21.)

37. The episcopal members of the Board of Governors of the Church Commissioners should set up a small group to look at the moral and ethical implications of investments and (after a debate in Synod) make recommendations to the Board. The Church Commissioners should thereafter have a separate section in their Annual Report giving an account of how their activities have reflected these recommendations. (12.40.)

38. In order to strengthen the responsibility required of the local Church, we propose that the Archbishop of Canterbury should set up an inquiry to make recommendations on the extent to which the Church Commissioners' work could be devolved to dioceses, and that the inquiry should report by the end of 1992. (12.54.)

39. A serious reappraisal should be made of clergy remuneration, with a view to the introduction of significant improvements to stipends. This reappraisal should include a reassessment of the arguments for and against length-of-service increments. It should be completed by the end of 1991. Its conclusions should be made widely available in popular form. (12.70.-12.73.)

40. Dioceses should review the measurable parish activities of clergy wives, and the parallel activities of the wives of senior clergy, particularly where they do not seek other paid employment, with a view

to paying a wife undertaking these duties an annual honorarium. We suggest something up to £2,000. (12.75.)

41. Archdeacons should ensure that the clergy are fully briefed on expenses and are receiving reimbursement at proper and realistic levels. (12.88.)

42. In view of the fact that our ancient churches are one of the country's greatest treasures and there is generally free access to them, the Churches should press the Government to make sufficient funds available to enable English Heritage to function efficiently and to provide 70% grants towards major repairs on all Grade I and II* listed churches as they do for redundant churches. (12.112.)

43. Repairs on all listed churches should be zero-rated for VAT (12.116)

44. The terms under which grants are given to churches should respect their function as places actively used for worship and as communal meeting-places. (12.112.)

45. Each archdeaconry (or, at the very least, each diocese) should have an advisory secretary, fully versed in English Heritage procedures, appointed to help parishes with their applications and to monitor progress. We have in mind someone like a retired architect or surveyor. (12.112.)

46. English Heritage should allow local congregations some freedom in the assessment of lighting positions, materials and style, ensuring that, within a general practice of conservation, and subject to the advice of the diocesan advisory committee, local interpretation with its lack of uniformity should be permitted. (12.112.)

47. The General Synod should budget for an officer and a secretarial assistant to be based at the Arthur Rank Centre to progress the recommendations of this report. (11.26)

Appendix A

Principal Evidence Received

During the visits to 41 dioceses the Commissioners spent time with the majority of diocesan bishops and many of their suffragan or area bishops. Similarly, time was spent in diocesan offices, meeting secretaries and representatives of the various boards. We also met large numbers of parish clergy and lay people. These have not been listed separately. A number of bishops have visited the Commission informally, or sent us memoranda, and their guidance has been much appreciated.

Each diocese appointed a diocesan link officer to work with the Commission and these gave invaluable help.

The deans and provosts of 40 of the cathedrals of England wrote giving evidence of their contacts with the rural parts of their diocese.

The following is a list of the principal evidence received from organisations and individuals:-

Sir Donald Acheson, Department of Health and Social Security
Action with Communities in Rural England (ACRE)
Mrs Hester Agate, Suffolk Historic Churches Trust
Age Concern
Agricultural and Food Research Council
Mr Colin Alves, General Secretary, General Synod Board of Education
Mr Julian Anderson, MAFF
Mr Bryan Anderson, Royal School of Church Music
Mr John Anfield, Peak National Park
Animal Christian Concern
Arkleton Trust
Very Reverend John Arnold, Dean of Durham
Mr David Arthur, Industrial Christian Fellowship
Arun Project
Asda Stores Ltd
Right Reverend J F Ashby, Bishop of Western Kansas, USA
Reverend Peter Ashby, Vicar of Eskdale, Carlisle Diocese
Reverend Canon Richard Askew, Salisbury Diocese
Association of Chief Police Officers
Association of County Councils
Association of District Councils
Right Reverend Peter Atkins, Bishop of Waiapu, New Zealand
Automobile Association
Mr Graham J L Avery, Director for Rural Development, European Commission, Brussels
Avon Community Council
Mr Alain Bain, Chief Executive, Bridgnorth District Council
Baptist Union of Great Britain
Reverend J R Barff, Vicar of Pining with Compton Greenfield, Bristol Diocese
Reverend David Barker, ACCM
Reverend Julian Barker, Vicar of Repton, Derby Diocese
Basset Law District Council
Reverend Canon Paul Bates, Director of Training, Winchester Diocese
Mr Trevor Baxter
Mr Albert Baxter, General Secretary, The Park Homes Residents' Guild
Mrs Louise Beaton, ACRE
Reverend Nicholas Beddow, Vicar of Escombe and Witton Park, Durham
Reverend John Belderson, URC Minister, Pateley Bridge, Ripon Diocese

Faith in the Countryside

Mr Richard Beman, Community College, Bishop's Castle, Herefordshire
Reverend G A G Bennet, Rector of Redenhall, Harleston, Wortwell and Needham, Norwich Diocese
Reverend Alan Billings, Ripon College, Cuddesdon.
Bishop Burton College of Agriculture
Reverend Chris Bishop, Chaplain, Stansted Airport
Reverend Robin Blackall, Rector of Edith Weston with North Luffenham and Lyndon with Manton, Peterborough Diocese
Reverend Bernard Blanchard, Rural Theology Association
Mr Chris Bland
Reverend Canon R P Bloy
Board for Social Responsibility of the General Synod
Board of Education of the General Synod
Mr T B Boden
Mr E J Bolton, Senior Chief Inspector, HM Inspectorate of Schools
Miss N M Bond
Venerable David Bonser, Archdeacon of Rochdale
Reverend Canon Michael Botting, Chester Diocesan Director of Lay Training
Mr Peter Boulter, Director of Education, Cumbria County Council
Canon P H Boulton, Director of Education, Southwell Diocese
Venerable Michael Bourke, Archdeacon of Bedford
Mrs M Bousted
Mr Brian Bowden, the Grosvenor Estate, Eccleston, Cheshire
Boys' Brigade
Reverend Dr Ian Bradley, Church of Scotland
Mr Harry Bramma, Director, Royal School of Church Music
Mr Desmond Brereton
Brighton Polytechnic Countryside Research Unit
British Coal
British Council of Churches
British Council of Churches Community and Race Relations Unit
British Geriatrics Society
British Horse Society
British Organic Farmers and Organic Growers Association
British Rail
British Telecom
Professor Dennis K Britton, formerly of Wye College, University of London
Broadland District Council
Reverend Charles Brock, Mansfield College, Oxford
Broken Rites
Brothers of Charity Services, Lisieux Hall, Chorley, Lancashire
Venerable Murray Brown, Archdeacon of Northam, Western Australia
Reverend Dr Allen Brown, Episcopal Church Center, New York
Mr Gilbert Brown, Torr Farm, Hathersage, Derbyshire
Buckinghamshire County Council
Professor Alan Budd, Barclays Bank
Mr Peter Burman, Former Secretary, Council for the Care of Churches
Professor Paul Burns, Cranfield School of Management
Business in the Community
Buswatch
Professor Neville Butler, Director, Youthscan
Dr Caroline Cahm, National Federation of Bus Users
Reverend Canon Douglas Caiger
The Earl of Caithness, Minister of State for Housing, Environment and the Countryside
Reverend Jean Calvert, Peterborough Diocese
Cambridgeshire County Council

Mr Charles Capstick, MAFF
Carers' National Association
Mr Eric Carter, Farming and Wildlife Advisory Group
Reverend G A Catchpole, Priest-in-Charge of Bradwell-on-Sea, Chelmsford Diocese
Mr Kevin Catchpole, Salisbury Diocesan Communications Officer
Central Council of Church Bellringers
Central Stipends Authority
Charity Commissioners for England and Wales
Chelmsford Diocesan Evangelical Association
Cheshire County Council
Cheshire Rural Community Council
Child Poverty Action Group
Mr John Chilvers, Archbishop's Commission on Urban Priority Areas
Christian Ecology Group
Church Action on Poverty
Church Action with the Unemployed
Church Commissioners for England: in addition to those who came to give oral
    evidence, and who are listed individually, various members of staff have given
    invaluable help in writing or by telephone
Church in Wales
Church of Ireland
Church of Scotland
Church Society
Cinderford Town Council
Mr David Clark, MP
Mrs Margaret Clark, Rural Development Commission
Venerable K J Clarke, Archdeacon of Swindon
Mr Roger Clarke, Countryside Commission
Reverend Harold S Clarke, Luton Industrial College
Mrs Sarah Clarkson, Herefordshire Self-Help Project
Cleveland Council for Voluntary Services
Cleveland County Council
Clifton Rural Rating Action Group
Mr Nigel Clutton
Mr Peter Codling
Colyton Team Ministry, Exeter Diocese
Commission of the European Communities
Common Ground
Community Council of Devon
Community Council of Lancashire
Community Council of Northumberland
Community Council for Shropshire
Community Council of Staffordshire
Community Council for Suffolk
Community Council for Wiltshire
Community Projects Foundation
Reverend Derek Conaber, Baptist Union, North Eastern Area
Conference des Eveques de France
Miss Moira Constable, Executive Director, NAC Rural Trust
Reverend Bede Cooper, Reader
Mr Nicholas Corbin, Norfolk Churches Trust
Cornwall County Council
Corporation of the Sons of the Clergy
Mr P G Cotgrove, Deputy Managing Director, British Coal Opencast Executive
Council for Christian Care, Exeter
Council for the Deaf
Council for the Protection of Rural England

Faith in the Countryside

Country Landowners' Association
Countryside and Rural Issues Group, Chelmsford Diocese
Countryside Information Systems, Shepton Mallet
Mrs Jean Craig, Reader
Reverend Bryant Crane, Honorary Director of Studies, Central Readers Conference
Craven District Council
Dr Christopher Cripps, Director ComTaw, Lydney, Gloucestershire
Reverend Michael Crowther-Green, Stewardship Adviser, Oxford Diocese
Mr Alan Croxford, Reader
Crusaders
Reverend Ian Cundy, Cranmer Hall, Durham
Dr John Cunningham MP
Mr David Curry, MP
Mr Hilary Daniel, Reader
Venerable & Very Rev David Woodworth, Rector and Dean of Cashel and Archdeacon
   of Cashel, Waterford and Lismore, Church of Ireland
Dr Grace Davie, University of Exeter, who was commissioned to write a paper (*The
   Rural/Urban Interface*)
Right Reverend J D Davies, Bishop of Shrewsbury
Mr Michael Davies, Redundant Churches Secretary, Church Commissioners
Right Reverend Peter Dawes, Bishop of Derby
Mr Nicholas Dean, Countryside Director, Housebuilders' Federation
Miss Eve Dennis, Church and Conservation Project, Arthur Rank Centre
Department of Education and Science
Department of Employment
Department of Health and Social Security
Department of the Environment
Department of Transport
Derbyshire Rural Community Council
Mr James Derounian, Northumberland Rural Development Programme
Devon County Council
Devon Land Bank Trust
Directorate General, Employment, Social Affairs and Education
Dispensing Doctors' Association
Reverend Canon Michael Dittmer
Mrs Maria Donizetti, Headmistress, Boyle & Petyt Primary School, Bolton Abbey,
   North Yorkshire
Reverend L W Doolan
Reverend C R Dormer, Convenor, Home Mission Committee, Scottish Episcopal
   Church
Dorset County Council
Dorset Community Council
Mr Michael Dower, Chief Officer, Peak National Park
Mrs B Downer, Bank End Farm, Roadhead, Carlisle
Durham Rural Community Council
East Northamptonshire and Huntingdonshire Rural Development Area
Ecclesiastical Insurance Group
Reverend Chris Edmundson
Very Reverend David Edwards, Provost of Southwark
Reverend Canon David Edwards, Rural Theology Association
Mr Martin Elengorn, General Purposes Secretary, Church Commissioners
Ellesmere Cottage Hospital League of Friends
Reverend Chris Elliott, United Reformed Church, Teeside District
Mr Mike Emmott, Director of Programmes for the Employment Service
English Tourist Board
Reverend Alun W Evans, Provincial Officer for Social Responsibility, Church in Wales

Dr David Eversley, who was commissioned to write a paper (*Changes in the Social Order and Policy Frameworks and their Implications for Rural Areas*)
Faculty of Community Medicine, Royal Colleges of Physicians
Farming and Wildlife Trust Limited
Dr and Mrs John Farrer, Clapham, North Yorkshire
Mrs Jill Faux
Reverend Pamela Fawcett, Norwich Diocese
Miss Jean Fawley, Teacher, Guilsland Primary School, Cumbria
Mr Jeremy Fennell, ACRE
Reverend Heather Fenton, Diocese of St. Asaph's, Church in Wales
Mr Barry Field MP
Mrs Juliette Fleming, ACRE
Reverend Sally Fogden, St Edmundsbury & Ipswich Diocese
Mrs Lilias Foggin, organiser of parish teas for tourists at St Gregory's Church, Tredington, Warwickshire
Venerable Anthony Foottit, Archdeacon of Lynn
Mr D W Ford, Chairman, Caddington and Slipend Parish Council
Forestry Commission
Mr Timothy Forse, Segal Quince Wicksteed Ltd.
Forum of Private Business
Mrs Sally Foulkes, South Northamptonshire District Council
Ms Harriet Frazer, Memorials by Artists
Friends of the Clergy Corporation
Frontier Youth Trust
Mr Douglas Fryer, Head of Statistics and Computer Department, Central Board of Finance
Reverend Canon John Fuller, Salisbury & Wells Theological College
Mr Peter Gardiner-Hill, Industrial Christian Fellowship
Reverend Paul Gatenby, Rector of Isham with Pytchley, Peterborough Diocese
Reverend Gordon Gatward, Ecumenical Chaplaincy of Lincoln & South Humberside
Mr John Gatwood, Housing Corporation
Reverend Dr John Gay, Director, Culham College Institute
Dr George Giarchi
Professor Alan Gibb, Durham University Business School
Reverend Canon William Gibbs, Priest-in-Charge of Cottesbrooke etc Peterborough Diocese
Venerable Kenneth Gibbons, Archdeacon of Lancaster
Reverend Mary Gill, Carlisle Diocese
Reverend Professor R Gill
Mrs Cecil Gillington
Girl Guides Association
Lieutenant Colonel R J Girling, Secretary for Special Service, Salvation Army
Reverend Jonathan Gledhill, Rural Dean of Canterbury
Gloucestershire Rural Community Council
Gold Fields Trust
Great Yarmouth Borough Council
Mr John Green
Mrs Sue Grey
Right Honourable John Selwyn Gummer, Minister of Agriculture
Reverend Sandy Gunn, Church of Scotland Rural Working Group
Captain Philip Haines, Church Army
Mr Richard Halsey, English Heritage
Reverend Roger Hamblin, Vicar of Cockerham, Blackburn Diocese
Hampshire Community Care Groups
Hampshire Council of Community Service
Hampshire County Council

Professor Charles Handy, Visiting Professor at the London Business School and
  Chairman, Royal Society of Arts
Right Reverend R M Hardy, Bishop of Lincoln
Mr Reg Harman
Mr G Harries-Jenkins, Dean, University of Hull School of Adult and Continuing
  Education
Ms S Harrison, DARSET Play and Learn Van
Reverend Michael Hart
Reverend David Hawtin, Ecumenical Officer for the Diocese of Durham
Mr Brian Hayes, Chief Constable of Surrey
Venerable Ben Helmer, Archdeacon of Kansas, USA
The Lord Henniker, Thornham Magna, Suffolk
Hereford & Worcester Advocacy Project
Hereford & Worcester County Council
Hereford & Worcester Rural Community Council
Hereford & Worcester Rural Housing Association
Mr John Herington, Department of Geography, University of Loughborough
Mrs Mary Heron
Reverend R J Hewetson, Diocesan Ecumenical Officer, Norwich Diocese
Reverend Francis Hewitt, Vicar of Lastingham, York Diocese
Reverend John Hill, Rector of Tingrith and Westoning, St Albans Diocese
Reverend Elizabeth Hodgkiss, Methodist Church, Member of Rural Theology
  Association
Reverend Tony Hodgson, Christian Rural Centre, Dovedale, Derbyshire
Mrs Christina Hodson
Mr John Hogg, Barclays Bank
Reverend Dr Simon Holdaway, Senior Research Fellow, University of Manchester
Reverend David Holloway, Ecumenical Officer, Bristol Diocese
Miss Jenny Holmes, Adviser in Religious Education, Salisbury Diocese
Home Office Voluntary Services Unit
Home Start (Ludlow)
Mr Peter Hood, Springhead Trust, Shaftesbury, Dorset
Housebuilders' Federation
Mr Brian Howard, Deputy Chairman, Church Commissioners Assets Committee
Mr Michael Howard MP, Minister for Planning and Water, Department of the
  Environment
Reverend C Hughes Smith, General Secretary, Methodist Church Division of
  Education and Youth
Mr Richard Hughes, Salisbury Diocesan Director of Education
ICI Fertilizers
Inner London Probation Service
Instant Muscle
Institute of Agricultural Medicine and Rehabilitation
Isle of Wight Rural Development Programme
Reverend Canon Bill Jacob, Lincoln Theological College
Reverend Martyn Jarrett, ACCM
Mr Tristram Jenkins, Hereford Diocesan Director of Education
Mr Keith Jenkins, Partner, Winckworth & Pemberton Solicitors
Reverend Prebendary D Jenkyns, Rector of Kington with Huntington, Old Radnor,
  Kinnerton etc, Hereford Diocese
Mrs Diane Johnson
Reverend Cliff Jones, Reader
Mr Ron Keating, National Union of Public Employees
Dr David Keeble, Department of Geography, University of Cambridge
Reverend Peter Keeling, Rural Dean of Fincham, Ely Diocese
Reverend Norman Kelly, Vicar of Canewdon with Paglesham, Chelmsford Diocese
Reverend Canon Jim Kelsey, North Michigan Diocese, USA

Kennet District Council
Kent County Council
Kerrier Council for Voluntary Services
Dr Charles Kightly, Diocesan Tourist Consultant, Lincoln Diocese
Mr Francis Kinsman
Reverend Andrew Kirk
Right Reverend J D G Kirkham, Bishop of Sherborne
Reverend David Kitching, Priest-in-Charge Graveley etc, Ely Diocese
Mrs Margaret Laird, Third Church Estates Commissioner
Reverend Keith Lamdin, Director of Ministy, Oxford Diocese
Lancashire County Council
Lancashire Forum for Rural Initiatives
Dr Richard Laughlin, University of Sheffield
Reverend Tom Leary, Vicar of Sutton New Town, Southwark Diocese
Mr Barry Leathwood, National Secretary, Agricultural Workers Section, Transport
    and General Workers' Union
Reverend Reg Legg, Priest-in-Charge of Dymock with Donnington and Kempley,
    Gloucester Diocese
Leicester Diocesan Board of Mission and Social Responsibility
Leicestershire County Council
Library Association
Dr David Lloyd
Venerable Trevor Lloyd, Liturgical Commission
Sir Douglas Lovelock, First Church Estates Commissioner
Reverend Jonathan Lumby, Priest-in-Charge of Milverton etc, Bath & Wells Diocese
Miss P Lutwyche, Adult Guidance Worker, Dorset County Council
Reverend David MacPherson, Rector of Chedgrave etc, Norwich Diocese
Malpas Deanery Synod, Chester Diocese
Reverend Clive Malpass, Vicar of Askrigg, Wensleydale, Ripon Diocese
Right Reverend Michael Mann, Formerly Dean of Windsor
Mr Adrian Mann, Director, Anglican Stewardship Association
Miss Henrietta Manners
Marches Development Research and Action on Rural Issues
Reverend Jack Mardon, former diocesan evangelist, Bath & Wells Diocese
Professor J S Marsh, Department of Agriculture, Economics and Management,
    University of Reading
Professor Leonard Marsh, Principal, Bishop Grosseteste College, Lincoln
Reverend Geoffrey Mason, Bishop's Adviser on Ministerial Development, Southwark
    Diocese
Mr Tim Mason, Swindon Archdeaconry Youth Service, Bristol Diocese
Mr Graham Mather, Institute of Economic Affairs
Reverend Philip McFadyen, Rector of Swardeston etc, Norwich Diocese
Mr Hector McLean, Archbishops' Appointments Secretary
MENCAP
Methodist Church
Metropolitan Police
Reverend J S C Miller, Abinger Hammer Village School Trust
MIND
Ministry of Agriculture, Fisheries and Food (MAFF)
Mr Peter Moffat
Reverend Nicholas Monk, Ashton Keynes
Mr B Moore-Smith, Consultant in Geriatric Medicine, East Suffolk Health Authority
Moravian Church
Reverend Canon L G Moss, Social Responsibility Officer, Hereford Diocese
Mothers' Union
The Lord Mottistone of Mottistone, Lord Lieutenant, Isle of Wight
Movement for the Reform of Infant Baptism

Myerscough Hall College of Agriculture and Horticulture
NAC Rural Trust
National Advisory Council for the Youth Service
National Association for the Support of Small Schools
National Association of Citizens Advice Bureaux
National Association of Local Councils
National Children's Bureau
National Council for Voluntary Organisations
National Council of Churches, Domestic Hunger and Poverty, New York
National Council of Women of Great Britain
National Economic Development Office
National Farmers' Union
National Federation of Sub-Postmasters
National Federation of Women's Institutes
National Federation of Young Farmers Clubs
National Institute of Adult Continuing Education
National Society (Church of England) for Promoting Religious Education
National Toy Libraries Association
National Trust
Nature Conservancy Council
Reverend J W Naylor, Rector of Chollerton with Birtley and Thockrington, Newcastle
    Diocese
Right Reverend John Neale, Partnership for World Mission
New Homes Environmental Group
Professor Howard Newby, Economic and Social Research Council
Right Reverend Philip Newell, Bishop of Tasmania
Monsignor Vincent Nichols, General Secretariat, Catholic Bishops' Conference of
    England and Wales
Reverend A C F Nicoll, Vicar of Longnor, Quarnford and Sheen, Derby Diocese
Captain Paul Niemiec, Church Army Youth Officer for Dorset
Norfolk County Council
Norfolk Rural Community Council
North Norfolk District Council
North Wiltshire Rural Churches Group
Northamptonshire County Council
Northumberland Rural Development Programme
Norwich Diocesan Council for Education
Nottinghamshire County Council
Nottinghamshire Rural Community Council
Mr Bill O'Brien, MP
Professor Timothy O'Riordan, School of Environmental Sciences, University of East
    Anglia
Office of Population Censuses and Surveys
Mr Steve Ongeri, Housing Corporation
Open Spaces Society
Mr Keith Orford, Public Transport Officer, Derbyshire County Council
Reverend Barry Osborne, Rural Sunrise
Mr J G Owen, Chief Education Officer, Devon
Mrs Susan Page, Archbishops' Commission on Church Music
Peak Park Joint Planning Board
Mr Robert Pearce, Christian Aid Area Secretary for Dorset, Wiltshire
Major John Pearce-Haydon, Salvation Army, Northern Division
Reverend John Peck, St Emundsbury & Ipswich Diocese
Mr Alec Peever, Stonecarver and Letterer
Mr David Peirse, Headmaster, St. Aidan's Church of England High School, Preesall,
    Lancashire
Mr Derrick Penrose, Chatsworth Estate Office, Derbyshire

Reverend David Perrett, Vicar of Ollerton, Southwell Diocese
Mrs Joyce Perry, URC Member of Portsmouth Diocesan Council for Social Responsibility
Mr Nigel Pett, Reader
Ms Carole Pickett
Mr George Pinker, President, Royal College of Obstetricians and Gynaecologists
Mr Ian Pitcher, Headmaster, Toftstead County Primary School, Amberhill, Lincolnshire
Mr Jonathan Porritt, Director, Friends of the Earth
Sir Laurens van der Post
Post Office Counters Ltd
Reverend E A Pratt, Vicar of St. Simon's, Southsea
Presbyterian Church in Ireland
Presbyterian Church of Wales
Mr Ian Purdy
Mr John Green
Radwinter Primary Church of England School, Saffron Walden
Ramblers' Association
Right Reverend T K Ray, Bishop of North Michigan, USA
Reverend John Reader, Vicar of Lydbury North, Hereford Diocese
Reverend Kathleen Reale, Carlisle Diocese
Redundant Churches Fund
Reverend Bruce Reed, Grubb Institute
Mr Robin Rees
Reverend Gavin Reid, Mission England and Church Pastoral Aid Society
REPLAN
Reverend Eric Richards, Vicar of Hutton Buscel, York Diocese
Reverend Charles Richards, Gloucester Diocese
Richmondshire District Council
Mr Allan Roberts, MP
Right Reverend Barry Rogerson, Bishop of Bristol, Chairman of ACCM
Roman Catholic Church in England and Wales
Romney Marsh and Rye Rural Development Area
Rosehaugh Self-Build Housing Initiative
Rothamstead Experimental Station
Royal College of Midwives
Royal College of Physicians of the United Kingdom
Royal Institution of Chartered Surveyors
Royal Pharmaceutical Society of Great Britain
Royal Society for the encouragement of Arts, Manufactures and Commerce
Royal Society for the Protection of Birds
Rural Affairs Group, Newcastle Diocese
Rural Development Commission
Rural Voice
Reverend Dr Brian Russell, ACCM
Mrs Kathy Russell, Organiser, District Nurses' Scheme, Lincolnshire
Reverend Canon Jesse Sage, Chaplain to Agriculture and Rural Society, Canterbury Diocese
J Sainsbury plc
Venerable Roger Sainsbury, Archdeacon of West Ham
Samaritans
Mr Robert Savage, County Planning Officer, Hampshire County Council
Reverend John Saxbee, South West Ordination Course
Mr Michael Scott, Eric Dring Farms, Holland Fen, Lincolnshire
Right Honourable N Scott MP, Minister for Social Security and the Disabled
Right Reverend Michael Scott-Joynt, Bishop of Stafford
Scottish Episcopal Church

Faith in the Countryside

Scout Association
Sea Fish Industry Authority
Mr K A Seals
Reverend Hugh Searle, Rural Dean of Bourn Deanery, Ely Diocese
Dame Joan Seccombe, Conservative Central Office
Sedgefield District Council
Miss Joan Selby-Lowndes, the *Church Times*
Shaw Trust
Mr Robin Sheldon, Director, Music in Worship Trust
Mr J E Shelley, Secretary, Church Commissioners
Shropshire Youth Service
Reverend Christine Sindall, Ely Diocese
Reverend Jane Skinner, Carlisle Diocese
Reverend David Slater, Vicar of Bulford, Figheldean and Milston, Salisbury Diocese
Small Business Development Centre, Cranfield School of Management
Small Farmers' Association
Small Firms Division, Department of Environment
Mr John Smallwood, Southwark Diocese
Right Reverend D J Smith, Bishop of Maidstone
Reverend Canon Alan Smithson, Director of Carlisle Diocesan Training Institute
Soil Association
Mr Clive Soley MP
Somerset Council on Alcohol and Drugs
Somerset County Council
South East Regional Planning Conference
South Norfolk District Council
South Shropshire District Council
South West Arts
Spar UK Ltd
Professor Colin Spedding, Centre for Agricultural Strategy, Reading University
Mr Ken Spencer, Institute of Local Government Studies, University of Birmingham
Spook Enterprises
Sports Council
Springhead Trust, Shaftesbury, Dorset
Staffordshire County Council
Very Reverend David Stancliffe, Provost of Portsmouth, Member of the Liturgical
    Commission
Standing Conference of the East Anglian Local Authorities
Reverend Canon D Staples, Vicar of West Haddon with Winwick and Ravensthorpe,
    Peterborough Diocese
Mrs Elizabeth Stead
Mr Geoffrey Steeley, Planning Officer, Hertfordshire County Council
Steeple Langford Church Aided Junior School, Salisbury
Mr George Stevenson, MEP
Reverend Canon John Stewart, Rector of Kingston, Langton Matravers and Worth
    Matravers, Salisbury Diocese
Stewartry and Dumfries Association of University Women
Reverend Jonathan Still, Agricultural Chaplain, Diocese of Hereford
Stone House League of Friends
Rev Michael Stonhouse, Alberta, Canada
Strategic Planning Society
Mr Lewis Stretch
Stroud District Council
Suffolk Historic Churches Trust
Reverend Alan Summers, United Reformed Church, Durham District
Reverend John Sumner, Vicar of Swallowfield, Oxford Diocese
Mr Jeremy Surr, Director of Adult Training Programmes, the Training Agency

Mr J P Swallow, National Association of Head Teachers
Mr R G F Swanton
Bishop Owen Swindlehurst, Roman Catholic Church
Tavistock Institute of Human Relations
Reverend Peter Taylor, Rector of Necton with Holme Hale, Norwich Diocese
Tenant Farmers' Association
Tesco plc
Mrs Rachel Thomas
Thomas Weatherald Ltd, Askrigg, Cumbria
Dr Mary Thornton, University of Southampton
Professor Sir Bryan Thwaites
Mr C C Tipple, Director of Education, Northumberland County Council
Reverend Dr Norman Todd, Archbishops' Adviser for Bishops' Ministry
Reverend Canon David Tonkin, Taumarunui-Ohura Parish, New Zealand
Father T Towers, Roman Catholic Church, Diocese of Hexham and Newcastle Town
    and Country Planning Association
Transport 2000
Mr Tony Travers, London School of Economics, who was commissioned to write a
    paper on *The Government of Rural England*
Mr David Trippier MP, Minister for the Environment and Countryside
Reverend Canon Timothy Tyndall, former Chief Secretary, ACCM
United Free Church of Scotland
United Reformed Church
University of Exeter, School of Education
Upper Waveney Valley Rural Bus Scheme
Village Halls Forum
The Lord Vinson, former Chairman of the Rural Development Commission
Voluntary Action Cumbria
Volunteer Centre UK
Dr Shailendra Vyakarnam, Silsoe College
Mrs J M Wagstaffe
Mrs Joan Walley, MP
Reverend Michael Ward, Vicar of Barkby and Queniborough, Leicester Diocese
Mr George Ward, Industrial Christian Fellowship
Sir Frederick Warner
Warwickshire Rural Community Council
Reverend Michael Watkins, Priest-in-Charge of Snitterfield with Bearley, Coventry
    Diocese
Reverend Edward Watson, Methodist Church, Darlington District
Reverend Geoff Watson, Priest-in-Charge of Shadforth, Durham Diocese
Wear Valley District Council
Reverend John Webb, Senior Chaplain, Catterick Garrison
Wensleydale Housing Forum
West Lancashire District Council
West Somerset CIB Advice Centre
Mr Richard West, Headmaster, Guilsland Primary School, Cumbria
Reverend Neil Weston, Rector of Stodden Churches, St Albans Diocese
Mr John Wheatley, Industrial Christian Fellowship
Mr R A Wheeler, Tewkesbury Borough Council
Reverend John Whitehead, Rural Theology Association
Mrs Beatrice Whitehouse, Little Shellford, Cambridge
Professor James Williamson, President, British Geriatric Society
Reverend Boyd Wilson, Clevedon Anglican Parish, New Zealand
Reverend Mervyn Wilson, Rural Theology Association
Mr John Wilson, St. John's Windlesham Car Scheme
Wiltshire County Council
Wiltshire Pre-School Playgroups Association

Wiltshire Rural Housing Association
Reverend David Winter, Priest-in-Charge of Ducklington, Oxford Diocese
Dr Michael Winter, Centre for Rural Studies, Royal Agricultural College, Cirencester
Reverend T Withers Green, Rector of Weldon with Deene, Peterborough Diocese
Women's Farm and Garden Association
Women's Royal Voluntary Service
Mrs Barbara Wood
Mr John Woods, Central Readers Conference
Worlebury School Support Committee
Sir Marcus Worsley Bt, National Trust
Wye College, University of London
Wyre Borough Council
Wyre District Youth Service
Young Men's Christian Association
Yortek Club, North Yorkshire
Young Enterprise

Appendix B

Principal visits (excluding the larger cities)

During the following visits the Commission met an estimated 6,000 people.

Abbotts Ann
Abinger
Addington
Aldford
Almley
Alveston
Alweston
Alwinton
Amport
Appleshaw
Ardington
Arncliffe
Asheldam
Ashton Keynes
Askrigg
Atherstone
Bakewell
Barnburgh
Barton
Barton Bendish
Beamsley
Beccles
Beckington
Beeston
Belchamp Otten
Belford
Bentham
Bentley
Birling
Bishop's Castle
Bishop's Caundle
Bishopsbourne
Bishopswood
Blakeney
Bleddington
Bletchingley
Blubberhouses
Blyth Hall
Boosbeck
Boot
Boroughbridge
Brading
Bradninch

Brampton
Bretherton
Bridgnorth
Broadway
Brockhurst
Bromyard
Brotton
Broughton
Bruton
Bulwick
Bunbury
Butterton
Caldecote
Cambourne
Castle Acre
Castleberg
Castor
Catterick
Catworth
Chapel Stile
Charltons
Chatsworth
Chellington
Chiddingstone
Chilham
Cinderford
Cleeve Prior
Colburn
Coldharbour
Coleford
Colyton
Coniston
Coniston Cold
Coombe Bissett
Coppenhall
Cornhill
Covington
Cowden
Cranbrook
Cranleigh
Crayke
Crediton
Cromhall

Crook
Cropton Magna
Crosby Garrett
Croston
Dalbury
Dalbury Lees
Dalston
Dartington
Dartmoor National Park
Debden
Dorchester
Driffield
Dunham on Trent
Dymock
East Kennett
Eaton
Edensor
Edwin Ralph
Elkstone
Elmley Castle
Ely
Epworth
Eskdale
Evenwood
Evesham
Ewelme
Ewhurst
Fewston
Figheldean
Finsthwaite
Fishburn
Flixton
Folksworth
Framlington
Frampton
Froxfield
Fulhope
Fyfield
Gilsland
Grassington
Great Barugh
Great Milton
Great Oxendon

Great Staughton
Greenfoot
Guilsborough
Haddon
Hale
Halebank
Harbottle
Harden Bridge
Harrogate
Harvington
Hathersage
Hatton
Hazelwood
Hedon
Helmsley
Henfield
Hexham
Highley
Hilborough
Hilston
Holmer
Holmfirth
Hope
Hordley
Hove
Huggate
Hurleston
Hurley
Hurstbourne Tarrant
Hutton Buscel
Idridgehay
Ilketshall St Margaret
Ingoldsby
Kendal
Kimpton
Kingsbury
Kington
Kington Langley
Kirkburton
Kirkby Malham
Kirkby Stephen
Kirkbymoorside
Kirton
Knighton
Lake District National Park
Lakeside
Langdale
Langtown
Leeming
Leigh
Leighterton
Leighton Buzzard
Leightonstone
Leintwardine
Leominster
Letcombe Regis
Leverington

Lexden
Leyburn
Lingdale
Lingrith
Little Comberton
Little Downham
Littleport
Lockinge
Loftus
Long Buckby
Longborough
Longhirst
Longnor
Lostwithiel
Luddenden
Lydbury North
Maldon
Malham
Malpas
Malton
Mappleton
Market Bosworth
Market Overton
Marlborough
Marrick Priory
Martin Mere
Marton
Mayfield
Meerbrook
Melbourne
Melbury
Merevale
Michelmersh
Middleton
Mildenhall
Milton
Mollington
Morborne
Moreton in Marsh
Morpeth
Much Hadham
Muncaster
Musgrave
Myerscough
Naseby
Nayland
Necton
Neston
Nether Wallop
Newchurch
Nidderdale
North Otterington
Norton
Norton St Philip
Oaksey
Oborne
Ockley

Oddington
Okeford Fitzpaine
Old Radnor
Ollerton
Ormskirk
Oswestry
Oundle
Over Wallop
Overseal
Oxenhope
Pateley Bridge
Patrington
Peak District National Park
Penistone
Penrith
Pershore
Petrockstowe
Pickering
Pluckley
Pontefract
Ponteland
Postlebury
Pudleston
Radwinter
Raveningham
Ringmore
Ringsfield
Riseley
Roadhead
Romford
Rossendale
Rothbury
Rumburgh
Ruston
Ryarsh
Ryedale
Saffron Walden
Saltburn
Sandringham
Sawtry
Scalby Mills
Sedgebarrow
Sedgefield
Settle
Shadingfield
Shawbury
Sherston
Sheviock
Shillingford
Shillingstone
Shrewton
Shudy Camps
Skilmoor
Skinningrove
Skipton
Slapewath
Somborne

South Croxton
South Darley
South Elmham
South Lafford
South Molton
South Otterington
Spilsby
St Mellion
Stainton
Stalmine
Stanhope
Stansted
Stanton
Staplehurst
Steens Bridge
Steeple Bumpstead
Steeple Langford
Stilton
Stiperstones
Stocksfield
Stockton
Storriths
Stretford
Sutton Cheney
Swaledale
Swardeston
Teesdale
Temple Normanton
Thornham Magna
Thornley
Thornton
Thornton le Beans
Thornton le Moor
Thorpe
Thurleigh
Tilbrook
Tirril
Townhead
Tredington
Trefonen
Trottiscliffe
Tunstall
Twigworth
Uffculme
Upham
Upper Hulme
Upper Poppleton
Urchfont
Waberthwaite
Wadborough
Walden
Walpole St Peter
Warcop
Warslow
Waterbeach
Watlington
Weardale

Wearhead
Weldon
Welney
Welton
West Lavington
West Meon
West Overton
West Walton
Westoning
Wetheral
Wiggenhall
Wigmore
Wirksworth
Witchampton
Witham
Woburn
Woder
Wolsingham
Wolvey
Wolviston
Woodmancote
Wootton
Wrockwardine
Wroughton
Wye
Wykeham
Yarpole
Yeaveley

Appendix C

Conservation and Environmental Pressures on the Countryside by Dr Michael Winter, Centre for Rural Studies, Royal Agricultural College, Cirencester

This paper provides a brief overview of environmental issues and is a much condensed version of an earlier submission to the Commission. The paper is divided into three main parts. The first reviews the origins of environmental concern and the main changes which have taken place in the rural environment in recent years. The second examines the various policy responses. The final part looks forward to the year 2000 suggesting a number of factors which will determine the management, utilisation and appearance of the English countryside.

Rural environmental concerns in England

Traditional environmentalism
Concern for the countryside is deeply rooted in English culture. The Commons, Open Spaces and Footpaths Preservation Society, was founded in 1865, and many conservation groups, such as the Royal Society for the Protection of Birds, date from the end of the last century (1). Several writers have commented upon the pull which the countryside exerts upon influential sections of English society (2). This is reflected in the treatment of rural landscapes in English literature and art (3), in the development of country sporting and residential estates (4), the growth of amateur natural history (5), and even the suburbanisation of cities (6). Britain's early industrialisation and the incorporation of many of its landowners into structures of power and influence alongside industrial and financial interests gave rise to both a strong vein of nostalgia for 'rural roots' and a respectability for rural and provincial life within England's ruling class. Thus while Britain was one of the earliest industrialised and urbanised countries, it was also one of the first in which rural living became a significant attraction for those whose wealth came not from the land but from manufacture and commerce (7). "Environmental concern was an integral part of the late Victorian intellectual reaction to many of the tenets of economic liberalism." (8) Consequently, British environmentalism has always contained strongly conservative strands (9), typified by the National Trust's concern with the preservation of quintessential aristocratic homes and estates (10).

The protection of landscapes, buildings and wildlife therefore characterises the traditional British approach. In practice this has meant a strong emphasis upon protection through planning designations and controls, epitomised by National Parks (11). Atlee's post-war government embarked upon a series of measures which established a comprehensive planning system, the protection of sites of landscape and nature conservation merit, and guaranteed support for agriculture (12). Environmental groups could not have attained their current level of political influence without a significant degree of popular support. Lowe and Goyder have estimated that between two and three million people in Britain belong to a local or national environmental group (13). Popular support derives from shared traditional values across a relatively wide cross-section of society. However, the existence of more radical and oppositional

Faith in the Countryside

strands as shown in the battle to secure access to the countryside, particularly between the wars in northern England, demonstrates a rather different aspect of environmentalism in Britain (14). Contrasts between radical and traditional environmentalism are not, therefore, entirely new although they have aquired a deeper significance in recent years.

The changing countryside

For the first two decades after 1945 the new measures for protecting the countryside were quietly implemented. Concerns were voiced over some issues, such as the impact of afforestation in the uplands, the removal of hedgerows and the demands for more land for urban expansion (15), and these concerns led to the Countryside in 1970 Conferences presided over by the Duke of Edinburgh in the 1960s (16). The spirit of these meetings was positive and largely focused on the means by which appropriate planning and management could cater for competing demands upon land. A consensus between agricultural and conservation interests generally prevailed (17). From the close of the 1960s this consensus began to break down with the emergence of a more radical environmentalism. The most devastating critique of all was published in 1980. Marion Shoard lambasted farmers for landscape and ecological destruction and concluded with a passionate plea for new and stronger planning controls to preserve the countryside (18). A spate of books followed which debated the means of controlling agriculture (19). The impact of agricultural intensification upon particular species of wildlife and distinctive wildlife habitats, many of which depended upon traditional farming, became widely recognised:

> The present generation is witnessing the most comprehensive and far-reaching change of the natural history and historical landscapes of Britain ever experienced in such a short period of time. What is so particularly alarming is that so little is understood about these changes - their magnitude and long-term consequences - yet what is known is sinmply appalling. The grim chronicle reads as follows: over the past 35 years, the nation has lost 95 per cent of lowland herb-rich grasslands, 80 per cent of chalk and limestone grasslands, 60 per cent of lowland heaths, 45 per cent of limestone pavements, 50 per cent of ancient woodlands, 50 per cent of lowland fens and marshes, over 60 per cent of lowland raised bogs, and a third of all upland grasslands, heaths and mires. (20)

Escalation of concern in the 1980s

In 1981 the Wildlife and Countryside Bill was passed after prolonged debate in Parliament (21). The Act provided an indication that the political strength of agriculture was on the wane. During the stormy passage of the bill, and more especially as a consequence of the growing environmentalist critique of agricultural methods in its aftermath, the farming industry faced an unprecedented level of public criticism, culminating in legislative ammendments in 1985.

The strength of feeling in environmental circles was matched by a growing view among monetarists and would-be EEC reformers that agriculture was an administrative and costly burden. A number of commentators, both supporters and detractors of the government, pointed to the high cost of agricultural support, particularly storing surpluses. It was claimed, somewhat opportunistically, that reducing agricultural support would have corresponding environmental benefits (22). The first move to reduce surpluses, milk quotas in 1984, was purely an agricultural measure (23). Subsequently, however, the British Government seized upon the opportunity to promote environmental measures as part of a package of CAP reform.

Meanwhile environmental concern has continued as further evidence of agricultural change has become available (24). Moreover, in the late 1980s some attention has switched - many would argue belatedly - from habitat and landscape change to issues of pollution and more broadly defined environmental quality.

Radical environmentalism

Whereas the traditional conservation bodies tended to concentrate on single aspects of environmental protection, the ecology movement, which emerged in the late 1960s, expressed a very different philosophy. Organisations such as the Conservation Society (1966) and Friends of the Earth (1970) articulated concern across the whole spectrum of human interaction with the environment, focusing on issues such as the depletion of the world's resources, pollution, renewable energy sources and organic agriculture. Many of the new ecologists also offered a vision of an alternative society and economy based on self-sustaining and self-determining small communities (25). The new groups were much more overtly political than the traditional conservation bodies, and Britain became the home to the first green party, launched in 1973 (26). In recent years the Friends of the Earth has worked more closely with some of the mainstream conservation bodies while maintaining its 'green' credentials (27). Moreover, concerns over acid rain, the greenhouse effect and so forth have, to some extent, broadened traditional British concerns.

Policies and prospects

The British approach to environmental issues

Any analysis of British environmental policy has to consider a paradox. On the one hand the British legislature has continuity and public acceptability. Thus Britain's body of environmental legislation dates back to the middle of the last century, and in land use planning and public health law Britain has been a forerunner (28). But on the other hand, British governments have been reluctant to formulate and implement national strategic policies of an interventionist and state regulatory nature except in very special circumstances (29). Britain has no national land use or environmental policies as such, rather a series of ad hoc measures some of which are rather weak.

In the absence of a strongly developed sense of state direction many government initiatives have depended upon a high degree of self-regulation and the principle of voluntarism, whereby the maximum freedom is given to owners and managers of land to interpret regulations. It is a principle intricately linked to notions of property rights and compensation and it pervades many recent policy intiatives (30). Thus policies which appear to have environmental objectives cannot always be implemented in ways likely to give the maximum environmental benefits. Moreover, environmental policies exist across a wide spectrum of government activity with different ministries and departments, not to mention boards, quangos, commissions and local authorities, holding different responsibilities.

The planning framework

In spite of recent attempts to encourage planning authorities to be more positive in their attitudes towards development in the countryside, most rural land is still protected from residential and industrial development (31), and this remains a key area for concern especially in green belt areas (32). In the open countryside the direct control exercised by planning authorities is strictly limited, as agricultural and forestry operations are largely exempt from planning controls (32). The prospects for any immediate change to this are not great (33). Traditionally, planning expertise and skills have been developed with regard to principles of design and the appearance of physical features, not the management of ecosystems. One of the few powers possessed by planners to control countryside change is through Tree Preservation Orders, but these have been criticised for preventing effective woodland management (34).

Planning authorities are consulted over afforestation schemes, where Forestry Commission grants are involved. Similarly the local planning authority is likely to be involved when the Nature Conservancy Council is negotiating with landowners over the management of Sites of Special Scientific Interest. Planning authorities play a central role in Environmental Impact Analysis (EIA), which is required for certain development proposals. It is possible that more agricultural and forestry operations may be brought under the auspices of EIA (35). Conversely planners are being urged to relax some controls, and to take a lead from MAFF which no longer opposes all building on good farmland (36). Whatever the inadequacies of the planning system, as a function of local government, it is relatively open and democratic. Moreover, its purpose is inherently broad, based on attempts to promote a balance between economic, social and environmental objectives.

Designated areas
Alongside planning protection of rural land, it was felt in 1947 that extra protective powers should be available for land of special landscape, archaeological and wildlife interest. Thus a number of designations were established, which have been extended or modified over the years. Landscape and recreation designations include the National Parks and Areas of Outstanding Natural Beauty. Nature conservation designations cover National Nature Reserves and Sites of Special Scientific Interest (37). In addition two areas - the New Forest and the Broads - have special protection outside the terms of these designations. In the case of AONBs, which comprise over 11% of the total area of England and Wales, the extra planning controls over development are relatively minor, and agricultural developments are virtually free from control. By contrast National Parks have a measure of control, through management agreements, consultation procedures (eg. in Forestry Commission and MAFF grant-aided schemes), and the operation of the National Park authority planning committees in which local authority representation is supplemented by members chosen by central government. In a number of National Parks, notably the Peak and the Lake District, innovative schemes have been financed by the Parks to encourage preservation of special landscape features.

The distinction between the protection in AONBs and that in National Parks would be understandable if the landscapes of AONBs were inferior or less suceptible to change. But this is not the case. Landowners in AONBs have been reluctant to countenance AONBs coming into line with National Parks, especially in the sphere of recreation provision. Indeed separate recreational measures had to be taken after 1968, through the provision of Country Parks in lowland areas (38). And yet the AONBs contain some of the most attractive and accessible countryside, including such areas as the Shropshire Hills, Malvern Hills, the Wye Valley, many areas of chalk downland, and the Cotswolds.

SSSIs and NNRs occupy a much smaller proportion of the land surface. They represent important examples of different types of wildlife habitat. As with the National Parks and AONBS, the SSSIs are mostly in private ownership, although the NNRs are usually owned and managed by the Nature Conservancy Council. The protection of SSSIs has been the subject of intense public debate. Although some continue to be lost the rate of loss has diminished. Certainly in the case of agriculture, the safeguards are reasonably strong and most landholders wishing to change the use of land designated as SSSIs are offered generous compensation under Management Agreements.

One problem with designation is that it may reduce attention to those areas not designated. This negative aspect of designation is a very serious problem and has prompted a number of authors, notably Richard Mabey, to make a passionate plea for the protection of local features, even if they are of no national importance (39). For example primroses may be common nationally, but if the last primrose bank in a parish is threatened then they become an endangered species in that community. Some would argue a case for standard measures of protection across the countryside. This would present problems, for clearly some sites do warrant greater protection than others, but there is a strong case for giving greater importance to the needs of local communities in the protection of their own cherished scenes, possibly through greater direct involvement in the management of community lands.

Conservation advice for farmers
While the NCC grappled with problems of SSSI protection (all sites had to be re-designated after the 1981 Act) the Countryside Commission produced evidence of continuing landscape change throughout the countryside (40). The renewed interest in the local significance of wildlife sites and landscape features prompted a closer look at

the wider countryside (41). The main policy response has been the provision of conservation advice and small-scale grants for farmers and landowners outside the designated areas. Grants are available from local authorities and the Countryside Commission for tree planting schemes and MAFF has removed its grants for hedge removal and replaced them with hedge planting grants. Many millions of trees have been planted in recent years, although the after-care and management has not always been good.

Additionally, there has been a growth in conservation advice for farmers. Most counties in England have a Farming and Wildlife Advisory Group (FWAG) adviser who is available to advise on all aspects of conservation and to direct farmers to other specialist sources of advice or grant aid (42). County FWAGs were formed in the 1970s comprising interested farmers, MAFF officials and representatives from the voluntary and public conservation groups. A number of counties began to offer advice to farmers and from 1984 many employed full-time specialist officers, with finance from the Countryside Commission, the Farming and Wildlife Trust (a national charity) and local subscriptions.

FWAG is a blend of public and private initiative with leading figures in the farming community heavily involved. It is thus 'acceptable' to many farmers in a way that official conservation agencies might not be. It is based very firmly on the principles of voluntarism and compromise (43). Farmers are encouraged to seek advice and great play is made of the agricultural knowledge and sympathies of those giving advice. Consequently a compromise between the needs of modern agriculture and conservation is stressed, which may in practice lead to purely cosmetic changes. Its capacity to provide advice is small with one adviser covering an entire county. FWAG has tended to concentrate on wildlife and landscape features with less regard to longer term ecological change or to recreation and access.

Reforming agriculture: diversification, alternative land uses and Environmentally Sensitive Areas

We now turn our attention to recent initiatives. The search for alternative land uses offers much promise for conservation, but has also highlighted prospects for new productive uses for the countryside, such as new cropping for biomass or exploitation of leisure opportunities, which may damage conservation (46). Although the key symbols of the debate - alternative land uses, diversification, value-added, agro-forestry etc - are very 'new', the style of the debate is surprisingly reminiscent of the heady days of the 1940s when the aim was to 'get agriculture moving'. The message is that land abundance presents new market opportunities, and that the role of government is merely to ease the transition for individual landholders. In reality this interpretation is fundamentally misconstrued and detracts from the real need to accommodate competing demands on land in ways that bring benefit to rural economies and the environment (47). Some initiatives arising from the farm crisis (48) are more promising for the environment. Set-aside, for instance, offers potential environmental advantages, with government indicating a wish for the scheme to be used for positive wildlife benefits. Yet this is left entirely to the managers of the land concerned, with no extra financial incentives for environmental enahncement except in the east of England (49).

The first six Environmentally Sensitive Areas (ESAs) were designated by the MAFF in 1986 and there are now eleven in England (50). They cut across existing designations but their purpose is quite different. They are not the designations of conservation or planning authorities. Instead they are an integral element in agricultural policy reflecting the need to cut surplus production. At the same time they reflect a widely held view that neither designations of special sites nor conservation advice can prompt the whole-farm management required to preserve an environmentally beneficial style of farming. Clive Potter has described this new departure as follows:

> ESAs signal a recognition that specific tracts or pieces of countryside can often only be effectively conserved by maintaining the traditional systems and styles of farming which lie behind them. . . . This indicates an important shift towards

husbandry as well as simply investment and project-based solutions to conflicts between agriculture and the environment (51).

In ESAs farmers may adhere to a management plan in return for annual payments on an acreage basis. The take-up of the scheme has been encouraging, for although the payments are not great the scheme is flexible and in many cases farmers are happy to receive payments for continuing to farm in a traditional manner. Although production levels cannot be directly controlled, limits on fertiliser applications or the extent of arable land taken into cultivation restrict increases in production.

Woodland and forestry

The relatively small proportion of England under woodland and the post-war decline in the extent and quality of ancient woodland has excited much concern (53). In the uplands, coniferous afforestation has reduced the number of sites of value to birds of prey and detracts from the openness and wide vistas of moorland landscapes. At the same time as the Forestry Commission came under pressure to review its upland policies (54) it also undertook a review of its broadleaved woodland policy resulting in the first grant scheme designed specifically to encourage the establishment and management of deciduous woodland (55). Although the impetus behind this move, which departed from established policy and silvicultural norms, was prompted by environmental considerations, it allowed the recipients of grant to determine aims and objectives on a continuum from fully commercial hardwood planting to amenity planting. No attempt has been made to determine the appropriate balance between different types of planting at a national level. Therefore a scheme publicised by Government as an example of its commitment to conservation could, in practice, result in monocultures of fast growing species such as Southern Beech or Sycamore (56). The recently introduced Farm Woodland Scheme rests on a similar principle of voluntarism in which coniferous planting is included as an option (57).

It has to be said that in both cases the Forestry Commission is obliged to consult local authorities and in certain instances other conservation agencies, on the desirability of planting schemes. This may allow modifications to some schemes according to environmental criteria but as each scheme is considered on its merits and no attempt is made to co-ordinate responses between authorities, no sense of overall planning emerges or, indeed, is intended.

Pollution

In very recent years pollution has emerged as a major cause of concern. On a global scale, damage to the ozone layer by chloro-fluoro-carbons and the 'greenhouse effect' caused by industrial waste gases, especially carbon dioxide, are now well recognised. The climatic consequences are hard to predict. Some have suggested that Britain may become cooler as world climatic patterns shift (58). However, the broad consensus is that temperatures will increase, with a possibility of longer drier summers and wet mild winters. The implications for agriculture and land use are still far from clear, but clearly there is the chance that arable farming will increase in extent with a greater range of more exotic crops (59).

Of more immediate concern to the rural environment are the pollutants which are already effecting environmental quality. Two are of particular importance: air pollution, and agricultural and freshwater pollution (60). In the case of air pollution the major concern is the increase of acidity in the atmosphere and resulting acid rain. There is evidence that soil acidity is increasing, especially in some upland areas, although this may be partly caused by the management of coniferous forests and fertilisers as well as by air-borne pollutants. The damage to trees in Britain has not been as extensive as in many parts of Europe, but recent surveys have produced contradictory evidence, with Friends of the Earth suggesting that damage to yew and beech trees in southern England is a result of air pollution (61).

Agricultural pollution through the application of pesticides and fertilisers and the direct pollution of water-courses by slurry or silage effluent has resulted in the deterioration of rivers in areas of livestock farming, notably the south west of England

340

(62), and the pollution of ground-water by nitrates (63). These usually derive from fertiliser applications and may take many years to effect water quality. Thus chalkland areas are now reaping the results of increased fertliser applications in the 1960s. Nitrates may also reach water courses through intesive livestock farming. Smell is another pollution problem associated with livestock farming and the trends towards intensive and concentrated production have greatly increased this risk. Finally, much concern has been expressed over pesticides - both the direct risks to those using them and the implications of residues for human and animal health generally (64). In most cases general legislation outlaws gross pollution, but in recent years special measures have been introduced to tackle agricultural pollution. Nitrate Sensitive Areas have been designated, where farmers are being urged to reduce fertiliser applications. Agricultural pollution promises to be the chief environmental issue of the 1990s in the way that habitat loss was the main focus in the 1980s.

Access
Access and recreation have often been neglected in rural policy discussions. True farm diversification, and the possible incomes to be gained from tourism and leisure (65), have slightly reversed earlier biases but on the whole the topic remains a contentious one. Yet rural leisure pursuits of all kinds figure highly in all surveys of recreation pastimes (66). Public footpaths provide one of the main means by which visitors, and indeed residents of rural areas, may enjoy the countryside. The maintenance of these paths has been an issue of contention for many years with groups such as the Ramblers Association pressing for much freer access and the Country Landowners' Association insisting on a need to rationalise the existing network of paths to take account of agricultural requirements.

Access and recreation should be more closely integrated into environmental considerations and policy. This should not be the role of the Countryside Commission and Tourist Boards alone, but an essential element in all land use policy. More effort could be put into securing access agreements where public money for conservation projects is involved. The whole issue of access needs to be broadened to go beyond the footpath debate. There has been scarcely any public debate on the establishement of a general right of access to rural land (67) or of re-establishing common lands for recreation and amenity purposes. As discussions of agricultural surpluses and alternative land uses continue it seems opportune to consider such options. The needs of existing rural residents, urban visitors, and minority interests, such as the requirements of travelling folk, all deserve attention.

The rural environment in the year 2000

Predicting the course of change, even over a dozen years, is very difficult. Current concerns over global warming make the task even more difficult. Further influences on environmental quality are equally unpredictable - election results, international trade, EEC directives, and so forth. The balance of power may shift within and between government departments. There may well have been further erosion of local government alongside an increasing role for European policy making. The world economy and the role of agriculture within it will have changed. Outside the realms of economics and politics, ecological processes are more predictable but even here many doubts remain. How seriously damaged are our waterways? How easily can habitats be re-created? How sustainable is modern agriculture? In seeking to speculate on some of these questions I have briefly developed two possible scenarios. A third, of course, would be a continuation of environmental deterioration - which might be termed the exploitation scenario - in which case we could expect a serious depletion of valued habitats, landscapes and possibly serious health risks and even a decline in the capacity of the natural environment to sustain itself.

Market green scenario
The first scenario assumes that the environment will continue to attract widescale

attention and command policy initiatives. It is assumed that these initiatives will be market-led and market interventionist, relecting current practice, in which the rhetoric of the market exists alongside modes of intervention which allow considerable freedom to economic agents.

In agriculture there will be a further decline in profitability and prices. In some instances land may be removed from agricultural production altogether, especially where government schemes to encourage woodland and other alternative uses are in operation. These schemes will increasingly have an environmental focus, but will continue to be circumscribed to some extent by the importance of private property rights and voluntarism in a market economy. The balance between self-regulation and external regulation of these schemes will determine just how 'green' this scenario is. In the realm of pollution control we can expect much tougher regulations, as the Government responds to public and EEC pressures. Farmers may find strict controls on fertiliser and pesticide applications. A proportion of them will shift to organic production to cater for the growing market for these products. As much as 5-10% of the land surface may be farmed in this way, with a further 30-40% under some form of designation in which environmentally sensitive farming is encouraged.

What are the problems with this scenario? Clearly much depends upon the balance of political power between the various actors which will determine the extent to which the environmentalist rhetoric is accompanied by major improvements in environmental quality. 'Hidden' environmental costs may continue, especially where detection of damage is difficult. Changing technologies of agricultural production for example may produce new pollutants which could remain hidden for many years. A further problem concerns the distributive aspects of this scenario. Continuing social and economic divisions and inequalities in society, both within rural areas and between urban and rural areas, will mean that while many habitats and landscapes may be improved, the benefits of this will not be equally shared. The issue of public access will remain contentious. Indeed it may be exacerbated as purchases of land for residential and recreational (ie. consumptive) purposes increase. Village and country houses with land holdings will become even more sought-after 'positional goods' (68). As a result environmental quality will improve, but the benefits will be unevenly distributed within society.

Radical green scenario

The second scenario rests on very different propositions altogether. Here I assume that the environment becomes a dominating concern, possibly as a result of new and dramatic evidence of environmental degradation or of a major economic crisis linked to einvironmental factors. At the same time the needs of people in the countryside will become of greater importance.

In a radical green future a combination of government regulation and political-social transformation will lead to reforms in agricultural production with organic farming playing a leading role. Pollution will be strictly controlled at source and all land uses will be designed to be environmentally beneficial. A wholesale reform of land designations will have occurred with much greater emphasis upon local protection policies for all parts of the countryside, including a role for community ownership and management of lands for multi-purpose use such as woodlands for firewood and recreation. Public access and recreation will be an important component of the new rural economy.

Conclusions

What are the main principles which should be borne in mind by those wishing to invent the future? Constructive reform must satisfy a number of criteria: sustainable utilisation, economic and environmental cost-effectiveness, social justice in countryside management, and political attainability (69).

The notion of sustainable utilisation was developed in the UK's response to the World Conservation Strategy (70). Sustainability encompasses both the maintenance of productive capacity and the continual enhancement of the cultural value of the countryside. Environmental management should reflect the need to avoid any risks to future production or to the educational, aesthetic and recreational qualities of the countryside. Countryside management is so sensitive and complex that sustainability demands a cautious approach to innovation. The environment is too precious for risk-taking.

Economic and environmental cost-effectiveness, or value for money, implies that policies designed to safeguard the environment must take account of the costs incurred. In particular public investment must be directed at socially desirable objectives and should not, as a general rule, be used to subsidise those whose activities have caused environmental degradation in the first place. The 'polluter pays' principle should be at the heart of cost-effectiveness. In other words the responsibility for the cost of cleaning up the environment should reside with those who have caused the damage rather than with those who have suffered.

Social justice in countryside management implies an overt recognition by all involved in rural affairs that there are rights of citizenship relevant to environmental management. First, all people have rights to a healthy and pleasing environment. Secondly, those living in the countryside have rights to an economic livelihood. Thirdly, those with direct property rights through landownership should exercise them through an ethic of stewardship (71). There is an urgent need for a debate on the social and political dimensions of rural issues, in which issues such as land reform and rights of access to land should figure highly.

Political attainability is perhaps a curious principle when we are indulging in inventing the future, but it is vital that all specific proposals for reform should be attuned to political realities. Opportunities for pragmatic and expedient reforms should be grasped in the hope that more far-reaching opportunities will ultimately be available. A number of such possibilities have been mentioned during the course of the paper. The reform of the Common Agricultural Policy, the improvement of countryside designations, the promotion of environmentally sensitive farming, the elimination of certain pollutants, are already high on political agendas. The Church alongside environmental lobbies should be looking for ways of increasing the pressure to secure rapid reform in these and other important areas.

FOOTNOTES
1. Lowe, P. and Goyder, J. (1983) *Environmental Groups in Politics*, London: Allen and Unwin. On the history of the National Trust see: Fedden, R. (1974) *The National Trust: Past and Present*, London: Cape.
2. See Wiener M.J. (1981) *English Culture and the Decline of the Industrial Spirit 1850-1980*, Cambridge: Cambridge University Press; Wright, P. (1985) *On Living in an Old Country*, London: Verso. Both books, written from very different perspectives, come to complementary conclusions about the significance of rural nostalgia for English economic and political life. David Lowenthal, though, drawing upon the work of Dellheim questions whether rural retrospect is in fact wholly pervasive or instead largely decorative with minimal impact on the worlds of economics and technology. See: Dellheim, C. (1982) *The Face of the Past: The Preservation of the Medieval Inheritance in Victorian England*, Cambridge: Cambridge University Press; Lowenthall, D. (1985) *The Past is a Foreign Country*, Cambridge: Cambridge University Press. For a review of some of the consequences of anti-urban sentiment, in terms of various back-to-the-land movements and experiments see: Marsh, J. (1982) *Back to the Land: The Pastoral Impulse in Victorian England from 1880 to 1914*, London: Quartet Books.
3. These trends in literature are examined in Williams, R. (1983) *The Country and the City*, London: Chatto and Windus. See also Keith, W.J. (1975) *The Rural Tradition*, Sussex: Harvester Press; Turner, K. (1979) *The Politics of Landscape: Rural Scenery and Society in English Poetry 1630-1660*, Oxford: Basil Blackwell.
4. Girouard, M. (1980) *Life in the English Country House: A Social and Architectural History*, Harmondsworth: Penguin.
5. Allen, D.E. *The Naturalist in Britain*, Harmondsworth: Penguin; Lowe, P. (1976)

Amateurs and professionals: the institutional emergence of British plant ecology, *Journal of Soc. Bibliogr. Natural History*, 7, pp.517-535; Sheail, J. (1976) *Nature in Trust: the History of Nature Conservation in Britain*, Glasgow: Blackie.
6. Thorns, D. (1973) *Suburbia*, London: Paladin.
7. See: Beckett, J.V. (1986) *The Aristocracy in England 1660- 1914*, Oxford: Basil Blackwell; Rubinstein, W.D. (1981) New men of wealth and the purchase of land in nineteenth century England, *Past and Present*, 92, pp.125-147; Thompson, F.M.L. (1973) *English Landed Society in the Nineteenth Century*, London: Routledge.
8. Lowe, P. and Goyder, J. op. cit. p.19.
9. Indeed attempts have been made to identify conservation with Conservatism. See for example: Sullivan A. (1985) *Greening the Tories*, London: Centre for Policy Studies.
10. For example the Trust owns 7.5% of all land in National Parks and 23.5% of the Lake District National Park. The implications of its land ownership role have been examined in: Tunbridge, J.E. (1981) Conservation trusts as geographic agents: their impact upon landscape, townscape, and land use, *Transactions of the Institue of British Geographers*, 6, pp.104-125.
11. MacEwen, A. and MacEwen, M. (1982) *National Parks: Conservation or Cosmetics?*, London: Allen and Unwin.
12. On the developments in this period see: Gilg, A. (1978) *Countryside Planning*, Newton Abbot: David and Charles.
13. Lowe, P. and Goyder, J. op. cit.
14. See: Hill, H. (1980) *Freedom to Roam*, Ashbourne: Moorland Publishing.
15. Some commentators have subsequently argued that post-war planning was overly restrictive in its land allocations for urban development during this period. See: Best, R. (1981) *Land Use and Living Space*, London: Methuen; Hall, P. Gracey, H. Drewett, R. and Thomas, R. (1973) *The Containment of Urban England*, London: Allen and Unwin.
16. Conferences were held in 1963, 1965 and 1970. They resulted in some practical conservation work especially with regard to the creation of new landscape features, and in promoting this approach were something of a precursor to the Farming and Wildlife Advisory Groups which have become so significant in the 1980s. On these developments see: Cox, G. Lowe, P. and Winter, M. (1990) *The Voluntary Principle in Conservation: A Study of the Farming and Wildlife Advisory Group*, Chichester: Packard.
17. Nan Fairbrother, an influential thinker at this time, painted a typically optimistic picture of scientific progress and advance. Agricultural, industrial and residential change is inevitable and offers opportunities for the creation of new landscapes, which must not be eschewed through unwarranted preservationism. See: Fairbrother, N. (1970) *New Lives, New Landscapes*, Harmondsworth: Penguin.
18. Shoard, M. (1980) *The Theft of the Countryside*, London: Maurice Temple Smith.
19. Shoard continued to advocate planning controls. A passionate plea for reform of the market is contained in: Bowers, J.K. and Cheshire, P. (1983) *Agriculture, the Countryside and Land Use*, London: Methuen. The contrasting approaches have been evaluated in Lowe, P. Cox, G. MacEwen, M. O'Riordan, T. and Winter, M. (1986) *Countryside Conflicts: The Politics of Farming, Forestry and Conservation*, London: Gower/Maurice Temple Smith.
20. Lowe, P. Cox, G. MacEwen, M. O'Riordan, T. and Winter, M. op. cit. p.55. It should be pointed out that the losses recounted here are caused by many factors, agriculture being the most significant but not the sole one. The main source on habitat loss is: Nature Conservancy Council (1984) *Nature Conservation in Britain*, London: Nature Conservancy Council. Other useful sources of information include: Adams, W.M. (1986) *Nature's Place: Conservation Sites and Countryside Change*, London: Allen and Unwin; Green, B. *Countryside Conservation* , London: Allen and Unwin; Pye-Smith, C. and Rose, C. (1984) *Crisis in Conservation: Conflict in the British Countryside*, Harmondsworth: Penguin; Rackham, O. (1986) *The History of the Countryside*, London: Dent.
21. See: Cox, G. and Lowe, P. (1983a) A battle not the war: the politics of the Wildlife

and Countryside Act 1981, *Countryside Planning Yearbook*, 4, pp.48-76; Cox, G. and Lowe, P. (1983b) Countryside politics: goodbye to goodwill? *Political Quarterly*, 54, pp.268-282; Cox, G. and Lowe, P. (1984) Agricultural corporatism and rural conservation, pp.147-166 in Bradley, T. and Lowe, P. *Locality and Rurality*, Norwich: Geo Books.

22. For example: Howarth, R.W. (1985) *Farming for Farmers?*, London: Intitute of Economic Affairs.

23. Nonetheless quotas were not without environmental implications in so much as they prompted farmers to maximise their grassland production (as opposed to purchasing concentrated protein feeds), thereby encouraging higher fertiliser applications and greater production of silage both of which can have detrimental consequences for levels of pollution in water courses. On the changes in farm management induced by quotas see: Halliday, J. (1987) *The Effect of Milk Quotas on Milk Producing Farms: A Study of Registered Milk Producers in the Honiton and Torrington Areas of Devon*, University of Exeter.

24. For example see the evidence on continuing landscape degradation in Wetmacott, R. and Worthington, T. (1984) *Agricultural Landscapes: A Second Look*, CCP 168, Manchester: Countryside Commission; Countryside Commission (1987) *Agricultural Landscapes: A Select Bibliography*, Manchester: Countryside Commission.

25. In this respect the early ecology movement had some of its ideological roots in anarchism. Of course, as with most utopian and radical thought, the movement was characterised by some diversity and it should be pointed out that at least one strand, represented by one of the Ecology Party's chief ideologues Edward Goldsmith, contained something of an authoritarian streak. See: Rudig, W. and Lowe, P. (1986) The withered 'greening' of British politics: a study of the Ecology Party, *Political Studies*, 34, pp.262-284.

26. The party was initially called the People Party before becoming the Ecology Party. In September 1985 it was renamed the Green Party. See: Rudig, W. and Lowe, P. op. cit.

27. The successful pursuit of such a delicate balance owes much to the political skills of FoE's former Director, and Green Party member, Jonathan Porritt, now widely recognised and respected as one of the leading exponents of radical environmentalism in Britain. However, the more 'respectable' FoE has perhaps lost some of its earlier direct-action campaigning edge to Greenpeace which is now very much at the forefront of local support for environmental radicalism. For a clear statement of modern green thinking see: Porritt, J. (1984) *Seeing Green*, Oxford: Basil Blackwell. For an example of co-operation between FoE and other more conservative environmental groups see: Skea, J. (1988) *Electricity for Life? Choices for the Environment*, London: CPRE and FoE.

28. A thorough background to the development of environmental law is given in Hughes, D. (1986) *Environmental Law*, London: Butterworths.

29. For an examination of the historical and political factors behind this characteristic of the British case see: Winter, M. (1990) Land use policy in the UK: the politics of control, *Land Development Studies*, 7, pp.3-14.

30. Cox, G. Lowe, P. and Winter, M. (1988) Private rights and public responsibilities: the prospects for agricultural and environmental controls, *Journal of Rural Studies*, 4 (4), pp.323- 337.

31. For discussions of Department of Environment circulars modifying planning control see issues of the *Journal of Planning and Environment Law*; also: Department of the Environment and Welsh Office. (1988) *Plannning Guidance: Index of Extant Circulars*.

32. Munton, R. (1983) *London's Green Belt: Containment in Practice*, London: Allen and Unwin.

33. Indeed the government has rejected an additional planning control which it had previously appeared to support - Landscape Conservation Orders in National Parks.

34. In truth the administration of TPOs varies enormously from district to district. Some authorities have achieved management objectives within the terms of TPOs.

Faith in the Countryside

Personal communications: C. Watkins and S.E. Westover. On the overall functions and activities of local authorities in nature conservation see: Tyldesley, D. (1986) *Gaining Momentum: An Analysis of the Role and Performance of Local Authorities in Nature Conservation*, Oxford: Pisces Publications.

35. Bichard, E. and Frost, S. (1988) EIA in the UK planning system, *Land Use Policy*, 5 (4), pp.362-364.

36. A recent report by the Council for the Protection of Rural England has shown how the Ministry of Agriculture, Fisheries and Food has significantly reduced its opposition to residential and industrial development even on the best quality agricultural land: CPRE. (1988) *Concrete Objections: The Ministry of Agriculture's Response to Applications for Development of Agricultural Land*, London: CPRE.

37. For a general description of landscape designations and their operation see: Poore, D. and Poore, J. (1987) *Protected Landscapes: The United Kingdom Experience*, Manchester: Countryside Commission; MacEwen, A. and MacEwen, M. (1982) *National Parks: Conservation or Cosmetics?*, London: Allen and Unwin. On SSSIs see: Adams, W. *Nature's Place*, London: Allen and Unwin.

38. For an overview of rural recreation policy see Curry, N. (1985) Countryside recreation sites policy: a review, *Town Planning Review*, 56 (1), pp.70-89.

39. Mabey, R. (1980) *The Common Ground*, London: Arrow Books.

40. Countryside Commission (1987) op. cit.

41. An important book encouraging local conservation initiatives is King, A. and Clifford, S. (1985) *Holding Your Ground*, London: Maurice Temple Smith.

42. The leading counties in this area were Gloucester, Kent, Somerset, and Suffolk.

43. See Cox, G. Lowe, P. and Winter, M. (1988) op. cit.

44. See: Winter, M. (1988) Information and advice to farmers: the development of conservation advice for farmers in England and Wales, pp.163-170 in Mormoint, M. Ed. *Environment and Agriculture*, Fondation Universitaire Luxembourgeoise.

45. See: Harvey, D. et al. (1986) *Countryside Implications for England and Wales of Possible Changes in the Common Agricultural Policy*, CAS, University of Reading; Lowe, P. and Winter, M. (1987) 'Alternative perspectives on the alternative land-use debate', in Jenkins, N. R. and Bell, M. *Farm Extensification: Implications of EC Regulation 1760/87*, Merlewood Research and Development Paper No.112.

46. Cox, G. Flynn, A. Lowe, P. and Winter, M. (1986) 'The alternative land-use debate: where are the conservationists?', *Ecos*, 7 (3), pp.16-21.

47. Lowe, P. and Winter, M. (1987) op. cit.

48. On the farm crisis see: Cox, G. Lowe, P. and Winter, M. (1989) 'The farm crisis in Britain', pp.113-134 in Goodman, D. and Redclift, M. Eds. *The International Farm Crisis*, London: Macmillan.

49. See: Centre for Rural Studies (1988) *Cereal Extensification in Lowland England: An Assessment of the Benfits for Wildlife*, Cirencester: Royal Agricultural College; Potter, C. Burnham, C.P. Green, B.H. and Gasson, R. (in press) *Agricultural Surpluses: Environmental Opportunities*, London: Routledge; Potter, C. Burnham, C.P. Green, B.H. and Gasson, R. (1988) *Set-aside as an Environmental and Agricultural Policy Instrument: A Summary Report*, Wye College: Occasional Paper.

50. The best available overviews are: Baldock, D. Cox, G. Lowe, P. and Winter, M. (1990) Environmentally Sensitive Areas: incrementalism or reform?, *Journal of Rural Studies*, 6 (2), pp.143-162; Potter, C. (1988) Environmentally sensitive areas in England and Wales, *Land Use Policy*, 5 (3), pp.301-313.

51. Potter, C. (1988) op. cit. p.301. 52. There is some evidence that there are continuing problems in some ESAs, for example the Somerset Levels. See Baldock, et al, (1990) op. cit.

53. Rackham, A. (1980) *Ancient Woodland*, London: Edward Arnold; Peterken, G. (1981) *Woodland Conservation and Management*, London: Chapman and Hall; Watkins, C. (1990) *Woodland Management and Conservation*, Newton Abbot: David and Charles.

54. See: MacEwen, A. and MacEwen, M. (1981) op. cit.

55. Watkins, C. (1986) Recent changes in government policy towards broadleaved

346

woodland, *Area*, 18 (2), pp.117-122.

56. This is not to say that commercial timber production is inherently incompatible with conservation, but compatible management techniques do need further research and development. See: Watkins, C. (1987) The future of woodlands in the rural landscape, in Lockhart, D. and Ilberry, B. eds. *The Future of the British Rural Landscape*, Norwich: Geobooks. pp.71-96.

57. The Broadleaved Woodland Scheme has now been merged with the Forestry Grant Scheme, but grants for deciduous planting remain at a higher level.

58. Gribbin, J. (1988) Britain shivers in the global greenhouse, *New Scientist*, 9 June, pp.42-43. See also: Krupa, S. and Manning, W .(1988) Atmospheric Ozone: formation and effects on vegetation, *Environmental Pollution*, 50, pp.101-137.

59. At present predictions about future agricultural change cover only very broad zones within continents.

60. I am indebted to my colleague, Dr Charles Watkins, for his guidance on the chief forms of pollution and their implications for rural conservation and landscapes.

61. For summaries of the casuses and effects of acid rain see: Innes, J.L. (1987) Acid rain : its effects its causes, *European Environmental Review*, 1 (5) pp.38-45; Innes, J.L. (1987) *Air Pollution and Forestry*, London: HMSO; Ling, K. and Ashmore, M. *Acid Rain and Trees*, Peterborough: Nature Conservancy Council; Mohnen, V.A. (1988) The challenge of acid rain, *Scientific American*, 259 (2), pp.14-22. For detailed studies of acidification in upland areas see: Kay, D. and Stoner, J. (1988) The effects of catchment land use on stream water quality in an acid-suceptible region of West Wales: the implications for compliance with EC drinking water and fishery dirtectives, *Applied Geography*, pp.191-205; Neal, C. Whitehead, P. Neale, R. Cosby, J. (1986) Modelling the effects of acidic deposition and conifer afforestation on stream acidity in the British uplands, *Journal of Hydrology*, 86, pp.15-26; Woodin, S.J. (1988) Acidic deposition and upland conservation - an overview and the way ahead in Usher M and Thompson D (eds) *Ecological Change in the Uplands*, Oxford: Blackwells. On the consequences for ground-water quality of upland forest management techniques see: Moofat, A.J. Forestry and soil erosion in Britain - a review, *Soil Use and Management*, 4 (2), pp.41-44.

62. On river pollution see: Hellawell, J. (1988) Toxic substances in rivers and streams, *Environmental Pollution*, 50, pp.61-85; House of Commons Environment Committee (1987) *Pollution of Rivers and Estuaries: Report*, London: HMSO; Water Authorities Association (1987) *Wate Pollution from Farm Waste*, Sheffield: WWA.

63. On nitrates in ground water see: British Geological Survey (1986) The Groundwater Nitrate Problem *Hydrogeological Report 86/2*; Croll, B and Hayes, C (1988) Nitrate and water supplies in the United Kingdom, *Environmental Pollution*, 50, 163-187; ECETOC (1988) Nitrate and drinking water, *ECETOC*, Brussels.

64. See: House of Commons Agriculture Committee. (1987) *The Effects of Pesticides on Human Health*, 379 - vols 1, 11, 111. London: HMSO.

65. For studies of various aspects of rural tourism see: Bouquet, M. and Winter, M. (1987) *Who from their Labour Rest? Conflict and Practice in Rural Tourism*, Aldershot: Avebury/Gower.

66. Patmore, J.A. (1983) *Recreation and Resources*, Oxford: Blackwell.

67. But see: Shoard, M. (1987) *This Land is our Land*, London: Paladin.

68. Hirsch, F. (1978) *Social Limits to Growth*, London: Routledge.

69. The remainder of this section draws on ideas contained in the final three chapters of our work in this area: Lowe, P. Cox, G. MacEwen, M. O'Riordan, and Winter, M. (1986) op. cit.

70. WWF et al (1983) *The Conservation and Development Programme for the UK: A Response to the World Conservation Strategy*, London: Kogan Page.

71. On how the farming lobby has used this notion in a defensive manner see Chapter 4 of: Lowe, P. Cox, G. MacEwen, M. O'Riordan, and Winter, M. (1986) op. cit. On the philosophical and theological dimensions of stewardship see: Black, J. (1970) *The Dominion of Man*, Edinburgh: Edinburgh University Press; Passmore, J. (1974) *Man 's Responsibility for Nature*, London: Duckworth.

Appendix D

Demographic Forces and the Reshaping of Rural England in the Late Twentieth Century by Dr Tony Champion (University of Newcastle upon Tyne) and Mr Alan Townsend (University of Durham)

* This is an abridged and updated revision of a report submitted to ACORA by the authors in September 1988. Dr Champion is Senior Lecturer in Geography at the University of Newcastle upon Tyne; Mr Townsend is Reader in Geography at the University of Durham.

Introduction

The traditional image of Rural England is one of depopulation, based on the fact that most parishes saw their number of inhabitants peak during the middle or later decades of the nineteenth century. The recent story, however, is very different, in the sense that the remoter largely rural districts now constitute the second fastest growing type of area in England and Wales and have done so for the past twenty years or so. Nevertheless, the population of rural areas, in aggregate, still retains many features inherited from the past, including an older-than-average age structure, natural decline, net outmigration of school leavers and a very low proportion of ethnic minority members. Moreover, the new-found growth is by no means evenly spread, either on a regional basis (with much stronger growth in the rural areas of southern England and in places which are relatively accessible to the large cities) or at a more local scale (with growth largely being concentrated in larger settlements at the expense of smaller villages and outlying areas). This diversity makes it very difficult to make valid generalizations, but essentially the elements of decline and growth both raise important social issues with challenging policy implications for those involved in catering for the needs and aspirations of people in the countryside.

Recent population trends

Population growth and decline
The key feature of the recent history of population change in Rural England is *its turnaround from decline to growth*. In the 1950s the more rural parts of the country, in aggregate, recorded overall loss of population, in spite of relatively strong national population growth. In the 1960s rural areas switched to substantial population increase, and subsequently they have broadly maintained their aggregate growth rate, in spite of the major reduction in the national rate of growth. This dramatic development, variously labelled the "rural population revival", "metropolitan migration turnaround" and "counterurbanization", is by no means unique to Britain, but has been observed in most countries of the more advanced Western World - though to differing extents and only in a few cases on such an intense and long-term basis (see Champion, 1989).

The beginning of a new decade, with the last Population Census over nine years away and with only months to go before the next (April 1991), is just about the worst time to assess the scale and significance of the latest trends. Table 1 uses population

349

estimates for aggregations of Local Authority Districts to summarize the main features of population change in the 1980s. Clearly evident is *the shift of population* from Greater London and the Metropolitan Counties into non-metropolitan England and Wales, as also is the prominent role of the less urbanized district categories in accommodating national population growth over the seven-year period up to 1988. Indeed, the most rural category of "remoter, largely rural districts" is believed to have recorded annual average growth of 9.3 per thousand, the highest rate of all eleven district categories recognised by OPCS (1990) except for "resort and retirement districts" (10.3 per thousand). Moreover, it can be seen that this growth was achieved entirely through net in-migration, since this category has been experiencing a slight surplus of deaths over births (Table 1).

At the same time, however, this strong growth has not occurred uniformly across Rural England, either regionally or on a more local scale. In particular, there is a *major contrast between the North and South* of the country. Northumberland and Cumbria, the two most rural counties in northern England, experienced population increases of only 0.7 and 1.7 per cent respectively between 1981 and 1988, compared to 5-6 per cent increases for North Yorkshire, Lincolnshire and Shropshire, the counties with the next lowest population densities in Britain, and 8-10 per cent increases for Cambridgeshire, Buckinghamshire, the Isle of Wight, Dorset and Cornwall (OPCS, 1990). These variations seem to be linked to a number of factors, including differential rates of economic growth in North and South generally during the 1980s, proximity to major urban centres (notably London), the greater problems faced by upland and livestock farming in adjusting to the new agricultural *regimes,* and the greater attraction of the "sunbelt" South for retirement and holiday-making (for more details, see Champion and Townsend, 1990, especially Chapter 11).

At the *more local scale,* comparison of data from the 1971 and 1981 Population Censuses shows that, even in more rural counties with relatively strong growth, a considerable number of parishes suffered *depopulation;* for instance, 41 per cent of both Shropshire and Lincolnshire, not surprisingly considerably more (55 per cent) in Northumberland, but impressively as many as 46 per cent in West Sussex, a county under great development pressure. This paradox of widespread occurrence of population decline at parish level despite overall gains in rural areas can be explained largely by reference to the particular circumstances of individual places. As pointed out by Weekley (1988) in a study of the East Midlands, it is due to a combination of restrictive planning policies and changing population composition. Town and country planning policies have aimed at curbing the spread of urban development into the deep countryside and at concentrating new building in "key settlements" which have a fuller range of existing services, including mains drainage, schools and public transport. At the same time, the essentially fixed supply of houses in most of the smallest settlements means that they are not able to accommodate as many people as previously because of falling household size, because houses have been taken over for use as second homes, or, in less pressurized areas, because houses have become vacant or fallen into disrepair.

Changes in population composition

Alongside the major changes in population distribution which are affecting Rural England, there have also been important developments in the structure and composition of the population of rural areas. Some of these are associated with the distributional changes described above, since migration has been tending to alter the age structure and social character of rural settlements. Others parallel national trends in birth rate, age structure, household composition and social characteristics, but are no less significant in that they can have more marked consequences for rural communities than for large cities, particularly with respect to the provision of local facilities and services.

In terms of age structure, Rural England has a *tradition of older average age,* with more elderly and fewer children than the country as a whole (see Bracey, 1970, and Lawton, 1982). This arose principally because of the out-migration of school-leavers and young adults in search of work, housing, better facilities, further education and military service, but in more recent decades was reinforced by the growth of retirement migration into rural areas. These two processes are still in operation, with most counties of Rural England continuing to experience a net loss of 16-19 year olds (and some also losing 20-24 year olds) and to attract a net inflow of people aged 60 and over. On the other hand, the "rural population revival" of the last twenty years has involved a major increase in the net in-migration of working-age people including large numbers of younger families with children as well as older pre-retirement couples (the latter often called "empty-nesters" because by this stage their children have left home for higher education or work).

As a result, the age profile for Rural England is, nowadays, *not far different from the national average* (Table 2). In 1988, 20.3 per cent of the people living in "remoter, largely rural districts" were of pensionable age compared to 18.4 per cent for England and Wales as a whole, while the respective figures for the under-15 year olds were 17.8 and 18.7 per cent. The "mixed urban-rural" category, which comprises substantial less urbanized parts of the country but also includes some large towns, has proved particularly attractive to younger families, as reflected in its rather younger-than-average age structure in 1988 (Table 2). At the same time, it must be recognised that these average figures mask wide local variations, often with the smaller rural settlements containing larger shares of older people and with families with school-age children tending to gravitate towards the local centres with better facilities and easier access to housing.

For rural areas as a whole, however, the most important developments in population composition do not arise from migration, but form part of changes taking place nationally, and indeed more widely in Western Europe and across most of the Developed World. This is as true for *age structure* as for some other aspects of rural demography. The rising proportion of the elderly in rural populations is a long-term phenomenon which parallels national trends in longer life expectancy. In the short-to-medium term, even greater changes in age structure have been occurring as a result of past fluctuations in numbers of births, most notably the strong acceleration in birth rate during the late 1950s and early 1960s and its equally dramatic fall through to the mid 1970s. Over the last thirty years, rural areas, like places elsewhere, have had to cope with the progression through school age, and, more recently, into working and marriageable age, of the "baby boom" and then come to terms with the subsequent "baby bust" with all its implications for schools in smaller settlements. The last few years of higher birth rate, partly resulting from the "coming of age" of the 1960s bulge, has served to re-open many of these contentious issues.

Some other major changes in the national population have been shared by rural areas, while others have not. Rural England has not escaped the general trend towards *smaller average household size,* produced by the increasing number of elderly people, smaller family size (in terms of numbers of children per family), rising rates of divorce and separation, and the acceleration in "household fission" (involving more people living as separate households rather than as part of a larger family group, particularly observed for the elderly and for young single adults). For Britain as a whole, average household size fell from 2.91 persons per household in 1971 to 2.70 in 1981 and is estimated to have shrunk to 2.48 in 1987. As mentioned above, this development has had a significant impact on the population size of rural settlements where little new house-building has been taking place, but it also raises more specific policy issues such as the problem of caring for elderly people with no younger family members at home or perhaps close by.

By contrast, Rural England generally tends to contain *much lower proportions of ethnic minorities and lone-parent families* than the country as a whole. The former have traditionally been highly concentrated in a small number of large cities and it is reckoned that, though their numbers have grown hugely (from around 200,000 in Britain in 1951 to an estimated 2.4 million by the mid 1980s), relatively few have moved into rural areas, either by choice or through lack of opportunity. Lone-parent families, usually characterized by low incomes, are also understood not to participate very fully in the population shift to rural areas, while those among them who are rural by upbringing tend to drift to the towns to find suitable accommodation and support. Up-to-date facts on these aspects of population change are hard to come by at the sub-national scale, but a much fuller picture will be available soon from the 1991 Census, particularly as this includes a question on ethnicity for the first time.

Population prospects for Rural England
It is clear that recent years have seen major changes in the size, structure and geographical distribution of population, although it is impossible to be too specific about the local-scale trends experienced since the 1981 Census. It is even more difficult to attach precise numbers to future trends with any great degree of confidence. This is not just because of moving forward from a poorly documented base but also because of the knowledge that previous projections have tended to be confounded by unexpected events. Not the least of these was the reversal of rural-to-urban migration shifts, but they also included the remarkable changes in national fertility rates during the 1960s which were largely unforeseen but have had significant consequences for age structure and household composition in rural areas and elsewhere. This section looks at the trends in population, households and age structure currently anticipated for the remaining ten years of this century.

Population projections
The latest official population projections relating to the decade up to 2001 are shown in Figure 1. They are based on the national assumptions relating to fertility and mortality, modified by local-area factors, and on past trends in migration adjusted by the Department of the Environment in the light of land-use planning policies and other relevant considerations. Not surprisingly in this context, therefore, the overall patterns of population change which the official projections suggest bear a strong resemblance to those of the last few years.

The *main features* of the changes expected for England during the 1990s are:
1) A continuation of population redistribution in favour of the South and more rural regions;
2) Substantial population decline in the main conurbations of the North, including Cleveland and the West Midlands, but some further population growth for London;
3) Modest growth in counties immediately around London and in the central Midlands, which are already heavily developed in relation to permitted building land;
4) Fastest population growth in counties fringing the more developed and industrial areas of southern England and the Midlands, particularly round the nothern and western fringes of the South East region;
5) Strong growth in some of the more remote counties in the South and Midlands, especially Cornwall, Lincolnshire and Shropshire;
6) Weak growth in the northernmost counties, and population loss in Durham and Humberside (though presumably mainly from their more urban and industrial areas).

Household projections
The 1985-based household projections produced by the Department of the Environment (DoE, 1988) follow a similar geographical pattern to those in Figure 1, but because of the trend towards smaller average size of household they suggest an *even greater rate of growth than the population projections*. Buckinghamshire and Cambridgeshire, for instance, are both expected to have one-third more households in 2001 than they had in 1985. *Increases in excess of 20 per cent* are anticipated in a band of counties stretching from Dorset and Hampshire in the south to Lincolnshire in the north. Not far short of this are most of the other counties in the South, but north and west of the Severn-Humber line the only counties expecting more than a 16 per cent

increase in household numbers are Shropshire, Hereford and Worcester, and North Yorkshire.

In all non-metropolitan counties, as for England as a whole, the *shift away from the traditional married-couple household* is expected to continue. Only those counties which are growing most rapidly or which attract predominantly young families rather than older people are likely to experience a substantial increase in numbers of married-couple households. Otherwise, the most significant growth in numerical as well as in percentage terms is expected in lone-parent, one-person and other households. Examples drawn from a range of counties are shown in Table 3.

Clearly, *large parts of non-metropolitan England, particularly in the South and Midlands, are facing substantial pressures* for housing development over this 16-year period, as in most cases they attempt to accommodate by 2001 between one and two extra households for every six that they had in 1985. Of course, it could be argued that shortage of housing in more rural areas could slow down the underlying trend towards smaller household size, or at least divert more building to the larger towns and cities, but these DoE figures are meant to have taken account of the changing age structure of the population, long-term trends in divorce rates and so on, and policy considerations concerning the most appropriate broad distribution of population in the future. There is also uncertainty over whether the extra households will generally aspire to the same type of housing as married couples and, if not, whether other types of housing will be available. It is up to the local and national planning machinery to be the final arbiter on the patterns and scale of new housebuilding, particularly the extent to which it is concentrated into the more heavily built up parts of these counties as opposed to taking place in smaller settlements and deeper into the heart of the countryside.

Age structure
These local considerations also affect the number and distribution of people in different age groups. Once again, the official projections provide the broad canvas of changes produced by the ageing of the base-year population and the trends in migration. The changes expected in a sample of counties are shown in Table 4.

Most non-metropolitan counties will be sharing the national trend towards *stabilization of the proportion of older people,* though the number of very elderly will be increasing in all cases. Indeed, because of the smaller cohorts now reaching retirement age and also because most non-metropolitan counties are now gaining more working-age people than older migrants, the proportion of those aged 60 years old and over is expected to fall significantly in several counties, particularly those with a traditional retirement role such as East Sussex, Dorset and Cornwall.

The other significant changes common to most non-metropolitan counties, as they largely follow the national trend between 1985 and 2001, are a reduction in the number - not just the proportion - of *young adults* (17-28 years old), except in counties experiencing the most rapid growth, and a massive increase in both the number and proportion of *29-59 year olds.*

There will also be *some growth in the number of children,* essentially reflecting the overall rate of population growth in these counties, though in some cases increasing their share of the total population. While this will lift the demand for child-related facilities above the very low levels to which they had sunk throughout Britain in the 1980s, there is no guarantee that this will lead to a widespread respite in the rate of school closure in rural areas. Housing market factors, particularly the fact that older couples can outbid young families for housing in the more attractive small communities, are likely to combine with school rationalization schemes to ensure that this increase in numbers of children will disproportionately benefit the towns and larger villages in rural areas.

The population challenge for rural areas
A number of important changes have been taking place in the size and structure of the population of Rural England over the past 15-20 years and are likely to continue at

least until the end of the century. There are, however, important regional and local differences in the scale, and in some cases in the nature, of these changes. Moreover, their impact will vary according to the inherited circumstances of particular areas and communities. In particular, rural areas differ in their degree of internal diversity - a source of potential conflict as well as a force for greater stability.

The key feature common to all broad areas of Rural England is *population growth*. This can be seen as beneficial in many respects, particularly in relation to the general confidence which it gives and to the ability of rural areas to support a wider range of services and to generate more service-orientated jobs. Such growth does, however, pose challenges for rural areas, because in general they face greater difficulties than more urbanized areas in meeting pressures arising from growth, whether for particular publicly-provided services or in terms of accommodating new building without detracting from the environment of the countryside or from the character of small settlements.

Further problems arise from the nature of population growth, particularly in relation to its age and social structure. The number of *very elderly people* in the countryside is growing extremely rapidly and will continue to do so well into the next century, as a result of the previous influx of retirement migrants as well as the national trend towards larger numbers in this age group. This will create even greater problems in rural areas than in the cities because of the problems of access to appropriate facilities from scattered settlements and the limited opportunities for scale economies.

Changes in the numbers of children and young adults also pose some uncertainties and potential problems. The projected *increase in the number of 0-16 year olds* in the 1990s could be considered an important positive development for rural areas. Yet this upward trend is likely to be fairly temporary, peaking around the end of the century. This will mean that difficult decisions will have to be made, for instance, concerning whether to re-open schools. Moreover, it is likely that some local areas will not share in the general rise in this age group because their populations are now dominated by older working-age people and the elderly.

The number of children in the future also depends on the migration behaviour of *school-leavers and young adults*. Traditionally rural areas have experienced net losses of this age group. One of the key features of the next few years is that this age group will contract substantially nationwide and, indeed, employers are already expressing concern over labour shortages in London and the South East, leading to the bidding up of wage rates. The projections already indicate that the number of 17-28 year olds will fall in all the most rapidly growing rural counties. It could well be that the situation in urban areas will lead to an acceleration in rural out-migration, unless escalating operating costs in the cities prompt employers to move to more rural locations.

The number and distribution of the younger half of the population also depends very much on *housing factors*. A major problem in recent years has been the bidding up of house prices by newcomers - often older and wealthier - to levels which cannot be afforded by young couples, not only local people but also other young families that might have moved in from the cities. This shortage of young-family accommodation has been compounded by the decline in tied cottages, the sale of council housing and the general contraction of private-rented housing, not only in the deep countryside, but also in the main centres in many rural areas. Unless steps are taken to reverse the decline of rented and low-cost housing, the trend for young couples to be displaced from smaller settlements into the larger villages and towns may intensify to the extent that more have to look further afield on marriage.

The diversity of rural areas and the need for flexibility

This report has concentrated on the more general features of rural population change, though where appropriate attention has been drawn to the extent of variation across Rural England. The forward projections described above should be handled with particular care, because the county scale masks some of the differences within rural areas and in many cases involves their amalgamation with places which could not be considered "rural" even under the most generous interpretation of the term.

Two aspects of diversity are most commonly recognized - the degree of "rurality" and type of socio-economic function, the two being to some extent related to each other. Research by Cloke (1986) has demonstrated the existence of a sliding scale of *rurality*, which is related first and foremost to distance from a substantial urban centre. This is also strongly associated with the ratio of households to dwellings (low in the most rural areas), proportion of second homes and holiday accommodation (high), proportion employed in farming (high), proportion aged 65 and over (high), availability of household amenities (low) and population density (low). The diversity of *socio-economic function* has been demonstrated well by the detailed work of Dunn, Rawson and Rogers (1981) on "rural housing profiles". This identified at least six types of rural areas differentiated by their distinctive elements which included high-status owner-occupiers, retired owner-occupiers, farmers, farmworkers, local authority tenants and members of the Armed Forces.

Care must therefore be taken in interpreting this report's observations on a more local scale. Some areas will share more fully in the trends outlined, depending on their openness to urban influences, their inherited demographic and social structures, and their local features, such as housing stock and planning status. As mentioned previously, it is particularly important to distinguish between deep countryside, containing only the smallest settlements and subject to strict planning controls, and areas where villages and towns have been selected as centres of concentrated growth.

The aggregate nature of most statistics also masks some of the problems which exist in rural areas. For instance, statistics on average gross weekly earnings of full-time male workers put the most remote and rural counties at the bottom of the national league table, with Cornwall, Lincolnshire, Shropshire, Devon, Northumberland, and North Yorkshire in ascending order from the bottom. This is primarily because of the low incomes earned in their predominantly agricultural and related primary production sectors. The higher average earnings for more heavily populated counties are more likely to be a reflection of the greater proportion of people working in urban areas than to be produced by higher incomes for rural workers, so in some respects the latter could well be at a greater disadvantage than their counterparts in more rural counties. This is particularly the case when they are being squeezed out of smaller settlements by wealthy newcomers and have to compete for housing against local townsfolk and against relatively low-income commuters who have had to look beyond the larger cities for affordable housing.

Anticipated population trends therefore raise some *delicate problems of balance* between people, jobs, housing and services. Given the nature of underlying market forces and the current degree of central control over public spending, these changes largely lie outside the control of local government. They therefore raise management issues which *must be addressed primarily at national level.*

From what has been said in the previous section, however, it should be clear that there is *no single set of rural problems that can be tackled with a single policy package.* This report has highlighted the major contrasts which exist between different parts of Rural England, most notably between North and South, between areas closer to the larger cities and those most remote, and more locally between the main settlements and the surrounding countryside. The fragmented nature of its settlements and the diversity of its people are among the major attractions of Rural England, yet they also pose a challenge for those attempting to anticipate local population trends and cope with their implications.

Acknowledgements and sources

Figure 1 is taken from Champion, A. G. and Townsend, A. R. *Contemporary Britain: A Geographical Perspective,* Edward Arnold, London, 1990. Tables 1-4 are derived from data which are Crown Copyright. The authors thank the OPCS for providing the unpublished data on which Table 4 is based.

For an account of recent trends and problems in rural Britain, see Chapter 11, "Outer Rural Areas", in Champion and Townsend (1990). More detailed treatments of aspects of rural life and change can be found in Champion and Watkins (forthcoming), including migration to the countryside, housing, employment, transport, community development, and issues relating to women and the elderly. Pacione (1984) and Phillips and Williams (1984) provide useful introductions to the geography and society of rural areas, while Bracey (1970), Newby (1979), Lewis (1979) and Bradley and Lowe (1984) focus on past and present aspects of social change in the countryside.

References
Bracey, H. E. (1970) *People in the Countryside,* Routledge & Kegan Paul, London.
Bradley, T. and Lowe, P. (eds) (1984) *Locality and Rurality: Economy and Society in Rural Regions,* GeoBooks, Norwich.
Champion, A. G. (ed) (1989) *Counterurbanisation: The Changing Pace and Nature of Population Deconcentration,* Edward Arnold, London.
Champion, A. G. and Townsend, A. R. (1990) *Contemporary Britain: A Geographical Perspective,* Edward Arnold, London.
Champion, A. G. and Watkins, C. (forthcoming) *People in the Countryside: Studies of Social Change in Rural Britain,* Paul Chapman, London.
Cloke, P. (1986) Rurality in England and Wales, 1986, *Regional Studies* 20, 289-306.
DoE (1988) *1985-based Estimates of Numbers of Households in England, the Regions, Counties, Metropolitan Districts and London Boroughs 1985-2001,* Government Statistical Service, London.
Dunn, M., Rawson, M. and Rogers, A. (1981) *Rural Housing: Competition and Choice,* Allen & Unwin, London.
Lewis, G. J. (1979) *Rural Communities: A Social Geography,* David & Charles, Newton Abbot.
Newby, H. (1979) *Green and Pleasant Land? Social Change in Rural England,* Hutchinson, London.
OPCS (1988) *Population Projections, England by Area, 1985-2001,* Series PP3, no. 7, HMSO, London.
OPCS (1990) *Key Population and Vital Statistics: Local and Health Authority Areas, 1988.* Series VS no. 15, PP1 no. 11. HMSO, London.
RGS (1989) *Population Projections: Scotland (1987-based),* Registrar General Scotland, Edinburgh.
Weekley, I. (1988) Rural depopulation and counterurbanisation: a paradox, *Area* 20, 127-34.
Welsh Office (1989) *1987-based Population Projections for the Counties of Wales,* Welsh Office, Cardiff.

Table 1: Population change, 1981-88, by types of district

| Type of District | 1988 | 1981-88 Change | | | | | |
| | Population | Total | | Natural | | Migration | |
	000s	000s	Rate	000s	Rate	000s	Rate
Greater London	6735.4	− 70.2	− 1.47	+ 144.0	+ 3.02	− 214.3	− 4.50
Metropolitan	11122.9	− 230.7	− 2.90	+ 129.3	+ 1.63	− 360.0	− 4.53
Non-metropolitan	32535.1	+ 1060.0	+ 4.81	+ 241.3	+ 1.10	+ 818.6	+ 3.72
of which							
Mixed urban-rural	9930.2	+ 429.8	+ 6.46	+ 149.4	+ 2.25	+ 280.3	+ 4.21
Remoter largely							
rural	5465.8	+ 334.6	+ 9.32	− 28.7	− 0.80	+ 363.3	+ 10.11
England & Wales	50393.3	+ 759.0	+ 2.18	+ 514.6	+ 1.48	+ 244.3	+ 0.70

Note: Rate is expressed in terms of annual change per 1000 people.

Source: Calculated from OPCS (1990).

Table 2: Estimated residential population, by age group, 1988

Age group	Remoter largely rural		Mixed urban-rural		England & Wales	
	000s	%	000s	%	000s	%
1- 4	323.4	5.92	623.9	6.28	3287.5	6.52
5-14	652.1	11.93	1229.6	12.38	6121.0	12.15
15-29	1211.7	22.17	2334.2	23.51	11837.4	23.49
30-44	1114.1	20.38	2141.6	21.57	10417.7	20.67
45-PA	1052.1	19.25	1916.9	19.30	9442.4	18.74
PA-74	693.1	12.68	1074.0	10.82	5834.8	11.58
75+	419.1	7.67	610.1	6.14	3452.4	6.85
Total	5465.8	100.00	9930.2	100.00	50393.3	100.00

Note: PA = Pensionable age (65 for men, 60 for women).

Source: Calculated from OPCS (1990).

Table 3: Projected changes in households, 1985-2001, for selected counties.

County/Year		Married couple 000s	Lone parent 000s	One person 000s	Other 000s	All households 000s	Average household size
Lincolnshire							
	1985	138	16	49	11	214	2.57
	2001	149	23	70	16	258	2.46
Northumberland							
	1985	73	9	26	4	113	2.61
	2001	69	11	39	5	123	2.49
East Sussex							
	1985	152	22	88	23	286	2.33
	2001	151	28	121	31	331	2.18
Cornwall & Isles of Scilly	1985	107	13	39	10	169	2.56
	2001	113	19	54	15	200	2.55
Shropshire							
	1985	92	11	32	8	142	2.70
	2001	99	17	49	11	176	2.57

Source: Department of the Environment, *1985-based Estimates of Numbers of Households in England, the Regions, Counties, Metropolitan Districts and London Boroughs 1985-2001,* Government Statistical Service, 1988.

Table 4: Projected changes in age structure, 1985-2001, for selected English counties.

County/Year Total		Under 17	17-28	29-59	60 & over	Total
Lincolnshire						
1985	000s	121.3	102.2	214.2	122.5	560.3
2001	000s	140.2	87.0	298.3	121.3	646.8
1985	%	21.6	18.2	38.2	21.9	100.0
2001	%	21.6	13.5	46.1	18.8	100.0
Northumberland						
1985	000s	66.5	52.6	117.1	64.5	300.7
2001	000s	68.7	44.9	129.9	68.2	311.7
1985	%	22.1	17.4	38.9	21.4	100.0
2001	%	22.0	14.4	41.7	21.9	100.0
East Sussex						
1985	000s	126.3	112.9	237.7	205.5	682.4
2001	000s	143.4	96.9	301.1	198.7	740.2
1985	%	18.5	16.5	34.8	30.1	100.0
2001	%	19.4	13.1	40.7	26.8	100.0
Cornwall & Isles of Scilly						
1985	000s	92.5	74.1	166.6	110.5	443.7
2001	000s	118.0	73.6	222.4	106.9	520.9
1985	%	20.8	16.7	37.5	24.9	100.0
2001	%	22.7	14.1	42.7	20.5	100.0
Shropshire						
1985	000s	90.4	74.6	148.8	76.5	390.3
2001	000s	109.1	67.0	199.5	81.3	456.9
1985						
%		23.2	19.1	38.1	19.6	100.0
2001	%	23.9	14.7	43.7	17.8	100.0

Source: Unpublished data provided by OPCS.

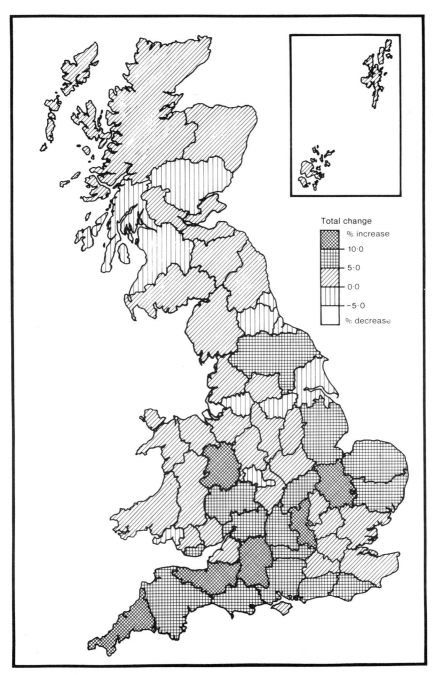

Figure 1. Projected population change, 1991-2001.

Source: Champion and Townsend (1990), Figure 12.1. Originally calculated from OPCS (1988), RGS (1989) and Welsh Office (1989).

Appendix E

Agricultural Restructuring: Current Trends and Prospects by Professor Richard Munton (University College London), Dr Terry Marsden (South Bank Polytechnic), and Dr Sarah Whatmore (University of Bristol)

Introduction

In the post-war period British agriculture has experienced dramatic changes in its social and economic organisation. Among the more important are the specialisation of production on farms and in particular farming regions (Bowler, 1985); a decline in the number of farm businesses, by approximately 40% to 250,000 since 1950; a reduction of almost 50% in the agricultural workforce over the same period to 600,000; and an unprecedented growth in agricultural productivity following the increased use of *agrotechnology*, including chemical inputs, machinery and genetic engineering techniques.

These new methods of production have been developed off the farm through agricultural research programmes undertaken in universities and specialist institutes, and by private industry (Munton *et al.*, 1990). They have been widely supported by government through direct investment in research and development and, indirectly, through the use of grants for capital improvements, tax relief on capital gains, and advisory agencies to facilitate the adoption of new methods by farmers. The rapid industrialisation of agricultural production has been the result of a successful alliance between industry, farming and government lasting half a century.

The very success of this alliance has brought in its wake the social and economic problems which now characterise the farm crisis. The term "crisis" is used advisedly to draw attention to the *structural* nature of the industry's economic problems and the increasing evidence for the *inherent* contradictions contained in post-war agricultural policy. For example, the state has been committed, at least in its rhetoric, to safeguarding the economic viability of traditional family farms while at the same time promoting a process of industrialisation which has rendered many of them economically marginal; public money has been invested heavily through price support while many smaller farmers and the hired workforce have remained among the most poorly rewarded groups; and it has supported private property rights, excluding agricultural land from most planning controls, in spite of widespread deterioration in the quality of the farmed environment. These contradictions have made it increasingly difficult for the government to legitimate existing policy, although it is important to stress that the crisis is not a peculiarly British phenomenon but is international in nature (see Goodman and Redclift, 1989). Equally, its effects are unevenly distributed throughout British agriculture, varying between different sectors of production, regions and types of farm.

The first section of the paper identifies two structural features which distinguish agriculture as a sector of the economy and examines the industrialisation process as a response to them. It is a process shaped by the economic strategies of vested interests and by the policies and practices of various state agencies which affect these interest groups unevenly. Farmers, it will be argued, represent an increasingly dependent and diminishing interest within a complex *agro-food* chain. Section Two examines the implications of this dependence for the social organisation of farming and, in particular, for its traditional family structure. The final section speculates on future developments in British agriculture and agricultural policy.

i. The industrialisation of agriculture

The industrialisation of farming is, in part, an outcome of two fundamental constraints. First, unlike other sectors of industry, the production of agricultural goods involves the biological processes of plant growth and animal gestation. To this extent the output and profitability of farming is dependent on "natural" conditions. Second, the consumption of agricultural products is relatively unresponsive to price differences and income changes (1).

In this context, the post-war period has experienced rapid growth in the non-farming sectors of food production and major modifications to the biological processes and the role of land in farm husbandry. The net effect has been to tie farming much more closely into a wider agro-food chain and to shift the balance of market power away from farming (see below). Today, the most important sectors are the industries producing and servicing technological inputs to the farm and, especially, the indutries processing and marketing farm products. Recent experience is only the culmination of long-term trends. Ever since the late nineteenth century both these sectors have grown in size and influence and become increasingly dominated by a small number of large national and multi-national corporations. For example, just three companies now control 95% of the UK market in nitrogenous fertilisers and three food processing companies account for 90% of the UK frozen food market (Ward, forthcoming).

The manufacture of technological inputs and the processing of farm products have been effectively removed from the farm. In both cases, the development of new technology is central to their profitability. The inputs industries, in particular, have a vested interest in an intensive agricultural system. De-intensification threatens their profits. For example, the imposition of milk quotas in 1984 produced a cut of some 30% in the size of the UK dairy-feed market. This led in turn to over-capacity among feed manufacturers and to renewed rounds of acquisition and price-cutting among the companies concerned.

Some 75% of farm produce is processed in some way before it reaches the consumer and the food processing industry is the fourth largest manufacturing sector in the UK. To overcome the consumption constraint on the profitability of food, the industry has concentrated on increasing the value-added element of its products. Farm products have been turned into raw material for further processing, using sophisticated biotechnologies (Goodman *et al*, 1987), and the food market segmented by introducing quality criteria which target high-income consumer groups. These changes have altered the relationships between the food industry, the consumer and the farming sector. As raw materials, farm products represent a declining share of the total cost of food products. For example, a higher proportion of the cost of a packet of potato crisps is made up from packaging, marketing and promotion (39%), than from its basic raw materials, potatoes and oil (35%). At the same time, where the product is to be sold to consumers largely in its farm "form" (eg frozen meat and vegetables), higher quality, more standardised produce is required from farms. This is often achieved through growing on contract where husbandry practices may be determined and monitored by the purchasing company, and the flow of products planned to meet the company's marketing strategy.

Farms have thus become tied to the food chain on increasingly unequal terms. Their survival is ever more dependent on industrial inputs, sources of technological and financial advice from off the farm, and externally defined production processes. The comparative market weakness of farming is reflected in the distribution of value added. Recent figures for the UK (excluding net imports) suggest that the food industry accounts for nearly 65% of the value added and the farming sector between 15 and 20% (Harvey, 1987). Thus, although farming is still undertaken predominantly by independent, family-owned businesses, their control over the production process is compromised by numerous indirect links with the corporate sectors of the agro-food chain. Farming may still be stereo-typed as an independent, autonomous occupation, but in reality this is far from the case.

Farmers' declining economic influence is reinforced by reduced public credibility and political support for the arguments which have justified post-war agricultural policy. The rising costs of CAP price support have not been brought properly under control, and represent a blatant challenge to a government committed to the twin goals of reducing public expenditure and exposing more of the economy to the rigours of unsupported markets. This is an unhappy coincidence for British farmers and a further blow to the already low status of the social goals of agricultural policy, such as protecting the incomes of small family farms. This largely economistic approach to agricultural support, which has been evident to varying degrees since the early 1950s, contrasts with the outlook of many of our EC partners.

ii. Changes in the social structure of English farming

A. *The agricultural workforce*
The industrialisation of agriculture has had profound consequences for the structure and size of the agricultural workforce. Most significantly, through the direct replacement of labour by capital it has led to a rapid decline in the labour requirements of the industry and the size of the workforce. The pace of decline has slowed somewhat from a loss of 28% of the workforce in the 1960s, to 13% in the 1970s and to 7% between 1975 and 1985.

To the 600,000 or so working on farms needs to be added the contribution to employment in rural areas of other sectors in the agro-food chain. This is very difficult to assess because these sectors are characterised by companies with diverse economic interests of which agriculturally-related production may be only one. Craig *et al*, (1986) calculated that in 1983 nearly 189,000 full-time job equivalents were associated with the manufacturing of farm inputs while the Department of Employment (1984) recorded 524,000 employed in the food manufacturing industry alone. But as Errington and Harrison (1990) point out, there have been major reductions in these occupations during the 1980s, particularly in the farm inputs industries. How much of this employment occurs in rural areas is impossible to determine. While it may be assumed that the majority of manufacturing jobs are based in urban areas, this is certainly not true for the servicing industries which are "more likely to be based close to their customers in rural areas" (Errington, 1987:21).

Aggregate trends in the farm workforce also disguise a number of other important changes to its internal structure. First, both the absolute number and proportion of family workers in farming is higher than it is for hired workers, and the rate of decline in family workers is slower, even showing a slight increase in places in the 1980s, than for hired workers. Between 1977 and 1987 the number of family workers fell by 6.7% while the number of hired workers declined by 19.4%, raising the share of the workforce consisting of family members to 62% in 1984 (Errington, 1985).

Second, there has been a growth in *intermittent* forms of farm labour (Ball, 1987a), particularly of seasonal and casual employment. Despite the acknowledged inadequacies of census data which lead to under-recording, the process of *casualisation* is reflected in the growth of seasonal and casual workers from 20.2% of the farm workforce in 1970 to 32.6% in 1987. Their work is generally associated with the more manual and least mechanised aspects of farm production and with poorer pay and employment conditions in a sector which is recognised as one of the lowest paid, with some 38% of adult male agricultural workers (the elite of the farm workforce) estimated to fall below the official poverty line in 1982.

Two sub-themes within this wider pattern are of particular note. The first is that a much higher proportion of seasonal and casual farm employment falls to women than is the case for full-time farm employment while the growth in the predominantly manual sector of intermittent employment is paralleled by an expansion in the area of highly mechanised contract labour. This sector often takes the form of "self-employed" workers, many of whom may also be part-time farmers who use their own equipment, who are hired on contract to undertake specific, machinery-related tasks. Ball (1987b) suggests that as many as 43,000 workers might be involved, concentrated in the arable sector.

Finally, it should be stressed that the full-time, hired workforce is thinly distributed yet concentrated on a small number of large holdings. In England and Wales, for example, in 1986, 1,400 holdings with ten or more hired workers (0.75% of all holdings) employed 24,000 full-time workers (21.7% of the full-time workforce).

B. *Farm businesses and family farming*

Britain has also experienced a substantial move towards a smaller number of larger holdings (2). Large farm units, defined as occupying more than 300 acres, grew from 4.3% of total holdings and 25.2% of total farmed area in England and Wales in 1951, to 13.7% and 54.3% respectively by 1983 (Grigg, 1987). The predominance of a small number of large holdings distinguishes Britain's farm structure from those of other EC countries. Accompanying this trend has been the concentration of farm output into fewer, larger enterprises. For example, between 1967 and 1987 the proportion of cereal output grown on holdings with more than 50ha of cereals rose from 60% to 74%, and milk from herds with more than 60 cows from 37% to 71% (MAFF, 1988a).

Associated with these trends have been changes to the forms of business and land ownership. At least 85% of land assets and 95% of business assets are "family" as opposed to corporately or publicly owned, but the forms family ownership now take are more complex, particularly on the larger, more economically significant units. Moves from sole proprietorships to family partnerships and to family companies are especially evident in those regions and sectors where large-scale, intensive methods are most advanced, to the point of incorporating non-family members (Munton *et al,* 1988). These changes are often made to reduce taxation burdens. They are, therefore, sensitive to legislative change, and can lead to increased instability in business and land holding.

About 90% of farmland is privately owned (Northfield Committee, 1979) and the balance is made up by public, corporate and charitable ownership. The ratio is not altering rapidly. On the other hand, the detailed pattern of *occupancy* is much more dynamic. Beneath the long-standing trend towards increased owner occupation, recent research reveals more composite forms of ownership, such as partnerships and trusts, largely within farm families (Whatmore *et al,* 1990). Moreover, the nature of the traditional relationship between landlords and tenants of agricultural land, as protected by the Agricultural Holdings Acts, also now appears more complex, with share-cropping and sale and leaseback arrangements emerging as new strategies (Marsden, 1986).

C. *Farm incomes and debt*

The escalating costs of the CAP have led to attempts to reduce the financial burden of price support, mainly through a lowering of the real prices paid to farmers. Combined with rising costs, the effect has been to reduce the industry's net income in real terms by nearly one half since 1976. However, this figure provides only one indicator of the industry's economic health and the living conditions of its members (see Hill, 1989). It only refers to income derived from agriculture. It does not include other on- or off-farm earnings by the farm operator; nor should it be confused with the *household* income of farm families. Moreover, because of the varying experiences of farms operating in different sectors of the agricultural economy, income trends vary regionally and significantly from year to year.

Perhaps the most important development in the 1970s was the growth in the proportionate and absolute cost of land and fixed investment, while in the 1980s, falling incomes and rising real interest rates have led to greater borrowing and debt. In the same period that farm incomes fell by 40% (1976-86), farm debt rose from

£2,400m to £8,500m. By 1986, debt liabilities were rising at a rate three times that of farm income, and had resulted in interest repayments absorbing 31% of farm business income.

Given the unusually high value of fixed assets in farming, particularly land and buildings (which represented some 70% of all farm assets in 1988), the industry's liability to asset ratio remains relatively modest. Although it rose during the 1980s as land prices fell in response to the loss of confidence in farming, the clearing banks - the major lenders - recognised that this modest ratio (about 15-18%) gave a false sense of security, failing to capture the real essence of the debt problem. In particular, it says little about the distribution of debt. A more sensitive measure of serious debt is to isolate those farms where total liabilities exceed total farm assets, *excluding* land and buildings. About 12% of all farms in England and Wales were estimated to be in this position in the mid-1980s, although Harrison (1989) regards this as a conservative figure. Between 1979 and 1987, farms in this category have increased from 3% to 14% of all dairy farms; from 3% to 10% in the upland and lowland livestock sectors, and from 3% to 10% in the cropping sector (MAFF 1988b). There is some suggestion of a rise in farmland values at the end of the 1980s, but primarily as a result of non-farming considerations (Johnson, 1990).

Faced with declining farm incomes and rising debts, farming *households* have increasingly pursued a number of strategies to supplement and diversify both business and household income. These strategies have been implemented for a variety of reasons but usually in order to allow the family to remain on the land or, in the case of the larger farm business, to invest profits in activities which represent a higher or more secure return to capital and/or labour.

D. *Alternative livelihood strategies*

In the UK, approximately 23% of farmers acquire additional incomes from other gainful activities than farming itself. While this proportion is considerably lower than in other EC countries (such as West Germany 43%; Italy 30%), it underestimates the significance of non-farm income to the livelihoods of farm families by failing to take account of the income earned by household members other than the farm principal. About 75% of farmers with second incomes earn their non-farming income as proprietors of additional businesses rather than from paid employment. Part-time farms are distributed throughout the size spectrum although they are concentrated amongst small farms where earnings from the farm business itself are lowest. The regional distribution of part-time farming also depends in part on the greater opportunities afforded by the densely populated and relatively affluent south, both for farming families to diversify and for non-farmers to reside on farms. But whatever its particular form, part-time farming should be viewed as an enduring characteristic of agricultural restructuring (Marsden *et al,* 1986).

The contributions of spouses to overall household income is highly significant. With farmers' spouses included, 31% of farm families in England and Wales are recorded as having a gainful activity other than farming. A further 8% have other family members in paid work but the extent of the overlap is unknown (Gasson, 1988). Women in particular are participating in diversification, turning their domestic household work skills into income-generating enterprises. These include providing bed and breakfast and other tourist services, making "home-made" produce which adds value to products for sale at the farm-gate, and dealing directly with specialist sectors of the high-quality food market.

iii. Conclusions and prospects

This report highlights the social interests and economic imperatives affecting changes observed in agriculture as well as some of the responses that the farming community has made to them. One of the most important issues is the inadequacy of many of the stereotypes held of the farming community by a public and media increasingly unsympathetic to it. For example, while farmers have become the scapegoats for food surpluses and environmental degradation in the countryside, the systems of production they have practised are not all of their own making and far from being in the interests of all sectors of the farming community.

The social consequences of industrialisation are identified most clearly by the increasing differences amongst farm businesses. On the one hand are a small elite who are closely tied into the agro-food system and manage a significant proportion of the land. They have maintained the most beneficial terms by adopting some of the characteristics of the corporate interests in the wider food chain with whom they deal regularly. On the other are the majority of farmers who are either tied into the technological treadmill on increasingly unfavourable terms, or are marginalised from commercial agricultural production because of the limited scale of their operations.

While it seems clear that policy support for the industrialisation of farming will slacken, in Britain this change is primarily motivated by a drive to reduce public expenditure. But unless such a reduction in total farm support is also more effectively distributed it will have little beneficial impact on the social and environmental problems which the existing system has created. Indeed, there is a risk of augmenting the treadmill effect in some areas, further concentrating output and income. This might extend the problems of falling incomes and rising debt over a wider range of farm businesses and households, as well as to other groups in the food chain. The aftermath of the introduction of milk quotas provides a case in point. Through the market in quota, production has tended to become more concentrated on a smaller number of larger dairy units. But the most serious effect has been felt among ancillary workers (as in creameries) who lost their jobs but without any of the compensation allocated to dairy farmers who voluntarily gave up quota (Cox *et al*, 1990).

The future outlook for farming seems set to continue in two main directions. First, there will be further intensification of production characterised by the kinds of social changes in the composition of the workforce and business-ownership of farming previously noted. Second, a diversification of economic activity amongst those either marginalised from the agricultural production process or sufficiently well off to be able to make the choice not to participate in it. This latter route may sustain more of the younger generation of farming families on the land, even if farming no longer supplies the majority of their income. The gap between these two very different groups within the farming community seems likely to widen and to bring with it new alliances between them and others with vested interests in the countryside, including those who do not earn their living from it.

Partly as a consequence of its own success, the farming population is now much less in control of its own destiny. Forced to be more dependent upon other parts of the food system and placed in an increasingly reactive position vis-a-vis Brussels, its strongly-held independence has dwindled. However stable their livelihoods seemed to be a decade ago, farmers are now facing mounting pressure in at least two directions, from a reformulated state policy which promulgates extensification, diversification and environmental regulation, and from an agro-industrial complex still largely promoting intensification and renewed rounds of technological change. In addition to this, and external to the farming industry itself, the deregulatory mechanisms being implemented by government, not least in attempting to modify the land-use planning system, are encouraging non-agricultural, private sector investment in the countryside. The traditional justifications and priorities associated with the protection of agricultural land are being progressively weakened by the notion of "surplus" agricultural land supply and a rising *demand* for other land uses (eg leisure facilities, conservation schemes, amenity woodland, residential and industrial development). The potential supply of "surplus" agricultural land and the associated (mainly urban-based) demands for it are, however, uneven and largely dependent on the vagaries of local labour market conditions.

Nevertheless, whatever the locally specific outcomes of this new set of conditions, it is likely that farmers' standing in the rest of the rural community will suffer as the justifications for, and legitimacy of, intensive agricultural production weakens. Farmers' attempts to maintain incomes through half-hearted diversification and set-aside schemes, or more particularly, the development of farm buildings and associated farm infrastructure, will do little to endear them to an increasingly socially heterogeneous village population. New alliances and conflicts will typify rural communities in the 1990s as the influence of traditional landowning and agricultural interests decline. After forty years when most of us have assumed the priorities of agricultural expansion, the rural community, and society at large, now face an agriculture in retreat.

Footnotes

1. This is not to underplay the significant differences that exist between the dietary composition of food consumed by different income groups.
2. Holdings are not the same as farms. They represent units for which an Agricultural Census form has been returned. Harrison's (1975) research suggests that the number of farm businesses approximates to 90% of the number of holdings returned in the Agricultural Census.

References

Ball, R, (1987a), Intermittent labour forms in UK agriculture: some implications for rural areas, *Journal of Rural Studies*, 3/2: 133-50.

Ball, R, (1987b), Agricultural contractors: some survey findings, *Journal of Agricultural Economics*, 38/1: 481-7.

Bowler, I (1985), *Agriculture under the Common Agricultural Policy*, University of Manchester Press, Manchester.

Cox, G, Lowe, P and Winter, M, (1990), The political management of the dairy sector in England and Wales, Chapter 4 in Marsden, T K and Little, J (eds), *Perspectives in the Food System*, Gower, London.

Craig, G, Jollans, J and Korbey, A (1986), *The Case for Agriculture: an independent assessment*, CAS Report No. 10, University of Reading.

Errington, A, (1985), The changing structure of the agricultural and horticultural workforce, *Agricultural Manpower*, 11/2: 21-28.

Errington, A (1987), *Rural Employment Trends and Issues in Market Industrialised Countries*, Report for the International Labour Office, Mimeo.

Errington, A and Harrison, L (1990), Employment in the food system, Chapter 5 in Marsden, T K and Little, J (eds), *Cultural Perspectives in the Food System*, Gower, London.

Gasson, R, (1988), *The Economics of Part-time Farming*, Longman, London.

Goodman, D and Redclift, M, (1989), *The International Farm Crisis*, Macmillan, London.

Goodman, D, Sorj, B and Wilkinson, J, (1987), *From Farming to Biotechnology*, Basil Blackwell, Oxford.

Grigg, D, (1987), Farm size in England and Wales from early Victorian times to the present, *Agricultural History Review*, 35: 179-89.

Harrison, A, (1975), *Farmers and Farm Businesses in England*, Department of Agricultural Economics and Management, Misc. Study No. 62, University of Reading.

Harrison, A, (1989), *The Changing Financial Structure of Farming*, CAS Report No. 13, University of Reading.

Harvey, D, (1987), *The Future of the Agricultural and Food System*, EPARD, Vol. 1, University of Reading.

Hill, B, (1989), *Farm Incomes, Wealth and Agricultural Policy*, Avebury, Aldershot.

Johnson, C, (1990), Farmland as a business asset, *Journal of Agricultural Economics*, 41/2, 135-48.

MAFF, (1988a), *Annual Review of Agriculture*, Cm. 299, HMSO, London.

MAFF, (1988b), *Farm Incomes in the United Kingdom: 1988 Edition*, HMSO, London.

Marsden, T K, (1986), Property-state relations in the 1980s: an examination of landlord-tenant legislation in British agriculture in Cox, G, Lowe, P and Winter, M (eds), *Agriculture: People and Policies*, 126-46, George Allen and Unwin, London.

Marsden, T K, Whatmore, S J, Munton, R J C, and Little, J K, (1986), The restructuring process and economic centrality in capitalist agriculture, *Journal of Rural Studies*, 2/4: 271-80.

Munton, R J C, Whatmore, S J, and Marsden, T K, (1988), Reconsidering urban-fringe agriculture: a longitudinal analysis of capital restructuring on farms in the Metropolitan Green Belt, *Transactions of the Institute of British Geographers*, 13/3: 324-36.

Munton, R J C, Marsden, T K, and Whatmore, S J, (1990), Technological change in a period of agricultural adjustment, in Lowe, P, Marsden, T K, and Winter, M (eds), *Technological Change in the Rural Environment*, Fulton, London.

Northfield Committee, (1979), *Report into the Acquisition and Occupancy of Agricultural Land*, Cmnd. 7599, HMSO, London.

Ward, N, (forthcoming), The British food system, *Food Policy*, November 1990.

Whatmore, S J, Munton, R J C, and Marsden, T K, (1990), The rural restructuring process: emerging divisions of agricultural property rights, *Regional Studies*, 24.

Appendix F

Beyond Farming: Economic Change in Rural Areas of the United Kingdom by Dr Graham Gudgin (Northern Ireland Economic Research Centre)

1. Introduction

The UK in the twentieth century is undergoing an unravelling of the nineteenth-century concentration of industry and population into cities. Decentralisation from the cities to the rural areas which began before the turn of the century, has been greatly accelerated in the second half of the century by improvements in motor transport, roads, electricity and telecommunications. These improvements fundamentally have shifted the balance of locational advantage away from urban nodes. Postwar planning restrictions on urban sprawl gave a further impetus to the resurgence of small towns and rural areas. The urban-rural shift as it is called is now well advanced and eventually most of manufacturing industry will be located in small towns and rural areas. Large cities are returning to their older, pre-industrial, function of providing services rather than goods. The aim of this paper is to describe the progress of the urban-rural shift over recent decades, and to provide a brief explanation of how and why it happens.

2. Definition of rural areas

There is no standard definition of rural areas, and the difficulty of deciding what constitutes 'urban' and 'rural' has been more difficult since the abolition of rural districts as administrative units in 1974. For the analysis below, rural areas have been arbitrarily defined first as local authority districts in which all settlements had fewer than 35,000 people in 1971. On its own this definition would be misleading since two types of area not truly rural would be included. The first are coalfield areas, with an urban character but in scattered settlements. The second are suburban areas where several local authorities cover what is essentially a single urban agglomeration. Both coalfield and small suburban areas have been excluded from the definition.

The remaining rural areas comprise 175 out of the total of 484 local authority districts in Great Britain and Northern Ireland. They include small market towns as well as villages and isolated settlements, and encompass areas well within commuting range of major cities as well as more purely agricultural areas and remote uplands. These areas contained close to three million employees in 1987 or 15 per cent of the total employment of the United Kingdom. The rural areas as defined here are those areas which might thus be considered to be wholly rural. Substantial areas of countryside are excluded, ie, rural areas which lie within local authority districts containing settlements of more than 35,000 people. Rural areas as defined here include 53 per cent of those employed in agriculture, forestry or fishing. A further third of agricultural employment is in districts with towns of 35-100,000 people. These latter districts are classified as 'small towns' in this report.

A number of urban categories are also included in some of the following tables to demonstrate the contrasts within the urban-rural shift. In each case the definition is determined by the size of the largest settlement within a local authority district or group of districts. Small towns have populations up to 100,000 and large towns have between 100,000 and 250,000 people. Free standing cities include all larger cities excepting London and the officially designated conurbations (West Midlands, Manchester, Merseyside, West Yorkshire, Tyne and Wear, and Clydeside).

The regional distribution of rural areas as defined here is shown in Table 1. Within England two thirds of the rural areas (measured in terms of employment) are in the three southern regions, South East, South West and East Anglia. In contrast only 14 per cent of rural employment in England lies within the most northerly regions, each of which is heavily urban. Total employment in English rural areas in 1987 was 2.4 million with a further 285 thousand in Wales, 420 thousand in Scotland, and 206 thousand in Northern Ireland.

In this and following sections the structure and performance of rural economies is described in terms of employment. The focus is on rural economies rather than rural dwellers. The location of employment is the workplace rather than residence. The jobs of commuters who live in rural areas but who work in towns and cities with populations of over 35,000 are thus excluded from the rural totals. No distinction is made between full-time and part-time employment. It should be borne in mind, however, that part-time working is important in some sectors, particularly within the private services.

3. The nature of rural economies

The most striking aspect of the economies of rural areas as defined in this report is how few people work directly in agriculture, forestry or fishing. Out of a total employment of a little over 3 million in 1987 only 189 thousand were employed in these primary sectors (Table 2). These figures understate the position since they exclude the self-employed who form a large proportion of all those occupied in farming and fishing. No direct figures exist for the self-employed in rural areas; however, estimates have been calculated (Table 3) using the assumption that the national ratio of self-employed to employed in each sector applies to rural areas. Even including the self-employed those occupied in agriculture, forestry and fishing still comprise less than one-tenth of the total working population. In the more remote rural areas this proportion can of course become much greater, but the total numbers of people living in such remote areas is relatively small.

The major sources of employment in rural areas as defined here are the same as those in urban areas. Almost two-thirds of employees work in the service sectors. Of these most are in the private services, a wide ranging sector including retail and wholesale distribution, hotels and catering, finance, business and professional services and a range of entertainment, leisure, and miscellaneous services. 'Transport and communication' is also included making the title 'private services' not wholly accurate since British Rail and the Post Office are both included.

Government services include health and education as well as public administration in both local and central government. Again the definition is not precise since private education and health are included. With one in five of all employees in government services, the rural areas have a similar proportion to that in the country as a whole. Two important aspects of government employment are stability, and uniformity in wage levels. Jobs are less vulnerable to recession and redundancy and add stability to local economies. Many public occupations are paid on national scales and hence the presence of a substantial public sector raises average incomes especially in remote rural areas where incomes in other sectors may be below the national average.

After the private services the second most important sector in rural areas is manufacturing which, as outlined in the next section, has grown steadily in importance in rural areas. A quarter of all employment is now in manufacturing (Table 2), a proportion only slightly lower than the national average. It is a little known fact that manufacturing is now as important a component of rural economies as it is of the economies of Britain's large cities. The range of manufacturing activities is very diverse. Few industries can now be considered exclusively urban. Only the largest highly integrated assembly activities require concentrations of labour which might be difficult to assemble in rural areas. The few remaining shipyards, and the major motor car, aircraft and locomotive assembly works are still predominantly urban activities. However, rising labour productivity and the associated falling requirements for huge concentration of labour will steadily make rural locations feasible for all manufacturing industry.

The employment structure of rural areas is surprisingly similar to that of the UK as a whole. Rural areas have close to 14 per cent of national employment both in total and in most individual sectors as defined in Table 2. Only in mining and quarrying is the proportion markedly lower, and in this case only because the rural areas are defined to exclude the major coalfields.

Within the range of economic activities, those capable of bringing income in from outside the individual rural area are of particular importance. These activities, sometimes termed 'basic' activities, include agriculture, forestry, fishing, mining and quarrying, and manufacturing. These activities underpin economic growth in the sense that overall growth or decline depends on the performance of these sectors in 'exporting' goods and services to other areas in return for the income needed to purchase 'imports'. Income earned in these activities subsequently supports those service sector activities which depend on local purchasing power.

Within private services a number of activities are potentially of more than local importance either because they can be traded outside the local area or because they support other activities which are traded in this way. One significant group of activities in this category are the so-called 'producer services'. These include parts of banking, insurance, finance, accountancy and similar professional services to industry and commerce. Such activities also serve consumer markets, but official statistics do not allow us to differentiate internationally or nationally oriented producer services (as in the City of London) from the branch banks and other locally oriented financial services. Using a more restricted definition of rural areas than that employed in this report, Gillespie and Green (1987) showed that in 1981 employment in producer services was under-represented in rural areas in Great Britain, especially in the northern half of the country. The dominance of London in these activities means that most other areas have a low proportion of total employment in producer services relative to the national average. Leaving London aside what emerges is a strong north-south divide. Southern areas have a proportion of employment in producer services only slightly below the national average. In the northern half of Britain the proportion is only two thirds of the national average. Within each half of the country rural areas appear to have similar proportions of producer service employment to urban areas.

In the same way as most private services depend on local purchasing power most government services are dependent on local needs, although in this case there is considerable scope for one area to subsidise another through fiscal transfers. The broad evidence suggests that government services are not in general subsidised by urban tax-payers although it would be impossible to test this conclusion rigorously. Rural areas do however have employment in government services in proportion to their total employment (Table 2). It is however likely to be true that the level of public services in some remote rural areas and in some peripheral regions is higher than could be supported by locally raised fiscal resources. This is certainly true for instance in Northern Ireland and is most likely also the case within Scotland.

4. Economic change in the 1970s and 1980s

The national economy has undergone profound changes in recent decades and in particular has grown significantly less rapidly since the oil-price shock of 1973 than in the decades prior to 1973. Slower growth in the national economy has meant that sectors with strong upward trends in labour productivity have shed large numbers of jobs. These include both agriculture and most industrial sectors (Table 4). Employment growth has been confined to the service sectors both public and private. These changes have affected different localities to various degrees but underlying the mosaic of change has been a general shift of economic activity and people to rural areas.

The urban-rural shift in employment is evident (Table 5). As a general rule the less urban an area the more it has gained jobs. The general economic trend of falling employment 1971-87 has been compounded in the cities by a shift of jobs to smaller towns and rural areas. Within the rural areas, however, national decline in employment has been offset by urban-rural redistribution to such an extent that these areas have gained substantial numbers of jobs. The latest employment figures for rural areas are available for 1987. Taking the period 1971-87, rural areas gained 496 thousand jobs (19.2 per cent). Over the same period the national experience was a loss of 318 thousand jobs (1.5 per cent). The rural areas were the only part of the UK to experience significant employment gains over this period of national employment decline.

Employment in rural areas has continued to grow at a relatively steady rate of around one per cent per annum through a range of contrasting economic circumstances. This included both the deepest national recession in at least half a century, in the early 1980s, and the longest sustained postwar economic boom, in the period since 1983.

National trends in employment change by sector have been reflected within the rural areas. The only sectors to have increased their employment nationally between 1971 and 1987 have been government services and private services. This has also been true within rural areas. The rise in service jobs in rural areas in this period was 672 thousand (Table 6). The remaining sectors taken together lost 144 thousand jobs.

The redistribution of economic activity out of the cities and into rural areas is clear when the growth of employment in each rural sector is compared with the national growth in that sector (Table 7). Rural areas have gained the greatest share of national activity in manufacturing. Manufacturing employment in rural areas grew 29 per cent faster than the national average. In 1971, 9.5 per cent of national manufacturing employment was in rural areas. By 1987 this had risen to 14.9 per cent. Rural areas also performed better than average in every other sector except agriculture where the difference was very slight.

It is the redistribution of tradable activities (mainly manufacturing) into rural areas that has led to a similar redistribution of non-tradable activities. The growth of employment within private services has been much faster in rural areas than in the United Kingdom as a whole (Table 7). Also, employment in the gas, electricity and water industries has also risen more rapidly. While the same is true of construction, in this sector the advantage of rural areas is lower. Employment in government services has grown less rapidly in the rural areas than in the UK as a whole. This suggests that the provision of public services in rural areas is lagging behind the increase of people and jobs. While this suggestion is plausible, more direct evidence is needed to prove it.

Other factors than lagging service provision may also influence the distribution of employment in government services. A major reorganisation of local government occurred in 1974 involving the switching of some administration between the county and district tiers. Since county council headquarters are often in towns, rather than rural areas as defined here, the reorganisation may have had some redistributive effects between urban and rural areas. It does however seem probable that at least some lag has occurred in the provision of additional public services in growing rural areas. In the period 1981-1987 which involved no reorganisation there was little difference between urban and rural areas in the growth of employment in government services. Yet in this period private sector jobs and people continued to move from urban areas into rural areas.

The north-south divide in employment prospects has been a marked feature of regional economic change in recent years. Although north-south contrasts have affected large cities and coalfields most strongly, rural areas have not been immune. Over the whole period 1971-1987 rural areas in the three southern regions, together with those in Yorkshire-Humberside, have grown most rapidly (Table 8). Rural areas elsewhere have grown at only half the national rate. However, rural areas in all regions have performed much better than cities and towns in the same region. The north-south contrast within the rural areas has been more marked in the 1980s than in the 1970s although the three southern regions performed best in both periods.

One reason for the better performance of southern rural areas is the greater importance of financial and business services in southern rural areas compared with rural areas further north. The national boom in this sector has helped southern areas most. Conversely rapid growth in government services in the 1970s was directed more towards areas of higher unemployment in the north of England, Scotland and Wales, than towards the south. Stagnation in government employment during the 1980s has removed one source of growth from the northern areas. Southern rural areas are also likely to have gained from the relative prosperity of southern towns. The gap in prosperity between north and south has led to large migration flows from north to south. In the 1980s over 250,000 more people of working age have migrated into the three southern regions than have left it. Even when people have moved to urban jobs many have come to live in rural areas. These have increased local demand for services in southern rural areas.

5. The urban-rural shift in manufacturing
The fact that economic growth has been faster in rural areas than in nearby urban areas has been largely due to the shift of manufacturing industry out of urban areas and into rural areas. Manufacturing jobs have decentralised rapidly out of cities in recent decades. This in turn has attracted population movements, and hence shifts in service sector jobs serving the rising rural population. Any explanation of the overall urban-rural shift thus needs to account primarily for the manufacturing shift.

Rural manufacturing employment grew rapidly between 1960 and 1974, increasing by over 130,000 jobs alone between 1967 and 1974. Thereafter the growth faltered (Table 9). The number of jobs slipped a little between 1974 and 1978, and fell substantially during the recession at the beginning of the 1980s. Only since 1984 has any small recovery occurred. Despite the recessionary losses, rural manufacturing employment in 1987 was still significantly higher than in 1960, and the rural areas' share of the national stock of manufacturing jobs increased steadily throughout the period.

The urban-rural contrast in manufacturing employment change is now well documented (2,4,9). Table 10, which shows employment change in different types of area, emphasises the scale of the contrast and illustrates the point that the growth in rural areas is in fact part of a wider shift in industrial location. As a general rule, the larger the settlement the greater the rate of decline in manufacturing employment. Rural areas, at one extreme of the urban hierarchy, have experienced the most favourable growth. The effect over a long period has been to modify substantially the industrial geography of Britain. For example, in 1960 rural areas in aggregate had only two manufacturing jobs for every five in London, but by 1987 rural manufacturing employment exceeded that in London by 50 per cent.

This shift of industrial jobs to rural areas has been largely unplanned. Most of the New Towns are in districts we have classed as' small towns' and their growth has therefore not contributed to trends in rural areas as defined here. Several Expanded Towns fall within rural districts, particularly in the South East and East Anglia, and their planned growth has boosted industrial employment, though it has been a small component of the overall growth in rural areas. The shift has been more than just short-distance relocation of firms out of cities to neighbouring rural areas. In fact, growth actually appears to have been fastest in more remote rural areas. Between 1960 and 1987 manufacturing employment in rural areas within 40 km of a conurbation increased by four per cent: it increased by 15 per cent in rural areas 40-80 km from a conurbation and by 38 per cent in areas more than 80 km away (6).

In all regions rural manufacturing trends have been better than the national average and, with the minor exception of the North West, rural areas in all regions experienced an absolute increase in manufacturing employment between 1960 and 1987. There are however some important regional differences, and the average growth in southern

373

England (the Midlands, East Anglia, the South East and South West) was considerably greater than the average growth in the rest of Great Britain. In the absence of regional policy the disparity would probably have been larger since many rural areas outside southern England have had assisted area status. Table 11 shows the changing pace of rural industrial expansion. The growth prior to 1974 and the subsequent decline, shown in the first part of the table, has already been noted. The second part of the table shows the employment change relative to the national average. This is measured as the difference between the change in manufacturing employment in rural areas and the change which would have occurred if their manufacturing employment had grown or declined at the national rate. It reveals uninterrupted relative growth in rural areas. During the late 1960s and early 1970s their manufacturing employment increased by over 24,000 jobs a year relative to the national average, markedly more than in earlier or later years. After 1978 the absolute loss of manufacturing jobs in rural areas masked a modest resurgence in their relative growth.

6. Causes of the urban-rural shift in manufacturing

One of the most surprising aspects of the shift of manufacturing to rural areas is that most of the shift is *not* due to the relocation of companies. Far more important is the fact that existing rural factories grow faster than their urban counterparts. Even if the opening of new branch plants is added to complete relocations of companies, the number of jobs involved still accounts for only a quarter to a third of the urban-rural difference in growth (2). It is also largely true that rural gains in manufacturing have little to do with the mix of industries in each area (1, 2, 7, 10).

The most plausible explanation of the urban-rural shift in manufacturing is that it is the outcome of two national economic trends:

(i) Rising capital intensity of industry leads to a reduction in the number of employees on any given area of factory floorspace. In 1964 there were on average 36 workers per thousand square metres of floorspace. By 1982 this had fallen to 21. The density of employees falls on average by around two per cent a year. This process affects existing factory floorspace in all areas, rural as well as urban.

(ii) Any expansion in industrial output requires an increase in the volume of factory floorspace. Most of this new floorspace is built outside the major cities. Rural areas receive a disproportionate share of new floorspace.

Increases in industrial output vary from year to year but average at around two per cent per annum. This leads to a long-term rise in the requirements for factory space of around one per cent per annum. In the cities planning constraints and competition from other land users prevent any significant increase in factory floorspace. Most of the expansion is thus located on the periphery of smaller towns or in rural areas. Between 1967 and 1982 rural areas increased their stock of factory floorspace by 50 per cent, while in the large cities the increase was negligible.

The joint result of these two processes is that manufacturing employment declines steadily in all locations unless new floorspace can be constructed to offset the losses caused by steadily rising output per employee. Only in the rural areas has the availability of industrial land been sufficient to lead to an actual rise in manufacturing jobs. At the other extreme in a large city like London, where there is no expansion in overall industrial floorspace, employment falls at the same rate as output per employee rises.

This explanation accounts for the apparent paradox that the shift of jobs out of the cities and into rural areas proceeds most rapidly in periods of high growth and high investment. For example, in the boom conditions of the period 1983-1989, London lost *over a quarter* of its entire manufacturing base. This is exactly as the theory would predict since high growth leads to rapid investment which in turn gives rising output per employee. With no possibility of increases in factory floorspace in London, manufacturing employment declines rapidly. The national expansion is instead located in less urbanised and rural areas. In the period 1973-89 Wales was the main beneficiary and manufacturing employment rose 17 per cent in only six years. Conversely in periods of national recession, urban areas suffer less disadvantage, and rural areas fare less well relative to the cities.

This theory of rural industrial development still attracts some controversy. Partly this is because it concentrates on a single issue, land availability, and partly it is because it does not emphasise cost factors including the cost of land or labour. Although costs can be important there is no strong or consistent pattern. Cities with relatively low land or labour costs still lose jobs to small towns and rural areas.

Finally, it should be stressed that the transfer of jobs occurs in complicated ways. It has already been stressed that the building of new factories by relocating firms is only a small part of the process. More important are differences in the rate of expansion of already existing firms. Rural firms usually have the space to build extra floorspace onto existing factories. Urban firms often have highly constrained premises hemmed in by existing development. If the latter consists of roads, railways, canals, schools, cemeteries or the like, it is not available for purchase at almost any price.

For these reasons rural industry has expanded and will continue to expand faster than the national average. The increase of industrial jobs attracts and retains population which brings with it incomes and purchasing power. This in turn stimulates demand for private services. The larger population leads eventually to an expanded local public sector. In this way the rural economies are quietly and steadily becoming revitalised. The process will one day come to an end, but not for several decades yet.

7. Unemployment in rural areas

The fact that rural areas have performed well in terms of employment growth does not necessarily mean that unemployment will be below average. Unemployment levels also depend on the degree to which commuting and migration compensate for tightness or slackness in the labour market. In general unemployment in rural areas has been below that in the more urbanised parts of the same region. This is true for instance in the Midlands and North of England. In the South East (where most of the major commuter districts are excluded) and East Anglia, rural unemployment rates are close to the regional averages. Throughout England, with the exception of Devon and Cornwall, it appears that the movement of people into rural areas has generally *not* outstripped the in-movement of jobs to such an extent that unemployment has risen above the regional average.

In contrast Wales, Scotland and the south of England all have unemployment rates in rural areas which are higher than the regional averages. In the South West high rural unemployment is largely confined to Devon and Cornwall. The common factor linking rural Wales, rural Scotland and Devon and Cornwall is environmental attractiveness. It appears that these areas tend to attract more immigrants than are warranted by the growth of jobs and high unemployment results.

8. Conclusion

Rural areas are in the midst of a process of reindustrialisation which is likely to last well into the next century. Manufacturing industry is steadily decentralising out of cities into small towns and rural areas. This in turn has led to population shifts and thus to relatively rapid increases in both the public and private service sectors in rural areas. Rural areas have not been immune from wider economic trends, including an absolute fall in manufacturing jobs and rising unemployment. However, the steady shift of economic activity into rural areas has meant that rural areas have escaped the worst impact of recession, and gain disproportionately in times of economic recovery. Partly as a result, unemployment tends to be lower in rural areas than in urban areas. The main exception to this rule is in environmentally attractive areas of South Western England, Wales and Scotland where an influx of people boosts unemployment rates.

References

1. Danson, M W, Lever, W F & Malcolm, J, 1980. The inner city employment problem in Great Britain, 1952-76: a shift share approach. *Urban Studies.* 17, 193-210.
2. Fothergill, S, & Gudgin, G, 1982. *Unequal growth: urban and regional employment*.

change in the UK. (Heinemann Education Books, London).

3. Fothergill, S, Kitson, M & Monk, S, 1983. The impact of the new and expanded town programmes on industrial location in Britain 1960-78. *Regional Studies*. 17, 251-260.

4. Fothergill, S, Kitson, M & Monk, S, 1985. *Urban Industrial Change*. DOE Inner Cities Research Programme. 11.

5. Fothergill, S, Gudgin, G, Kitson, M & Monk, S, 1984. *Scottish Journal of Political Economy*. 31, 72-91.

6. Fothergill, S, Gudgin, G, Kitson, M & Monk, S, 1985. Rural Industrialisation Trends and Causes in Healey and Ilbery *Industrialisation of the Countryside*. Geo Books.

7. Keeble, D, 1976. *Industrial location and planning in the United Kingdom*. (Methuen, London).

8. Keeble, D, 1980. *Industrial decline, regional policy and the urban-rural manufacturing shift in the United Kingdom*. Environment and Planning A. 12, 945-962.

9. Lonsdale, R, 1985. The Case of the USA in Healey and Ilbery (eds). *Industrialisation of the Countryside*. Geo Books.

10. Moore, B C, Rhodes, J & Tyler, 1986. *The Effects of Government Economic Policy*. HMSO.

11. Gillespie, A E and Green A E. The Changing Geography of Produce Service Employment in Britain. *Regional Studies*. 21, 379-411.

Table 1: Rural areas in the United Kingdom 1987

Region	No of Rural Districts	Total Employment (000s)	% of Region's Empl. in Rural Areas 1987
South East	21	699.5	9.5
East Anglia	14	291.1	39.4
South West	29	607.5	37.3
East Midlands	14	262.1	17.4
West Midlands	11	177.3	8.9
North West	2	61.5	2.6
Yorkshire-Humberside	9	111.8	6.3
North	9	156.7	14.6
Wales	18	284.8	30.8
Scotland	31	419.7	22.3
Northern Ireland	17	205.9	40.6
United Kingdom	175	3277.9	15.2

Source: Department of Employment, NOMIS

Table 2: Employment in rural areas in the UK 1987

Sector	Rural Areas		% of UK total in each sector
	(000s)	**(%)**	
Agriculture, forestry & fishing	188.5	5.8	54.2
Mining and quarrying	14.7	0.4	7.3
Manufacturing	775.7	23.7	14.9
Construction	172.3	5.3	16.8
Gas, electricity water	48.8	1.5	15.9
Private services	1346.2	41.1	13.5
Government services	731.7	22.3	15.4
Total	3277.9	100.0	15.1

Source: Department of Employment, NOMIS

Table 3: Estimated self-employed in rural areas 1987

Sector	(000s)	(%)
Agriculture, forestry, fishing	147.7	34.0
Mining and quarrying	—	—
Manufacturing	41.7	9.6
Construction	94.9	21.8
Gas, electricity, water	—	—
Private services	150.6	34.7
Government services	—	—
Total	434.5	100.0

Source: Department of Employment, NOMIS

Table 4: Employment change in the UK by sector 1971-87

Sector	(000s)	(%)
Agriculture, forestry, fishing	− 100.5	− 22.4
Mining and quarrying	− 197.0	− 49.4
Manufacturing	− 2881.8	− 35.6
Construction	− 184.9	− 15.3
Gas, electricity, water	− 86.6	− 22.1
Private services	2122.2	27.1
Government services	1010.7	27.1
Total	− 317.9	− 1.4

Source: Department of Employment, NOMIS

Table 5: Employment change in the UK by urban-rural category 1971-87

	1971-81 %	1981-87 %	1971-87 %
London	− 10.5	− 0.2	− 10.6
Conurbations	− 12.2	− 4.8	− 16.4
Free standing cities	− 4.0	− 2.4	− 6.3
Large towns	3.1	3.1	6.3
Small towns	3.4	3.5	7.0
Rural areas	11.4	7.0	19.2
United Kingdom	− 2.4	1.0	− 1.5

Source: Department of Employment, NOMIS

Table 6: Employment change in UK rural areas by sector 1971-87

	(000)	(%)
Agriculture, forestry, fishing	− 57.3	− 23.3
Mining and quarrying	− 12.5	− 46.0
Manufacturing	− 56.1	− 6.7
Construction	− 16.2	− 8.6
Gas, electricity, water	− 2.2	− 4.3
Private services (1)	477.3	54.9
Government services	194.5	36.2
Total	527.5	19.2

Source: Department of Employment, NOMIS

Note: (1) Includes public sector services in transport and communication.

Table 7: Employment change in rural areas relative to the UK (1971-87)

	(%)
Agriculture, forestry, fishing	− 0.8
Mining and quarrying	3.4
Manufacturing	28.9
Construction	6.7
Gas, electricity, water	17.8
Private services	27.8
Government services	9.1
Total	17.8

Source: Department of Employment, NOMIS

Table 8: Total employment change in rural areas by region

Regions	1971-81 %	1981-87 %	1971-87 %
South East	17.6	14.6	34.7
East Anglia	11.7	9.5	22.3
South West	11.9	6.9	19.6
East Midlands	8.3	4.0	12.7
West Midlands	9.0	6.1	15.6
North West	2.2	17.9	20.5
Yorkshire-Humberside	12.8	10.3	24.4
North	6.0	5.0	11.4
Wales	7.7	3.7	11.7
Scotland	11.8	− 3.4	8.0
Northern Ireland	8.5	6.1	15.2
United Kingdom	11.4	6.8	19.0

Source: Department of Employment, NOMIS

Table 9: Manufacturing employment in GB rural areas 1960-87

	(1960 = 100)	% of GB Total
1960	100.	6.6
1967	115.5	7.4
1974	140.6	9.6
1978	138.1	10.2
1981	124.3	11.1
1984	118.6	12.0
1987	120.3	14.3

Source: Department of Employment

NB: Definition of rural areas differs slightly from that in previous tables.

Table 10: The urban-rural contrast in manufacturing employment change Great Britain 1960-87

	Change in number of manufacturing jobs (000s)	as % 1960
Rural areas	104.0	19.7
Small towns	− 136.0	− 8.3
Large towns	− 275.0	− 29.9
Free standing cities	− 551.0	− 41.4
Conurbations	− 1272.0	− 55.7
London	− 882.0	− 61.5
Great Britain	− 3012.0	− 37.5

Source: Department of Employment

Table 11: Manufacturing employment change in UK rural areas

	1960-67	67-74	74-78	78-81	81-84	84-87
Actual Change (000s)	11.7	19.0	−6.2	−19.8	−11.2	3.2
%	(2.2)	(3.1)	(−0.7)	(−2.4)	(−1.4)	(0.4)
Relative to UK (000s)	10.3	24.1	16.3	19.1	18.8	13.6
%	(2.0)	(4.0)	(2.0)	(2.6)	(2.6)	(1.8)

Source: Department of Employment, NOMIS

Note: Northern Ireland is excluded prior to 1974.

Appendix G

The Governance of Rural England by Professor Ken Young and Dr Liz Mills (Institute of Local Government Studies, University of Birmingham)

1. Introduction

This paper is concerned with a neglected topic, that of local government in rural England. Its principal concern is with the twin problems of rural governance: establishing a framework for the effective representation of the interests of people who live in rural England; and defining a role for representative institutions within the growing network of statutory and non-statutory, local and national organisations all of which have a part to play in tackling rural problems.

2. Rural local government today

The origins of the system
The structure of local self-government in rural England is essentially that established in the closing decades of the last century. Representative government came late to the rural areas, more than fifty years having elapsed between the reform of the municipal corporations in 1835 and the creation of county councils in 1889. Radical reformers entertained high hopes of county reform leading to the political emancipation of the rural people. But, as has been argued elsewhere, there was an equally strong and better-founded expectation that elective self-government would consolidate the rural social order by confirming the gentry in their role as social leaders (Young, 1989).

The first county council elections were hard-fought, with high turnouts and an unexpectedly high proportion of contested seats; many county contests were conducted on clear party lines (Game and Leach, 1989). Thereafter, county politics fell into a period of quiescence, being conducted with little partisanship and with relatively few contested elections throughout the entire period from 1892 until the first elections to the reorganised counties 71 years later. The parties retreated into their respective spheres of influence, acknowledging the status quo and avoiding the cost and uncertainty of electoral contests.

Much the same pattern prevailed for the more local bodies established under the Local Government Act of 1894. At both rural district council and parish council level, the first elections saw a surge of hope and activism, followed by disappointment and withdrawal. The greater political hopes of popular government had attached to the districts and parishes. But from the early decades of the twentieth century, it was the county councils which steadily gained power relative to the more local bodies, and the machinery of community government fell into obscurity.

The impact of party competition
Of the many social, economic and political factors which have worked to transform the nature of local government over the past twenty-five years, none has had so pervasive an influence as the spread of party politics. On the face of it, this appears to be true of rural as well as urban areas, and the reorganisation of local government under the 1972 Act did much to bring about this politicisation.

Faith in the Countryside

At the *county level*, the incorporation of the larger towns into county areas and uncertainty over the ultimate control of the new, socially mixed, counties led both major parties to extend their campaigning and their organisation into rural areas, competing with each other and with the remaining independent candidates (Young, 1986). But in contrast to the situation prevailing in 1889, this was no mere episode, the process of continued politicisation being vividly dubbed 'the nationalisation of local politics'.

The creation of larger *district councils* under the 1972 Act created a similar uncertainty, the tendency being for the practices of the already partisan areas to be extended to the former non-party areas with which they merged. Even at the *parish* level, re-organisation seems to have stimulated the growth of partisanship, with parties looking to parish politics for both issues and candidates capable of being drawn into the ambit of the principal authorities.

The ubiquity of party politics made a considerable impression upon the Widdicombe Committee on the Conduct of Local Authority Business, whose 1986 report accepted that the business of even the smaller and more rural district had come to be conducted on much the same lines as that of the county borough council of twenty years before (Widdicombe, 1986). More recent research (Young and Davies, 1990) suggests that this was an over-interpretation, that the impact of party politics on rural areas is more ambiguous than hitherto believed, and that rural areas retain something of their own distinctiveness.

In the remainder of this paper, frequent reference will be made to 'rural' and to 'largely rural' areas, whose characteristics will be compared with those of 'urban', 'largely urban' and 'mixed' areas. These distinctions refer to *district councils* only, although the broad patterns discussed apply similarly to county councils. The assessment of rurality is made on the basis of proportions of the population living in settlements of fewer than 5,000 persons in 1981.

Party representation and party control

Despite what the Widdicombe Committee called 'a tidal force of politicisation' independent politics persist in rural areas. Although political parties are represented upon almost all local authorities in England (the exceptions all being rural areas) there is an important distinction to be made between party *representation* and party *control*. In over half of the most rural authorities and in 13 per cent of all authorities in England, power and influence over the decision-making process are not exercised through the medium of a political party or parties in majority, minority or coalition control but through some other form of status system. In most cases - and especially in rural areas - this takes the form of an 'inner circle' of senior and respected councillors.

It is also the case that the institution of party has a different meaning in urban and rural areas. In urban areas, and particularly in Labour authorities, the wider party – elected and appointed officials, branch office-holders, delegates and activists – typically play a part, varying in importance, in council business. In rural areas in contrast, even among those authorities which are under party control, the party comprises for practical purposes only those elected councillors who share a common membership.

These urban-rural differences show up strikingly in respect of that quintessential instrument of party government, the election manifesto. Elections are fought on the basis of manifestos in more than three quarters of the urban and largely urban authorities, but in only half of those largely rural, and in no more than a third of those rural authorities which are under party control. Only in urban areas are manifestos used as guidelines for policy and provision made in council procedures for monitoring their implementation.

Turning to the control of council business, and confining the discussion to those authorities which are controlled by a political party, it is notable that only in the most rural districts do governing parties deviate significantly from the long-standing practice of the majority party taking all committee and sub-committee chairmanships and vice-chairmanships, there being a greater willingness in rural areas to share at least the less powerful posts with councillors of other parties or of none.

Similarly, the cohesion and discipline exacted by the party group differs markedly in rural areas from what is widely assumed to be the norm for party control of local councils. In 1989 it was reported that members of the controlling party always vote as a group at council meetings in a third of the two most urban types of authority, while no rural authority reported that this was the practice. More than four out of ten of the more urban authorities reported that majority party members never vote with the opposition in council meetings, with only one in ten rural authorities reporting this to be the case. Councillors are considered to be routinely bound by party group decisions in nine out of ten urban authorities, this practice declining in prevalence along the continuum from urban to rural areas, being virtually unknown in the most rural type of authority. The national figures on these measures indicate that considerable increases in party cohesion and discipline have occurred since 1985, but closer inspection shows that the increases are almost entirely concentrated in urban areas.

So the *presence* of political parties on rural councils does not everywhere amount to *party control;* nor, it seems, does party control in rural areas resemble more than superficially the practices which have become familiar in the larger cities. When due account is also taken of the fact that more than half of the most rural, and a small number of the largely rural authorities are not controlled by political parties, the overall picture is far from one of rural areas engulfed by a wave of politics. Rather, the spirit of independence, in all its senses, appears to survive, and it is apparent that people active in rural political life cherish this tradition.

The council and the public

Rural councillors behave in a distinctly more independent fashion than their urban counterparts, even when they share allegiance to the same national party. They are more likely to be in closer touch with their constituents, to be better-known as individuals within their community, and to be the first port of call for the constituent with a complaint than are urban councillors. In these senses, the representative linkages work better in rural than in urban areas; this, then, is one of the strengths of rural local government.

In other respects, however, rural authorities fall far short of the standards set in more urban areas. Three indicators of the quality of representative government in rural areas are noteworthy: the practice of holding day-time meetings; the publication of information; and the opening of meetings to public questioning.

One of the long-standing issues in rural government has been the propensity of councils at all levels to hold day-time, rather than evening, meetings. In the late nineteenth century this practice was attacked as likely to exclude working people from the opportunities of council membership. This point may well still have some force, but it is amplified by the effective exclusion of members of the public who may wish for whatever reason to attend council and committee meetings. Only a third of the most rural district councils hold their meetings after 5 pm, compared with three quarters of the most urban.

While authorities are now obliged by law to publish more information about their activities and expenditure, many authorities have gone beyond this requirement to provide civic newspapers or information sheets. The rationale is often to inform and to involve, sometimes to foster a more positive view of the authority itself. As many as 70 per cent of the most urban authorities published some form of newspaper or information sheet in 1989, this proportion declining steadily down the urban-rural continuum to a low of 13 per cent in the most rural districts. A very few authorities have gone beyond this form of one-way communication and have introduced a facility for public questioning at council or committee meetings; this novel practice similarly declines through the urban-rural continuum, being almost unknown in the rural authorities.

Councillors and officers

There is one further respect in which rural local government differs from its urban counterpart, and this concerns the relative influence of councillors and officers. This

Faith in the Countryside

issue has attracted considerable attention during the last decade, with more assertive councillors sometimes coming into conflict with intransigent officers. In some instances there have been apparent abuses of member power, and the evidence of friction contributed to a climate of concern that culminated in the appointment of the Widdicombe Committee.

As Widdicombe and the government have acknowledged, however, there are gains as well as losses from this new assertiveness. Those authorities where decisions are left in officer hands may drift a long way from the standards of accountability that are increasingly expected. And commentators sometimes characterise rural authorities as being more reluctant than most to take a corporate or strategic view of the issues they face, councillors being less inclined in these areas to take the reins of power into their own hands.

The evidence generally confirms the supposition that urban and rural authorities differ in this regard. The formulation of committee agenda is more likely to be left to chief officers in rural than urban authorities, while the arrangements made in some urban authorities to secure closer interlocking relationships between members and officers are far less prevalent in rural areas. Thus, while chief executives and treasurers attend party group meetings to assist policy formulation in half of the 'urban' and 'largely urban' authorities, they do so in only a small minority of those rural authorities where a party group exists.

The quality of rural government
Whether, in sum, rural local government can be judged 'better' or 'worse' than that which prevails in more urban areas is a matter of personal judgement. But we can offer a balance sheet. On the one side, the open-mindedness and respect for individuality of rural authorities is something to be prized. Rural councillors enjoy a closer relationship with those they represent and their connections are less likely to be mediated by party organisation. The smaller scale of rural life enables something of a face-to-face society to survive, in which people can be judged more for personal qualities than as adherents of national parties.

On the other hand, rural authorities pay little attention to communication and involvement with the larger public. They remain relatively inaccessible and few have shown much sign of tackling the problems in ways which are becoming commonplace in urban areas. Finally - though here the judgement is necessarily tentative - rural local authorities, at least at district level, seem less inclined to establish clear policy frameworks and to express their priorities through councillor control of business.

Government at the grass-roots: the parish
Much less is known about parish government, a topic largely neglected by researchers. The failure of parish councils to meet the expectations levelled at them by nineteenth century reformers was compounded by their steady eclipse by the principal authorities in the twentieth century. Only after World War II did the signs of a revival of parish government appear, while interest has quickened in recent years.

From a slow start, participation in parish affairs began to increase with the formation of the National Association of Parish Councils (NAPC) in the immediate post-war period marking the maturity of a grass-roots rural institution. The claim made in 1949 by Sir Leslie Scott, first President of NAPC, accurately reflects the parish council role as it developed under the impetus of post-war planning legislation. The powers conferred on rural local authorities, he said,
> are rightly on a diminishing scale; but no powers, big or little, can be well-exercised without knowledge of the needs they are designed to serve. The powers of your tier are naturally the smallest; but in many ways your knowledge is the greatest. It is the parish council which has its ear closest to the ground, and can give to the other tiers information about facts and people of the countryside, without which rural government could not be good (Scott, 1949: 209).

As late as the 1950s consideration was given to the abolition of parish councils (they were abolished in Scotland under the Local Government Act of 1929). But they were even then poised to enjoy a revival of support. With their consultative role in development control (to be given statutory backing in 1972), parish councils stood to gain from the general increase in social activism and participation which characterised the 1960s and from the growth of neighbourhood associations and ad hoc single-issue groups seeking to resist unwelcome development in the countryside.

The Local Government Act of 1972 lowered the population threshold at which a parish council could be formed. District councils are now obliged to create a parish council when called upon to do so by a parish meeting where there are between 150 and 200 electors and have the discretion to do so where they number less than 150; there are at present four parishes with less than 90 electors, the smallest being Hesleyhurst in Alnwick with 27. In 1974 there were 7,600 parish councils in England and Wales and a further 3,200 parishes without councils. About a further 1,000 parish councils have been created since then, a number which includes some non-statutory neighbourhood councils. Of the 296 shire districts in England, 57 currently have no parish councils, while 136 are only partly parished. Of the 36 metropolitan districts, 21 have parishes in part of their area. The late 1980s have witnessed the rise of an active parish movement in the National Association of Local Councils (as it now is) which seeks to achieve the complete parishing of non-metropolitan England.

The re-organisation of local government in 1972 had the additional effect of increasing the relative importance of the parish council, for the number of district councillors was reduced at a stroke as a consequence of the amalgamation of districts. Since that time the number of parish councillors has seen a steady increase to its present total of around 65,000.

Parish councils, then, seem set to enjoy a revival, due partly to the continuing growth of grass-roots involvement in local issues, and partly to the growing recognition that, by international standards, British local government is large-scale and remote. A new interest in 'micro-democracy' may well lead to an increased role for parish government in the future. Much will depend upon the outcome of current debates on the future shape of non-metropolitan government and upon the possibility of enhancing the vitality and public standing of parish councils (see Collingridge, 1988; Perks, 1977).

While a DoE circular of 1977 emphasised the importance of parish councils as 'a unit of community feeling', in the identification of which 'a prime consideration should be the feeling of the local community and the wishes of the inhabitants' they are no longer the only local bodies able to pose such a claim. Arguably, while the parish has gained strength from recent developments, other agencies - statutory and non-statutory - have developed in parallel to the extent that they may well rival the parish council in importance and effectiveness.

The wider framework

The development of a wider framework of institutions has added complexity to the rural scene without achieving a comprehensive approach to rural problems. Several reports have highlighted the fragmented and conflicting nature of government policies impacting upon rural areas, the lack of co-ordination and integration of policies and the existence of major policy gaps (see Hodge, 1985). Into these gaps have stepped a number of organisations, including the Rural Development Commission, the Countryside Commission and the local authority associations, and - representing more directly the interests of the people who live and work in rural areas - the national lobbying organisation Rural Voice, the secretariat of which is provided by Action for Communities in Rural England (ACRE), the umbrella organisation for Rural Community Councils (RCCs).

Changing agricultural policies and practices, a growing recognition of the recreational importance of the countryside and increased public concern for the environment have underpinned some shifts in the national approach to rural areas. There is now a recognition, shared by the Ministry of Agriculture and the Department of the Environment, that the countryside is a setting for multiple forms of economic and recreational activities, and is not just the preserve of agriculture (Blunden and

Curry, 1988). While agricultural and environmental issues have acquired a high profile, there has been relatively little progress on the social policy front, where rural communities are rather expected to tackle their own problems.

Awareness of the unsatisfactory and contradictory impact of national and local government policies on the countryside has found a focus in the notion of *integrated rural development*. The Development Commission (redesignated as the Rural Development Commission (RDC) in 1988) has for some time been seeking the closer integration of the work of government agencies, local authorities, and the voluntary and private sectors, aiming for a closer reconciliation of initiatives with one another and with the needs and aspirations of people living in rural areas. To this end, 27 Rural Development Areas (RDAs) were established in 1984 as priority areas for the targeting of initiatives (McNab, 1984).

County councils were accepted as the lead agencies under this scheme, collaborating with other bodies to prepare Rural Development Programmes (RDPs) as local strategies for action (RDC, 1989). Although changing economic conditions have undermined the original designations, and no new RDAs are likely to be created, the commitment to integrated development has become generally accepted. The trend is towards local experiment outside the RDAs, with RCCs often taking the lead with backing from the RDC and with variable levels of support from the local authorities concerned (Martin et al, 1990).

The extent of the move towards joint working at the local level is signified by the steps taken by the Countryside Commission to take forward the debate on the future of the countryside via the establishment, in 1986, of a Countryside Review Panel and by the subsequent proposal that county councils should prepare comprehensive countryside strategies 'covering economic, social, environmental and recreational objectives as well as land-use policies' (Countryside Commission, 1987). Through this initiative, the Countryside Commission has further broadened the view of what integrated rural development should encompass.

Through the development of an integrated approach to rural problems, in which the complementary roles of the RDC and the Countryside Commission - the one with its social and economic remit, the other with its concern for natural beauty and access to the countryside - are readily apparent, the plethora of local responsibilities has gained a sharper focus, with the county councils playing a key role at the centre of the network (Countryside Commission, 1989).

Reviews of integrated rural development (see for example Tricker et al, 1989) have stressed that there is no universal solution to the diverse problems of rural areas, success depending very much upon the involvement of local communities in identifying both needs and solutions. Increasingly, economic and community development objectives are seen as overlapping and mutually reinforcing.

The second major issue of institutional development in rural England, then, concerns *community development*. Some county councils have played a pioneering role in attempting to promote this (Broady and Hedley, 1989), but the focus of initiative lies naturally at the grassroots level, and here the RCCs have played a leading role.

RCCs are independent county-level voluntary bodies with a particular concern for the welfare of rural communities, expressed through the encouragement of self-help initiatives. The first RCC was established in 1921 and every county now has one. Financial support is drawn from RDC grant, from local authorities, and from the membership subscriptions paid by local voluntary organisations.

RCCs enjoy a strategic location within the network of rural organisations, working closely with parish councils and usually providing the secretariat for their county association. The central position which RCCs enjoy in rural affairs stems partly from an initiative by the then Development Commission in 1973, under which the Commission met the costs of appointing 16 countryside officers (rising to 30 in 1984) attached to RCCs principally to 'develop .. co-operative efforts of voluntary bodies and their links with local authorities, especially in the development and conservation of the countryside', to 'assist local communities in formulating views on their needs' and to 'promote and assist voluntary projects' (Williams, 1984).

The appointment of the first countryside officers coincided with the re-organisation of local government, and one of their early tasks was to assist parish councils in their new statutory role in the planning process. Recent years have seen greater RCC involvement in 'self-help' solutions to local problems and, more radically, helping local communities to organise themselves so as to gain more control over scarce resources. One unintended consequence of this pattern of institutional growth is that it is the RCCs, as voluntary bodies, which possess the concentration of professional capacity for local-level development work. Parish councils have arguably lagged behind in this respect, and a DoE-sponsored study argued for improved training for parish council clerks and members (Smart and Wright, 1983).

Moreover, there is a tension between the role of the parish council as a legitimate representative body (however constrained by low participation and the absence of political competition) and that of the RCC as essentially a county-based committee of institutional participants. Moseley (1988) argues that the tension is a creative one, in which RCCs enjoy

> a breadth of view. While the big battalions and QUANGOs and the departments of local authorities by and large have a vertical view of the world ... RCCs have learned to look laterally, that is to say across all of the services and across all of the rural community.

The publication by Rural Voice in 1987 of its *Rural Strategy* has sought to build upon this lateral perspective to provide cohesion and a sense of overall direction within voluntary-based rural social development.

Conclusion

The governance of rural England retains its distinctive flavour. The habits and practices of independent local politics survive there with remarkable vigour, even within the partly-established system of party politics. The expectations of nineteenth-century reformers, that the establishment of first the county, and then the district and parish councils would lead to a flowering of popular participation have not been met, although there is some evidence that local government is better understood, better regarded and its members more accessible there than in the towns and cities. Where rural local authorities have notably failed is in the area of public information and access to meetings. Here older practices have not changed to the same degree as in urban England.

The future of rural local government remains uncertain. Proposals for county council abolition continue to surface from time to time, although the renewed interest in micro-politics raises the possibility that the districts might themselves be the vulnerable tier, caught between the strategic overview of the county operating in partnership with the national Commissions and the grass-roots representative role of the parish, operating in partnership with the RCCs.

The role of the parish council is a critical one, for whatever its shortcomings, it remains the sole popularly-elected body at the community level. Since the 1970s it may have been somewhat overshadowed by the growth of the Rural Community Council movement which, while county-wide, has a local focus. The network of statutory and non-statutory bodies has been energised by the recent concern for co-ordinated social and economic development. Their respective roles are essentially complementary, and none is likely to claim pre-eminence; but all would benefit from a clearer conception of the parish council's place in the future system of rural governance.

References
Blunden, J and Curry, N (1988) *A Future for Our Countryside* (Oxford: Basil Blackwell)
Broady, M and Hedley, R (1989) *Working Partnerships: Community Development in Local Authorities* (London: Bedford Square Press)
Collingridge, J H (1988) *Parish Government in Rural England: A Study of Present-day Trends and Practices* University of Birmingham, unpublished PhD thesis.
Countryside Commission (1987) *Shaping a New Countryside: the Commission's*

Response to the Countryside Review Panel (Cheltenham: Countryside Commission).

Countryside Commission (1989) *Planning for a Green Countryside* (Cheltenham: Countryside Commission)

Game, C and Leach, S (1989) 'The County Councillor in 1889 and 1989' in K Young (ed) *New Directions for County Government* (London: ACC/INLOGOV)

Hodge, I (1985) *Countryside Change: A Review of Research* (London: ESRC)

McNab, A (1984) *Integrated Rural Development in Britain* Gloucestershire Papers in Local and Regional Planning No 22 (Gloucester: GLOSCAT)

Martin, S J, Tricker, M J and Bovaird A G (1990) 'Rural Development Programmes in Theory and Practice' *Regional Studies*

Moseley, M (1988) *One Countryside - One Community?* Paper to the 1988 Rural Life Conference, Durham (Cirencester: ACRE)

Perks, H (1977) 'The Rural Dimension' in R Darke and R Walker (eds) *Local Government and the Public* (London: Leonard Hill)

Scott, Sir L (1949) 'Presidential Address' *Parish Councils' Review* 1949-50

Smart, G and Wright, S (1983) *Decision-making for Rural Areas: A Research Report to the Department of the Environment* (London: Bartlett School of Architecture and Planning, UCL)

Tricker, M J, Bovaird, A G, and Hems, L C (1989) *The Peak District Integrated Rural Development Experiment: an Evaluation Report* to the Steering Committee (Bakewell: Peak Park Joint Planning Board)

Widdicombe, D (Chairman) (1986) *Committee of Inquiry into the Conduct of Local Authority Business: The Conduct of Local Authority Business* (London: HMSO)

Williams, G (1984) *Rural Self-help: Institutional Instrument or Policy Objective in Rural Development?* Gloucestershire Papers in Local and Regional Planning No 23 (Gloucester: GLOSCAT)

Young, K (1986) 'Party Politics in Local Government: an Historical Perspective' in Committee of Inquiry into the Conduct of Local Authority Business, *The Conduct of Local Authority Business: Research Volume IV: Aspects of Local Democracy* (London: HMSO)

Young, K (1989) 'Bright Hopes and Dark Fears: the Origins and Expectations of the County Councils' in K Young (ed) *New Directions for County Government* (London: ACC/INLOGOV)

Young, K and Davies, E M (1990) *The Politics of Local Government Since Widdicombe* (York: Joseph Rowntree Memorial Trust, forthcoming)

Appendix H

The Structure of the Church of England by the Reverend Canon Dr Paul Welsby

1. Very early in its history the whole of this country became covered by a network of **parishes,** each with its own parish priest or **incumbent,** who for historical reasons was given the title **rector** or **vicar,** although today there is no practical difference between the two. For nearly a thousand years, until the Industrial Revolution, the parochial system remained virtually unchanged. In the nineteenth century, however, new parishes were created and churches built in the large towns all over the country, and this development has continued until the present day. Since the last war major schemes for the reorganisation of the parochial system have been put in hand and this process has been accelerated by the shortage of clergy and the constraints of finance. During this period a number of benefices and parishes have been united. A **union of benefices** means that the identity of parishes remains intact, each with its own parish church and parochial organisation, but their combined incumbencies become a single office, held by a single incumbent whom they share. A **union of parishes** involves not only a union of the benefices concerned, but each of the parishes loses its separate identity which is merged into a single new parish.

2. Any proposed union of benefices or parishes is effected by a pastoral scheme under the Pastoral Measure 1983. This measure also provides for the creation of team and group ministries. A **team ministry** is the sharing of the cure of souls in a specified area by a team of ministers consisting of the incumbent (who is known as the team rector) and one or more other ordained ministers (known as team vicar(s)). A **group ministry** is where the incumbent of a benefice within the established group of parishes will, in addition to attending to his own benefice, have legal authority to assist the incumbents of the other benefices in the group. Finally, under the Church of England (Ecumenical Relations) Measure 1988, a **Local Ecumenical Project** can be set up in a parish or area. This is an area where, under responsible authority, certain denominational traditions are suspended for a period of years in order that new patterns of worship, mission and ministry can be undertaken. There is considerable variety of structure in these areas, but they all come within the definition accepted by the major churches that "a local ecumenical project may be said to exist where there is at the level of the local church a formal, written agreement, affecting the ministry, congregational life and/or buildings of more than one denomination; and a recognition of that agreement by the appropriate denominational authorities".

3. The **incumbent** of a parish is chosen and presented to the benefice by the **patron.** Just under a quarter of the benefices in England are in the gift of private patrons, including various trusts. Of the rest, about 3,700 are in ecclesiastical patronage (e.g. bishops, cathedral chapters), about 850 are in the patronage of the universities and colleges and between 700 and 800 are in the patronage of the Crown. Under the Patronage (Benefices) Measure 1986, apart from those cases where the Crown is patron, the bishop and representatives of the parochial church council are closely involved with the patron in the choice of a new incumbent, and any candidate chosen by the patron must have their approval. Once he is instituted and inducted to a benefice an incumbent possesses a freehold and cannot be removed against his will unless he seriously neglects his duties or unless he is guilty of unbecoming conduct - a

vague notion, and one that does not apply to any question of doctrine, ritual, or to the incumbent's social or political views. Normally, no clergyman over the age of 70 may continue to hold a benefice (except the small number already in office prior to the passing of this law in 1976). The bishop may, however, on grounds of pastoral need and with the consent of the parochial church council authorise his continuance in office for an extra period not exceeding two years.

4. The chief lay officers of a parish are the **churchwardens** (usually two in each parish), appointed by the joint consent of the incumbent and a meeting of parishioners. Unless the bishop permits otherwise, they must be communicant members of the Church of England. They are the officers of the bishop, are admitted to office by the bishop or archdeacon, and it is their duty to answer such questions as are put to them about the condition of the parish. They should also at any time report to the bishop any irregularity or failure of duty of which he ought to be informed. In the parish it is their duty to maintain order in church and to provide seats in church for the parishioners. In addition to these legal obligations, the churchwardens usually take a leading role among the laity. At least one of them is normally present at every service to supervise arrangements and very often one of them is elected vice-chairman of the parochial church council. During a vacancy in the benefice it is usually the churchwardens who are responsible for the maintenance of the services and for the engagement of clergy and readers for that purpose. In an emergency, when no ordained minister or reader is available, a churchwarden has authority to conduct Morning and Evening Prayer. The churchwardens should try to ensure that the incumbent is relieved of administrative work in connection with the maintenance of the church and churchyard.

5. The **parochial church council** (PCC) is the legal administrative body in the parish and its membership ensures that the laity of the parish have a voice, jointly with the incumbent, in the affairs of the church. It consists of the incumbent, other clergy and lay workers in the parish, the churchwardens and a number of lay members (who must be actual communicants of 17 years of age and upwards) elected by the Annual Parochial Church Meeting. The latter must be held each year not later than 30th April and all persons on the **electoral roll** of the parish are entitled to attend and to vote. The electoral roll contains the names of all those lay persons who are baptised, who are members of the Church of England or a church in communion with the Church of England, who are 16 years of age and upwards, and have signed a form of application for enrolment. They must be resident in the parish, or they must have habitually attended public worship in the parish during six months prior to enrolment. The essential work of the PCC is to co-operate with the incumbent "in promoting in the parish the whole mission of the Church, pastoral, evangelistic, social and ecumenical". Its functions also include "consideration and discussion of matters concerning the Church of England and any other matters of religious or public interest" and it is the duty of the incumbent and PCC "to consult together on matters of general concern and importance to the parish." (Synodical Government Measure, 1969, Sec. 6.) The PCC is responsible for the financial affairs of the church, together with the care and maintenance of the church and churchyard. It has the power to acquire and manage property for ecclesiastical and educational purposes. The PCC, jointly with the incumbent, chooses which form of service (i.e. 1662 Prayer Book or Alternative Service Book) is to be used in the parish church at Holy Communion and at Morning and Evening Prayer. If they are unable to agree, the form of service in the 1662 Prayer Book must be used, subject to one proviso - if another form of service has been used continuously in the course of the previous four years, the PCC (but not the incumbent) can require the use of that form.

6. The parish is not an isolated unit, but an integral part of the Church of England which is divided into the two **provinces** of Canterbury and York, each presided over by an **archbishop.** The Archbishop of Canterbury also has a relationship with the world-wide Anglican Communion, where he has great spiritual and moral authority. He is constantly asked for advice and counsel by overseas bishops and he is President of the Lambeth Conference, held every ten years, but he makes no claim to a primacy

of universal jurisdiction. Each province consists of a number of **dioceses** (30 in the province of Canterbury; 14 in the province of York), each under the jurisdiction of a **bishop.** A diocesan bishop is usually assisted by a **suffragan bishop,** and some dioceses have been divided into episcopal areas and the diocesan bishop has legally delegated certain of his powers to an **area bishop.** The bishop is head of the diocese pastorally as well as administratively. However much work he may delegate, he is the final authority on many matters. The financial affairs of the diocese, the committees and councils guiding the various spheres of church work in the diocese, the creation of new parishes and the reorganisation of existing ones, and a hundred and one other matters, come ultimately under the responsibility of the diocesan bishop. Moreover, as the leader of the Church of England within the area covered by his diocese, he has a certain responsibility to represent the Church vis-a-vis local secular bodies. Pastorally, the bishop will choose fit persons for the ordained ministry and play a leading part in appointing suitable men to vacant benefices. Moving about the diocese for confirmations, institutions and other engagements, he gets to know the clergy and laity, their needs and their problems. There is the less congenial, but nonetheless necessary, task of exercising discipline over the clergy in the case of moral offences, neglect of duty or offences against the doctrine of the Church of England and its law of public worship. Moral persuasion, admonition, and censure are the chief means employed by the bishop in dealing with these delinquencies; very rarely is it necessary for him to take legal action against the offender.

7. Every diocese is divided into two or more **archdeaconries,** each of which will contain a fairly large number of parishes, presided over by an archdeacon, appointed by the bishop. The archdeacon is responsible for inspecting the fabric and contents of churches within his archdeaconry. Under the Inspection of Churches Measure 1955 he is responsible for the enforcement of the provisions of the quinquennial inspection of churches. In these days, however, his role is increasingly seen as a pastoral one, assisting the bishop in the care of the clergy and the parishes. Finally, each archdeaconry is divided into **rural deaneries,** or small groups of parishes, over which presides the rural dean, one of the local incumbents who undertakes his rural deanery duties on a part-time basis. Each rural deanery has regular meetings of the clergy within the deanery to discuss and take action on matters of common concern. The rural dean is also Joint Chairman of the Deanery Synod (see below). He is a valuable channel of communication between the bishop and the parishes, and it is his task to make known to the clergy the wishes of the bishop and to represent the wishes of the clergy to the bishop.

8. Thus every parish lies within, and is related to, a rural deanery, an archdeaconry, a diocese, and a province.

9. A word must be said about **cathedrals,** where a **dean** or **provost,** together with a small number of **residentiary canons,** are responsible for the spiritual and temporal concerns of the cathedral church. A cathedral is not subject to the same ecclesiastical controls as parish churches, although it is the mother church of the diocese, and the place where services particularly associated with the bishop are held. Today a cathedral is the venue for a large number of special services and other events. It is increasingly a place of pilgrimage, and every cathedral has its evangelistic and educational opportunities among the mass of sightseeers. A number of cathedrals have provided ancillary facilities such as gift shops, guides in various languages, visitors' centres, treasuries, refectories, and exhibition areas.

Synodical government

10. The government of the Church of England is by synod, which operates at three levels:-

(i) The **General Synod,** which is a legislative body promoting Measures affecting the life and work, the finance and administration, of the Church which, when they have passed through all their stages and have received the royal assent, have the force of statute law. It was in 1919 that Parliament delegated most of its legislative authority in ecclesiastical affairs first to the Church Assembly and then, in 1969, to the General Synod. Nevertheless, ultimate legislative control remains with Parliament, for when a measure has passed through all its stages, Parliament can still debate it and must either accept or reject it. It is through Measures dealing with such matters as pastoral reorganisation, clergy stipends, ecumenical co-operation, etc, that the evangelistic and pastoral work of the Church at the parochial level has been facilitated. The Synod is also a liturgical body, and it was the Synod which produced the Alternative Service Book and other authorised services. In addition, it acts as a forum for expressing Christian views and insights on major public issues and for discussing and settling central Church business. It initiates and makes decisions about Church unity schemes, ecumenical co-operation and working arrangements with other churches.

(ii) The **diocesan synod**, which considers matters concerning the Church of England and makes provision for such matters in relation to the diocese, is a forum for the expression of Christian opinion on any matter of religious or public interest, advises the bishop on any matter on which he may consult the synod, and makes provision for the financing of the work of the diocese.

(iii) The **deanery synod**, whose task is officially defined as to "generally promote in the deanery the whole mission of the Church, pastoral, evangelistic, social and ecumenical". To this end, it brings together the views of the parishes of the deanery on common problems, discusses and formulates common policies, and fosters a sense of community and interdependence among those parishes. It can consider and express an opinion on any matter of religious or public interest.

11. What is the relationship between these three bodies and between them and the parishes?

(i) Each parish elects one or more representative(s) to serve on the deanery synod. The clergy and the laity on the deanery synod elect their representatives on the diocesan synod. The laity on the deanery synods elect the House of Laity of the General Synod, while the House of Clergy of the General Synod is elected mainly by the parochial clergy in each diocese. There is thus considerable opportunity for reporting back from the General Synod to the diocesan and deanery synods and thus to the parishes. At the same time, in theory at least, the elected members of the General Synod are sufficiently near the 'grass roots' to be aware of local opinion.

(ii) Certain measures have to be sent to diocesan synods for approval before a final decision can be made by the General Synod, and on other important matters the diocesan synods are consulted. Many of these matters are passed down by the diocesan synods to the deanery synods, and the parish representatives on the latter may wish to consult their PCCs.

(iii) It is possible for a parish to send resolutions for debate and discussion in the deanery synod. The latter can pass resolutions up to the diocesan synod, and they can go on to the General Synod.

The Church Commissioners

12. The Church Commissioners came into existence in 1948 when Queen Anne's Bounty (established in 1794) and the Ecclesiastical Commissioners (formed in 1836) were united. It is a large body representative of both Church and State, but the main work is monitored by the Board of Governors, which consists of the two archbishops, the three Church Estates Commissioners and twenty-three members appointed by the Commissioners. The work of the Church Commissioners is extremely varied, but for convenience it can be divided as follows:-

(i) The management of the historic resources of the Church, which means that they own a considerable amount of agricultural, urban and commercial property, together with a large and diverse portfolio of securities, all of which is managed to secure good income growth for present and future generations.

(ii) The primary call on the Commissioners' income is the payment of clergy stipends. In 1988 they provided 40% of the money for stipends, which is distributed among the dioceses on a selective basis according to perceived need.

They also make capital grants of up to 50% for the provision of parsonage houses, and may also assist by allocating funds for providing churches, church halls and housing of the clergy in new housing areas. An increasing call on the Commissioners' money is the payment of pensions of retired clergy and clergy widows.

(iii) Under the Pastoral Measure 1983 the Commissioners are responsible for dealing with proposals for pastoral reorganisation initiated by diocesan authorities, and they also have to decide whether churches which have been declared redundant should be made available for suitable other uses, be preserved, or be demolished.

Voluntary offerings

13. Voluntary contributions have to cover such large items as the portion of clergy stipends not covered by the Commissioners' grants, the training of men and women for ordained and lay ministry, the mission of the Church at home and abroad, the upkeep of the fabric of churches and cathedrals, together with their running expenses. Income and expenditure can be regarded as being on three levels - the parochial, the diocesan and the central - the link between them being the **quota system.** In each diocese, every parish is assessed for a contribution to the diocese (the parochial quota); each diocese is assessed for a contribution to central funds (the diocesan quota). The quota represents not an imposition or a levy but the share which the parish or diocese pays towards the work of the whole Church, of which each diocese and each parish is itself an integral part.

Appendix I

The Care of All the Churches

The following chart was designed to give some indication of the life of one united rural parish in late 1988. The incumbent, Canon John Seymour, tells us that there have been some changes since it was drawn, although the broad picture still stands. The most significant of these is that he is now also Rural Dean of a mixed urban/rural deanery of 38 congregations and 19 clergy with, this summer, five vacancies. In this capacity he has no additional help, although he receives an annual sum towards expenses.

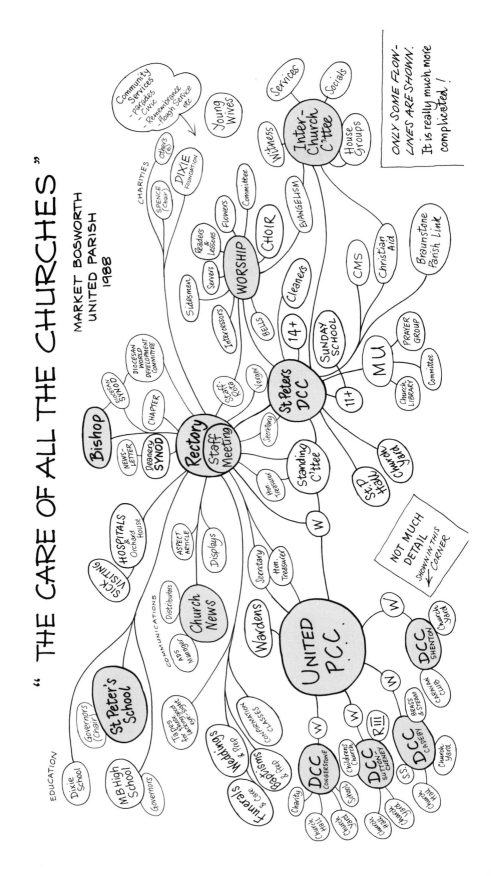

" THE CARE OF ALL THE CHURCHES "

MARKET BOSWORTH
UNITED PARISH
1988

ONLY SOME FLOW-
LINES ARE SHOWN.
It is really much more
complicated!

NOT MUCH
DETAIL
SHOWN IN THIS
CORNER

Appendix J

Useful Addresses

Action with Communities in Rural England (ACRE)
Stroud Road
Cirencester
Glos
GL7 6JR

Arthur Rank Centre
National Agricultural Centre
Stoneleigh
Kenilworth
Warwickshire
CV8 2LZ

NAC Rural Trust
35 Belgrave Square
London
SW1X 8QN

Memorials by Artists
Snape Priory
Saxmundham
Suffolk
IP17 1SA

Music in Worship Trust
151 Bath Road
Hounslow
Middlesex
TW3 3BU

The Royal School of Church Music
Addington Palace
Croydon
CR9 5AD

Appendix K

Abbreviations

ACCM	Advisory Council for the Church's Ministry
ACORA	Archbishops' Commission on Rural Areas
ACRE	Action with Communities in Rural England
ACUPA	Archbishops' Commission on Urban Priority Areas
AEI	Average Earnings Index
ARC	Arthur Rank Centre
ASB	Alternative Services Book
BCP	Book of Common Prayer
BItC	Business in the Community
CAB(x)	Citizens Advice Bureau(x)
CAP	Common Agricultural Policy
CIO	Church Information Office (now Church House Publishing)
CLA	Country Landowners' Association
CME	Continuing Ministerial Education
CP	Community Programme
CPAS	Church Pastoral Aid Society
CPRE	Council for the Protection of Rural England
CSA	Central Stipends Authority
DBF	Diocesan Board of Finance
DEC	Diocesan Education Committee
DES	Department of Education and Science
DoE	Department of the Environment
DSS	Department of Social Security
DTI	Department of Trade and Industry
EC	European Community
ESA	Environmentally Sensitive Area
ESG	Education Support Grant
ET	Employment Training
GATT	General Agreement on Tariffs and Trade
GNP	Gross National Product
GS	General Synod
HMI	Her Majesty's Inspectorate (of Schools)
HMSO	Her Majesty's Stationery Office
LEA	Local Education Authority
LEP	Local Ecumenical Project
LNSM	Local Non-Stipendiary Minister
LOM	Local Ordained Minister
MAFF	Ministry of Agriculture, Fisheries and Food
NACRT	National Agricultural Centre Rural Trust
NALC	National Association of Local Councils
NASSS	National Assocation for the Support of Small Schools
NCSS	National Council for Social Service
NFU	National Farmers' Union
NFWI	National Federation of Women's Institutes

NOMIS	National On-Line Manpower Information System
NSM	Non-Stipendiary Minister
OECD	Organisation for Economic Co-operation and Development
PCC	Parochial Church Council
PSU	Pastoral Studies Unit
PSV	Public Service Vehicle
RCC	Rural Community Council
RCP	Rural Church Project*
RDA	Rural Development Area
RDC	Rural Development Commission
RSCM	Royal School of Church Music
RSG	Rates Support Grant
RSPB	Royal Society for the Protection of Birds
RTA	Rural Theology Association
SERPLAN	South East Regional Planning Conference
SPCK	Society for the Promotion of Christian Knowledge
TEC	Training and Enterprise Council
UBR	Uniform Business Rate
UMEX	Upland Management Experiment
UPA	Urban Priority Area
URC	United Reformed Church
WCC	World Council of Churches
WRVS	Women's Royal Voluntary Service

* The Rural Church Project is based jointly at the Centre for Rural Studies, Royal Agricultural College, Cirencester and the Department of Theology, University of Nottingham. From 1988-1990 the project was funded by the Leverhulme Trust and ACORA to carry out surveys in five dioceses.

Copies of these reports and further information about the Rural Church Project are available from the Centre for Rural Studies, Royal Agricultural College, Cirencester and the Department of Theology, University of Nottingham.